SOCIETY FOR NEW TESTAMENT STUDIES

MONOGRAPH SERIES

General Editor: G. N. Stanton

64

FAITH AS A THEME IN
MARK'S NARRATIVE

Faith as a theme in Mark's narrative

CHRISTOPHER D. MARSHALL
Lecturer in New Testament
Bible College of New Zealand

The right of the
University of Cambridge
to print and sell
all manner of books
was granted by
Henry VIII in 1534.
The University has printed
and published continuously
since 1584.

CAMBRIDGE UNIVERSITY PRESS

CAMBRIDGE
NEW YORK   NEW ROCHELLE   MELBOURNE   SYDNEY

Published by the Press Syndicate of the University of Cambridge
The Pitt Building, Trumpington Street, Cambridge CB2 1RP
32 East 57th Street, New York, NY 10022, USA
10 Stamford Road, Oakleigh, Melbourne 3166, Australia

© Cambridge University Press 1989

First published 1989

Printed in Great Britain at
the University Press, Cambridge

British Library cataloguing in publication data

Marshall, Christopher D. (Christopher David), *1953–*
Faith as a theme in Mark's narrative.
1. Bible. N.T. Mark – Critical studies
I. Title. II. Series
226'.306

Library of Congress cataloguing in publication data

Marshall, Christopher D.
Faith as a theme in Mark's narrative / Christopher D. Marshall.
    p. cm. – (Monograph series / Society for New Testament Studies)
Based on the author's thesis (doctoral) – University of London, 1985.
Bibliography: p.
ISBN 0 521 36507 4
1. Faith – Biblical teaching. 2. Bible. N.T. Mark – Criticism,
interpretation, etc. I. Title. II. Series: Monograph Series
(Society for New Testament Studies)
BS2545.F3M37 1989
226'.306 – dc19   88-25788   CIP

In memory of my mother
Jenny Marshall
with loving gratitude

ὦ γύναι, μεγάλη σου ἡ πίστις *(Mt 15:28)*

CONTENTS

PREFACE

It is almost a commonplace these days to read of the 'rediscovery' of Mark by recent scholarship. The earliest evangelist, who in the past has been considered as a somewhat simple-minded collator or rather artless redactor of discordant traditions, is being increasingly recognised as an author of considerable theological and literary competence. Many would now feel that the comparatively low estimate of Mark's literary abilities that has coloured much form critical and redaction critical analysis of his gospel, simply attests to a failure by scholars to appreciate the stylistic features and rhetorical integrity of his text. Hopefully the present study of Mark's faith-theme will further corroborate this more positive evaluation of his capacities as an author.

This book is based on a doctoral thesis, prepared under the supervision of Professor G. N. Stanton and accepted by the University of London in December 1985. The revision was largely carried out during a short stay in London over the Christmas period of 1987–1988. I am grateful for a grant from the E. M. Blaiklock Memorial Fund that made the time in London possible and for the generous hospitality offered to my family and myself by the London Mennonite Centre. In carrying out the revision I was helped by the comments made on the thesis by its examiners, Dr John Muddiman and Dr Cyril Rodd, and especially by the detailed written criticisms offered by Professor Ernest Best, who recommended my work for inclusion in the SNTSMS series. To have at hand the comments of such a highly respected Markan specialist as Professor Best was invaluable in provoking me to further reflection on the subject and greater clarity of expression. I would also like to thank Professor Stanton for his guidance during the period of research and for his advice and encouragement during the preparation of the work for publication.

I am very conscious of how much my work owes to the love, support and generosity over many years of family and friends, both in New Zealand and in the United Kingdom. They are too numerous to name but without their contribution in so many different ways, my research on Mark would have never seen the light of day. I am especially grateful to my parents who have exemplified in their own lives many of the qualities of faith described in the following pages. Sadly my mother's life was claimed in a car accident before the book was published, and it is to her memory that I gratefully dedicate this study in Mark's gospel. A special word of thanks to my wife, Margaret, and my little boy, Peter, for sacrificing their summer holiday in the New Zealand sun to enable me to undertake preparation of the typescript in the mid-winter chill of London.

ABBREVIATIONS

AnBib	Analecta Biblica
BAG	Bauer, W., Arndt, W. F., Gingrich, F. W., and Danker, F. W., *A Greek English Lexicon of the New Testament*
BDF	Blass, F., and Debrunner, A., trans. and revised by Funk, R. W., *A Greek Grammar of the New Testament and Other Early Christian Literature*
BETL	Bibliotheca ephemeridum theologicarum Lovaniensium
Bib	*Biblica*
Bill	[Strack, H. L.] and Billerbeck, P., *Kommentar zum Neuen Testament aus Talmud und Midrasch*, I–VI, 1926–61
BJRL	*Bulletin of the John Rylands University Library of Manchester*
BR	*Biblical Research*
BTB	*Biblical Theology Bulletin*
BZ	*Biblische Zeitschrift*
BZNW	Beihefte zur Zeitschrift für die neutestamentliche Wissenschaft
CBQ	*Catholic Biblical Quarterly*
ExpT	*Expository Times*
FRLANT	Forschungen zur Religion und Literatur des Alten und Neuen Testaments
Fs	Festschrift
HTR	*Harvard Theological Review*
IDB	Interpreter's Dictionary of the Bible
IDB supp	Interpreter's Dictionary of the Bible Supplementary Volume
IrBibStud	*Irish Biblical Studies*
Int	*Interpretation*
JAAR	*Journal of the American Academy of Religion*

JBL	*Journal of Biblical Literature*
JR	*Journal of Religion*
JSNT	*Journal for the Study of the New Testament*
JSNTSS	JSNT Supplement Series
JTS	*Journal of Theological Studies*
JournTheolSAfr	*Journal of Theology for Southern Africa*
NIDNTT	New International Dictionary of New Testament Theology
NovT	*Novum Testamentum*
NTS	*New Testament Studies*
RelS	*Religious Studies*
RevExp	*Review and Expositor*
SBT	Studies in Biblical Theology
SJT	*Scottish Journal of Theology*
SANT	Studien zum Alten und Neuen Testament
SBLDS	Society of Biblical Literature Dissertation Series
Sem	*Semeia*
SNTSMS	Society for New Testament Studies Monograph Series
SNovT	Supplement to Novum Testamentum
SUNT	Studien zur Umwelt des Neuen Testaments
SWJT	*Southwestern Journal of Theology*
TBT	*The Bible Translator*
TDNT	Theological Dictionary of the New Testament
Theol	*Theology*
TToday	*Theology Today*
TZ	*Theologische Zeitschrift*
WUNT	Wissenschaftliche Untersuchungen zum Neuen Testament
WMANT	Wissenschaftliche Monographien zum Alten und Neuen Testament
ZNW	*Zeitschrift für die neutestamentliche Wissenschaft*
ZTK	*Zeitschrift für Theologie und Kirche*

INTRODUCTION

Interpreters of Mark have long recognised the value of studying the constituent themes of the gospel as a way of determining the evangelist's distinctive theology. Numerous studies have been devoted to such typically Markan concerns as messianic secrecy, the incomprehension of the disciples, his Son of Man christology, Galilee and the Gentile mission, miracles and their relation to *theios aner* conceptions, his concept of 'gospel', and many others besides. A theme which has attracted comparatively little attention however, and one which Mark himself indicates is fundamental to understanding his work, is the theme of faith.

That faith is one of Mark's basic theological concerns is evident in various ways. Statistics can be misleading and should be used with caution, but the relative frequency of πίστις, πιστεύειν terminology is significant since, as we will see, verbal repetition is an important device for underlining points of emphasis. Taking 16:8 as the intentional ending of the narrative,[1] Mark employs the word group seventeen times in his gospel, in ten different episodes spread throughout his narrative.[2] This compares favourably with other topics widely held to be of particular importance in Mark. The term εὐαγγέλιον, for example, which Marxsen deems 'the main concept of the work',[3] occurs only seven times.[4] There are only three explicit parousia sayings,[5] twelve references to Galilee,[6] and fourteen

---

[1] See below, n. 1, p. 150.

[2] 1:15; 2:5; 4:40; 5:34,36; 6:6; 9:19,23,24; 10:52; 11:22,23,24,31; 15:32. A variant reading of 8:17 includes the term ὀλιγόπιστοι (P⁴⁵ W Θ Φ Ψ 28 125 565 700 syᵐᵍ geo² arm).

[3] Marxsen, *Introduction*, 137.

[4] 1:1,14,15; 8:35; 10:29; 13:10; 14:9.

[5] 8:38; 13:26; 14:62.

[6] 1:9,14,16,28,39; 3:7; 6:21; 7:31; 9:30; 14:28; 15:41; 16:7.

uses of the phrase 'Son of Man'.[1] Even the notorious commands to silence occur, on a generous reckoning, only nine times.[2] The subject of faith then is one which Mark addresses with comparative frequency.

Another indicator of its importance is the location of a call to faith in the programmatic summary of 1:14f. We shall argue in chapter 2 that the effect of this placement is to highlight the role of faith throughout the narrative and to provide the reader with a yardstick to use in evaluating subsequent developments in the story. The fact that Mark matches this faith reference at the beginnning of Jesus' activity with another one at the very end of his life (15:32), to create a bracket around his earthly ministry, is a further indication of the hermeneutical significance of the theme. More evidence for this will emerge as we proceed, but already enough has been said to confirm that 'Mark's Gospel is rich in the importance it gives to faith.'[3]

The numerous faith references in the gospel have not, of course, been totally ignored by scholars. The material has been examined both in general works on the subject of faith and in various essays and monographs on Mark.

(i) A number of scholars have investigated the faith language of the synoptic tradition, often with the aim of arriving at an understanding of Jesus' own conception of faith – with or without a critical sifting of the material for authenticity. This area was pioneered by A. Schlatter, whose monumental study, *Der Glaube im Neuen Testament* [1885, 5th ed., 1963], has influenced all subsequent literature on the subject. His claim that the New Testament doctrine of faith originated in the time of Jesus was not taken up by Old Liberalism or the *religionsgeschichtliche Schule*, and with the advent of form criticism scholarly interest shifted decisively to the post-Easter community. Bultmann's almost classic article in the *TDNT* [6, 174–228] does not even raise the question of Jesus' teaching on faith.

New impetus was given to the question, however, by G. Ebeling's essay, 'Jesus and Faith' [1958, ET. 1963], which sought to establish the historical distinctiveness of Jesus' faith language. There are now available a considerable number of studies which address the exegetical, historical and theologi-

[1] 2:10,28; 8:31,38; 9:9,12,31; 10:33,45; 13:26; 14:21,41,62.
[2] 1:25,34,44; 3:12; 5:43; 7:36; 8:26,30; 9:9.
[3] Martin, *Evangelist and Theologian*, 108.

cal issues raised by the synoptic faith references. Among these are the works cited in the bibliography by Shearer, Benoit, Fuchs, O'Connor, Heijke, [43ff], Bornkamm [*Jesus*, 129–33], Perrin [*Rediscovering*, 130–42], Marxsen [*Beginnings of Christology*, 57–68], Gogarten [38–41, 46–51, 239–44, 255–60], Jeremias [*Theology*, 1, 159–65], Goppelt [149–57], Roloff [152–73], Maisch [71–6], Glöckner [75–94], M. Cook, Lohse ['Glauben', 89–102], and others.

While offering indispensable insights, the main limitation of this work, from our perspective, is its failure to explore the distinctive configurations of the faith motif in the individual gospels. This is either because researchers have simply assumed there is no basic difference in the understanding and use of faith among the different evangelists, or because they have been primarily concerned with traditio-historical questions.

(ii) The literature available specifically on the place of faith in the Markan tradition is notable for its sparseness and its brevity. In his 1923 study of Pauline influence on Mark's gospel, M. Werner devotes a short section to distinguishing Markan and Pauline conceptions of faith [*Einfluss*, 106–18], an area also covered briefly in Fenton's essay 'Paul and Mark' [1955, pp. 106–9]. J. A. Finlay [*Jesus* (1921), 102–8], J. M. Robinson [*Problem of History* (1957) 73–8] and R. P. Martin [*Evangelist and Theologian* (1972) 108–11, 155f, 173, 175f, 207f] provide useful summaries of the place of faith in the gospel, which they all regard as one of Mark's special emphases. Schreiber identifies faith as 'Das Zentrum der markinische Theologie' (p. 235) and gives an eight-page account of the way Mark redactionally reorients the *Wunderglaube* of his tradition to serve his theology of the cross [*Theologie des Vertrauens* (1967) 235–43]. In addition to these works, monographs on the miracle stories and on particular themes often include short accounts of Mark's understanding of faith, as do excursuses in the more substantial Markan commentaries. A few short essays have also been devoted to the subject. The two most significant[1] are by D. Zeller ['Jesus als Mittler' (1968)] and F. Hahn ['Verständnis des Glaubens' (1982)]. Zeller works

---

[1] Despite the promising title, Schweizer's 'The Portrayal of the life of Faith in the Gospel of Mark' (1978) has comparatively little exegesis of the faith references in Mark. Mention may also be made of a brief survey of the data by M. A. Beavis, 'Mark's Teaching on Faith' (1986).

from the final text and summarises Mark's view of faith under five headings. Hahn considers the main references individually and discusses redactional and traditio-historical issues as well. Both scholars accept that Mark has successfully integrated different traditions on faith into his overall composition.

If this is so, then we would propose that the available treatments of Mark's faith theme suffer from two methodological shortcomings: first, a tendency to focus exegesis solely on the faith logia themselves, in isolation from the narrative context in which they occur and from which they derive their meaning; and secondly, an almost exclusive concentration on the conceptual aspects of the theme, with little consideration being given to the literary and dramatic methods employed by the narrator to convey his message on faith to his audience and to integrate it into his overall story.

The following investigation departs from the existing literature in both these respects. In the first chapter we propose an approach that endeavours to combine a theological and a literary analysis of the theme, and the organisation of the ensuing chapters is intended to facilitate this aim. While there is always a danger of systematising Mark's data in a way that gives a false impression of his perspective, some degree of categorisation is essential. Ideally it should be simple and correspond as far as possible to what emerges from the material itself; exegesis should prevail over mapping out complex structural patterns. Therefore, after an analysis of Mark 1:14f (chapter 2) and a review of the place of miracles in the theme of faith (chapter 3), we consider the remaining data in three groupings – the portrayal of faith of supplicants in the miracle stories (chapter 4), the place of faith in discipleship (chapter 5), and the depiction of unbelief (chapter 6). In the final chapter we attempt to summarise the main conceptual lines of Mark's understanding of faith.

Our focus throughout will be on faith as *a narrative theme*. We will not attempt to use the form and content of the gospel to arrive at an understanding of the historical and social setting of Mark's own community. Such an interest is legitimate in itself, even if there are real methodological difficulties entailed in using a story set in the historical past to reconstruct the present situation of the author's first audience. But socio-historical investigation is a different and separate task from literary analysis, and our concern is principally with the latter.

Having said that, it remains true that the more we can know of the cultural, sociological and linguistic context in which literature, especially ancient literature, has emerged, the better equipped we are to appreciate its function and meaning. Moreover, as we note in chapter five, there are points at which Mark expressly addresses the real life situation of his readers (especially 13:14,23,37), so that some reflection on what that situation is becomes inescapable. It may be helpful therefore, before narrowing our attention to a single theme in the narrative, to comment briefly on current scholarly opinion on the life-setting of the earliest gospel.

The gospel itself is of course anonymous, and in that sense the author is unknown; anonymity indeed is what the author intended. The reliability of the early tradition that identifies the author as the Mark mentioned elsewhere in the New Testament[1] and makes him dependent on the preaching of Peter in Rome, is evaluated differently by scholars.[2] After reviewing the evidence, R. E. Brown concludes that 'The role of Peter as the source for the gospel is the most dubious element; but Mark as the author and Rome as the site cannot be quickly dismissed as implausible'.[3] The majority of scholars would probably still opt for a Roman provenance for the gospel, although some weighty voices have argued for a location in Galilee[4] or in Syria.[5] The main difficulty with a Palestinian setting, apart from the dubious interpretations of Markan eschatology that often bolster the view, is explaining why Mark should need to explain Jewish customs (7:3,4,11,19), convert local currency (12:42) and translate Aramaic (5:41; 7:34; 15:22,34) for such an

[1] Ac 12:12,25; 13:13; 15:36–41; Phlm 24; Col 4:10; 2 Tim 4:11.

[2] Opinion covers the spectrum from 'historically worthless' (W. Marxsen, *Introduction*, 142f) to 'rests on an old tradition which we can trust' (M. Hengel, *Studies*, 3f, 47–50).

[3] Brown, R. E. and Meier, J. P., *Antioch and Rome*, 191–201 (quote from p. 197). For more vigorous defences of all three elements of the tradition – Markan authorship, a Roman provenance, and dependence on Peter – see Hengel, *Studies*, 1–30, 47–53, and Senior, '"Swords and Clubs"', 10–20.

[4] E.g., Lohmeyer, *Galiläa und Jerusalem* (1936); R. H. Lightfoot, *Locality and Doctrine* (1938); Marxsen, *Introduction*, 143f; idem, *Mark the Evangelist*, 54–95, 102ff, 166ff; Kelber, *Kingdom*, 21f, 51–3, 59, 62, 64f, 129–32, 138–44; idem, *Mark's Story*, 13ff.

[5] Kee, *Community*, 103–5.

audience.[1] There are comparable problems with locating the gospel in a hypothetical community in rural Syria,[2] and in our opinion the case for accepting Rome as the place of composition remains compelling.[3] An origin sometime during or immediately after the Jewish War of AD 66–70, with its heightened eschatological temperature, provides the most plausible life setting for chapter 13, which is the linchpin for all attempts to date and locate the composition.[4]

Mark's purpose is best understood as broadly pastoral;[5] it is to instruct and strengthen the faith of his readers by involving them in the story of Jesus in such a way that those features of his teaching and example which Mark has chosen to narrate are experienced as directly relevant to their present needs. R. M. Fowler suggests that in interpreting Mark it is not necessary to assume that first readers knew anything of Christian history and tradition.[6] But this is surely not the case. Not only does Mark seem to presume a Christian understanding on the part of his readers from his very first verse, but his use of irony and dramatic paradox virtually requires it.[7] On the other hand, Mark's story should not be regarded as esoteric teaching intended exclusively for Christian initiates; the author no doubt wanted his main story-line to be comprehensible to those outside the church as well as those within. D. E. Aune has recently made the suggestion that the gospels were addressed to Christian households (some of which functioned as church centres), but which still included non-believing members and still made recourse to pagan values and customs. The gospels were consciously designed therefore both to reinforce Christians in the personal and social impli-

---

[1] Other difficulties include Mark's lack of clarity on Galilean topography and his pronounced Gentile bias. See Achtemeier, *Mark*, 114–16; Perrin, *Introduction*, 150, 163; Kee, *Community*, 102f; Cook, *Jewish Leaders*, 13f. For a more general critique of Kelber and Kee, see Via, *Ethics*, 71–6.

[2] See the factors mentioned by Hengel, *Studies*, 28f; Senior, '"Swords and Clubs"', 13f; Martin, 'Theology of Mark's Gospel', 28.

[3] See n. 3, p. 5 above, and also Cook, *Jewish Leaders*, 10–12.

[4] See Hengel, *Studies*, 14–28.

[5] See Best, 'Purpose', 19–35; idem, 'Mark; Some Problems', 84–92; Hooker, *Message of Mark*, 88f, 104, 116f.

[6] Fowler accepts that Mark's readers were Christians but says that it is impossible to tell how familiar they were with the Jewish Scriptures or Christian tradition. *Feeding Stories*, 41f, cf. 182f.

[7] See Best, *Gospel as Story*, 18–20.

cations of belief in Jesus and to persuade non-Christians of his ultimate religious significance.[1] If such was the case with Mark, then the call to faith, which we will see looms large in his composition, is to be understood as directed at both Christian and non-Christian hearers. To this theme we now turn.

[1] Aune, *Literary Environment*, 59f.

1 METHODS FOR EXPLORING THE THEME

The aim of the present study is the description and interpretation of one of the constituent themes in the gospel of Mark, the theme of faith. Our objective is to understand both the 'what' and the 'how' of the theme – what Mark understands by the notion of faith and how he succeeds in communicating this understanding to his readers through the medium of his gospel narrative. In pursuing this aim, the first question is one of method. What critical procedures are best suited to the task in hand?

Although there has been a tendency towards a polarisation of approaches, it has become increasingly clear that an adequate treatment of the complexities of Mark's text requires a methodological pluralism.[1] No one method can answer all the questions; all methods – source criticism, redaction criticism, rhetorical criticism, and so on – are valuable in complementing, correcting and controlling each other. In fact, a hard and fast distinction between different approaches to Mark is today more and more difficult to maintain.

In this chapter we will propose a somewhat eclectic method that offers the possibility of elucidating both the theological and the literary dimensions of Mark's faith-theme. Our basic contention is that the interpretation of Markan themes is best served by using the tools and insights of literary or narrative criticism, while still taking into account what redaction criticism has taught us about the composition and character of the gospel. The first section of the chapter briefly discusses the inherent limitations of a conventional redaction-critical approach to Mark; the second section outlines the procedures and

---

[1] See J. Dewey, *Public Debate*, 38; Petersen, 'Introduction' to *Semeia* 16 (1980), 1–5; Perrin, 'Christology of Mark', 173–87; idem, 'Evangelist as Author', 5–18; idem, 'Historical Criticism . . .', 361–75; idem, 'Interpretation' (1967), 361–75. For a brief survey of recent methodological approaches to Mark, see Fuller and Perkins, *Who is this Christ?*, 67–80.

principles of gospel narrative criticism; and the third section
touches upon some principles of lexical semantics, since our
access to the faith-theme is primarily by means of the πίστις,
πιστεύειν word group.

1. The limitations of Markan redaction criticism

The advent of modern *Redaktionsgeschichte* in the 1950s constituted a reaction against the prevailing understanding of the
gospel writers as mere compilers of community traditions.
Redaction criticism insisted instead that the evangelists were
theological authors in their own right who had not simply
collected traditional materials together, but through a process
of judicious selection, careful arrangement and creative adapt-
ation, had stamped these materials with their own theological
and pastoral imprint. The aim of redaction criticism then is to
trace the editorial process of the evangelists in order to determine the theological concerns that lie behind their use of tradition. Its central procedure is to make a detailed study of all
the observable changes made by the gospel writers to inherited
tradition. Although redaction criticism is also interested in the
selection and thematic arrangement of material, it is the concern to differentiate source and redaction that is particularly
distinctive of the method, and it is this aspect we shall focus
upon. In what follows then, 'redaction criticism' refers specifically to the attempt to isolate the evangelist's personal contribution to his text.

In the case of Matthew and Luke this is, assuming the two
source hypothesis, a relatively straightforward matter.[1] In the
case of Mark, however, the lack of a readily discernible *Vorlage* makes it much more problematic. Indeed, although in
principle redaction criticism offers a workable methodology for
evaluating the Markan theme of faith, in practice not only is
the feasibility of accurately distinguishing source and redaction strictly limited, but the hermeneutical value of doing so is
open to question.

First, the issue of viability. The kind of minute analysis that
endeavours to define the actual words and phrases, even
moods and tenses,[2] incorporated by the evangelist presupposes

---

[1] But note the cautions expressed by Hooker, 'In His Own Image?', 3f.

[2] F. C. Synge, for example, uses 'alien aorists' in a string of present indi-
catives to identify the hand of a pre-Markan redactor, 'A Matter of Tenses',
ExpT 88 (1977) 168–71.

a fairly accurate picture of the sources being edited. Yet with
Mark we have no independent picture of the sources he used;
they must be conjectured from the available text. This is especially difficult with respect to oral source material, for while
the shape and content of the oral traditions known to Mark
were probably fairly stable,[1] the exact wording is liable to have
varied with each telling.[2] The attempt to reconstruct the precise wording of oral sources from the written text is, therefore, a most hazardous undertaking. Without having Mark's
sources in hand, determining what the redactor has created,
what he has retold in his own words, what he has transmitted
unaltered, and what he has modified, remains a matter of
informed guesswork.

Even the usual considerations that inform this guesswork[3]
are not without difficulty. For example, many of the form
critical assumptions underlying redaction criticism, such as
the existence of 'pure' forms, the operation of predictable laws
of oral transmission, and the circulation of most pericopae in
complete isolation, are now considered highly dubious[4] and
must be used with care in locating the redactional level in a
passage. Linguistic and stylistic considerations often bear the
burden of proof in separating source and redaction in Mark.
But the statistical tests used are an uncertain guide. A particular word or construction may be frequent in the gospel
either because Mark included it, or because it was widespread
in his sources, or because of a redactional extension of traditional usage. Even if Mark's stylistic preferences are determined principally from the vocabulary and syntax of seams,
summaries, and 'insertions', it is questionable whether such a

---

[1] See Best, *Gospel as Story*, 113f.

[2] See Kelber's recent discussion of orality and textuality in *Oral and
Written Gospel* (1983). He notes that each oral telling is a new, authentic
speech act, a recreation, if not a fresh composition, of the account. 'In
orality, tradition is almost always composition in transmission.' (p.30)
Kelber exaggerates the significance of this however.

[3] See the criteria listed by Stein, 'What is Redaktionsgeschichte?', 45–56;
idem, 'Markan Seam', 70–94; idem, 'Proper Methodology', 81–98.

[4] Stanton remarks that, 'nearly all aspects of form criticism are overdue for
serious consideration', 'Form Criticism Revisited', 13; Kelber likewise
comments: 'Today it is no exaggeration to claim that a whole spectrum of
major assumptions underlying Bultmann's *Synoptic Tradition* must be
considered suspect.', *Oral and Written Gospel*, 8. See especially the extensive critique of form criticism by E. Güttgemanns, *Candid Questions*
(1979).

limited range of data can yield a full enough picture of the evangelist's style to be used as an accurate measure for distinguishing source and redaction elsewhere.[1] The infrequency of a linguistic usage may be as much a feature of an author's style as frequency.

The very presumption that significant, discernible linguistic and stylistic differences *ought* to exist between the evangelist and his sources itself warrants examination. If the material Mark drew upon belonged to the Christian tradition of his own community, and if Mark learnt his style at least in part from his own participation in church tradition,[2] then should we not expect there to be a marked similarity, though not necessarily an identity, in vocabulary and style between redaction and tradition? Indeed, the chief obstacle to using linguistic arguments for establishing redactional material is that we must reckon with a complicated two-way interpenetration of style and terminology having taken place between the evangelist and his sources.

On the one hand, in retelling traditional accounts it would have been practically impossible for him to avoid using some of his own words and idioms. Even solidly traditional material would thus have been 'markanised' to some degree. Moreover, if before writing the gospel Mark himself had handled his sources in the capacity of an oral storyteller, which is quite plausible,[3] or if while writing he had to translate or paraphrase some Aramaic material,[4] then reflections of redactional style in traditional material would be even more widespread. On the other hand, Mark's 'own redaction may not have been uninfluenced by linguistic usages already belonging to the tradition'.[5] As we will see, many of the stylistic traits in the gospel are best explained as a redactional imitation of linguistic usages natural to oral tradition, so that we should

---

[1] We may note, for example, that Acts has a significant number of constructions which are rare in Luke alone and alters the view we would have of Luke's style if we only had his gospel. How much more hazardous then it is to judge Mark's characteristic style on the basis of a handful of passages.

[2] As Pryke suggests, *Redactional Style*, 8, 30.

[3] What was Mark doing before he wrote his gospel? What qualified him to write down a definitive record of the stories about Jesus? Surely the evangelist had a thorough familiarity with, and participated in, the oral life and traditions of the community.

[4] Cf. Pryke, *Redactional Style*, 31; Rigaux, *Testimony*, 64f.

[5] Pryke, *Redactional Style*, 31.

expect there to be traditional terms and expressions repeated and used in editorial material.

The complex interaction between the evangelist and his sources at both oral and written levels has served to produce a sort of homogeneity in the Greek style of the finished gospel. This makes it extremely difficult to determine with any degree of accuracy the precise limits of source and redaction. Frans Neirynck classifies this homogeneous style under the rubric of 'duality'. Duality refers to the repetitions, pleonasms and duplications found at nearly every level of Mark's composition, ranging from individual words, phrases and sentences up to larger scale pericope-doublets and sandwich arrangements. Whereas such duplicate features in Mark have been customarily regarded as evidence of diverse sources, Neirynck finds that duality is 'one of Mark's most characteristic features of style',[1] acting as a 'two-step progressive device' in which the second item adds clarity or precision to the first. In this case, great caution is needed in using repetition and duplication as criteria in redactional investigation.

The wide divergence of results achieved by scholars using redaction critical methodology illustrates the practical difficulties encountered. Donahue's comparison of recent German work on the Markan passion narrative, for example, reveals not only a wide disagreement about almost every verse, but 'a fragmentation of the text which rivals the attempts early this century to divide the Pentateuchal narrative into a multitude of J's, E's and P's'.[2]

Quite apart from these practical problems is the question of whether the crucial task of discerning Mark's theological concerns and emphases, and of determining how these are conveyed in the gospel narrative, is best served by reconstructing Mark's sources and tracing his redactional activity. We would suggest that the hermeneutical value of such a procedure for elucidating Mark's understanding of faith, for example, is limited in two main respects.

First, it rests on the mistaken assumption that establishing the evangelist's uniqueness in relation to his sources offers the most profitable access to his theological thought-world. What the evangelist has added or changed in his sources is considered to be more significant than what he has passively accepted from tradition. It may be conceded that this

[1] Neirynck, *Duality in Mark*, 49.
[2] Donahue, 'Passion Traditions', 15.

distinctiveness is only part of his total theology, but in practice most value is attached to redactional *modifications*. The evangelist thus becomes a critical commentator on tradition and his own theology is cast in dialectical tension with it. However Mark's theological position is not best disclosed by documenting his modifications of tradition, but by studying his gospel in its entirety. For it is the final text in its totality that Mark employs as the vehicle of his theological message. Determining the special emphases of that completed text is, furthermore, a logically distinct procedure from ascertaining the critical pedigree of the material within it. Additions and changes to source material do not in themselves reveal the concerns and emphases of the evangelist. They may reflect only a passing concern, or be of minor stylistic importance, or even be inadvertent. Alternatively, the writer may incorporate tracts of tradition without alteration but tailor his work to show that this material is centrally important and has a significance beyond what it had in previous tradition.[1] Whatever the critical status of the component parts, therefore, it is only analysis of their place in the written composition as a whole that reveals the evangelist's theological perspective.

This means that primary exegetical respect is owed to the completed text as a literary reality. However – and this is our second point – the redaction-critical procedure of dissolving the extant wholeness of the text into an array of pre-literary sources and redactional touches in order to trace its compositional prehistory is ill-suited to appreciating the final text as a literary phenomenon. The basic principle for interpreting a literary work is that it must be accepted in the form in which it stands, for this is how the reader encounters it. It has a validity and integrity of its own, independent of its prehistory, just as a tapestry has a reality that goes beyond the collection of its threads. However, instead of evaluating significant features in the text, such as repetitions or ambiguities, in terms of their literary function in the finished composition, redaction criticism uses them as an occasion for delving behind the text to the hypothetical stage prior to its completion. It focuses much more on the redactor at work than on the text he has published. By too readily citing source dependence as the reason for apparent inconsistencies and duplications in the text, redactional methodology makes it difficult for interpreters to appreciate the rhetorical and stylistic intricacies in the

[1] Tannehill, 'Disciples in Mark', 386.

narrative Mark has produced. Redaction criticism on the contrary begins with the assumption of a flawed, somewhat incoherent text.

To sum up, both the problems of performing an accurate separation of source and redaction in Mark's gospel, and the inherent hermeneutical limitations of doing so, mean that redactional analysis is an inadequate method for elucidating the theological and literary contours of the theme of faith in the gospel. In order to do so, Markan redaction criticism 'must mutate into a general literary criticism'.[1]

2. Narrative criticism

The inability of conventional redaction criticism to cope adequately with the literary and theological integrity of Mark's gospel has led a growing number of scholars, especially in America,[2] to turn to secular literary criticism and related disciplines associated with the nature of language for the necessary tools and insights to interpret the earliest gospel. For even if the gospel contains successive layers of tradition and redaction, the final product is still an intentional and coherent verbal construct, and thus amenable to genuinely

---

[1] Perrin, 'Interpretation' (1967), 120.

[2] Two scholars in particular stimulated this interest in the evangelist's narrative skills: E. Auerbach, *Mimesis. The Representation of Reality in Western Literature* (Princeton University Press,1953), 40–9, and A. N. Wilder, *Early Christian Rhetoric. The Language of the Gospel* (1964). The seeds for a more literary approach to Mark were sown in the works of R. H. Lightfoot and E. Lohmeyer (see bibliography). Lightfoot insisted that the gospel must be treated as a literary unit and each part interpreted in light of its place in the whole, and Lohmeyer's was the first commentary to pay particular attention to the evangelist's literary activity. Both scholars drew attention to various compositional techniques and to the symbolic use of geographical references. The form critical evaluation of Bultmann and Dibelius was in some respects a backward step from such an appreciation of Mark's literary role. Vorster, ['Mark: Collector . . .', 55], nominates Weeden's book [*Traditions in Conflict*, 1971] as marking a transition, at least in theory, from the customary diachronic approach of redaction criticism to the more synchronic methods of literary analysis. Norman Perrin pointed the way forward in many significant essays in the early 1970s (see bibliography). On Perrin's own contribution, see Seal, 'Norman Perrin and his "School"', 87–107; Kelber, 'The Work of Norman Perrin', 452–67, and Mercer, *Norman Perrin's Interpretation* (1986). On the influence of various types of literary criticism on New Testament scholars, see the works cited in n. 3, p. 15 below.

literary analysis. Such analysis of biblical writings entails, in Robert Alter's words,

> manifold varieties of minutely discriminating attention to the artful use of language, to the shifting play of ideas, conventions, tone, sound, imagery, syntax, narrative viewpoint, compositional units and much else; the kind of disciplined attention, in other words, which through a whole spectrum of critical approaches has illuminated, for example, the poetry of Dante, the plays of Shakespeare, the novels of Tolstoy.[1]

The methods used in interpreting a literary text vary according to the type of literature it is, whether drama, poetry, history, treatise, and so on. While there is much disagreement over the precise literary genre that best accommodates Mark's gospel, or whether it is in fact *sui generis*,[2] all would agree that the fundamental category to which it belongs is that of *narrative*. By narrative we mean a story or an account of events and participants who move through time and space, a recital with a beginning, middle and end. The most fruitful literary approach to Mark, then, is one which takes seriously the narrative or story mode he uses to communicate his message, an approach which may be called *narrative criticism*.

Now literary or narrative analysis is far from being a well defined, monolithic discipline. It embraces an almost chaotic variety of methods and interests, some of which are mutually exclusive.[3] In this section, we will outline the categories and procedures of a type of narrative critical approach which, we suggest, does justice to the historical, theological and literary character of Mark's composition. Then we will consider the utility of such a method for exploring Mark's faith theme.

A narrative may be said to operate on two levels[4] – the story

---

[1] Alter, *Art of Biblical Narrative*, 12f. Such literary criticism is to be distinguished from the so-called 'literary criticism' practised by earlier source critics; see Petersen, 'Literary Criticism in Biblical Studies', 25–50.

[2] On Mark's genre, see e.g., Kelber, *Oral and Written Gospel*, 117–29; Best, *Gospel as Story*, 140–5; cf. also Guelich, 'The Gospel Genre', 183–219; Aune, *Literary Environment*, 17–76.

[3] See Dertweiler, 'After the New Criticism'; McKnight, 'Contours and Methods', 53–69; idem, *The Bible and the Reader*, passim; Mercer, *Norman Perrin's Interpretation*, 46–70.

[4] See Chatman, *Story and Discourse*, 19 and passim; Rhoads and Michie, *Mark as Story*, 4; Rhoads, 'Narrative Criticism', 414ff; Petersen, *Literary Criticism*, 47f; Stock, *Discipleship*, 31–3.

level and the discourse level. In simple terms, the story is the 'what' or content of the narrative, all the events, characters, settings and actions that make up the account. The discourse or rhetoric level is the 'how' of the narrative, the way the story is told to have the desired effect on the reader. Narrative criticism inquires into the relationship between the content of the story and the stylistic, compositional and rhetorical features[1] of the narrative that convey the story to the reader. Embracing such an approach to Mark, in preference to the exclusive use of a classical redactional or traditio-historical approach, involves a revision of understanding or shift of emphasis on three fronts: with respect to the author, to the text, and to the events in the narrative.

(a) The author

With regard to the author it entails a shift from clumsiness or artlessness to literary competence. This is significant, since the view one holds of Mark's literary capability will very much influence how one interprets features in his text. For a long time Mark was thought of as a clumsy, somewhat simplistic writer, not really in control of his material and, 'unworthy of mention in any history of literature'.[2] This accounted not only for his unpolished Greek but also for the ambiguities and inconsistencies in his narrative, the awkward, unexplained transitions, the obscure geographical schema, the inability to sustain the secrecy motif, the redundancies and duplications of episodes, and so on. Narrative criticism however, begins with the assumption that Mark was at least capable of telling a coherent story, and argues that he has, in fact, displayed considerable skill and artistry in doing so. The ambiguities, repetitions, and logical tensions in the text are not merely vestiges of poorly assimilated sources but are narrative strategies intended to involve, enthrall and surprise the reader or hearer. Instead of despising such features, we should see them as effective dramatic devices and allow them to have their full impact.

---

[1] Rhetoric is the art of using language in such a way as to produce a desired impression upon the hearer or reader. In the present study we use the term 'rhetorical' to denote the dramatic, literary and stylistic techniques Mark engages to convey his message. On the definition of rhetoric, see Kennedy, *Rhetorical Criticism*, 3.

[2] Trocmé, *Formation*, 72.

Such a positive assessment of Mark's literary skill does not go unchallenged. J. C. Meagher cites examples of clumsiness in Mark's technique and warns against 'the misguided attempt to project finesse into the awkward performance of an ordinary, weak, if talented and creative storyteller'.[1] Others maintain that Mark could not have possibly intended all the elaborate patterns and strategies detected by literary critics. It is true that Mark is not a self-conscious literary author, nor is his work a classical achievement in terms of literary aesthetics. Yet three factors should be borne in mind when evaluating the more generous estimate of Mark's literary capabilities allowed for by narrative criticism.

(i) To begin with, it should be remembered that literary creativity is not solely the function of an author's conscious intent. Mark need not have been aware of *all* the patterns he was creating or devices he was employing, for the human mind has ways of imposing order on experience unconsciously. (Nor incidentally does the reader or hearer need to be consciously alert to the symmetry, balance and architectural patterns in a text in order to experience their impact; indeed such unmediated experience of the text is primary, and the critical distillation of the devices that account for this experience is a secondary matter.) This observation should not be taken to imply a surrendering of concern for the author's intention in determining the arrangement and meaning of the text; it is simply to recognise the innate nature of human creativity. It should also be noted that none of the stylistic or rhetorical devices detected in the gospel are unique to Mark, but belong to a pool of techniques available to all narrators.[2] Some of Mark's ways of doing things would have come to him from tradition; some would flow naturally from his innate gifts as a storyteller; some would have been unconsciously imbibed from his cultural milieu. With respect to the latter point, Kennedy points out that even if Paul and the evangelists had no formal training in Greek rhetoric, they would

> have been hard put to escape an awareness of rhetoric as practised in the culture around them, for the rhetorical theory of the schools found its immediate application in

---

[1] Meagher 'Principle of Clumsiness', 466. More fully, idem, *Clumsy Construction*, passim. Meagher's target is actually redaction criticism; how much greater would be his objection to recent literary criticism.

[2] Dewey, *Public Debate*, 8, 29.

almost every form of oral and written communication:
in official documents and public letters, in private correspondence, in the lawcourts and assemblies, in speeches
at festivals and commemorations, and in literary composition of both prose and verse.[1]

The yield of literary analysis, therefore, should not be rejected
on the grounds that no single author could have consciously
intended everything that is detected in the text.

(ii) But how can equally competent scholars reach such opposite conclusions regarding Mark's literary capabilities? The
self-same features cited as proof of Mark's ineptness as a
writer are called upon by others as evidence of his literary
skill. How can this be explained? At least part of the answer
lies in the extent to which allowance is made for the fact that
Mark's style is that of a speaker rather than a literary writer,[2]
and that his gospel was written not principally for private
reading but for public recitation, probably in its entirety at one
sitting. Indeed the written gospel could well be the result of
Mark writing down, more or less verbatim, the story which he
had already told several times in oral form. Many of the
features of Mark's style, then, are not the result of strenuous
efforts to produce a sophisticated written work but are con-
cessions to the needs of oral communication. The expressive
looks and dramatic gestures, the hand motions and pregnant
silences, the variations in tone and pitch of voice and speed of
delivery – all of which are essential to effective oral communication – have as far as possible been verbally integrated in the
text,[3] so that the effects of oral performance could be renewed at
every public reading of the gospel. Features intended to appeal
to the ear in oral story-telling may now sometimes offend the
eye as written prose. But what is lost in literary smoothness is
more than made up for in dramatic effect.

The demands of oral delivery help explain Mark's vernacu-

---

[1] Kennedy, *Rhetorical Criticism*, 10. J. P. Pritchard suggests that while
Mark himself was not a stylist bound by the laws of literary genre, his
selection and arrangement of material suggests he had the assistance of a
trained rhetorician, *Literary Approach*, 38.

[2] So Pesch, *Markus*, I, 25; Pryke, *Redactional Style*, 25; Rigaux, *Testimony*, 66; Best, *Gospel as Story*, 18; Rhoads and Michie, *Mark as Story*, 2;
Meagher, 'Principle of Clumsiness', 465.

[3] See Stock, *Discipleship*, 72–5; Kelber, *Oral and Written Gospel*, 44f;
Theissen, *Miracle Stories*, 189–95.

lar Greek and his vivid style. Single episodes are linked together into a jolting paratactic narrative that creates a sense of urgency and excitement, catching up the readers and pro- pelling them from one event to the next. This tone is produced by Mark's 'activist syntax' [Kelber], especially his excessive use of the historic present,[1] of pleonastic ἄρχεσθαι and of εὐθύς and πάλιν, which together give the prose a breathlessness that corresponds to the effect of the story upon its hearers. Other features, such as the prolific use of the third person plural instead of the passive, a propensity for triadic patterns, the clustering together of like materials (such as controversy stories in chapters 2–3, and parables in chapter 4) and a pref- erence for direct speech, are all in keeping with the popular style of storytelling. Repetition and duality, so characteristic of Mark, are also essential strategies in oral communication. Whereas a reader can digest a written text at his or her own pace, pondering its words and comparing passages, a listener has only one hearing in which to receive the speaker's mess- age. The reiteration of words, clauses and themes is the oral substitute for the reader's ability to return to what was written before and link it up with what is being repeated now, and so grasp the author's emphases.[2] Even the notorious awkward- ness of Mark's geography and chronology may result partly from the fact that in oral performance time and place notation can be signalled as much by non-verbal means as by explicit references, although only the latter are readily reducible to written form.

This is not to say that all the textual features of the gospel are explicable in terms of oral needs. Even if the gospel was intended for public reading, Mark took a decisive step in choosing the written medium. The comparative slowness of written composition opens to an author a range of literary possibilities not available to the oral performer,[3] and Mark is

[1] Cf. however, Osburn's interesting discussion on the historic present in Mark, 'The Historical Present in Mark', 486–500.

[2] See Kelber, *Oral and Written Gospel*, 64–70, 80. This is not the *only* function of repetition in biblical narratives; see Alter, *Art of Biblical Nar- rative*, 88–113.

[3] Cf. Güttgemanns, *Candid Questions*, 196–200; Best, *Gospel as Story*, 17f, 107; Kelber, *Oral and Written Gospel*, 95f, 109–55, 217f. Kelber vastly over- states the antithesis between orality and textuality in the development of New Testament tradition; see the review of his book by J. D. G. Dunn, *Int* 40 (1986), 72–5, and the critique by Gerhardsson, *The Gospel Tradition*, esp. 30–9.

able to exploit these as well, while even those devices deriving from or intended for oral delivery have their function extended once transposed to written form.

(iii) The third point to note is that Mark's creative authorship does not automatically entail a denial of his dependence on prior tradition, nor even his conservative manner of handling this tradition. 'Creativity' is not the same thing as invention, nor does 'authorship' mean composition from scratch. It is rather to recognise the evangelist's supervening role in the publication of a work of considerable literary complexity.

Mark's authorship lies in the creation of something which did not exist before, a single, co-ordinated, *written* narrative about the earthly Jesus, indeed the gospel form itself.[1] This unitary narrative was not the inevitable outcome of processes inherent in the tradition, as Bultmann thought,[2] but was the result of a deliberate, innovative step taken by Mark. In creating this sequential account, Mark has *chosen* to write in subordination to existing tradition, to be controlled by it. His creative skill lies not in the freedom he has exercised over the content of his sources but in the way he has set incidents in relationship to each other by means of two related processes of arrangement. The first is the arrangement of pericopae (and complexes) into a linear sequence to form a coherent plot with its own space and time. The second is the arrangement of a complex web of relationships between incidents by the use of a wide range of compositional, stylistic and literary techniques: repetitional devices, such as two-step progression, three-fold patterns, reiteration of key words; parenthetical constructions, such as intercalations, 'insertions', framing passages, and the use of *inclusio*; symmetrical patterns, such as chiasmus, ring composition, and parallelism; techniques of foreshadowing and retrospection; and extensive use of the dynamics of parabolic speech, such as role reversal, paradox and irony. Through these two processes, Mark provided a new way of interpreting familiar Jesus-traditions, not by theological exposition and commentary, but by their relationship to one another and their place in the overarching story of Jesus.[3]

---

[1] Cf. Guelich, 'The Gospel Genre', 213.

[2] On this, see Güttgemanns, *Candid Questions*, e.g., 95–124; 334–42; Kelber, 'Mark and Oral Tradition', 8–15; idem, *Oral and Written Gospel*, 1–43.

[3] See Achtemeier, 'Mark as Interpreter', 115f; idem, *Mark*, 22. See also, Theissen, *Miracle Stories*, 198–228.

Our mode of literary interpretation, then, must be conditioned by this peculiar mode of composition. Inasmuch as Mark's gospel is not a completely free authorial creation, we cannot assume he has an equal investment in every word, sentence and unit, as we could if we were reading a novel. We must beware of an overly-subtle exegesis that invests every word and detail with symbolic or theological significance. On the other hand, inasmuch as Mark has successfully integrated diverse materials into a new, carefully crafted whole, only after attempts to assign features of the text semantically to their context have failed or become implausible are we justified in claiming Mark's unthinking or clumsy use of prior tradition.

In summary, while Mark has worked in conscious dependence on what went before him, narrative criticism has good grounds for regarding him as an author[1] of considerable literary skill who, regardless of his sources, bears full responsibility for the shape and structure of the final product.

(b) The text

As we have seen, redaction criticism entails a breaking up of the text into its component parts in order to trace the compositional processes that gave rise to the text as we have it. Yet it was clearly Mark's intention that the recipients of his work would encounter it as a single, unified story, not just as an assemblage of various, subtly modified traditional units. Individual pericopae were no longer to be experienced simply as separate tales, but also as cumulative episodes or scenes in

[1] Some scholars are uneasy with the term 'authorship' for describing Mark's activity because it implies greater compositional freedom than Mark was able to exercise (e.g., Pryke, *Redactional Style*, 29; Hickling, 'A Problem of Method', 345f). E. Best prefers to think of him as an artist who creates a collage or a composer who forms a new work out of existing tunes, *Gospel as Story*, 118, 121f; idem 'Mark: Some Problems', 82. However, in contemporary usage the term 'author' is not confined to writers of fiction who have a free hand in the development of character and plot. It is also used for writers who present well known material in a fresh way, such as writers of biography or recent history. Besides, not even writers of fiction are completely free agents. All authors are subject to some constraints: constraints of genre and structure, of culture and language, of upbringing and ideology, of readers' credulity and expectations. Describing Mark as an author has the virtue of granting him recognition as one who, irrespective of his dependence on prior tradition, is to be credited with the shape of the final narrative.

a single tale or story. Narrative criticism therefore calls for a shift away from fragmentation as an interpretative procedure and toward an appreciation of the wholeness of the completed text.

Now it is not enough simply to assert the unity and coherence of the final text; some interpreters deny that Mark's story has genuine coherence,[1] so it must be shown what it is that makes Mark a *bona fide* narrative, a single story and not just a collection of unrelated pieces. Narrative criticism approaches this task from a number of angles.

From one angle, it is the *narrator*[2] that confers unity on the work. The narrator's task is to tell the story, and to do so in a way that guides and shapes the reader/hearer's evaluation of what is described. As Petersen explains,

> Through what he tells and shows, both by commission and omission, the narrator evokes images as well as ideas in the reader's imagination, requiring the reader to see, however determinately, characters and their actions, settings and movements, and to feel with and about the actors, to make judgements about them and their motives, even to raise questions in anticipation of answers expected as the narrative process continues to its end. Throughout all of this the reader's imagination is controlled by what the narrator says and does not say, making the act of reading both imaginative and controlled. It is through the control exerted by the narrator, himself the puppet of an author, that the reader also becomes a participant in the formation of the work and its imaginative world.[3]

Mark functions consistently as a third-person, intrusive (and reliable) narrator. As the 'third person voice', he is external to the story and narrates the entire gospel from beginning to end

---

[1] See n. 1, p. 17 above

[2] Literary theorists distinguish between the 'real author', the 'implied author', and the 'fictional narrator' (see, e.g., Booth, *Rhetoric of Fiction*, 70–7; Chatman, *Story and Discourse*, 147–51; also McKnight, *Bible and Reader*, 101-3; Petersen, 'Literary Criticism in Biblical Studies', 37–9). As there is no discernible difference in the perspectives of each of these in Mark, it is not important to maintain these distinctions (so Rhoads and Michie, *Mark as Story*, 148 n.14; Rhoads, 'Narrative Criticism', 420; Vorster, 'Mark: Collector...', 59; Kingsbury, *Christology*, 1 n.1). Klauck finds it analytically useful to do so however, 'Erzählerische Rolle', 1–26.

[3] Petersen, 'Literary Criticism in Biblical Studies', 38f.

as an outsider. As an intrusive narrator, he is invisibly present in every scene, even when Jesus is alone (14:35ff), telling us
everything he considers we need to know about the agents and
events recorded. Furthermore the Markan narrator evaluates[1]
all the occurrences in his story from a consistent perspective or
'point of view',[2] a standard of judgement that corresponds to
the values, beliefs and attitudes displayed by the central
character, Jesus.[3]

The consistent role and ideological standpoint of the narrator is one means whereby Mark creates a unified narrative
out of sundry sources. Another means is by the careful *plotting*
of his narrative and the creation of an intelligible story-world.
Plot designates the way an author arranges events at the
discourse level in terms of time and causality to produce the
desired effect.[4] If plot denotes the *pattern* of events narrated,
narrative world refers to the *totality* of events referred to,
whether or not they are part of the plotted narrative.[5] Now
Mark has linked once separate units by geographical and
temporal designations into an extended sequential plot built
around a dichotomy between Galilee and Jerusalem and
Jesus' movement from one sphere to the other. The story as a
whole has a clear dramatic structure that builds towards
climax and resolution and has a projection into the future. The
narrative world embraces such unplotted items as creation
(10:5), Old Testament history (1:2f), Jesus' resurrection (14:28;
16:7), and the eschatological consummation (8:38: 13:26; 14:62).

Perhaps the clearest evidence that Mark has consciously
distilled a definite plot from his sources is the complex inter-
connections he establishes between episodes.[6] One way he does
this is by a network of backward and forward references of
various kinds[7] that bring plotted, and some unplotted, episodes

---

[1] See Tannehill, 'Disciples in Mark', 389–92, for the major ways the author
expresses evaluation.

[2] On 'point of view', see Chatman, *Story and Discourse*, 151–61; Berlin,
'Point of View', 77–113; eadem, *Poetics and Interpretation*, 43–82; Petersen, 'Point of View', 97–121.

[3] So Petersen, 'Point of View', 107; Tannehill, 'Disciples in Mark', 391;
Rhoads, 'Narrative Criticism', 421.

[4] See Matera, 'Plot of Matthew's Gospel', 235–40, and the literature cited
there.

[5] See Petersen, *Literary Criticism*, 40, 47, 49–52.

[6] See Petersen, *Literary Criticism*, 49–80.

[7] E.g. forward references may be divided into fulfilled and unfulfilled

into relationship to one another. Forward references anticipate and interpret what is to come as the narrative advances (e.g. 3:6; 4:1; 8:31; 9:31; 10:32; 11:2f; 14:18,43ff; 14:27,66f). Retrospective references require the reader or hearer to recall what has gone before and to reflect on it in light of current developments (e.g. 8:18ff; 11:21; 14:72). In this way the author combines a forward momentum in his plot with a transcending of the linear sequence of episodes to suggest relationships and meanings in events that go beyond their immediate context.

Plot is one of the two basic requirements for a narrative. The other is *characterisation*, and here too we find a consistency that spans the entire work. Guiding his audience to either a negative or a positive evaluation of the words and actions of his characters is one of Mark's main ways of achieving his purpose. Mark develops characterisation in a variety of ways: by recounting the words and deeds of the people in his story; by describing their interaction; by juxtaposing character depictions to create comparisons and contrasts; and occasionally by commenting directly on the inner life of the participants in different episodes (e.g., 2:6f; 5:27f; 6:26). This last way is worth noting since it is frequently denied that biblical narrators describe the interior life of their characters.[1] The characters often express points of view that clash with the evaluative point of view of the narrator and it is this that creates irony, ambiguity and pathos in the story.

The major narrative figures – Jesus, the disciples, the authorities, demons, the crowd – reappear in successive scenes in the gospel. There is a consistency in the roles these characters fulfil and the tasks they undertake from one scene to the next. On the other hand, there is a progressive enrichment of what is known about these figures. Certain episodes reinforce what is understood about them from earlier scenes; other scenes reveal new characteristics; still others indicate significant shifts and development.[2] Those aspects of characterisation that emerge from any one scene therefore are enriched and

prophecies and predictions; backward references into explicit and implicit retrospection.

[1] Berlin discusses this common misconception, 'Point of View', 90f, and *Poetics and Interpretation*, 37f. See also her discussion of the techniques of characterisation, 'Point of View', 88–102; eadem *Poetics and Interpretation*, 23–42, 59–73.

[2] See Tannehill, 'Disciples in Mark', 388f; Klauck, 'Erzählerische Rolle', 3f. On the implications of this for gospel christology, see Chouinard, 'Gospel Christology', 21–37; also Boring, 'Christology of Mark', 125–53.

extended when seen in relationship to all other scenes. Characterisation will prove of particular importance for the understanding of faith in the gospel. By and large it is supplicants for healing that exemplify the faith Jesus calls for. What it is that constitutes this faith only becomes apparent from analysis of the attitudes and behaviour of these characters.

Through the medium of story, Mark seeks to communicate a certain message to his audience, and at this *conceptual* or theological level too there is a consistency throughout the narrative. Of course Mark is not a theologian in the technical sense of being a systematic religious thinker. He is pre-eminently a storyteller, and his theological viewpoint (in the sense of definite convictions about God, humankind and salvation) is implicit in the way he tells or interprets the story of Jesus.[1] To speak of theological coherency in Mark is not to expect a logical precision or an ordered exposition of certain beliefs. In presenting his views in narrative form, Mark makes great use of riddle, irony, and paradox that resist easy systemisation. Much remains open-ended, and seemingly contrary viewpoints, such as revelation and secrecy, universalism and particularism, are left standing in unresolved tension.[2] Nevertheless, right across the spectrum of episodes lies a consistent depiction of sin, the human plight, the rule of God, and the challenge to men and women in light of God's work in Jesus. One of our tasks is to investigate the extent to which such consistency exists in Mark's depiction of faith and unbelief.

Finally, a certain homogeneity of *style* and repeated use of the same range of literary devices throughout the gospel also verifies its unitary nature. The main features of Mark's style are well known and need not be rehearsed here.[3] We have already mentioned his characteristic 'duality', and cited some of his literary techniques. The significant point to note is that

[1] 'There are more ways of telling a story than we usually realise. The narrator chooses the way that fits his purpose or limits his purpose to the narrative forms at his disposal, and so his purposes are mirrored by his stories', Tannehill, 'Disciples in Mark', 387f.

[2] See Burkill, *New Light*, 121–79.

[3] For convenient summaries, see Taylor, *Mark*, 44–66; Haenchen,*Weg Jesu*, 29–37; N. Turner, *Syntax*, 11–30, Vol. 1 in J. H. Moulton, *A Grammar of New Testament Greek* (Edinburgh: T. & T. Clark, 1965). The narrative vividness of Mark's account is well demonstrated by Findlay, *Jesus*, 27–38.

such features recur throughout the entire narrative. Consistency of style is not the same thing as total uniformity however. Narrative style need not be the same throughout a single work, and Mark varies his style to suit his ends. For instance, in describing the call of the disciples (1:16–20), his style is terse and concise, reinforcing the immediacy and authority of Jesus' call. In many of the miracle stories, conversely, especially those mentioning faith, his style is diffuse and wordy, partly because such descriptive details serve to illustrate nuances of meaning in the idea of faith being depicted. Mark also varies the tempo of his narrative. Early in the story the action shifts rapidly from one location to the next and covers a longish period of time, but at the end of the story it slows to an hour by hour account of the crucifixion in a single location, Jerusalem.

To summarise: at the levels of narrator, plot, characterisation, theology and literary style, one can discover a unity and integrity in the gospel that makes it both appropriate and necessary to study the work as a genuine narrative, as a single, coherent, intelligible story. By implication, the apparent discrepancies and contradictions in the text can often be resolved when examined in the context of Mark's storyline, character development, literary style and thematic progression. 'What looks like a flawed text, controlled by disparate pre-Markan traditions, may well prove to be under Markan control if we persist in reading the text within the Markan theological framework.'[1]

(c) Narrated events

The third shift of focus occasioned by narrative criticism is from the category of 'history' to the category of 'story' in treating the events recorded in the gospel. The concern that has governed virtually all modern synoptic research has been that of history. The gospels have been viewed principally as historical witnesses either for the time of Jesus, or of the primitive church, or of the evangelist. By contrast, narrative criticism is essentially ahistorical in the sense that questions of the historical foundations or accuracy of the gospel stories, or of the authenticity of Jesus' words, are considered extraneous to the task of appraising the gospels as imaginative works. For even if the author intends his account to be histori-

---

[1] Kelber, 'Hour of the Son of Man', 42.

cally true to the people and events portrayed, his narrative still functions as a narrative regardless of how successful he has been in achieving that aim.

Even though Mark's gospel is based on actual historical events, the world constituted by the narrative is nonetheless a literary creation, with an independent existence of its own quite apart from the real world events of Jesus' time or Mark's time. The real world and the narrative world are *distinguishable* realities, as a work of historical fiction shows. The story world is a self-enclosed entity with its own space and time, its own values and universe of meanings, its own internal network of references. It is this created reality that conveys the author's message. Statements in the narrative refer in the first instance to people, places, and events in the story, and derive their meaning primarily from this context, not from the historical verities of the real world.

At this point, we must lay an important caveat. Even if our interpretative focus shifts onto the narrative world, this does not mean that the gospel can be understood in a complete vacuum. Considerations drawn from real world history cannot be dispensed with altogether. Mark uses sources rooted in historical events and adopts an historical mode of narration, and there is no indication that he himself doubted that the events he records actually happened. Indeed he chooses the medium of story because he regards these events as so significant that he wishes to transport his readers/hearers back into the past and enable them to become part of what transpired then. For narrative, as a literary form, has the effect of drawing the audience into the action, engaging their emotions, encouraging identification with the narrative figures, so that they themselves experience what the characters experience in the story. Mark creates a narrative world in order to allow real world events and people of the past to impinge existentially on the present of his readers or hearers. The characters and events in the gospel thus belong at once to a self-contained story world and represent to the readers/hearers external historical realities. The degree of congruence between these two worlds is a problem for historical criticism, but that Mark intended a congruence seems clear.

Since Mark's narrative world is composed of people and events that also belong to the real world, it cannot be seen as *autosemantic* in any absolute sense. While there is an important sense in which every creative work has a certain aesthetic autonomy, the gospel narrative (or any other narrative for that matter) cannot be read in complete isolation. Basic to any literary communication is a pool of shared experiences, information, and concepts between author and readers. The greater this commonality, the more the author can rely on allusion, suggestion, and innuendo to convey his meaning. Sound hermeneutical procedure therefore will take into account not only the written text itself but also the cultural and conceptual horizons of the writer and audience. This is where background studies and even research on the historical Jesus have a valuable role in gospel literary criticism.[1] They help to illuminate the 'universe of possible meanings' open to the reader/hearer, and show whether particular ideas or associations would have been conceivable then.

This means that when Mark quotes or alludes to Old Testament concepts for example, or presumes his audience has knowledge in common with other Christians of their day so that he does not need to spell things out explicitly, we are justified in assuming this knowledge when interpreting the text. Thus we may presume that Mark's readers took 1:8 to refer to Pentecost, and 14:28 and 16:7 to denote resurrection appearances, even though these events are not narrated in the plot itself. Having said this, efforts must still be made to allow Mark to speak his mind without forced harmonisation with the other gospels or theological understandings culled from the epistles. The same applies to *religionsgeschichtliche* antecedents and parallels to Markan themes and procedures. Analysis of such parallels is a valid field of enquiry, but identification of a possible parallel usually contributes little to discerning how Mark himself treats the matter, which is the primary goal of exegesis.

(d) Summary

The narrative critical methodology outlined above is eclectic in the sense that it endeavours to take into account what redaction criticism has taught us about Mark's gospel, especially in two respects. First, while Mark's gospel is a literary narrative, redaction criticism reveals that it is also more than a narrative. It is a historical and theological communication

---

[1] The relationship between literary and historical analysis in biblical criticism is discussed frequently in the literature. See for example many of the essays in Part II of Spencer, *Orientation by Disorientation*. Also, Geller, 'Through Windows and Mirrors', 3–40.

with a pastoral purpose – features that reach out beyond the work itself and mean that it cannot be considered as totally self-interpretative. And secondly, while the gospel is a literary composition, redaction criticism reminds us that it is not a completely free authorial creation. Mark has worked in conscious dependence upon, even subordination to, tradition, and our mode of literary interpretation must be conditioned by Mark's particular mode of composition. However, narrative method surrenders any attempt to distinguish source and redaction, or to evaluate the authenticity of Jesus' logia, since these are of only peripheral significance to the interpretation of the author's message.

Inasmuch as it approaches the gospel writer's theological perspective through the medium of story, narrative criticism offers a promising method of combining a literary and conceptual analysis of Mark's faith theme. Our particular subject matter does, however, pose something of a challenge to narrative method. One issue to be tested is whether narrative-critical categories are appropriate for elucidating such a distinctly 'theological' matter as faith, and for investigating an element in Mark's story which does not itself advance the plot but functions rather as a kind of repetitive commentary on the action. A further challenge is posed by the fact that whilst narrative criticism stresses the importance of interpreting Mark in its entirety as one coherent, progressively developing story, we can only discover what Mark means by faith and the devices he uses to communicate it, by analysing the individual episodes in which faith is depicted. This necessitates a pericope by pericope approach. But in view of the fact that Mark's narrative structure has a clear 'scenic' quality in which the action is broken up into a sequence of discrete episodes, there is no reason why narrative critical categories and insights should not be applied to the smaller stories which make up the larger story, as well as to the overarching patterns of the narrative as a whole. Indeed Mark's consummate success as a creative author lies in his combining of a variety of independent stories into a unified whole with its own message, while at the same time leaving his traditions free to operate as small narratives in their own right, making their own points.

Accordingly, we will use narrative procedures at two levels of Mark's composition – at the level of individual passages that treat faith, and at the level of their integration into the larger gospel framework. We will seek to interpret the faith references within the integrity of the episodes in which they occur and from which they derive their meaning, and also in relation to the major progressive themes of the story with which they are interwoven. Because we will be devoting primary attention to the explicit faith pericopae, certain other pericopae of crucial significance in Mark's total narrative structure, such as 8:27–33, can be dealt only with in passing. This is not to deny the importance of these episodes; it is simply to focus our interest on one component theme of the larger story.

3. Isolating the theme: some semantic issues

As already noted, in exploring faith as a narrative theme we shall be primarily focusing on those pericopae which employ the πίστις, πιστεύειν word group. But this raises the question as to whether all that Mark wants to say about faith can be confined to these passages, and, conversely, whether his πίστις, πιστεύειν terminology always signifies faith and not something else. We will only be able to answer these questions in the course of our study, but three general observations may be made by way of introduction.

(i) A thematic study must start somewhere, and it seems reasonable to begin with the assumption that Mark uses the πίστις, πιστεύειν group of words – already semi-technical terms in his day[1] – as the primary lexical signal for material relevant to the notion of faith. To begin with some general definition of faith and then find places in the gospel which express this idea, would not only risk importing non-Markan meanings, but would also make it difficult to limit the scope of the study.

Yet it would be unjustified to assume that the πίστις, πιστεύειν material represents the sum total of what Mark wishes to say about faith. It is a basic semantic fallacy to think there is a one-to-one correspondence between words and concepts.[2] The absence of the word 'faith' does not necessarily mean that the idea of faith is also lacking, for it could be expressed by various other word combinations, or by synonyms, or be implicit in the way action is described.

---

[1] On the connection between early Christian understandings of faith and Old Testament-Jewish tradition, see Lührmann, 'Pistis in Judentum', 19–38; idem, Glaube, 85–99; Lohse, 'Emuna und Pistis', 147–55; idem, 'Glauben', 78ff.

[2] Barr, Semantics, 21–37; Louw, Semantics, 7, 39–42; Silva, Biblical Words, 19, 26f, 29 n.48.

There are no recurring synonyms[1] in Mark for the generic terms πίστις, πιστεύειν. Mark's stylistic preference is to overwork a limited range of important words rather than employ a variety of equivalents. Nonetheless, it is possible to extend our appreciation of Mark's conception of faith by attention to narrative context and by tracing the wider usage in the gospel of some of the more significant words that are brought into association with faith in the faith-pericopae. For example, since 11:23 identifies the heart as the seat of faith, other references to the heart, such as to hardness of heart (3:5; 6:52; 8:17), are brought potentially within the semantic orbit of faith. The same may be said for references to prayer in the narrative, in light of the link between prayer and faith in 9:28f and 11:24. Or again the association between 'seeing' and faith in passages such as 2:5; 5:22; 15:32 means that seeing (and 'hearing') becomes an important metaphor for faith and may well function this way in passages that do not employ the πίστις, πιστεύειν terminology, such as 4:12; 8:18;15:39. Care must be taken not to collapse too much into the one concept by reading every case where faith-associated words recur as an implied commentary on faith; the same word may have quite different significance in different contexts. Yet such verbal linkages do show that Mark's concept of faith is interwoven with a number of related ideas and cannot be treated in total isolation.

It may also be the case that the concept is implied in the way Mark describes certain episodes. Most commentators believe that he uses the story of the Syrophoenician woman (7:24–30) as a typical example of faith amongst the Gentiles; the word itself is not used, but the woman's insight, persistence and confidence exemplify its true nature. The same could be said of most other healing stories in the gospel, as well as such stories as the approach of the rich man in 10:17–21. The problem here lies in deciding whether information on faith is implicit in these accounts or is deliberately omitted, which is a crucial difference. Since some think that Mark had good reasons for *not* mentioning faith in these contexts,[2] we will prejudge less if we take as normative for the author's concept those passages where he explicitly mentions the subject, if only to provide

---

[1] Synonymity is where there is such a high degree of similarity between words that, in certain contexts, they may substitute for each other with no change in meaning. Absolute synonymity probably does not exist.

[2] Cf. Hull, *Magic*, 73f. Also, Sugirtharajah, 'The Syrophoenician Woman', *ExpT* 98 (1986), 14.

some standard for detecting implicit reference to it elsewhere. Thus, even if it does not represent the full extent of Mark's reflection on faith, examination of the πίστις, πιστεύειν material is a prerequisite for any attempt to range more widely over the gospel.

(ii) Although we shall follow a verbal motif through the gospel, we are engaged in a literary or thematic study, not in lexical analysis as such. Biblical lexicography is a specifically linguistic task concerned with determining the meaning of words and their translation equivalents in different contexts. We are less concerned with the narrower job of definition than with the contribution to the meaning of these terms made by the narrative context in which they occur, and vice versa. Obviously lexical and literary analysis are interdependent but each has a distinctive emphasis.

It is a mistake in exegesis to assume that individual words are the basic carriers of meaning. The meaning of a word depends not on what it is in itself, but on its relationship to other words in a sentence, and on the relationship of the sentence to its context. It is context in the broadest sense – linguistic, literary and situational – that determines the meaning of words.[1] Of course words do possess a relatively stable semantic core, without which communication or lexicography would be impossible. This core marks out the 'latitude of correctness' or boundaries of meaning usage must observe. But actual meaning, in contrast to semantic potential, is a function of conventional usage. Furthermore, since a term may carry different senses in different contexts, it is wrong to speak of the 'proper' or 'basic' meaning of the word, especially if this is linked with its alleged etymology.[2] One particular meaning may be most frequent in current usage, or be less 'marked' (i.e. less dependent on context for immediate comprehension), but this sense is not intrinsic to the word itself, nor determinative for other senses.[3]

By implication, we cannot determine what Mark means by 'faith' by attempting to discover the 'real' or 'inner' meaning of the words πίστις and πιστεύειν, but only by considering the

---

[1] On the role of context in meaning, see Silva, *Biblical Words*, 137–56; Louw, *Semantics*, 47–66 and passim; Taber, 'Semantics', 802f; Caird, *Language and Imagery*, 49–53.

[2] On etymologising and the root fallacy, see Barr, *Semantics*, 100–59, 163–8; Louw, *Semantics*, 23–31; Silva, *Biblical Words*, 35–51.

[3] Louw, *Semantics*, 33–7; Taber, 'Semantics', 29f.

entire passages that treat the subject. We also need not attempt to reduce all the uses of the word 'faith' to a single precise definition. There may be common elements in each usage, but there is little to be gained by formulating a definition that will cover all aspects. 'Faith', like 'love', may be an inclusive or generic term embracing a variety of specific senses which find concrete expression in different circumstances. Besides, as Findlay observes, while 'something like a definition of faith is given us in our Lord's saying as reported in Mark xi,22,23 . . . Mark's interest does not lie in definitions but in instances'.[1]

(iii) Finally, a comment on translation: It is clear even from a cursory reading of Mark that he uses πίστις and πιστεύειν as nominal and verbal markers for the same essential reality (e.g. 9:23; 11:22f). There is nothing in the words themselves to suggest that the verb always signals intellectual belief and the noun existential faith (as is often the case in English usage). The verb πιστεύειν could be translated 'to have faith', and where this appears to be Mark's meaning, we may use the English noun 'faith' to convey the sense implied by the Greek verb.[2] Having set out the main methodological principles we will employ in our study, we now turn to the analysis itself.

---

[1] Findlay, *Jesus*, 102.

[2] In their translation of Mark's text, Rhoads and Michie always use the term 'faith' when rendering the πίστις, πιστεύειν word group into English.

2 THE CALL TO FAITH (Mark 1:14-15)

The theme of faith in Mark's gospel takes its point of departure in the very first words found on the lips of Jesus. After the scene is set with information on time ('after John was handed over'), place ('Jesus came into Galilee') and theme ('preaching the gospel of God'), Jesus is quoted as declaring:

> The time is fulfilled and the kingdom of God is at hand;
> repent and believe in the gospel. (1:15)

The declaration falls into two parts: a two-fold indicative stating the kingdom's advent, and a double imperative summoning a response to this event of repentance and faith.

The appearance of the kingdom of God constitutes the *leitmotiv* of the entire gospel. As the theme unfolds in the following narrative, it becomes apparent that Mark's concept of the kingdom of God resists easy definition. It is bound up in paradox and mystery, and is the subject of cryptic parabolic discourse (4:1–34). The underlying idea, however, seems relatively clear, especially against the backdrop of Isaianic prophecy which the author first evokes in 1:2f. Fundamentally, in Mark's account, God's kingdom represents the definitive manifestation of his ruling power to put things right in the world, to bring in the promised age of eschatological salvation. It is not primarily a spatial or a temporal category but a dynamic event: God himself is approaching 'with strength' (Isa 40:10 LXX; cf. Mk 1:7) to establish his dominion over sin, sickness and hostile powers.[1]

Notwithstanding this, the first kingdom saying in Mark is unique for its powerful, double temporal qualification of 'fulfilment' and 'nearness'. The verb ἐγγίζειν can mean both, 'to arrive' and 'to come near'. Vigorous discussion has centred

---

[1] The background literature on the kingdom of God is voluminous. One of the most substantial recent studies is by G. R. Beasley-Murray, *Jesus and the Kingdom of God* (1986), which cites most other relevant literature.

on the temporal force of the verb in Jesus' proclamation.
C. H. Dodd championed the former option and W. G. Kümmel
the latter,[1] and subsequent scholarship has tended to favour
Kümmel's view. But the issue has often been obscured by a
failure to differentiate between the semantic potential of ἐγγίζειν
when treated in isolation, and the actual semantic value of the
verb in its Markan context. When viewed in context, the disputed phrase signifies the definitive arrival rather than the
imminent future of the kingdom.[2]

The clause ἤγγικεν ἡ βασιλεία τοῦ θεοῦ stands in synthetic
parallelism with Πεπλήρωται ὁ καιρός. They are mutually
interpretative expressions. The first clause indicates that the
divinely measured time (καιρός) of expectation (vv 2f) has
ended; the old era has now passed away. The second clause
announces the dawn of the new era; for if the time of waiting
for the kingdom is over, then the time of the kingdom must
have begun. The fact that both verbs precede their subjects and
are in the perfect tense further indicates that a completed
action with continuing implications is being enunciated.[3] The
only other place that Mark uses the perfect form ἤγγικεν is
instructive. At the end of the Gethsemane episode, Jesus
declares: 'my betrayer is at hand (ἤγγικεν)' (14:42). Significantly, it is while Jesus is still speaking (καὶ εὐθὺς ἔτι αὐτοῦ
λαλοῦντος) that Judas appears (v 43). From Mark's perspective, then, Jesus' first public utterance in Galilee constitutes
the threshold of the in-breaking kingdom. The sovereign action
of God to transform the world has been initiated in his
proclamation, and this event brings with it the corresponding
demand for repentance and faith.

The very fact that it is Jesus himself, the central, 'reliable'
character in the narrative, who singles out repentance and
faith as the fundamental response required to the announcement of eschatological salvation, invests faith with considerable significance. It is the first indication given of how the

---

[1] C. H. Dodd, *The Parables of the Kingdom* (Collins, 1961²), 36ff; W. G.
Kümmel, *Promise and Fulfilment* (London: SCM, 1956), 19–36. See the
summary in Kelber, *Kingdom*, 6–9; Beasley-Murray, *Kingdom of God*, 72–
3. Cf., also Sander's evaluation of the evidence, *Jesus*, 123–56.

[2] So Pesch, *Markus*, I, 101f; Gnilka, *Markus*, I, 68; Schmithals, *Markus*, I,
102f; Kelber, *Kingdom*, 9f; Via, *Kerygma and Comedy*, 82; Ambrozic,
Hidden Kingdom, 4; Kee, *Community*, 108f, 145; Zeller, 'Jesus als Mittler',
279; Beasley-Murray, 'Eschatology in Mark', 39f.

[3] So Kelber, *Kingdom*, 11; Ambrozic, *Hidden Kingdom*, 21f; Beasley-
Murray, 'Eschatology in Mark', 39; idem, *Kingdom of God*, 73.

readers are meant to evaluate the various reactions they will encounter as the story of the kingdom's impact proceeds. However, the full value faith is given at this early juncture can be most clearly seen by an examination of the literary function of the narrative unit in which the call to faith occurs (1:14–15). This unit performs a number of different tasks in Mark's narrative, as a result of which faith, as one of its constituents, acquires a degree of importance not apparent at first sight. After considering this narrative role, we will examine the meaning and content of faith in 1:15.

1. The narrative function of 1:14–15

Mark 1:14f is the first and foremost of Mark's *Sammelberichte*. Many of the central concepts of the gospel – preaching, handing over, fulfilment, gospel, Galilee, repentance and faith – are piled up into a kind of abstract or summary of what is to follow. Both this theological overload and the conspicuous positioning of the summary at the outset of Jesus' ministry set these verses apart as having a unique role in Mark's narrative programme. We may distinguish four main ways in which the unit functions.

(a) Introductory function

First of all, in terms of literary structure, the unit acts as an introduction to the Galilean ministry of Jesus. There is a difference of opinion over whether 1:14f should be read as the conclusion to the prologue or as the introduction to the Galilean section of the narrative.[1] Those who argue the former option point to how the 'fulfilment of time' terminates the period of anticipation and preparation outlined in vv 2–13, and the repetition of εὐαγγέλιον in vv 1,14f acts as an *inclusio* marking off the whole section.[2] However, there are stronger indications that Mark intends vv 14–15 to function primarily[3]

---

[1] See Keck, 'Introduction to Mark's Gospel', 353–62. Dautzenberg objects to calling vv 1–15 a 'prologue', since it does not conform to that literary *Gattung*, 'Zeit des Evangeliums', (I) 229–31. For a different view, see Stock, *Discipleship*, 49f; Standaert, *Marc*, 41–3, 504–9.

[2] Dewey, *Public Debate*, 13; Reploh, '"Evangelium" bei Markus', 111–12; Dautzenberg, 'Zeit des Evangeliums', (I) 231.

[3] This does not preclude the possibility of it also serving a transitional function, as Perrin proposes, *Introduction*, 144f. So too Robbins, 'Mark 1:1–20', 225. But see the critique of this by Hedrick, 'Summary Statements', 310f.

as an introduction to Jesus' public ministry as a whole. Whereas previous sentences are linked together with καί and ἐγένετο, v 14 begins with a temporal designation (μετὰ δέ) that separates the unit temporally from the previous episodes. It is also separated in spatial terms. Whereas the action narrated in vv 2–13 takes place in the wilderness (vv 2,4,12,13) and at the river Jordan (vv 5,9), the inauguration of Jesus' ministry occurs in Galilee[1] (v 14b). The reiteration of Γαλιλαίας in v 16a implies a unity, on the other hand, between v 14–15 and what follows. There is also a change in the nature of Jesus' activity. In vv 9–13, he is the passive recipient of baptism, the heavenly address, the descent of the Spirit, and propulsion into the wilderness, whereas in vv 14f he actively initiates the proclamation of the kingdom and remains the chief actor throughout the remainder of the story.

The repetition of εὐαγγέλιον in vv 14f serves as a literary device to encourage retrospection or flashback to v 1 after the parenthetical digression in vv 2–13. That this material is a parenthesis[2] is suggested by the use of framing temporal markers (ἀρχή and μετὰ δέ) and by the unique occurrence here of καθώς at the commencement of a sentence or pericope (v 2; cf. 4:33; 9:13; 11:6; 14:16,21; 15:8; 16:7). By encouraging a mental reversion to v 1, Mark indicates that the 'gospel of Jesus Christ, Son of God' finds its ἀρχή, not with John the Baptist, but here in Jesus' first proclamation in Galilee (vv 14f). This means that vv 14–15 cannot be regarded simply as one summary among many of Jesus' work, or as defining only the opening phase of his ministry in Galilee (to 3:6). Rather, vv 1,14,15 together provide an introduction to the entire ministry of Jesus, at least up until his final departure from Galilee in the last weeks of his life.[3]

---

[1] Mark sees a distinction between Galilee and the wilderness. Jesus goes out of Galilee to John in the desert (v 9), and comes into (ἦλθεν ... εἰς v 14) Galilee after leaving the wilderness (v 12).

[2] Dautzenberg calls vv 2–13 a type of 'Verschachtelung', 'Zeit des Evangeliums', (I), 228.

[3] Mark's Galilee–Jerusalem dichotomy, in which Jesus first appears in Jerusalem in 11:1 to go to his death, means that 'Galilee' in 1:14 could represent his public ministry as a whole. Before he appears in Jerusalem his ministry is not confined to Galilee, but he always returns to Galilee after journeys beyond the region.

(b) Programmatic significance

The fact that this is the only instance in Mark where the precise content of the 'gospel' is expressly spelled out endows the message of vv 14f with a programmatic significance. Three factors in particular enable it to function in this way.

(i) Its position at the beginning of Jesus' ministry means that it affects the reader's understanding of the entire narrative. All aspects of the story must be viewed in its light.

(ii) Jesus' words are not addressed to any specific group of characters in the story, and the present participles suggest that the proclaiming and speaking are on-going or repetitive. One of the functions of Mark's *Sammelberichte*, furthermore, is to indicate that Jesus' ministry extended over a wider area than the few regions that constitute the main setting of the plot.[1] All this means that the influence of Jesus' initial proclamation is universal, embracing all the figures who appear in the narrative.

(iii) The use of several key words and concepts in the summary which are reiterated at strategic points elsewhere in the narrative evokes a whole series of cross-referents that permit the message of vv 14–15 to reverberate throughout the narrative. This technique relieves the narrator of the burden of having to repeat the content of Jesus' words every time he depicts him speaking.

This last point is the key to appreciating how Mark extends the initial call to faith across his narrative. When, for example, Jesus is again described as 'preaching' in 1:38f, the reader is invited to supply the general content of 1:14f as the substance of his message. The same applies, by extension, to the twenty or so references to Jesus teaching. Whatever it is that differentiates κηρύσσειν and διδάσκειν in Mark,[2] it is clearly not their content. In 6:12,30, both words are used to depict the same event, and the phrase, 'speaking the word' serves as an equivalent for both preaching (1:15,45; cf. 14:9) and

---

[1] See Hedrick, 'Summary Statements', 289–311.

[2] On this issue, see Achtemeier, *Mark*, 51–4, 60–70; Baarlink, *Anfängliches Evangelium*, 153f; Meye, *Twelve*, 52–60; Best, *Temptation and Passion*, 72, 64; Schweizer, 'Anmerkungen', 92–7. The only real difference is that teaching is especially characteristic of Jesus (only in 6:30 is it used of anyone else, and here as an aorist, not an imperfect), while preaching is also an activity of those about Jesus (1:4,7,45; 3:14; 6:12; 7:36; 13:10; 14:9; cf. 1:14,38f for the application to Jesus).

teaching (4:33; 8:32; 9:31). Furthermore, faith is given as the desired response not only to preaching (1:15), but also to teaching (cf. 2:2,5; 6:2,6). Baarlink is therefore correct in considering that 'the content of the opening proclamation in 1:14 is also meant as an indication of the content of the διδαχή of Jesus in general'.[1]

The call to faith, then, is implied every time in the story Jesus is described as addressing an audience. Moreover if, as Achtemeier proposes, the programmatic use of κηρύσσειν in 1:14 is intended to subsume everything Jesus subsequently says and does under the rubric of 'proclamation',[2] then his *deeds* also constitute an implicit summons to repentance and faith (cf. 1:45; 2:10; 6:6a). In some respects Jesus' words and deeds are virtually interchangeable in Mark. Just as his words of command are imbued with power to bring about their own realisation (e.g. 1:27,41; 4:39; 5:41; 9:25f; 11:14 etc.), so his actions are infused with didactic power that qualifies them as preaching (1:39) and teaching (1:27; 8:14–21) in their own right. A similar pattern is discernible with the kingdom motif. Because the initial authoritative kingdom announcement includes a demand for repentance and faith, all later refer- ences to the mystery of the kingdom (4:1–34), to entering the kingdom (9:47; 10:14f; 10:23–5; 12:34), and to the futurity of the kingdom (9:1; 14:23; 15:43), are to be viewed through this prism.

(c) Paradigmatic significance

This cross-referencing technique is also the means of dis- cerning a third way in which 1:14–15 functions in the narrative, viz., paradigmatically. The activity of Jesus – his proclamation of the kingdom and summons to faith – provides a precedent or pattern which others in the story world, and beyond, are to emulate.

This is most apparent with the disciples, whose role is described in terms that repeatedly refer the reader back to 1:14f. The disciples are first called to follow Jesus (1:16–20; 2:14). Then they are commissioned to do what Jesus does in 1:14f – to preach (κηρύσσειν); and also to cast out demons (3:14; cf. 1:39). When sent out on a mission, their message is, like

---

[1] Baarlink, *Anfängliches Evangelium*, 153.
[2] Achtemeier, *Mark*, 51–4; cf. Schmithals, *Markus*, I, 97.

that of Jesus, one of repentance (6:12). We are not told in so
many words that it included a summons to faith, but ἐκήρυξαν
ἵνα μετανοῶσιν is probably intended to recall the full content of
1:15. The description of them healing the sick (ἀρρώστους . . .
ἐθεράπευον 6:13) also implies the involvement of faith; it is a
close verbal parallel to the account of Jesus' healing activity in
Nazareth, which the disciples observed (6:1) and where the
extent of Jesus' work was limited by a lack of faith (ἀρρώστοις
. . . ἐθεράπευσεν 6:5).[1]

Just as the disciples' present role is an extension of the
ministry of Jesus set out in 1:14f, so is their predicted future
role. They are given the same essential message and the same
sphere of action that Jesus adopts at the beginning. In 13:10,
Jesus entrusts his followers with the proclamation (κηρύσσειν)
of the εὐαγγέλιον to all nations as a prelude to the End (cf. 14:9).
Within the logic of the narrative, 'the gospel' can be none other
than that first announced by Jesus, although now enriched
with additional content supplied in the intervening material.
There is a consistency in the universal dimensions of 1:14f and
the worldwide preaching of 13:10. Even more significant are
the two instances where we are told that after his resurrection,
Jesus will lead or go ahead of (προάγειν) his disciples to Galilee, to the place where the gospel was inaugurated (14:28; 16:7).
Within the story, these verses imply a restoration of the 'scat-
tered' disciples (14:27) beyond the end of the actual narrative.
Returning to Galilee, they will 'see' the risen Jesus, not only in
a literal sense but also in the sense of gaining true insight into
his real identity. For 'seeing' in Mark often symbolises spiritual perception (cf. 2:5; 4:12; 8:18; 15:39), something which has
eluded the disciples so often in the preceding story.

But why does Mark emphasise, by repetition and by climactic
placement at the end of chapter 16, that this reunion must take
place in Galilee? What is the significance of the Galilean setting? One suggestion is that 'Galilee' is shorthand for 'Galilee
of the Gentiles' (cf. Isa 8:23 LXX; Mt 4:15), and that in 14:28
and 16:7 Mark's readers are being summoned to the Gentile
mission.[2] Yet nowhere does Mark speak of Galilee of the
Gentiles, and if he does insinuate the Gentile mission at all in

---

[1] These are the only two cases of ἄρρωστος in Mark. The term is found elsewhere in the New Testament only in Matt 14:14; 1 Cor 11:30; Mk 16:18.

[2] Boobyer, 'Galilee and the Galileans', 334–48; Evans, 'I Will Go Before
You', 3–18; see also Lightfoot, Gospel Message, 106–16, which represents a
revision of his view in Locality and Doctrine (n.3, p. 41 below).

his story,[1] it is through Jesus' travels to foreign lands surrounding Galilee, not his Galilean ministry as such.[2] Another
suggestion is that Galilee is a symbol for eschatological fulfilment[3] and that 14:28 and 16:7 actually refer to the parousia of
the Son of Man.[4] Mark's readers are being encouraged to
assemble in Galilee in view of the impending eschatological
climax.[5] Some combine the Gentile connotation of Galilee with
the parousia interpretation of 14:28 and 16:7 and believe that
Mark is identifying the Gentile mission as the locale of the
parousia.[6] However, it is quite unlikely that Mark is referring
to the parousia in these texts. The case for seeing them as a
reference to a resurrection appearance of Jesus is far more
compelling.[7]

The main difficulty with the above explanations is that they
pay insufficient attention to the rhetorical or narrative function
of these final references to Galilee. In rhetorical terms, the
emphasis on Galilee functions as a device to encourage the
reader mentally to return to the beginning of the Galilean
narrative (1:14–20),[8] where the disciples were first called, and
to reconsider these events as paradigmatic for the experience
of the disciples after Easter. The anticipated restoration and
ministry of the disciples will correspond to their experience at
the beginning. Just as their initial response to Jesus was one
of repentance and faith, so will their restoration entail repentance and renewed faith in Jesus. Just as the earthly Jesus

---

[1] See Kilpatrick, 'Gentile Mission', 145–58, who argues that Mark is
remarkably reserved with regard to the Gentile mission.

[2] Schreiber, *Theologie des Vertrauens*, 170–84, argues that Galilee in Mark
includes Tyre, Sidon, etc. to emphasise its Gentile character. But see
Malbon, 'Galilee and Jerusalem', 251ff, for the distinction in Mark between
Jewish Galilee and the foreign lands surrounding.

[3] Lohmeyer, *Markus*, 355f; idem, *Galiläa und Jerusalem*, 10ff; Lightfoot,
Locality and Doctrine, 49–67; see the critique of this position in Burkill,
Mysterious Revelation, 252–7.

[4] See Perrin, 'Towards an Interpretation', 26f for arguments.

[5] Marxsen, *Introduction*, 139–43; idem, *Mark the Evangelist*, 74–92, 151–
206.

[6] Perrin, 'Towards an Interpretation', 26–30; idem, *Introduction*, 148, 150;
Gaston, *No Stone*, 482.

[7] Stein, 'Short Note', 445–52; Best, *Temptation and Passion*, 157f, 173–7;
idem, *Gospel as Story*, 72–8; Burkill, *Mysterious Revelation*, 255f; Stock,
Discipleship, 60ff; Tannehill, 'Disciples in Mark', 83; Petersen, *Literary
Criticism*, 77f.

[8] On 1:14–20 as a literary unit, see below, pp. 135–6.

went ahead of his followers (δεῦτε ὀπίσω μου 1:17) in Galilee proclaiming the gospel and calling for faith, so will the risen Jesus go ahead (προάξω, 14:28) of the disciples proclaiming, through them, the same message; προάγειν, as the counterpart to ἀκολουθεῖν, is a discipleship term (10:32; 11:9; cf. 6:45). There is, thus, a direct continuity indicated between the activity and message of Jesus before Easter and that of his disciples after Easter, through whom the risen Lord speaks.[1]

The faith content of 1:15 now takes on a significance that transcends the temporal limits of the narrative world itself. The narrative reaches its literal end in 16:8, but by transporting his readers back to 1:14–15, where the risen Jesus takes up the proclamation of the gospel through his reconstituted community of followers, Mark indicates the continuing validity of the demand for faith.

(d) Parenetic function

Within the self-contained world constituted by the narrative, Jesus' announcement of the kingdom and call for conversion and belief are addressed to all the characters who populate the story world: the crowds, disciples, opponents and prominent individuals. There is also a sense, however, in which 1:14f is addressed directly to Mark's readers/hearers. The recipients of Jesus' address are not specified; in one way Mark's audience is the first audience Jesus preaches to. They are the first to receive his injunction to repent and believe. By placing these imperatives at the beginning of his narrative, Mark makes it clear at the outset what consequences he wants his readers or hearers to deduce from what follows. In the opening verse, Mark identifies the theme of his story as 'gospel', so when Jesus calls for faith in the gospel (v 15), the readers or hearers are being tacitly invited to respond in this way to what they hear or read.

By the time the readers or hearers reach Jesus' first words in 1:14f, they have been given sufficient information about Jesus to accord his words unique authority. He has been identified as Messiah and Son of God (v 1), as the κύριος of Isaiah's prophecy and fulfiller of Old Testament hope (vv 2–3), as one 'stronger' than John (v 7), the baptiser in the Holy Spirit

---

[1] 'In some sense the Marcan experience of Jesus' Galilean ministry seems to be proleptic of the post-resurrection experience of the followers of Jesus', Malbon, 'Galilee and Jerusalem', 250.

(v 8), the beloved son in whom God delights (v 11), the victor over Satan (v 13), and the herald of God's reign (v 14). Being equipped with such knowledge – which no character in the story, except demons, possess – has a paradoxical effect on Mark's audience. It enables them to align with Jesus, the chief character, to see things from his perspective, to side with him in his interactions with others, even to share his experiences of success and rejection. Yet it also establishes a radical distinction between Jesus and themselves. The readers or hearers are constrained by the description of Jesus in vv 1–14, validated by God himself (v 11), to ascribe to him a unique, authoritative position. Inevitably, they would feel the full weight of Jesus' double demand in v 15 impinging directly upon their own situation. This does not necessarily mean that the recipients of Mark's story were mainly non-Christians whom he calls to faith in Christ. It is more likely that he is addressing a predominantly Christian community and is reasserting selected aspects of the earthly Jesus' teaching and ministry, perhaps over against a tendency to ignore, neglect or deny such features in his church. In view of the full message presented in his work, conversion and faith are required.

(e) Summary

In Mark 1:14f, Jesus becomes active in Mark's story for the first time, after being identified in a way that leaves the reader/hearer in no doubt of his uniqueness and authority. His first words announce the dawn of a new era and climax in a call to repentance and faith. The occurrence of these words at the very outset of the narrative and repeated allusions back to them in the subsequent story suggest that the main purpose underlying Jesus' whole public ministry is to bring about a change in the direction of peoples' lives (repentance) and to awaken faith in view of the manifestation of God's ruling power. This task he shares with his first disciples and renews after Easter through his re-established following. This continuity gives Jesus' demand for faith a continuing relevance that impinges directly on the reader's own life. Alertness to the narrative functioning of 1:14–15 confirms that faith is a fundamental theme in Mark's story.

2. The nature of faith in 1:14–15

So far we have examined the extensive role which faith acquires in the narrative due to its inclusion in a literary unit that is a crucial passage for understanding the gospel.[1] Now we must look more closely at the shape and content of the faith-concept represented in 1:15.

(a) The object of belief

Mark 1:15 is one of the very few places in the gospel where πίστις or πιστεύειν is expressly referred to an object (cf. 11:23,31), giving it special significance for elucidating Mark's conception of faith. Although this is the only instance in the New Testament where πιστεύειν is followed by ἐν,[2] there are a number of examples of the construction in the LXX[3] and on this analogy, the Markan locution is best taken as a case of translation Greek with ἐν marking the object of faith.[4]

Yet in the past, New Testament scholars (especially Protestant scholars) have been reluctant to accept this conclusion, partly due to the influence of Pauline usage where the gospel is the ground of faith, not its object, and partly out of a desire to avoid the implication of faith being equated with the acceptance of doctrine. They have therefore suggested taking πιστεύειν absolutely and translating ἐν with an instrumental, causal, or local force, such as: 'in the sphere of' (Deissmann; early Moulton); 'on the basis of' or 'by means of' (Schlatter, cf. Lohmeyer); 'in connection with' (Lenski) or 'bei' (Wohlenberg).[5] Such efforts, however, amount to special pleading. The LXX precedent, the artificiality of the substitutes proposed, and the natural implications of the Markan context have convinced

---

[1] For a traditio-historical analysis of Mk 1:14f, see Chilton, *God in Strength*, 29–95.

[2] Jn 3:15 and Eph 1:13 are both ambiguous. It is possible to hold that the verb stands absolutely both times. See *BAG*, 661; C. F. D. Moule, *An Idiom-Book of New Testament Greek* (London: CUP 1959[2]), 80f.

[3] 1 Kgs 27:12; 2 Chron 20:20; Pss 77:22; 105:12 [A,B,ℵ]; Jer 12:6; Dan 6:24 [Θ]; Mic 7:5; Sir 35:21.

[4] So also: Doudna, *Greek of Mark*, 79; Taylor, *Mark*, 167; Harris, 'Prepositions and Theology', 1212; Cranfield, *Mark*, 68; Pesch, *Markus*, I, 103; Schnackenburg, '"Das Evangelium"', 320; Baarlink, *Anfängliches Evangelium*, 56; Dautzenberg, 'Zeit des Evangeliums', II, 78.

[5] See the summaries in *BAG*, 660; Harris, 'Prepositions and Theology', 1212; O'Connor, *Faith*, 23f; Doudna, *Greek of Mark*, 79.

most contemporary exegetes that ἐν τῷ εὐαγγελίῳ is presented as the object of the call to faith. The real question is what meaning or content Mark gives the term 'gospel' in 1:15.

(b) The meaning of 'gospel' in v 15

The word εὐαγγέλιον occurs seven times in Mark, twice in narrative material, both of which are qualified by a genitive (1:1,14), and the remainder in sayings of Jesus, where it is always used absolutely (1:15; 8:35; 10:29; 13:10; 14:9). Numerous studies have been devoted to determining Mark's particular understanding of what is clearly a leading concept in his work. Although there are variations in emphasis and detail in the findings of such studies, the general conclusion is that Mark uses the term in roughly the same way as it was used in the early Christian mission – i.e. as a technical term for the message of salvation through the death and resurrection of Christ.[1] He may be credited with innovatively expanding the concept to include not just the message of the cross, but the whole historical ministry of Jesus, and John the Baptist as well, as warranting a full response of faith.[2] By heading his work, 'the beginning of the gospel of Jesus Christ, Son of God' (1:1) and by placing the term 'gospel' on the lips of Jesus, Mark's intention is to suggest an equivalence between the preaching of Jesus and that of the church. 'What the one who goes to the cross preaches is the same as what is preached through the church by the risen Christ.'[3] The references to the gospel in 1:14f may stem from a different traditional source than the later absolute references,[4] but the redactional connection with 1:1 indicates that Mark wishes his readers to see Jesus or the risen Christ proclaiming the church's kerygma and, at least implicitly, summoning faith in himself (although it is possible argue that Mark wants to *contrast* rather than identify the conceptions of the gospel in 1:1 and 1:15).[5]

---

[1] This is clearly argued by Schnackenburg, who stresses that the 'gospel' in Mark is not just general missionary preaching but specifically the proclamation of Jesus' death and resurrection, '"Das Evangelium"', 309–24.

[2] Reploh, '"Evangelium" bei Markus', 113; Lohse, *Glauben*, 90f.

[3] Best, *Gospel as Story*, 139; cf. idem, *Following Jesus*, 40ff.

[4] See Pesch, *Markus*, I, 106 (cf. 76 n.6).

[5] See Lemcio, 'Intention of Mark', 189, 200f. Beasley-Murray stresses that a unity between 1:1 and 15 is not the same thing as an identity between them, *Kingdom of God*, 71, 75.

Now the interpretation that reads the content of the church's kerygma into Mark's use of 'gospel' owes more to traditio-historical judgements about the provenance and redactional pedigree of the expression, than to analysis of the meaning of the term in the context of the Markan narrative. From a narrative perspective, a sounder procedure is to regard the two genitive constructions in the early narrative material (1:1,14) as the narrator's commentary upon or explanation of the absolute usage of the term by Jesus in 1:15 and subsequently in the story. The retrospective and prospective functioning of εὐαγγέ-λιον in vv 1,14,15 indicates that Mark brings the first three references to the gospel into a mutually interpretative relationship. This not only discloses his own characteristic understanding of the concept, it also constitutes the basic fund of information called to mind thereafter each time the term recurs.

The gospel in which faith is summoned in 1:15 is, in context, the 'gospel of God' (v 14) which has a definite content: the fulfilment of time and the proximity of the kingdom. The phrase τὸ εὐαγγέλιον τοῦ θεοῦ probably means 'good news from God', although it could also mean 'good news about God', since Mark would see no significant distinction between the rule of God and God himself[1] (cf. 9:1 and 14:62). To appreciate how this gospel functions as an object of faith, we need to grasp that Mark does not conceive of Jesus' εὐαγγέλιον simply as a verbal message *about* God's reign; it is an integral aspect of the reality it depicts, the very means by which the kingdom is now being established. As we have already noted, a dominant trait in Mark's characterisation of Jesus is his capacity for powerful speech. 'His voice carries the power of action. It calls into discipleship, calms the sea, creates friend and foe, cures the sick, and ruins the fig tree.'[2] The very first words Jesus utters have this causative power. He does not simply inform people that a new age has come; he actually inaugurates the time of the End by his first public utterance in Galilee.[3]

---

[1] Cf. 1:15 and 11:22. Chilton finds the closest parallel to Jesus' usage of 'kingdom of God' in Targumic diction, where 'the kingdom of God refers to God himself, as it were, personally' ('Regnum Dei Deus Est', 266). See also idem, *God in Strength*, 28–95, on Mark 1:14f, and his conclusion that in dominical usage the kingdom denotes 'the saving revelation of God himself', 283. See also Beasley-Murray's discussion of the theophanic nature of kingdom expectation, *Kingdom of God* 3–62. It seems probable that Mark would share this understanding.

[2] Kelber, *Oral and Written Gospel*, 65.

[3] This portrayal of Jesus corresponds to the description of the 'Bearer of Good

Mark's 'event-full' conception of Jesus' gospel means that 'to believe in the gospel' is to respond in faith to the manifestation of God's kingdom as it is being brought about by the preaching of Jesus. We may go further, for in Mark's view, Jesus is able to initiate the kingdom precisely because in his own person he bears or embodies its reality. The saving presence and power of God become operative in the succeeding story only in and through Jesus (cf. 5:19,20). His words and deeds, his demeanour and destiny, constitute for Mark the hidden beginning and proleptic realisation of God's final glorious rule (Mk 4). Consequently, when Jesus calls for faith in the gospel, he is drawing attention to the eschatological revelation of God now being made evident in his own person and activity. There is therefore a sort of implied christology in the stated object of the faith demand.

This christological component is underlined by a flashback to the opening verse where Jesus is identified as the Christ, the Son of God. If the phrase τοῦ εὐαγγελίου Ἰησοῦ Χριστοῦ [υἱοῦ θεοῦ] is intended as an objective genitive ('the gospel about Jesus Christ'), as most exegetes think, then it is conceivable that Mark is prompting his readers to see implicit in the demand of Jesus a call for faith in himself as Messiah, Son of God and risen Lord. Yet, a more coherent picture of the narrator's line of thought emerges if we take τοῦ εὐαγγελίου Ἰησοῦ Χριστοῦ [υἱοῦ θεοῦ] as a subjective genitive:[1] 'the beginning of the gospel (of God's eschatological salvation) which Jesus Christ, Son of God, proclaimed'. This is grammatically

News' in Second Isaiah, which seems to provide the backdrop for Mk 1:1–15. In the depiction of the messenger in Isa 61:1–11, Westermann observes that the verbs, 'somewhat oddly combine the prophet's task with its purpose or results – "to proclaim . . . to declare . . . to bind up . . . to comfort . . . to give." All that he has to do is speak. Nevertheless, in and through this proclaiming he is to effect a change on those to whom he is sent', *Isaiah 40–66* (London: SCM OT Library, 1969), 366. Because it is God who speaks through the messenger, his message is effective speech, a word that brings its own fulfilment, that inaugurates the era it describes.

[1] Cf. Dautzenberg, 'Zeit des Evangeliums', I, 221f, 228 n.45; Beasley-Murray, 'Eschatology in Mark', 37. Not a few exegetes argue that it is both an objective and a subjective genitive (e.g., Best, *Temptation and Passion*, 63f; idem, *Gospel as Story*, 39f, 139; Anderson, *Mark*, 67; Gnilka, *Markus*, I, 43). Linguists point to semantic problems with such a combining of options, (see Louw, *Semantics*, 35; Taber, 'Semantics', 802f; Silva, *Biblical Words*, 148–56), although Dormeyer uses literary and linguistic considerations for refusing to choose between subjective and objective constructions, 'Kompositionsmetapher', 461f.

possible; it corresponds with the natural sense of vv 14f; it is intrinsically more probable in view of the fact that elsewhere in the narrative the gospel is always something which Jesus speaks about; and it accords with the conceptual background of Isaiah 40, the passage which the narrator draws upon in v 3. Here Yahweh's special messenger (ὁ εὐαγγελιζόμενος) pronounces eschatological salvation, the coming of God in power (Isa 40:9f). The content of the gospel in Mk 1:15 again recalls the description of the 'bearer of good news' in Second Isaiah who announces salvation and peace and proclaims, 'Your God reigns' (Isa 52:7; cf. 40:9; 41:27; 61:1f; Pss 68:11; 96:10f).

The narrator therefore paints a consistent picture of God as the author (v 14), Jesus as the herald (vv 1,14), and the arrival of the kingdom of God as the content (v 15) of the εὐαγγέλιον. In this people are enjoined to place their faith. Such faith therefore has a sort of crisis-quality about it. It is not simply a call to a settled trust in God, but a specific injunction to respond with believing acceptance to the concrete manifestation of God's saving action as it is being triggered, so to speak, by Jesus' proclamation and realised proleptically in all his words and deeds.

Mark establishes such an intimate connection between Jesus and the kingdom that the standing of characters with respect to the kingdom is somehow determined by their attitude to Jesus. To reject Jesus' proclamation is unbelief (6:1–6), and to equate his deeds with Satan is to be excluded from eternal life (3:28–30). One's fate at the final judgement is determined by one's acceptance or rejection of Jesus (8:35–8), while following Jesus has rewards in this life and the next (10:28–31). Thus, those who respond favourably to Jesus are 'not far from the kingdom of God' (12:34) or 'waiting for the kingdom' (15:43). Jesus himself 'is the crucial term by which belief and unbelief come to function'.[1]

Finally, for the sake of completeness, we should note that later uses of 'gospel' in the narrative presuppose the foundational definition in 1:1,14f. But in light of developments in the plot the concept is enriched in two main ways. The message of eschatological salvation is focused on the need for Jesus to suffer and die (8:35; cf. 8:29–38; 14:9); and fidelity to Jesus and his gospel entails suffering and loss for his followers, both in the story (10:29), and beyond it (8:35; 13:9f). Here the indissoluble connection between Jesus and the gospel indicated in

[1] Lane, *Mark*, 66.

1:1,14f is further underlined (ἕνεκεν ἐμοῦ καὶ τοῦ εὐαγγελίου
8:35; cf. 10:29; 13:9), for the gospel is the declaration and demonstration that ultimate salvation has dawned with the coming
of Jesus.

(c) The dimensions of faith

Until now we have spoken in terms of πιστεύετε ἐν τῷ εὐαγγελίῳ
denoting a 'response of faith' to Jesus' declaration. We should
now consider more carefully what Mark conceives the experience of faith consists of. What sort of response to Jesus'
preaching does Mark count as faith or 'belief in the gospel'?

Some interpreters maintain that since the object of the call to
believe is a verbal message, it would be artificial to take the
clause to mean anything more than 'believe that my words
about the coming kingdom are true'.[1] Support for this view is
sometimes derived from the similarity of the formula with the
terminology of the early Christian mission where, it is said,
faith was not so much a matter of trust as of rational acceptance of the message about Christ.[2] Now inasmuch as the
gospel in 1:15 is indeed a verbal statement, belief in the gospel
obviously calls in the first place for acceptance of the truthfulness of what is said. Without such assent we could scarcely
talk of faith in this context at all. But this does not exhaust its
meaning. To limit the demand entirely to the cognitive side of
faith would constitute a drastic impoverishment of the conception of belief depicted here. Indeed, consideration of the context
and actual formulation of 1:15 reveals that nearly all the ways
in which the faith motif is developed in the ensuing narrative
are present in embryonic form at this initial mention of the
subject.

(i) The prepositional construction πιστεύειν ἐν implies a
deeper, existential relationship between the believer and the
object of faith than mere intellectual assent. In the LXX,
this prepositional phrase conveys the sense of firm, trustful

---

[1] So Shearer, 'Concept of "Faith"', 5; Lake, *Stewardship of Faith*, 25f.;
Werner, *Einfluss*, 111f. A number of others come close to this position;
Burkill, *New Light*, 133; Keck, 'Introduction to Mark', 359; Taylor, *Mark*,
167.
[2] Maisch, *Heilung des Gelähmten*, 73f. Cf. Bultmann, *Theology*, I, 89f;
Conzelmann, *An Outline of the Theology of the New Testament* (SCM,
1969), 61.

reliance[1], as do the parallel prepositional constructions in the
New Testament. Had Mark wanted primarily to stress the
aspect of rational conviction, he could have omitted ἐν or composed a clause using πιστεύειν ὅτι (cf. 11:23f).

(ii) We have found that the gospel in 1:15 is not simply a
verbal message but is also a personal event, the presence of
God's saving power in Jesus. Two things follow from this.
First, the inescapable 'belief that' component in the demand is
not limited to the truth of Jesus' words but extends to his
identity as the one in whom God's reign is active and through
whom God's power is available. For the people who encounter
Jesus in the ensuing narrative, this is not initially a matter
of confessing his messiahship or divine sonship, but rather of
recognising his function as the instrument of God's eschatological dominion. Secondly, the summons to faith is not
primarily a preparation for the coming apocalypse but constitutes a response to the rule of God *already* being made
manifest.[2] Faith is therefore essentially an eschatological
reality. It is a response to the divine initiative, on the one hand
made possible by that initiative, and on the other demanded in
light of it. It is a gift inasmuch as Jesus' eschatological proclamation has the power to evoke a reply of faith; it is a demand in
that people remain free to accept or reject this power.

Faith is held out in 1:15 as the means by which individuals
may appropriate in the present (cf. 2:5,10) the powers of
salvation proffered in the gospel. Mark thus provides his
audience with an important clue as to how they should view
the role of faith in the healing stories that follow and in the
sayings that ascribe virtual omnipotence to faith (9:23; 11:23f;
cf. 10:27). The works of power are evidence of the in-breaking
kingdom.[3] But the soteriological efficacy of this event is not
automatic; there must be the engagement of faith. Faith for
Mark then is not simply a therapeutic requirement, but is the
means of gaining a share in God's reign and all that this
implies.

Such faith is rooted in a perception of the kingdom's presence despite apparent evidence to the contrary. For although
the kingdom's beginning is announced in 1:15, the subsequent
story shows that the manner of the kingdom's arrival is covert
and mysterious (4:11f), and its overt consummation remains

[1] Cf. Warfield, *Biblical Doctrines*, 476.
[2] Cf. Pesch, *Markus*, 102f; Gnilka, *Markus*, I, 67; Kelber, *Kingdom*, 14.
[3] This is discussed in chapter 3 below.

an object of anticipation (e.g. 9:1; 13:7; 14:25; 15:43). According to 4:26–33, the author's general conception seems to be that the first local manifestation of God's kingdom in Galilee is related to its ultimate cosmic triumph as sowing is to harvest. Present fulfilment and future consummation are held together by the activity of Jesus. He sets the process in motion; he establishes, through repentance and faith, a 'colony of the new age' (Kee) in the interregnum which has access to the benefits of salvation in advance of the End; and he will bring the process to a climax when he returns as Son of Man (8:38; 13:26; 14:62).

(iii) The call to faith does not stand on its own but is coupled with the demand μετανοεῖτε. The radical nature of the repentance envisaged forbids limiting faith to giving credance to Jesus' words. The New Testament use of μετανοεῖν parallels the use of *shub* in the Old Testament prophetic tradition and means not simply a change of mind or a feeling of remorse, as in profane Greek, but the redirection of the entire manner of life, both individually and corporately. It suggests an about-face on the wrong road and a return to God, a conversion involving a change of understanding and of conduct in both ethical and religious terms.[1] Although the terminology is not frequent in Mark (1:4,15; 6:12; cf. ἐπιστρέψωσιν 4:12), the radicality of the concept is underlined throughout the gospel, especially in the demands incumbent on the disciples (as we shall see in chapter 4). For them conversion means leaving home and occupations (1:16–20; 10:28–31), a readiness to become as little children (10:15f) and slaves (9:35f; 10:42–4), even a willingness to lose their lives in order to find them (8:35ff). It means total abnegation of their own desires and claims in face of the claims of the kingdom of God (cf. 8:34).

The eschatologically motivated demand for repentance is one of the strands of continuity[2] Mark establishes between the activity of Jesus and John the Baptist (1:4,15). He may be suggesting that Jesus takes up John's work, or simply that both men belong to the prophetic tradition. However, Jesus' call for repentance is differentiated from John's by the fact that it is complemented by a new element – the call to faith. It may be true that an element of trust or faith is implicit in the demand of John (and the Old Testament prophets) for repentance (cf. 11:31) – viz., confidence in God's readiness to remit

---

[1] See Behm, *TDNT*, 4, 975–1008; Goppelt, *Theology*, I, 34f; see also Sanders, *Jesus*, 106–13, 206; Lane, *Mark*, 593–600.

[2] See below, p. 199.

sins.[1] But the fact that faith explicitly emerges as a distinct demand only in Jesus' mission suggests that Mark conceives of faith not simply as the inner dynamic of repentance, but as the eschatological goal to which repentance leads. Faith, then, must exceed rational conviction or even the decision to return to God underlying repentance. M. Werner, reducing belief in the gospel to such dimensions, concludes that Mark presents ethical repentance as the only requirement for entry to the kingdom of God.[2] But if this were true, one would expect conversion to be the product of belief ('believe me and repent') rather than the other way around. For Mark, repentance is not an end in itself but the first part of faith, which brings one into the sphere of existence opened up by the gospel.

The dual formula also means that repentance is considered a necessary requirement for faith. Belief in the gospel presupposes this comprehensive break with the past and change in understanding and conduct. This means that faith itself must be the resulting expression of this radical reorientation of life in both its ethical and religious dimensions. Thus, in Mark's view, repentance and faith are inseparable.[3] Repentance, which as Schlatter notes, is at heart the abandonment of trust in one's self (Selbstvertrauen),[4] must lead to faith, a new condition of trust in God's ultimate disclosure. Faith, conversely, cannot exist without such conversion. This means that we are justified in assuming the presence of repentance where faith is active in the story,[5] and its want where unbelief is encountered.

(iv) The fact that faith is *demanded* indicates that Mark considers it a voluntary response, a free act of obedience. Hence its presence can be praised and rewarded (5:34; 10:52) and its absence rebuked and lamented (4:40; 9:19). Belief in the gospel is not something spontaneously engendered by the facts, as is purely cognitive belief,[6] nor is the evidence for Jesus' cosmic assertion so compelling that the appropriate reaction is self-evident. Indeed, the evidence is so ambiguous (cf. 6:2f) and

[1] Cf. Burkill, *New Light*, 135.

[2] Werner, *Einfluss*, 111f.

[3] Via suggests that while Mark distinguishes faith and ethics, he maintains 'the organic inseparability of the two factors', *Ethics*, 84f.

[4] See Schlatter's extensive discussion of repentance and faith, *Glaube*, 94–8, 144f, and passim.

[5] So too Branscomb, *Mark*, 46; Rhoads and Michie, *Mark as Story*, 110.

[6] Cf. Swinburne, *Faith and Reason*, 25f; cf.198–200.

paradoxical (cf. 10:23ff), the manner of the kingdom's advent so unexpected and veiled (cf. 4:11f) that it is necessary to specify the way those who hear Jesus are to respond – by turning and believing.

There is a striking paradox in Mark's characterisation of Jesus in 1:14f, and elsewhere. His words have power to inaugurate the kingly reign of God, to control the forces of nature (4:35–41), and to subdue demons (e.g. 3:11). Yet he has to invite repentance and faith, for he has no authority from God to subdue people or to force understanding on them. His relationship with people is non-coercive. The eschatological powers resident within him thus usually await the free response of receptive faith before they become operative on the human level.

(v) Finally, even at this first reference to faith, Mark indicates that he does not regard it as a once-for-all acceptance of the kerygma but as a continuing 'condition of being' into which the believer must enter. This may be implied in the use of the present continuous tense for the imperatives (i.e. 'be believing'), although the sense could also be repetitive in keeping with the summary format of 1:14f. However, as we will see later, the fact that Mark follows 1:15 with the call of the first disciples is a plain indication that he considers both repentance and faith to be an on-going experience. If faith is an initial act of obedient trust in the gospel, then it is also a continuing state of trusting obedience, a readiness to do whatever the will of God requires (cf. 3:35;9:42–50;10:21f etc.). It is this radical faith that Mark locates at the foundation of the new community that Jesus calls into existence.

3. Conclusion

The traditio-historical connection between what might be termed 'kerygmatic faith' on the one hand (i.e. faith understood as reception of the message of salvation), and 'miracle faith' on the other (i.e. confidence in and exercise of the miracle-working power of God) has occasioned much discussion in the literature. In Mark's gospel, 1:15, 9:42 and 15:32 are taken as examples of kerygmatic faith, and the remaining texts as miracle faith.[1] Pursuing this traditio-historical question falls outside the scope of our study, but something can be said about Mark's perception of the issue.

From his perspective, the faith demanded in the kerygma of

[1] See, e.g., Barth, 'Glaube und Zweifel', 269f; Luz, 'Die Jünger', 154f.

the kingdom's advent cannot be reduced to a predominantly intellectual acceptance of the truth of the message. It is rooted in this, but goes beyond it to involve a whole-hearted response of trust in Jesus as the one who discloses God's sovereignty, and obedience to the ethical demands of the impinging kingdom. More significantly, Mark would accept no fundamental distinction between the *structure* of kerygmatic faith and miracle faith. The kerygma inaugurates the kingdom, and reception of it brings one into the realm of eschatological power. People are called to entrust themselves to this power and the disciples are specially authorised to exercise it, through faith, on behalf of others. Both dimensions of faith belong together and are mutually interpretative. This will become increasingly clear as we proceed.

By summoning belief in the gospel then (1:15), Mark is not thinking of belief in the narrow sense of a mental acceptance of a proposition or statement. He is thinking rather of belief in the comprehensive sense, a response that embraces both the mental action and the habit or condition of trusting in and relying upon the person who speaks.

4. Excursus: 'belief in' and 'belief that'

The peculiar syntax of Mk 1:15b, πιστεύετε ἐν τῷ εὐαγγελίῳ, which on the one hand employs a prepositional phrase that suggests a personal, existential involvement with the object of faith, yet on the other hand supplies a propositional statement as that object, rather neatly encapsulates one of the fundamental issues in any examination of the notion of faith, whether it be exegetical, theological or philosophical in orientation. This is whether the attitude designated by πίστις, πιστεύειν (or their translation equivalents) is to be understood as an intellectual 'belief that' (i.e. the mental acceptance that certain propositions, such as the existence of God or the messiahship of Jesus, are true) or as a more personal, affective 'belief in' (i.e. an attitude of active trust that is directed towards a person and establishes a relationship between persons). In biblical Greek, πίστις, πιστεύειν can denote both belief and trust, and the question arises as to what the relationship between these two attitudes is, and whether either or both should be regarded or translated as 'faith'.

This is a vast and complicated issue and one that lies at the heart of the dispute between Protestant and Catholic theology,

as well as different schools within these traditions.[1] Although
an over-simplification, we could say that in the Thomist view,
faith is a matter of rational assent to the existence of God and
certain credal propositions about his nature and activity.
According to the Lutheran position, faith includes both theoretical beliefs *and* personal trust in God, though primacy is
given to trust (*fiducia*). In addition some recent writers have
attempted to develop a notion of faith as trust or existential
decision without any or an absolute minimum of 'beliefs-that'.[2]
Such varying evaluations of faith have, understandably, found
expression in exegetical as well as in dogmatic writings. It is
beyond the scope of the present study to explore fully the
theological and philosophical dimensions of the notion of faith.[3]
But as we will be confronted with the question of belief versus
trust at a number of points in Mark, a few general comments
are in order.

The first thing to say is that the theoretical distinction
between belief and trust is a valid one. Certain features differentiate each attitude. For example, rational belief is essentially
involuntary; a person cannot arbitrarily choose to believe on
the spot; it is something that happens to him or her in light of
the evidence. Trust, however, is voluntary, an act of the will.[4]
Or again, belief can exist without it immediately affecting
one's conduct, whereas trust requires certain consequent
actions in order to exist.[5]

Though distinguishable, they are nevertheless inseparable
in operation. All belief involves at least a modicum of trust (e.g.
trust in one's cognitive powers), while an act of trust would be
absurd without some minimum convictions about the character of the one being trusted or the benefits inherent in the act of
trusting itself. Every human judgement, in other words, has a
complex character involving both rational and non-rational
elements, in varying proportions depending on the circumstances. This is especially the case when it comes to religious
faith, where belief and trust are directed towards transcendent
and, in the case of Christianity, personal realities. Indeed, the

---

[1] See Dyson, *We Believe*, 16–37; Swinburne, *Faith and Reason*, 104–24.

[2] This is an aspect of the larger question of the relationship between faith
and history; see M. L. Cook, 'Call to Faith', 679–87.

[3] See, e.g., Evans, 'Faith and Belief', 1–19, 199–212.

[4] Swinburne, *Faith and Reason*, 25f, 199f.

[5] Although consideration should be taken of Swinburne's discussion on
belief and action, *Faith and Reason*, 8–13, 26–32.

classical disputes between different Christian traditions over
the nature of faith have been more due to differences of
definition and the relative weight given to the intellectual and
personal constituents of faith, than to fundamentally opposing
conceptions of the psychological structure of faith itself.[1] In
practical terms, all Christian conceptions of faith have in
common an unavoidable 'belief that' basis, plus a concrete
expression of belief in action of some kind that expresses trust
in the one about whom things are believed. Of course, differences of substance remain, especially over the content and
extent of the beliefs necessary for faith and the relative merit
accorded to consequent actions. But today there is a widespread
agreement that, 'only a mixed intellectual-existential account
of faith can begin to do justice to the character of faith as a lived
attitude'.[2]

We have seen that such a mixture of mental conviction and
existential commitment is inherent in the depiction of faith in
Mark 1:15, although it remains to be seen whether this is true
at other places in the gospel as well. Yet even a preliminary
glance at a pericope such as 11:20–25 would suggest that it is.
Here the narrator combines an injunction to 'have faith in
God' (πίστιν θεοῦ, v 22) with the instruction that, when praying,
'believe that (πιστεύετε ὅτι) you have received it and you will'
(v 24; cf. 23). Even if the texts which denote belief, and those
which describe trust, derive from different sources[3] (which
seems unlikely), Mark sees them as inseparably bound
together under the general conception of faith. For Mark, faith
is rooted in belief (or, better, in insight into God's presence in
Jesus) and fructifies in trusting reliance upon him. One attitude calls for the other. Belief which does not lead to trust is
sterile and does not experience the power conveyed by Jesus (cf.
8:27–30 and 9:18ff). Trust, which requires at least a minimum
of belief to come into being, must be accompanied by a growth
in understanding (4:13) or it will fail in dire circumstances
(4:35–41). We will explore this in more detail in the following
chapters.

---

[1] See Swinburne, *Faith and Reason*, 118–24.

[2] Dyson, *We Believe*, 31.

[3] Hatch attributed the trust element in Christian faith to the Hebraic influ-
ence and the belief element to Hellenistic influence, *The Pauline Idea of
Faith* (1917) and *The Idea of Faith* (1925). M. Buber also sharply contrasted
Hebraic *emunah* and Greek *pistis*, but see the discussion of this by Lohse,
'*Emuna* und *Pistis*', 147–63.

3 THE PLACE OF MIRACLES IN THE CALL TO FAITH

Mark commences his account of Jesus' ministry by announcing the dawning of God's kingdom and by singling out repentance and faith as the fundamental response sought to this great event. We have seen how, in light of the literary functioning of 1:14f, the initial call to faith is implied every time we subsequently find Jesus addressing an audience. Furthermore, since Jesus is portrayed as a figure of integrity, whose words lead to corresponding action and whose actions exemplify his words, Jesus' *deeds* also embody an inherent challenge to repentant faith.

Among Jesus' deeds, the miracles have a particularly prominent place in the development of the faith theme. The majority of the explicit references to the subject are found in or related to miraculous happenings. In later chapters we will examine these miracle episodes in some detail to discover what they contribute to Mark's conception of faith. But lest we are tempted to regard each account as an isolated unit unrelated to the overall sweep of the narrative, we should first consider in more general terms the significance of the miracles in Mark's work, and in particular their relationship to the call to conversion and faith. This will help set the general narrative context for the closer exegetical work in subsequent chapters.

Miracles are quite clearly of enormous importance in Mark This is obvious from the sheer amount of space devoted to them, proportionately more than any other early Christian document. Nearly one-third of the gospel[1] is given over to miraculous events of some kind — or about half of the first ten chapters, in which all but one of the eighteen distinct miracle stories are located. Of these eighteen, some thirteen are works of restoration (nine healings and four exorcisms) and five are so-called 'nature miracles', although these are somewhat

---

[1] Richardson calculates that 209 out of the 666 verses in Mark are devoted to the miraculous, *Miracle-Stories*, 36.

arbitrary distinctions. The great range of miracles worked is
another indication of their importance to Mark, as is the fact
that he enhances the overall impact of the miraculous through
periodic summary statements which speak of large numbers
of people being healed (1:32–4; 3:7–12; 6:53–6).

Why, then, does the author include so many miracles in his
story and to what ends does he use them? No doubt part of the
reason is that individually the miracle stories cover various
matters of 'doctrinal' interest, such as forgiveness of sins,
sabbath observance, ritual impurity, dealings with Gentiles,
and so on.[1] They would also have been of practical value for
Mark's community in its own practice of healing and exorcism
(cf. 1 Cor 12:9f,28f). Furthermore, in structuring his literary
composition, Mark has been able to turn many of the accounts
to rhetorical effect, using them to foreshadow later events in
the plot, or to symbolise important thematic developments. The
raising of Jairus' daughter (5:21–4,35–43), for example, foreshadows the resurrection of Jesus; the feeding miracles (6:35–
44; 8:1–10) anticipate and interpret the Last Supper; and the
two cures of physical blindness, which flank the central
discipleship-instruction section of the gospel (8:27–10:45), serve
to symbolise the need for spiritual insight.

But in addition to the value of the accounts individually, the
miraculous, as a particular dimension of Mark's composition,
fulfils a special didactic function with respect to faith. Mark
establishes the didactic purpose of Jesus' miracles program-
matically at the first opportunity so that it may be extended, by
implication, to all subsequent works of power. He does this by
bracketing the first miracle Jesus performs with the first two
references he makes to Jesus' teaching activity (1:21,27). As a
result of this, and by not specifying the actual content of Jesus'
words, the miraculous deed itself takes on the character of a
'new teaching' (1:27), the burden of which is qualified by the
message of Jesus in 1:15: the advent and demands of God's
kingdom. Because the miracles function in such a didactic
manner, it is quite fitting for Jesus to be addressed as 'teacher'
in miracle contexts (4:38; 5:35; 9:17; 10:51) and for miracles to
call forth the same response of awe and amazement as his

---

[1] See Burkill, *Mysterious Revelation*, 57f; Best, *Discipleship*, 194f. D.-A.
Koch lists some ten different messages the miracle stories convey, 'Die
Verschiedenheit der Überlieferung bleibt damit auch in der markinischen
Redaktion sichtbar', *Wundererzählungen*, 180f.

teaching does (e.g. θαμβεῖσθαι [cf. 1:27 and 10:24]; ἐκπλήττεισθαι (cf. 7:37 and 1:22; 6:2; 10:26; 11:18).

The miracles stand in a two-fold relationship to faith. On the one hand, they illustrate the concrete benefits afforded faith by the realisation of kingdom power in Jesus. On the other hand, they represent an implicit summons to repentance and faith for those who witness or hear of them. This first relationship will be our focus in the next chapter when we examine five separate faith miracles. Here we shall concentrate on the second connection, one which a few scholars mention in passing, but which has not to my knowledge been explored before in any substantial way.

1. The miracles as a summons to repentance and faith

That the miracles operate as a challenge to faith is not immediately obvious. Within the story, faith is never explicitly demanded because of Jesus' miracles, and in fact Mark displays considerable ambivalence towards the value of miracles for faith.[1] They often lead to hostility towards Jesus (2:1–12; 3:1–6,22–30; 6:1–6); the disciples fail to grasp their significance (4:35–41; 6:51f; 8:14–21); those healed are sometimes forbidden to speak of their experience (1:44; 5:43; 7:36; 8:26); Jesus refuses to work signs to validate his mission (8:11–13; 15:29–32); and a candid warning is given against credulity towards the claims of wonder workers (13:21f). Some commentators even think that Mark polemicises against the over-valuation of miracles by showing that they cannot lead to genuine faith at all.[2]

Yet, on the other side, Jesus' works of power are one of the main ways in the story in which the kingdom of God is concretely realised; and, as we noted in the previous chapter, it is the definite realisation of the kingdom, not just its future coming, that provides the ground for the initial call to conversion and faith (1:14f). Consistent with this, at a number of places Mark indicates a kind of 'apologetic' role for Jesus' miracles (e.g. 1:27; 1:44; 2:10,12; 3:3ff; 4:40f; 5:19; 6:2f; 7:36f).

---

[1] See esp. Koch, *Wundererzählungen*, 180–93.

[2] This is the view of scholars who claim Mark is combating a 'divine man' christology centring on the miracles, most notably, Weeden, *Traditions in Conflict*; idem, 'Heresy', 45–58. For an assessment of this view, see Theissen, *Miracle Stories*, 293–98. See also Lane, 'Theios Aner Christology', 144–61.

Most importantly, the very fact that the proper expectation of miracle is called 'faith' surely suggests that Jesus' miraculous activity is meant, at least in part, to excite this expectancy or faith. In this context the miracle stories constitute one of the devices the author uses to issue and reissue the demand for faith implicitly throughout the story.

But how does this device work? How can Mark use the miracles to convey a challenge to faith, yet remain so equivocal with respect to the effect of miracles on those who witness them? The key to this lies in the observation that in Mark the miracles display a markedly similar character to the parables. The miracles are to Jesus' actions what the parables are to his teaching: messages or puzzles that require interpretation. Mark himself signals the parabolic function of the miracles at a number of important places.

The first time Mark expressly mentions Jesus speaking ἐν παραβολαῖς (3:23a; but cf. 2:19–22) is in connection with his miracle ministry, specifically the charge of the Jerusalem authorities that he casts out demons by Beelzebul (3:22–30). In this account, not only is Jesus' reference to the strong man a parable about the meaning of his exorcisms, but the exorcisms themselves are parabolic of the clash of kingdoms occasioned by the appearance of Jesus. Since Satan does not cast out Satan something greater must be at work (cf. 1:24). Significantly it is in the general context of the dissension over Jesus' miracles, which involves his relatives as well as the scribes (3:20–35), that Mark first introduces the distinction between those 'around Jesus' and those 'standing outside' (vv 32–5), which he picks up again in the parable chapter (4:10f). Jesus' parabolic actions as well as his parabolic words effect a division between insiders and outsiders.

The explanation Mark gives for Jesus' use of parables in 4:10–12,33f seems angled to embrace actions as well as words. The term παραβολή can have various nuances, but most commentators agree that here it carries the dominant sense of riddle or enigma, in accord with the Semitic *mashal* tradition.[1] Those 'around Jesus' (v 10) have been given the mystery of the kingdom of God, but for 'those outside' ἐν παραβολαῖς τὰ πάντα γίνεται. Mark does not mean here that Jesus

---

[1] See, e.g., Kelber, *Kingdom*, 32ff; Rhoads and Michie, *Mark as Story*, 55ff; Kermode, *Genesis of Secrecy*, 23f; Jeremias, *Parables*, 16; Beasley-Murray, *Kingdom of God*, 105.

speaks to outsiders *only* in formal parables; on many occasions in the gospel he speaks plainly to them (e.g. 2:25; 7:6–13; 8:12f, etc.). He means rather that to outsiders everything (τὰ πάντα)[1] that Jesus says and does (the citation in v 12 mentions both hearing and seeing) remains (γίνεται) mysterious or enigmatic: riddles demanding interpretation. Apart from such enigmas, Jesus does not address outsiders (4:33f). Both his διδαχή and his δυνάμεις are complementary ways in which the mystery of the kingdom finds expression. Mark therefore parallels the parable collection in 4:1–34 with a miracle collection in 4:35–5:43, which begins in the same boat from which Jesus spoke the parables (4:1: 'a boat'; 4:36: '*the* boat').

At two other points, the parabolic function of Jesus' miracles is made especially clear. In 6:52, the miracle of the loaves (6:31–44) is an event to be apprehended parabolically, and the failure of the disciples to understand its meaning accounts for their fear at Jesus' miraculous walking on water. Again, in 8:14–21 Jesus chides the disciples for failure to understand the feeding miracles. In both cases, Jesus uses the same language distinctively introduced in 4:10–12 to describe the failure of outsiders to understand the parables. Two other verbs are also used which hitherto have only appeared in connection with the imperviousness of Jesus' enemies to the inner meaning of his miraculous deeds: πωροῦν (6:52; 8:16; cf. 3:5) and διαλογίζεσθαι (8:16f; cf. 2:6,8; later in 9:33; 11:31).

Within Mark's story, then, the miracles function as acted parables. And it is because they display the same logic and internal dynamics as parabolic discourse that they can implicitly summon those who witness them to repentant faith. What then is the nature of parabolic communication?

2. Miracles and parabolic communication

Much could be said about parabolic speech, but two qualities in particular are characteristic of parables, especially in Mark: their metaphorical or referential nature, and their discriminating or sifting effect. Both these dimensions may be applied equally to the miracles.

---

[1] Boobyer argues that τὰ πάντα includes parables, teaching and miracles, 'Redaction of Mark IV,1–34', 61–4.

(a) Referential function

The essential quality of all parables is their metaphorical character: they are not meant to be taken at face value but point beyond themselves to another level of meaning. In this way they function as mysterious speech and require interpretative involvement from the hearer. They call for explanation and are not complete until the hearer renders a satisfactory answer. In this sense they are riddles, 'hermeneutically unfinished stories'.[1] Their interpretation is not immediately clear, but some clue to their intended meaning is usually contained within the story.

As enacted parables, the miracles in Mark are not isolated phenomena but are signs of the presence of God's kingly power in Jesus. In Mark, the phrase 'kingdom of God' above all else means God's rule evidenced in the operation of eschatological power. The future consummation of the kingdom is spoken of in terms of δύναμις (9:1; 13:26; 14:62; cf. 12:24; 13:25), and Jesus' works of power, or δυνάμεις[2] (5:30; 6:2,5,14; cf. 9:39), are intended to point beyond themselves to the present in-breaking of this future kingdom in his own person. This is also clear from the eschatological content and instructional context of the miracles in Mark. All the Isaianic miracles are illustrated (cf. 7:37):[3] the blind see again, the deaf hear and the lame walk, sinners are forgiven and lepers cleansed, even the dead are raised. The feeding miracles typify eschatological feasting, while the calming of storms symbolises the reassertion of God's eschatological sovereignty over rebellious nature. Mark can therefore place miracles in a teaching context, even though the content of Jesus' words is not recorded, because the deeds themselves are declarative of the coming of God's kingly power.

The present assertion of God's power has a double effect in Mark. It constitutes, on the cosmic level, the plundering of

---

[1] Kelber, *Oral and Written Gospel*, 62.

[2] See Robbins, 'Dynameis and Semeia', 5–20. On the general question of the New Testament terminology for miracles, see: Moule, *Miracles*, 235–7; Baltensweiler, 'Wunder und Glaube', 246–8; and especially Remus, 'Does Terminology Distinguish Miracles?', 531–51.

[3] Koch minimises the significance of Old Testament language in Mk 7:37 because it is traditional, not redactional, *Wundererzählungen*, 175. But the critical pedigree of material does not determine its significance in the final text.

Satan's βασιλεία through the power of the eschatological Spirit (3:20–30; cf. 1:10–13).[1] On the human level, it involves the liberation of men and women from the effects of sin, sickness and demonic possession. Hence Mark distinguishes between, yet joins together, exorcisms and healings (1:34; 3:10f; cf. 6:7 and 6:13). They have a functional similarity in that they are both parabolic of the advancing kingdom, but they are differentiated by their orientation.

To say that the δυνάμεις are parabolic of the kingdom is decidedly not to say that Mark 'spiritualises' them, so that bodily deliverance becomes merely symbolic of the inward experience of spiritual salvation.[2] For Mark, bodily restoration and the physical provision of food and safety belong to the perfection of the future kingdom as much as the assurance of forgiveness and eternal life. Even if he uses the miracles to foreshadow and interpret such 'spiritual' events as the Last Supper and the death and resurrection of Jesus, this is not intended to deprive the miracles themselves of their tangible, material significance. On the contrary, the link between, for example, the feeding miracles and the Last Supper cuts both ways. It not only gives a eucharistic dimension to the miraculous deed, but also adds a social and ethical dimension to the eucharist. The eucharist becomes the mandate or context for satisfying both the spiritual and the physical needs of people in view of the messianic provision.

The broad range of miracles in Mark points to the power of Jesus over all the representative areas of human existence. Mark pictures God's reign as a kind of 'salvation energy' that impinges on maladjustment in all areas of life – the spiritual and the physical, as well as the ethical, the social and the political. Indeed the content of the miracles not only points to the presence of comprehensive salvation; it simultaneously points to the ethical and social implications of God's reign for those who respond to it. By his power Jesus removes the various forms of defilement – leprosy, deformity, ritual

---

[1] Koch sees no connection between the Spirit and the kingdom of God in 3:27 (*Wundererzählungen*, 175). But in the prologue it is only after receiving the Spirit (1:10) that Jesus defeats Satan (1:12–13) as a prelude to announcing the kingdom (1:14f).

[2] Schmithals, *Wunder und Glaube*, 25 and passim; Richardson, *Miracle Stories*, 57; idem, *IDB*, 4, 78; Best, *Discipleship*, 195. For a valuable corrective to such 'spiritualisation', see Theissen, *Miracle Stories*, 32, 249–53, 298–302.

uncleanness, racial prejudice, death – that have cut individuals off from social intercourse with the wider community. His healing of bodies makes possible the 'resocialising' of those who were marginalised by their physical condition (e.g. 1:44; 5:15,43). That God's reign reveals itself as a protest against the suffering caused by human isolation, as well as by illness and disease, imposes corresponding obligations on those who submit to this rule.[1] In this way the miracles embody not only a call to faith but also to conversion, to that radical break with current values and practices exemplified in the character of Jesus' deeds of power.

Interpreters frequently contrast the original eschatological significance of the historical Jesus' miracles with their current christological role in the gospels,[2] and D.-A. Koch flatly denies that Mark uses the miracles as signs of the kingdom.[3] But, from Mark's point of view, this is to set up a false dichotomy. In Mark's narrative, the miracles certainly have a dominant christological orientation. The question of Jesus' identity is first explicitly raised after the stilling of the storm: 'Who then is this, that even the wind and sea obey him?' (4:41). Every time in the subsequent narrative there is a mention of people's amazement at Jesus' miracles, there is an echo of this question[4] (see 5:15,20,42; 6:2f,14f,50–2; 7:37; 11:21). But the christological component does not supersede the eschatological; it is incorporated in it. The christological roll call in the prologue, as we have seen, provides the necessary backdrop for understanding the eschatological announcement of the kingdom in 1:14f. The miracle narratives are christological through and through precisely because in Jesus alone God reveals his eschatological power.

The miracles in Mark's story, then, are dramatic parables which refer beyond themselves to the manifestation of God's kingly power in Jesus and to its radical implications for those who respond to its demands. Like the spoken parables, the miracles are only complete when those who witness them move beyond the external occurrence to grasp the deeper

---

[1] Theissen argues that the early Christian communities understood the miracle stories as imposing obligations on them physically to provide for the needs of those in distress, *Miracle Stories*, 251ff, 302.

[2] E.g. Fuller, *Miracles*, 39–42, 46f, 66–8; Best, *Discipleship*; 177; Maisch, *Heilung des Gelähmten*, 127.

[3] Koch, *Wundererzählungen*, 173–6.

[4] Theissen, *Miracle Stories*, 213.

significance of the kingdom's coming and its concomitant demand for conversion and belief.

(b) Discriminating effect

The metaphorical nature of parabolic speech – the way it beckons the recipient to a more transcendent level of meaning – means that parables can be understood at two levels. This double-meaning effect gives parables an important sifting or discriminating impact. Some hearers perceive the real meaning being disclosed; others do not. Hence the *Weckformel*: 'He who has ears to hear, let him hear' (4:9,23ff; cf. 7:14; 8:18). 'Parables, it seems, may proclaim a truth as a herald does, and at the same time conceal truth like an oracle.'[1] It all depends on how one hears.

However we understand the so-called 'parable theory' in 4:10–12,33f, the underlying principle seems to be that for someone who already perceives the hidden reality of God's rule in the events surrounding Jesus – those who have been given the mystery of the kingdom of God – the parables should further clarify that rule. But for those who do not discern God's presence in Jesus, the parables only obscure matters further.

> Take heed what you hear; the measure you give will be the measure you get, and still more will be given you. For to him who has will more be given; and from him who has not, even what he has will be taken away. (4:24f)

Similarly with the miracles; although they are concrete signs that Jesus is the one who inaugurates the kingdom of God, they are nonetheless ambiguous signs, open to various interpretations. Jesus' ability to work miracles is not itself unique (13:6,21f). Whilst the description of huge crowds from Galilee, Judea and even foreign lands beyond flocking to Jesus because of his powerful deeds (1:32–4; 3:7f; 6:56 etc.) would suggest that the quantity, range and success of Jesus' miracles sets him apart from other contemporary wonder-workers (cf. 7:37), the evidential value of the deeds themselves is not sufficient to demand a particular conclusion about Jesus' status as kingdom bearer (cf. 6:14–16; 8:27f). They serve to raise the question of the source and ultimate significance of Jesus' power (1:27f; 2:7,9; 3:21ff; 4:41; 6:2,14–17; cf. 11:28ff) and to give clues to the

---

[1] Kermode, *Genesis of Secrecy*, 47.

correct answer, but they do not prove beyond all doubt his true identity.

Just as the parables create a line of demarcation between insiders and outsiders (4:10–12; cf. 3:32–5), so the miracles have a decidedly divisive effect upon characters in the story. Some see in Jesus' deeds the saving power and compassion of God himself, and respond in repentant faith. Others react negatively, a fact that Mark lays considerable stress on. At least four ways of reacting to the δυνάμεις are presented in a critical light, and it is worth spelling these out as it will allow us to see with greater clarity the positive nature of faith in our examination of the faith-pericopae in chapter four as well as setting the context for our discussion of unbelief in chapter six.

(i) *Hostility*: The religious authorities react with hostility and hatred to Jesus' miracles. They see in them blasphemy (2:1–12), the desecration of the Sabbath (3:1–6), the activity of Satan (3:22–30), and the self-inflated posturing of a man of common origins (6:1–6a). In a similar vein, Jesus' relatives see in them signs of madness (3:20f). It is noteworthy that the hostility of Jesus' opponents, unlike the inadequate responses of other characters in the story, expresses itself as direct criticism of the miracle worker himself.

(ii) *Incomprehension*: The disciples often respond to Jesus' miracles with incomprehension and misunderstanding. Their ready response to Jesus' call into discipleship indicates an initial perception of Jesus' eschatological role, which the first miracles they witness no doubt confirmed. But they repeatedly fail to penetrate the fuller significance of Jesus' deeds, particularly the unusual ones.[1] They are slow to discern his unique status (4:41; 6:51f; 8:14–21), and they fail to grasp the way in which divine power is meant to operate in their own activity (9:17f,28f; cf. 4:35–41 [?]; 11:20ff). The miracles do not guarantee full understanding.

(iii) *Sign-seeking*: The third false response to Jesus' miracles is one that demands demonstrations of power for wrong motives (cf. 10:35–41) or in order to validate disinterestedly Jesus' identity (8:11–13; 15:29–32; cf. 13:22). The fact that Mark places the Pharisees' request for a 'sign from heaven' (8:11–13)

---

[1] 'The setting for misunderstanding is mainly unexpected and unusual miracles: raisings of the dead, rescue and gift miracles. These are the least expected', Theissen, *Miracle Stories*, 56. In Mark, it is such miracles that underline Jesus' unique status, which the disciples are slow to comprehend.

straight after a long list of δυνάμεις (7:24–8:10), and has them demanding not a δύναμις but a σημεῖον, indicates that they are seeking something other than, or in addition to, Jesus' usual miracles. The only other place Mark mentions 'signs' is in the eschatological discourse, notably in connection with false messiahs leading people astray by apocalyptic signs and wonders (13:22; cf. 13:4). It would appear then that the Pharisees are insisting on some kind of portentous heavenly wonder to authenticate Jesus' authoritative status.[1]

Such a demand is flatly rejected. It betokens a separation of Jesus' miraculous deeds from his message of God's reign, and constitutes an evasion of the demand for repentance and faith addressed to them in Jesus' past words and deeds. The rejection of the demand for a sign is not a denial of signs as such; the narrator describes the occurrence of signs from heaven during the crucifixion (15:33,38), which ironically fail to move Jesus' enemies. What is being repudiated is the blindness of unbelief that fails to see the 'signs' already given in Jesus' δυνάμεις, and lays down its own conditions for belief. Moreover by demanding compelling proof as a condition for responding in faith to Jesus' message (cf. 15:32), the Pharisees effectively violate the nature of faith itself. For faith must be a morally free decision, not a response coerced by overwhelming proof 'from heaven'. The δυνάμεις make faith conceivable, but not inevitable.

There is a further reason why Mark scorns such a demand. The Pharisees' request, coming at the end of a major miracle collection, expresses, *in nuce*, a more widespread problem in the story relating to Jesus' exercise of divine power. In Mark, all of Jesus' miracles entail bringing the saving, healing, liberating and forgiving power of God to bear on human need. Such power is not for personal aggrandisement (10:35–45), nor for the avoidance of personal pain (14:32–42), but for the service of the powerless (10:45). This is why Mark groups the miracle stories in the first half of his gospel. All but three precede the main passion announcements and only one, the cursing of the fig tree (!), takes place after Jesus reaches Jerusalem. By this arrangement, Mark makes it clear that the miracles must be viewed in light of the cross and resurrection – and also the humiliation of the cross in light of Jesus' possession of

[1] So Robbins, 'Dynameis and Semeia', 15–17; Polhill, 'Miracle Stories', 393; Theissen, *Miracle Stories*, 296 n.35; Anderson, *Mark*, 199.

miraculous power. He also indicates this by actually sowing
the seeds of the passion in the early miracle stories (cf. 2:7f and
14:64; 3:6 and 11:18; 14:1). It is not *in spite* of the miracles, but
because of them that Jesus is rejected (cf. 15:31). Mark's intention therefore is not, as Weeden claims,[1] to supplant a false
thaumaturgical christology in the first half of the gospel with a
genuine paschal christology in the second. Rather, he wishes
to demonstrate the paradoxical character of the kingly power of
God manifest in Jesus.[2]

Despite his endowment with transcendent might, Jesus does
not come to rule as king, but to work as servant of all (10:45).
He uses his power to the full to triumph over the demons,
danger, death and disease that afflict the powerless, but he
does not use it to defend himself from betrayal, torture, crucifixion and death. The Son of Man who heals and forgives (2:10)
is also the Son of Man who suffers and dies (8:31; 9:31f; 10:33ff);
the Son of God who vanquishes demons (1:24; 3:11) is also the
Son of God who expires on the Roman cross (15:39). This un-
precedented pattern applies to the disciples as well. They are
expected to trust Jesus for deliverance from life-threatening
danger (4:35–41), yet are told to take up their crosses and follow
on the way of suffering (8:34–7). They have power over demons
(3:15; 6:7,13), yet will experience powerlessness at the hands of
human authorities (13:9–13).

This paradoxical combination of power and powerlessness is
resolvable in terms of the ethical-soteriological considerations
that condition the present operation of divine power. The power
to heal and the apparent powerlessness of suffering are united
by their redemptive intent. In fact, to endure suffering requires the operation of the same divine power that heals the
sick and equips for discipleship (cf. 14:36; 9:23; 10:27). In Gethsemane Jesus seeks God's enabling in order to accept the
powerlessness of torture and death, for in losing his life he will
save others (cf. 15:31 and 8:35). The power of the kingdom is not
the power of wealth (10:17–27; cf. 12:41–4), force (14:43–9; cf.
11:7f) and domination (10:42–5), but the power of suffering love.

---

[1] Weeden, *Traditions in Conflict*; idem, 'Power in Weakness', 115–34;
idem, 'Heresy', 145–58.

[2] For an excellent brief comment on the three main ways of accounting
for the shift in christological perspective from the first to the second half
of Mark (the polemical, the synthetic and the paradoxical), see Kelber,
'Passion Narrative', 176–9.

Mark would not agree with those who claim that Jesus' miracles are unmotivated in his story.[1] For the whole orientation of his power to those in need, as well as references to his compassion (1:41; 6:34; 8:2; 10:21; cf. 9:22) and to his touching of the sick[2] (1:31,41; 7:32f; 8:23,25; cf. 10:13), reveals a motivation of redemptive love. The power of such love will ultimately triumph because the healing and suffering Son of Man is the same Son of Man who rises from death (9:9; cf. 16:6) and will return in power as cosmic Judge (8:38; 13:26f; 14:62).

The disciples often fail to grasp the moral and redemptive conditioning of Jesus' power (8:31f; 10:35–45; cf 9:38–41). And for the religious authorities this dimension counts for nothing (2:5–10; 3:1–6). Instead of seeing the inherent character of Jesus' δυνάμεις as evidence for the saving presence of God, they demand a self-interested display of naked power to legitimise his claims (8:11–13). Indeed at the very point when Jesus is actually pouring out his life for 'the many', they deridingly demand that he prove himself by abandoning his soteriological mission through descending from the cross (15:29–32).

The miracles, then, have positive value only when understood in the context of Jesus' message of God's redemptive activity. This helps explain why we often find Jesus seeking to escape the teeming masses (e.g. 1:35ff,45; 3:7; 6:31,46), and why some of the miracles are concluded with commands to secrecy (1:44; 5:43; 7:36; 8:26) while others are not. Not all who throng Jesus have perceptive faith (e.g. 5:30–4) and the dissemination of miracle reports, divorced from their didactic context, is not considered an appropriate means of proclaiming the kingdom's presence and demands. To do so will simply promulgate misunderstanding. Accordingly, when on the other hand the Gadarene demoniac is sent away under instructions to declare openly his restoration, he is specifically enjoined to tell how much God has done for him (5:20), which the narrator labels κηρύσσειν (cf. 1:14f). Or again, even though the cleansed leper is forbidden to speak of his healing (1:44f), it is not an absolute prohibition, for he is to show himself at the

---

[1] E.g. Richardson, *Miracle-Stories*, 32; Stock, *Discipleship*, 75f.

[2] Even if the healing touch is a formal feature of miracle stories (cf. Theissen, *Miracle Stories*, 62f, 92f), it is still possible that Mark takes it as a sign of Jesus' loving-kindness, so Trocmé, *Formation*, 46. Cf also, F. J. Moloney, *Woman: First Among the Faithful* (London: DLT, 1984), 10–12.

temple 'as a witness to (or against) them'[1] – that is, as a sign of God's eschatological saving activity.

(iv) *Amazement*: The display of fear and amazement is also not considered an adequate response to Jesus' miraculous doings. The double motif of fear and astonishment pervades the entire gospel and features in all the main aspects of the story: the miracles, the teachings, the passion predictions and the so-called epiphanies. At least a dozen different words are used for this theme in more than thirty-four places in the narrative.[2] These invest the story with a numinous quality which corresponds to its central theme: the concentration of God's personal presence and eschatological power in the person of Jesus, his own beloved Son.

J. M. Robinson believes that Mark is hostile to the numinous response to Jesus *per se*, and equates it with misunderstand-stand and unbelief.[3] But this is improbable. Not only is such a response comparatively uncommon from the religious enemies of Jesus (11:18; 12:17f; cf. 6:2), but Jesus himself exhibits wonder and amazement (6:5; 14:33), and for others it can lead to praise of God (2:12; cf. 5:42). Furthermore, the recurrent stress on the awe-filled response by different characters to Jesus has the intended effect of producing in the reader a similar experience of holy dread as the appropriate and enduring legacy of Mark's story (16:8).[4]

Mark's thematic use of fear and astonishment is governed neither by blanket disapproval nor by unqualified approval. Inasmuch as it constitutes the inevitable reaction of people to divine revelation and activity (e.g. 1:22,27; 2:12; 5:42; 9:6; 10:24 etc.), fear and wonderment are ambiguous and provisional. They represent in Mark, 'a glimmer of conversion, faith and

---

[1] The meaning of the phrase, εἰς μαρτύριον αὐτοῖς in 1:44 (and in 6:11; 13:9) is disputed (see Van der Loos, *Miracles*, 487–9). But for the point being made here, it makes no difference whether it is meant positively or negatively (i.e. a witness against, a sign of judgement and rejection, as suggest Lohmeyer, *Lord of the Temple*, 25f and Budesheim, 'Jesus and the Disciples', 195–8). It still serves as a proclamation of miracle.

[2] For a full presentation of the data, see Pesch, *Markus*, II, 150–2. See also Theissen, *Miracle Stories*, 69–72, 152–73.

[3] Robinson, *Problem of History*, 70.

[4] For a similar thought, see Pesch, *Markus*, II, 151f; Donahue, 'Parable of God', 161. Theissen comments, 'The people in their praise and the disciples in their confession are waiting for the reader to take his place beside them and join their praise', *Miracle Stories*, 167.

understanding',[1] but they are only the first impulse in this direction and must be developed further to become such, and thus prove valuable. Sometimes awe and dread are bound up with faith (5:33f,36; 10:49; cf. 2:12; 14:33–6), or they occur in the context of continued, obedient following of Jesus (10:32). But elsewhere amazement issues in scandal and offence (6:2f); and fear leads to a rejection of Jesus (5:15–17; 11:18; cf. 15:5,44), to the paralysis of faith and understanding (4:40f; 6:50–2; 9:32), and to disobedience (7:37; 16:8[?]). And despite constant references to the fear and amazement of onlookers, they still arrive at inadequate estimates of Jesus' identity (6:14–16; 8:27f). Fear and astonishment, therefore, are an appropriate, yet incomplete reply to Jesus' miraculous deeds. They underscore both the difficulty and the necessity of moving beyond the visible to discern the mystery of the revelation of God's kingdom and then responding in intelligent faith.

3. Conclusion

A number of recent interpreters of Mark have suggested that the author is a rigorous parabolic thinker who, beyond the inclusion of a few formal parables, has extended the logic and dynamics of parabolic speech right across his narrative. His entire composition is a parable or metaphor of the mystery of God's kingdom, and he characterises Jesus himself as a 'parable of God'.[2] Whether or not this is a helpful way to read the gospel, we have found strong internal evidence that Mark uses the miracles as enacted parables of the secret invasion of God's kingly might in the person of Jesus. Recognising this has afforded us fresh insight into how the author can regard the miracles as an implicit summons to repentance and faith, while at the same time showing critical reserve towards their value in evincing genuine faith.

The miracles are not incontrovertible proof of Jesus' role as the messianic envoy of God's kingdom since they are amenable to various, even to sinister, interpretations. By soliciting interpretative involvement from those who witness them, the

---

[1] Ambrozic, *Hidden Kingdom*, 59. Bertram describes amazement as, 'the preliminary stage of faith', *TDNT*, III, 39f. Cf. Theissen, *Miracle Stories*, 76f.

[2] E.g. Donahue, 'Parable of God'; Hamilton, 'Parable of God', 438–41; Kelber, *Kingdom*, 32f; idem, *Oral and Written Gospel*, 117–31, 215–20. See also Malbon, 'Mark: Myth and Parable', 8–17.

miracles, like the parables, are essentially subversive in strategy. They disallow academic detachment but instead expose the instinctive reactions of the heart, especially to the moral character of God's activity.

The unimpressive appearance of Jesus (6:2f), the self-imposed ethical-redemptive limitations on the display of divine power (8:11–13; 10:35–45; 15:31f), and the paradoxical combination of strength and weakness, all force a decision about whether God's end-time power is indeed at work, as Jesus claims. Some are offended; others are merely dazzled; many are content with inadequate answers. But for those who perceive God's saving presence in Jesus, the δυνάμεις invite a response of conversion and of active faith in the one who brings them to pass. 'Miracles are inseparable from the message. They demonstrate the in-breaking of the kingdom of God, but only to the one who responds with the confession of faith.'[1]

One further question should be addressed before moving on. At first sight, the wording of Mk 4:11f, which follows the Targumic paraphrase of Isa. 6:9f, makes it appear as if the parables are actually intended (final ἵνα) to prevent outsiders from understanding the truth, lest (μήποτε) they should repent (ἐπιστρέψωσιν) and be forgiven. Many interpreters even speak of a Markan *Verstockungstheorie* in which the parables are divinely ordained to harden, in a temporary or definitive way, the hearts of those that hear them so that the truth becomes inaccessible to all but the elect.[2] If this is so, it would suggest that the miracles too, given their parabolic character, are aimed at obscuring rather than revealing the truth.

Attempts to avoid such an implication by emending the text of 4:11f,[3] or by translating ἵνα in a consecutive ('so that'), causal ('because'; cf. Mt 13:13), or imperatival ('may they') sense and rendering μήποτε as 'perhaps' instead of 'lest', are less than compelling.[4] Yet the explanation that almost treats the parables as instruments of divine punishment also encounters

---

[1] Polhill, 'Miracle Stories', 394.

[2] For convenient summaries of this view, see Baarlink, *Anfängliches Evangelium*, 161–71; idem, 'Antijudaismus', 188f; Kelber, *Kingdom*, 31–5.

[3] As does T. W. Manson, *The Teaching of Jesus*, (Cambridge: CUP, 1951) 74–80.

[4] For convenient summaries of this view, see: Turner, *Grammatical Insights*, 47–50; Burkill, *Mysterious Revelation*, 113–15; Kermode, *Genesis of Secrecy*, 29–34.

severe problems in light of the wider context of the parable chapter, not to mention the narrative as a whole.

According to 4:21ff, the reason for things being hidden (in cryptic, parabolic form) is not to obscure or withhold the truth but, on the contrary, to bring it to light. And this is not at some future point in time (the ἵνα clauses are purposive), but here and now, to those with ears to hear (v 23).[1] Concealment is, paradoxically, to facilitate comprehension. Hiddenness is the very strategy of revelation. Again, in the parable of the sower, which is both exemplary of and the hermeneutical key to Jesus' entire mode of parabolic communication (cf. v 13), the point at issue is not the intentions or didactic methods of the sower, but the influences which prevent proper 'hearing' at the receiver's end. Emphasis lies on human responsibility, not on divine causality (cf. v 15!). The repeated injunction to responsible hearing (vv 3,9,23f; cf. 33) also sits uneasily with any suggestion that some recipients are preordained not to hear, a judgement executed by means of parabolic discourse. Certainly there is a tension between divine sovereignty and human responsibility expressed throughout the parable chapter.[2] But the divine action is primarily related to bringing forth the harvest (cf. v 26ff), not to preventing germination!

In a comparable way, the ἵνα clauses in v 11f deal with the motivations of those who hear and witness parabolic communication, not with some perverse intention on the part of the parabolic speaker. In v 10, the questioners do not ask Jesus why he speaks in parables, but more generally concerning (περί) the parables as such. The answer given in v 11f, likewise, does not specify the purpose of Jesus' teaching method, but the reason why for some people everything appears or remains (γίνεται)[3] enigmatic, the riddles insoluble. Outsiders hear but do not comprehend, see but do not attain true insight, for fear that (μήποτε), if they did, they might have to repent and be forgiven.[4] Their inability to penetrate the significance of Jesus' parabolic message is rooted in their desire to evade its demand for repentance. They wilfully keep themselves in a

---

[1] See Kirkland, 'Jesus' Use of Parables', 12f. Dewey finds that vv 21f represent the interpretative centre of the concentric arrangement of ch 4, *Public Debate*, 147–52. Also Via, *Ethics*, 183.

[2] See Dewey, *Public Debate*, 147–52; Stock, *Discipleship*, 101–4; Standaert, *Marc*, 212f.

[3] See J. Jeremias, *The Parables of Jesus*, (London: SCM 1972³) 16f.

[4] See Carrington, *Mark*, 104f.

state of blindness and deafness, since genuine 'hearing' involves not just deciphering the message (cf. 12:12), but also obeying its implications.

There is no need then to posit a clumsy contradiction between 4:10–12,33f and the surrounding context, as many redaction-critical analyses do. There is instead a profound irony that emerges from the parable collection as a literary unit. Jesus conceals his message in parabolic form in order to invite an interpretative involvement from his audience that will lead to the revelation of 'the mystery of the kingdom of God' (v 10), namely its hidden presence in Jesus.[1] But for outsiders, Jesus' chosen mode of revelation becomes a means of concealment because they are unwilling to face their need for repentance and forgiveness. Whether parables reveal or conceal depends on whether the recipient chooses to be among 'those around Jesus' or among 'those outside'. And the dividing line is not the possession of secret instruction (v 13 implies this should not be necessary), but of perceptive faith, since this is the condition laid down at the only point previously in the narrative (cf. δέδοται 4:11) where the kingdom of God has been mentioned (1:14f). Faith sees beneath the surface and turns the concealing word into the revealing word, bringing to open manifestation what is secret and hidden. Applying this interpretation to the miracles, we may say that they too are intended as a mode of revelation leading to repentance and forgiveness. But to those who harden their hearts in unrepentance (3:5), the miracles conceal the truth behind a veil of incomprehensibility. Only the perception born of faith can penetrate this veil and receive the mystery of God's kingly presence in the works of Jesus.

---

[1] On the meaning of μυστήριον here, see Beasley-Murray, *Kingdom of God*, 103f.

4 FAITH AND THE POWERLESS

So far we have seen how, in Mark's presentation, both the content of Jesus' verbal proclamation and instruction, and the inherent character of his deeds of power, give expression to one fundamental reality: the dawning of the kingdom of God and the consequent need for repentance and faith. The day of God's ruling power has arrived in the person of Jesus, and the unfolding drama traces the manifold impact of this phenomenon on different characters in the story. There are a number of episodes in the Markan narrative in which the author presents in positive terms the relationship between human powerlessness and the power made available to genuine, receptive faith. These episodes are all miracle stories and involve the interaction of Jesus with minor, usually unnamed characters. The miracle context provides the dramatic setting within which faith is portrayed, and characterisation is one of the major devices the author uses to expound his conception of faith. In this chapter we shall examine five separate narratives which exemplify the author's understanding of the connection between faith and extreme human need. Before doing so, however, we should consider the place of plot and characterisation in these accounts in bringing out the essential qualities of the faith depicted.

1. Plot and characterisation in the faith narratives

Coherency of plot and consistency in characterisation are two of the main factors that qualify Mark's finished composition as a *bona fide* narrative. In the material relating to Jesus, the disciples, and the opponents there is a progressive development of character and plot that spans the entire work and climaxes in the events of passion week. It is out of the interplay of these two elements that the constituent themes of the story are spun. Plot and characterisation are also important at the level of individual episodes, and with respect to narrative figures who themselves appear only once in the story but who together constitute a more or less unified character group. This is the case in the miracle stories.

In the healing and exorcism narratives, there is no progressive development in plot or character from one account to the next. Each story is complete in itself; the need is raised and resolved in the same episode. The same basic event, with the same essential significance, is repeated over and again, with no material continuity between the figures who stand opposite Jesus in each discrete occurrence. The pattern is not progressive but iterative. However, as Tannehill points out, 're-iteration makes possible a different kind of development. Reiteration of a basic pattern allows and encourages variation of details. Points of emphasis can vary and various possibilities for filling the roles can be used.'[1] Although each of Mark's miracle stories conforms to a recognisable compositional structure or form, there is, as Kelber observes, a remarkable variability in the use of the basic elements of structure. 'There is ample room for narrative maneuvering, and no single story is quite like any other.'[2] The elements may be arranged, for instance, so that one motif is emphasised at the expense of others. Or the structure may be altered in the direction of a different literary genre, such as a call account or a conversion story.[3] In a number of the stories it is the faith motif which is given prominence. The wealth of descriptive detail found in these accounts should not be dismissed as uncontrolled secondary growth or unnecessary decoration, but accepted as a traditional feature or latent potential[4] which the author has been able to exploit in order to bring his understanding of faith to life and to illustrate different facets of the concept.

As well as heightening dramatic tension in the plot, such detail is often crucial to the author's characterisation of the supplicants for healing. These figures belong to a wider group of minor characters in the story who respond positively to Jesus. As well as those seeking help, it includes the children Jesus embraces, the poor widow in Jerusalem, the woman who anoints Jesus' body, Simon of Cyrene, the women at the cross, Joseph of Arimathea, and the centurion at Jesus' execution. Almost all these figures, many of whom are women,

---

[1] Tannehill, 'Narrative Christology', 67.

[2] Kelber, *Oral and Written Gospel*, 49.

[3] See Betz, 'Early Christian Miracle Story', 69–81.

[4] Cf. Theissen, *Miracle Stories*, 183–5.

display similiar traits: childlike trust, a capacity for sacrifice, and a lack of or disregard for personal status and power.[1] Inasmuch as they exemplify only a limited range of traits, they are 'flat' characters (unlike Jesus or Peter for example, who are more complex, 'round' characters).[2] Yet collectively the minor characters fulfil an important literary function in the narrative. They are the ones who measure up to the standards of judgement Jesus proclaims in the story, and thus serve as foils to other characters who do not measure up.

Those who figure in the healing and exorcism stories are characterised in particular by powerlessness in face of overwhelming need, frequently compounded by social and religious powerlessness as well. The full richness of Mark's conception of faith becomes apparent when we examine the attitudes and behaviour of those powerless ones who are specially commended for their faith. Even if the functioning of a limited number of set roles is more important in miracle stories than the precise delineation of individual characters,[3] there are nonetheless sufficient differences between the actors cast in the role of Jesus' opposite number and significant enough variations in the way Jesus interacts with them to justify analysis of each case separately. The fact that a succession of different individuals, in a variety of circumstances, exemplify true faith draws the reader's attention to the importance and feasibility of such a response. Furthermore, the conversion and faith of these radically powerless individuals serves as a foil for the behaviour of the disciples and the religious authorities. No direct comparison is made, but the juxtaposition of episodes, as well as elements within episodes, brings out the contrast. The progressive enrichment in the characterisation of the disciples and the opponents is partly achieved by the cameo appearance of minor characters who display the very qualities they lack.

The importance of the categories of power and authority in Mark's story has been recognised by a number of recent interpreters.[4] According to Dorothy Lee-Pollard, 'to explore the

[1] See Rhoads and Michie, *Mark as Story*, 129–36. Also see Rhoads, 'Narrative Criticism', 419.

[2] On various character types in biblical narratives, see Berlin, *Poetics and Interpretation*, 23–32.

[3] Kelber, *Oral and Written Gospel*, 51; Theissen, *Miracle Stories*, 4f, 43–6.

[4] See for example Senior, '"Swords and Clubs"', and the literature cited by him (p.14); Weeden, 'Power in Weakness'; Myers, 'Obedience and

dynamic relationship that exists between power and powerlessness within the structure of the gospel is essential for
understanding Mark as a theologian and an author'.[1] With
this in mind, we turn to look in detail at five faith miracles in
which individuals who are impotent in face of extreme need,
exhibit a quality of faith that wins the intervention of divine
power. We are interested both in what Mark conceives such
faith consists of, and how he conveys this to his readers or
hearers through the medium of the miracle narrative.

2. The faith of minor characters

The faith of the paralytic (2:1–12)

The account of the healing of the paralytic is the first occasion
after the initial call to faith in 1:14f that the subject is explicitly
raised again, and in many respects the story constitutes a
dramatic enactment of the main elements of Jesus' opening
message. Jesus appears at home in Capernaum 'speaking the
word'; ὁ λόγος here is a synonym for τὸ εὐαγγέλιον.[2] The
exercise of eschatological forgiveness 'upon the earth' demonstrates the fulfilment of time (cf. Isa 33:24; Jer 31:34); those
who come to Jesus exemplify the response of faith; and the fact
that the paralytic is granted forgiveness indicates an act of
repentance on his part (cf. 2:17; 4:12). The story is also the most
graphic example we have of the discriminating or double-sided
effect of Jesus' miracles. The self-same event causes some to
respond with praise of God (v 12) and others with accusations
of blasphemy (v 7).

(a) Composition, structure, and theme

Mark's account falls readily into two parts: one part describes
the interaction between Jesus and those seeking help (vv 1–5,
11–12), and the other records the interchange between Jesus
and the hostile scribes (vv 6–10). This double structure is conventionally seen as the result of the secondary expansion of a
straightforward healing story by the interpolation of a contro-

---

Upheaval'; Lee-Pollard, 'Powerlessness as Power'; Shaw, *Cost of Authority*,
190–268.

[1] Lee-Pollard, 'Powerlessness as Power', 173. Lee-Pollard makes little
mention of this motif within Mark's miracle stories, which is the focus of
what follows here.

[2] So too in 1:45; 4:14,15,16,17,20,33; 8:32; cf. 9:10,32.

versy apophthegm.[1] Various observations are advanced in support of this:[2]

(i)   When the controversy section is removed, the remaining verses (vv 1–5,11f) form a pure miracle story containing all the typical elements of the genre.

(ii) The appearance of the scribes in v 6 is unanticipated, and the abstract theological content and literary style of the controversy discourse contrasts with the vivid, concrete details of the healing narrative.

(iii) There is an awkward syntactical break in v 10. The final clause introduced by ἵνα peters out and there is a change of addressee. The repetition of λέγει τῷ παραλυτικῷ (v 10b; cf. v 5b) provides a cumbersome parenthesis around the insertion.

(iv) Verses 11–12 form a suitable conclusion only for the miracle story, not the composite narrative. There is no reference to the preceding discussion; the experience of forgiveness, unlike healing, cannot be 'seen' (v 12b); and the 'all' who praise God could scarcely include Jesus' enemies.

(v)   The combination of healing story and controversy transforms the miracle into a unique proof-miracle or *Schauwunder*, unparalleled elsewhere in the synoptic tradition.

Some account for the present composite form by postulating the combination of two independent traditions.[3] Others argue that the excised controversy could have never existed on its own, and see it as a creative expansion of a traditional healing narrative, either by Mark[4] or by a pre-Markan editor.[5]

[1] This view has been widely advocated since Wrede's work on the pericope, 'Heilung des Gelähmten', 354–8.

[2] For the most detailed listings of the main arguments, see: Maisch, *Heilung des Gelähmten*, 29–39; Klauck, 'Sündenvergebung', 225–31; Mead, 'Healing of the Paralytic', 348f. Also, Koch, *Wundererzählungen*, 47f.

[3] E.g. Bultmann, *History*, 14–16; Fridrichsen, *Problem of Miracle*, 129f; Schweizer, *Mark*, 60; Lohmeyer, *Markus*, 50; Klostermann, *Markus*, 21f; Sundwall, *Zusammenungsetzung*, 12–14; Rawlinson, *Mark*, 25; Taylor, *Mark*, 191f; Burkill, *Mysterious Revelation*, 127f; Nineham, *Mark*, 90–2; Fuller, *Miracles*, 35,50; Kuhn, *Ältere Sammlungen*, 53f; Budesheim, 'Jesus and the Disciples', 190–2.

[4] E.g. Kee, *Community*, 35f; Kelber, *Kingdom*, 18; Koch, *Wundererzählungen*, 49f; Johnson, *Mark*, 55; Patten, 'Thaumaturgical Element', 238; Pryke, *Redactional Style*, 49.

[5] E.g. Dibelius, *Tradition to Gospel*, 67; Schmithals, *Markus*, I, 151; Klauck,

Scholars also differ over the precise limits of the interpolation. One group follows Bultmann and includes the saying about forgiveness in the secondary expansion (vv 5b–10).[1] Another group follows Dibelius and ascribes the pronouncement of forgiveness to the original healing narrative.[2] Most take the linguistic break between v 10 and v 11 as marking the end of the insertion, although many see v 10 itself as a redactional insertion.[3] The result of the combination of elements is a pericope of mixed form in which the faith healing recedes into the background[4] and attention focuses on the christological dispute about Jesus' authority to remit sins.

Now narrative criticism is pre-eminently concerned with the text as it presents itself to the reader. Whatever the compositional prehistory of the narrative, it gives primary exegetical respect to the final form as possessing a genuine integrity of its own and as constituting the actual vehicle the author has chosen to convey his message. Thus even if the story of the paralytic is made up of two or more dissimilar components, knowledge of this fact is not essential (or even conducive) to grasping the author's message. On the other hand, many of the features of the pericope which have encouraged source division can be equally explained by taking into account three factors: the demands of oral storytelling, the narrator's characteristic heightening of dramatic tension, and the

'Sündenvergebung', 232, 242–4; Achtemeier, *Mark*, 75; Anderson, *Mark*, 99; Pesch, *Markus*, I, 149ff; Hultgren, *Adversaries*, 107; Doughty, 'Authority of the Son of Man', 162f; Kertelge, *Wunder Jesu*, 76ff; Gnilka, *Markus*, I, 96; idem, 'Elend vor dem Menschensohn', 206. Cf. also Reicke, 'Synoptic Reports', 319–29, whose findings would point in the same direction.

[1] Bultmann, *History*, 14–16, 212f; Schmid, *Markus*, 59; Klostermann, *Markus*, 22; Sundwall, *Zusammensetzung*, 13; Taylor, *Mark*, 191f; Maisch, *Heilung des Gelähmten*, 47f; Burkill, *Mysterious Revelation*, 127f; Haenchen, *Weg Jesu*, 104; Koch, *Wundererzählungen*, 47f; Schmithals, *Markus*, I, 96, 99; Gnilka, 'Elend vor dem Menschensohn', 202; Marxsen, *Introduction*, 114; Kertelge, 'Vollmacht des Menschensohnes', 207.

[2] Dibelius, *Tradition to Gospel*, 66; Branscomb, *Mark*, 44f; Pesch, *Markus*, I, 153, 156; Kelber, *Kingdom*, 18; Fuller, *Miracles*, 50f; Schweizer, *Mark*, 60; Kertelge, *Wunder Jesu*, 77; Ernst, *Markus*, 87; Theissen, *Miracle Stories*, 164; Klauck, 'Sündenvergebung', 236; Johnson, *Mark*, 55; Colpe, *TDNT*, 8, 431 n.235.

[3] See below, p. 183.

[4] So Schmid, *Markus*, 57; Haenchen, *Weg Jesu*, 99–103; Kelber, *Kingdom*, 18; Johnson, *Mark*, 55; Kee, *Community*, 36; Achtemeier, *Mark*, 76.

requirements of the literary integration of the unit into the broader gospel context. By heeding such considerations as these, we are better able to appreciate the narrator's strategy and intentions in the unitary account, especially with respect to the role of faith.

(i) Repetition and duality are essential strategies in oral communication; they create 'oral echoes' that underline points of emphasis. The central section of the paralytic story is permeated with verbal duplications:

(1) v 5a   λέγει τῷ παραλυτικῷ
     10b   λέγει τῷ παραλυτικῷ
   cf. 9a   εἰπεῖν τῷ παραλυτικῷ
(2)   5b   ἀφίενταί σου αἱ ἁμαρτίαι
     9b   ἀφίενταί σου αἱ ἁμαρτίαι
(3)   6b   διαλογιζόμενοι ἐν ταῖς καρδίαις αὐτῶν
     8a   διαλογίζονται ἐν ἑαυτοῖς
     8b   διαλογίζεσθε ἐν ταῖς καρδίαις ὑμῶν
(4)   9b   ἔγειρε καὶ ἆρον τὸν κράβαττόν σου καὶ περιπάτει
     11b   ἔγειρε ἆρον τὸν κράβαττόν σου καὶ ὕπαγε

These repetitions are not an indication of a multiplicity of sources or insertions,[1] but rather, as Kelber suggests,

> Mark may be treating an oral story for it to remain functional for the ear more than for the eye. By duplicating the key phrases, he has in effect told the controversy twice. The impact of reiterating verbal clauses allows the ear to recall and hear its way through the unconventional passage. Despite deviation from the norm of healing story, healing and controversy can now be heard as a narrative whole.[2]

The broken syntax of v 10 is also somewhat less problematic when seen in light of oral delivery. In dramatic performance (and in everyday speech generally), a sudden break in a sentence in order to address a different person, while keeping in view the original addressees as well, is quite common, and even functional for enhancing the tempo and dramatic impact of the exchange. Although strictly an anacolouthon, v 10a is perfectly intelligible as everyday speech, and both Matthew and

---

[1] As Doughty claims, 'Authority of the Son of Man', 163–7; also see Donahue, *Are You the Christ?*, 81f.

[2] Kelber, *Oral and Written Gospel*, 67. He comments: 'the gospel's proximity to oral life may warrant reflection on Lord's proposition: "I do not believe in interpolators any more than I believe in ghosts, even less!"'.

Luke take it over, although elsewhere they rectify Mark's grammatical slips and obscurities. Verse 10b is a kind of stage direction or parenthetical aside by the narrator explaining the change of addressee at this point in the action.

(ii) A heightening of dramatic tension is generally characteristic of Mark's style,[1] and a number of aspects of the present story serve this end. For instance, the pronouncement of forgiveness (v 5b) at this point in the narration is unexpected and generates surprise. The subsequent abrupt shift of focus to the questioning scribes before the healing is recorded creates suspense, as the audience is left wondering whether Jesus will be able to accomplish the cure in view of official hostility. The debate with the scribes is by no means a ponderous theological discussion at variance with the vivid healing account. It is a dramatic interchange centring on the emotive accusation of blasphemy, which is in effect an implicit death threat (cf. 3:6; 14:63–5). The climactic shift back to the paralytic in v 10f resolves this tension; the healing is performed and the scribal objections are simultaneously refuted.

(iii) Contrary to what is often said, the conclusion to the story is in fact more suited to the unitary account than to the healing alone. The story no longer stands in isolation but has been integrated into a larger narrative setting by backward linkages to the so-called 'day at Capernaum' (1:21–34) and forward linkages to the following *Streitgespräche*.[2] In this wider context, the Capernaum crowd has already witnessed Jesus' extensive healing and exorcising activity (1:27,33f), so that the cry, 'we have never seen anything like this' would be somewhat extravagant for a simple healing. Their reaction suggests they have witnessed something which goes beyond what has been seen before, namely a healing performed through the granting of eschatological forgiveness.

It is unlikely that the 'all' who respond in praise of God is meant to include the hostile scribes.[3] V.12 recalls 1:27 where 'all' denotes the people of Capernaum *in contrast* to the scribes, inasmuch as they compare their scribal leaders un-

---

[1] Theissen, *Miracle Stories*, 183f.

[2] The backward linkages are: place name ('Capernaum'); time reference ('again'); location ('before the door'; cf. 1:33); and theme ('authority'; cf. 2:10 and 1:22,27). The forward linkages to 2:13–17 are the mention of sin and healing (cf. 2:17) and the scribes (cf. 2:16).

[3] Contra Lane, *Mark*, 99. Matthew interprets it as a reference to the crowds (Matt 9:8).

favourably to Jesus (1:22). Within the broader Markan context, it is also an exaggeration to describe 2:1–12 as a unique proof miracle and to set it at odds with 8:11–13; 15:29–32. We have already seen how the miracles in general have the role of evoking a response of faith. The story of the healing of the leper (1:40–4), which immediately precedes 2:1–12, provides an interesting parallel to the Capernaum episode in two respects. First, the use of the term 'cleansing' (καθαρίζειν), also used in Christian circles for the purging of sin,[1] may suggest an implicit link between healing and forgiveness here too. Secondly, after Jesus heals the leper he sends him to the temple, not only to fulfil the necessary cultic requirements but also as a witness to (or against)[2] the priests. That miracle too is to serve as evidence for Jesus' eschatological claims. In the healing of the paralytic, both these elements are continued and expanded upon. The chiastic arrangement of hook words between 1:45 and 2:1ff serves to tie both episodes together thematically.[3]

1:45 τὸν λόγον, ὥστε μηκέτι . . . εἰσελθεῖν
2:1f εἰσελθὼν . . . ὥστε μηκέτι . . . τὸν λόγον

There is no contradiction between 2:10 and the situation pictured in 8:11ff and 15:29ff. Unlike these later episodes, at Capernaum Jesus' opponents do not *demand* a confirmatory work of power; the healing is offered spontaneously by Jesus as a sign of his mission and in response to the presence of active faith (2:5).

The various features which permit source division, therefore, can be shown to fulfil rhetorical or theological tasks in the unitary narrative. In addition, dividing the narrative in two disturbs the balanced, symmetrical structure of the existing account, a structure which helps us determine the hermeneutical significance to be ascribed to the faith reference. The text has a chiastic or concentric arrangement.[4]

---

[1] Cf. Acts 15:9; 2 Cor 7:1; Eph 5:26; 1 Jn 1:7,9 etc. See the discussion and references given by Best, *Temptation and Passion*, 106f; idem, *Gospel as Story*, 61; idem, *Discipleship*, 188.

[2] See above pp. 70 n.1 on this point.

[3] Cf. Dewey, *Public Debate*, 67; Sundwall, *Zusammensetzung*, 11f.

[4] There are various forms of chiasmus, of which concentric arrangement is one. See Dewey, *Public Debate*, 32ff, 66ff. Maisch also notes the concentric structure of 2:1–12, *Heilung des Gelähmten*, 55. More generally, see Stock, 'Chiastic Awareness', 23–7; Breck, 'Biblical Chiasmus', 70–4. The basic work on chiasmus is N. W. Lund, *Chiasmus in the New Testament* (Chapel Hill, N.C., University of North Carolina Press, 1942).

    (A)   Introduction (vv 1–2)
    (B)   Healing focus (vv 3–5)
    (C)   Controversy (vv 6–10)
    (Bi)   Healing focus (vv 11–12a)
    (Ai) Conclusion (v 12b)

The central controversy section is separated off by the duplicate framing verse: λέγει τῷ παραλυτικῷ (vv 5b,10b). Yet it is also united with the surrounding material in two ways: by hook words (αἴρω [v 9; cf. vv 3,11,12]; κράβαττος [v 9; cf. vv 4,11]; παραλυτικός [v 10; cf. vv 3,5]; ἀφιένται ἁμαρτίας [vv 7,9; cf. v 5]; also cf. λαλεῖν, λέγειν [vv 2,5,6,8,9,10,11,12]), and by content: healing and forgiveness are intertwined with each other in both the interchange with the sick man (vv 5,11) and with the scribes (v 9). Jesus' words to the paralytic lead to the scribes' question (v 7), whilst Jesus' question to the scribes (v 9) leads back to an address to the paralytic (v 11).

There are, then, as conventional criticism recognises, two elements in the story: the central controversy and the surrounding material. But they cannot be divided along form critical lines on the basis of content. Nor is it true that the controversy pushes the miracle into the background. For concentric patterning serves to *interrelate* elements in a story in a more complex or dramatic fashion than is possible in a straightforward linear narration. It may be used to emphasise the central element, to compare or contrast it with the surrounding material, to hold opposite ideas in tension, to express paradox, or to add depth to the development of the plot line. In the present case, the outside framing material provides an interpretative commentary, by way of comparison and contrast, on the central portion. On the one hand, it demonstrates the parallel between physical healing and the forgiveness of sins, and on the other, it sharply contrasts the attitude of those seeking help and those reasoning in their hearts. Since the former display πίστις (v 5a), the attitude of the latter is implicitly diagnosed as ἀπιστία.

The repetition of λέγει τῷ παραλυτικῷ reinforces this contrast between faith and unbelief. J. Donahue first noted Mark's widespread use of similar or identical framing verses. He considered it a redactional 'insertion technique', in which the duplicated phrases draw attention to the importance of the free-floating material Mark has intruded, 'much in the same fashion that a modern writer would use italics or an asterisk'.[1] While Donahue has pinpointed an important literary feature of Mark's narrative, there is no reason why the enclosed material should always be considered an interpolation, nor why the replicated framing verses should only serve to emphasise the intervening material. As a rhetorical rather than simply an editorial device, such repetition may serve other ends as well, such as drawing the reader's or hearer's attention back to an earlier phase in the story after a parenthetical aside, or making comparisons or contrasts between aspects of the story. In our story, the repetition of λέγει τῷ παραλυτικῷ in v 10b has a double effect. Structurally, it resumes the healing account, and thematically it recalls the faith response of the paralytic, to whom forgiveness and healing are granted, as a foil for the unbelief of the scribes, to whom only riddles are posed. It also, incidentally, qualifies the 'apologetic' nature of the miracle. The healing indeed confirms Jesus' authority to forgive sins, but by the allusion back to the receptive faith of the lame man (λέγει τῷ παραλυτικῷ) and the emphatic individualising of the interaction between him and Jesus (σοὶ λέγω), the miracle remains conditional on the active faith of one in need. It is a δύναμις, not a cold-blooded σημεῖον.

In sum then, our analysis of the literary structure of the pericope confirms the judgement made some time ago by M. D. Hooker, who wrote:

> Although it falls into two sections it cannot be split in two as the form critics demand, because its two themes are intertwined, and the whole point of the story is that we find forgiveness where we expect healing and vice versa. The faith of the paralytic's four friends, and the words spoken to him by Jesus in response to that faith, stand in contrast to the disbelief of the scribes, and the words of Jesus to the paralytic which are occasioned by that disbelief.[2]

The division is a *thematic one between faith and unbelief*, not a generic one between miracle and controversy, or between healing and forgiveness.

---

[1] Donahue, *Are You the Christ?*, 81 (see 77–84). See also Synge, 'Intruded Middles', 329–33, for similar observations.

[2] Hooker, *Son of Man*, 85f.

Now accepting 2:1–12 as a dramatically structured whole[1] is not necessarily to deny that it represents a fusion of distinct elements; traditio-historical and rhetorical explanations for textual phenomena do not have to be mutually exclusive.[2] Some of the awkward and abrupt transitions in the text could owe their origin to such a combination, but their retention in the available account is not due to the literary ineptitude of the final redactor but because Mark recognised their capacity for enhancing the rhetorical or theological functioning of the completed entity. Furthermore, the two elements could have always belonged together and the current format be the result of a stylistic rearrangement for rhetorical effect.[3] Mark shows a fondness for intercalations, and the present structure is really a smaller scale 'sandwich arrangement'.

Be that as it may, the existing account has its own literary integrity and deserves to be treated as such. 'It is', notes Carrington, 'a magnificent example of that classical effect, the story within the story, which permits of surprise, suspense, and solution. Faith is rewarded, criticism rebuffed; Jesus is vindicated; the man picks up his bed and walks out. The power of the story is gone if you divide it in two . . .'[4]

(b) The portrayal of faith in 2:1–12
In the finished narrative, the narrator is not only concerned to underline the ἐξουσία of Jesus to pronounce 'on the earth' the forgiveness of sins, but also to demonstrate the divergent ways in which people respond to this fact, the integral connection between healing and forgiveness, and the individual dis-

---

[1] Some of the scholars who defend the original unity, more or less, of 2:1–12 include: Schniewind, *Markus*, 22–7; Mead, 'Healing of the Paralytic', 348–54; Berger, *Exegese des Neuen Testaments*, 29–32; Van der Loos, *Miracles*, 440–9; Cranfield, *Mark*, 96ff; Lane, *Mark*, 97f; Carrington, *Mark*, 58; Polhill, 'Miracle Stories', 396f; Colpe, 'Argumentationen zu Aussagen Jesu', 232–6. See also the comments of: Theissen, *Miracle Stories*, 164f; Hooker, *Son of Man*, 81–93; Dewey, *Public Debate*, 66–79; Branscomb, 'Thy Sins are Forgiven', 59; idem, *Mark*, 47; Boobyer, 'Healing of the Paralytic', 115–20. Maisch lists and evaluates negatively the arguments for unity in *Heilung des Gelähmten*, 29–39.

[2] Berlin notes that even if literary criticism is an exercise in 'synchronic poetics', it should still be possible to write a 'historical poetics' showing the changes in structure and discourse that a text has undergone over time, *Poetics and Interpretation*, 111.

[3] See, e.g., Hooker, *Son of Man*, 87.

[4] Carrington, *Mark*, 58.

position necessary to win such benefits. The hermeneutical key to these concerns lies in the double-sided portrayal of faith and unbelief. We shall postpone examining the presentation of unbelief in this episode until chapter 6. Here we shall only consider the positive portrayal of faith.

By this stage in Mark's story, Jesus' popularity is such that he tries to avoid appearing openly in the Galilean cities, although even in the desert places people seek him out (1:45). He manages to return quietly to a house in Capernaum (cf. 1:29ff), but after several days news of his presence spreads and once again the crowds swarm to him (2:1f). Among them is a παραλυτικός, a man whose condition is characterised by extreme physical and social powerlessness. Unable to move, he is carried by four companions on a κράβαττος, a poor man's bed mentioned no fewer than three times in the account (vv 4,9,11). Prevented from approaching Jesus because of the crowd, the stretcher-bearers climb onto the roof, dig through, and lower the paralytic down.

At no point does the sick man or his friends verbalise their desire for healing or their trust in Jesus. Yet Jesus 'sees' in the trouble they take to reach him an internal posture of faith (v 5a). This is evidently because the men were driven by the overriding goal of reaching Jesus, and had refused to be deflected from doing so, either by the human obstacles that blocked the door or by the physical barrier of the roof that separated him from them. It is striking that the faith of the whole party (τὴν πίστιν αὐτῶν) is acknowledged, not just that of the paralytic. It is possible that Mark intends this as an example of vicarious faith (5:36; 9:17ff; cf. 7:26ff), but most commentators see no grounds for excluding the faith of the paralytic from the formulation. In any event, at a later point in the narrative the sick man is required to make a personal venture of faith by taking up his bed and walking. The explicit recognition of the contributory faith of the wider group does suggest however that faith is important for all who seek the operation of divine power, whether for themselves or for others.

In the view of H.-J. Klauck, the faith of the men 'is naive trust in the power of the miracle worker (cf. 5:28,34), with all the ambiguity inherent in such an attitude', though it is possibly deepened to a more fundamental encounter through the word of forgiveness.[1] But is this adequate? Even before

---

[1] Klauck, 'Sündenvergebung', 235.

Jesus' word of pardon, we are encouraged to see more than a mere *Wunderglaube* in the attitude of the men. By delaying the arrival of the suppliants (v 3) until he has constructed a didactic context (v 2b), and by stressing that their sole intent was to reach Jesus himself (ἔρχονται . . . πρὸς αὐτόν), the narrator indicates that their faith was conditioned by an apprehension of the kingdom message and by a corresponding conviction that God's kingly power was somehow concentrated in, and available through, Jesus alone. (In the Markan context, this conviction need not have arisen through Jesus' preaching on this occasion, for his διδαχή and δυνάμεις were already well known in Capernaum: 1:22,34). Although all five exhibit faith, only the sick man is addressed by Jesus, and the words spoken to him confirm that his faith exceeds 'naive trust in the power of a *Wundermann*'. The address τέκνον is a term of endearment (cf. 5:34,41) and, at very least, indicates the establishment of a personal bond with the man. More than this, it is the address used elsewhere for the disciples (10:24), expressing their childlike reception of the kingdom (10:13–16 cf. 9:36f,42) and their membership of Jesus' true family composed of those who 'do the will of God' (3:34f). Its connection here with the pronouncement of divine forgiveness, moreover, indicates God's acceptance of the man's repentant faith.[1] There are no real grounds, then, for equating such faith with a simple *Wunderglaube*.

As well as establishing a personal bond with the man, Jesus answers his faith with a word of forgiveness (v 5b) and an act of healing (v 11). A causal connection between sin and sickness was common belief in contemporary Judaism and in ancient religion generally.[2] It is unclear here however whether Mark

---

[1] 'Die Anrede ist liebvoll, väterlich, göttlich', Schmithals, *Markus*, I, 156. Τέκνον is used literally for children in Mk 7:27; 10:29f; 12:19; 13:12.

[2] In the Old Testament, healing and forgiveness are closely related, e.g. 2 Sam 12:13; 2 Chron 7:14; Ps 103:3; 147:3; Isa 19:22; 38:17; 57:18f; Zech 3:4, and in translation are sometimes almost interchangeable, e.g. Ps 41:4; Jer 3:22; Hos 14:4; cf. 2 Chron 30:20. The Jewish belief that sickness was due to sin is attested in Job 4:7; 22:5–10; Lk 13:4; Jn 9:2 – and a non-Jewish belief in Acts 28:3,4. Of particular interest is a comment in the Talmud that says, 'No one gets up from his sick bed until all his sins are forgiven' (B.Ned 41a). Some commentators cite as a parallel to Mk 2:5 the prayer of Nabonidus at Qumran: 'I was afflicted [with an evil ulcer] for seven years . . . and an exorcist pardoned my sins' (4Q Pr Nab 1:4 – Vermes' translation). But the translation is unsure. On healing in the Old Testament and Jewish tradition, see Kee, *Medicine, Miracle and Magic*, 5–26.

envisages that the man's paralysis was due to the general human condition of sinful separation from God,[1] or stemmed from his own specific sins[2] (the latter seems implied in the individual focus of the phrase (σου) and the use of the plural form 'sins'). But the point in the present story is not primarily the link between sin and sickness (which is presupposed); it is the inseparable connection that exists between healing and forgiveness within the activity of Jesus. The unusual procedure of healing the man by first informing him of God's immediate[3] forgiveness is intended to make it clear that Jesus' work of healing transcends physical restoration alone to include, at the same time, the imparting of divine acceptance and pardon. For Jesus has authority not just to teach and heal (1:22,27), but to establish 'on the earth' full eschatological salvation, the last great act of which was generally held to be the forgiveness of sins.[4] This perspective on Jesus' healing ministry is laid down early in the narrative so that in all the subsequent healing accounts physical recovery may be viewed as evidence of the forging of a new relationship of the recipient with God; the formulation of 2:10 plainly transcends the immediate episode. Because the particular faith Jesus recognises is 'repentant faith' in light of God's kingdom, the gift of healing is always accompanied by the gift of forgiveness and reconciliation to God (cf. Jas 5:15). In Mark's story, when Jesus heals bodies he reaches to the heart of the person's spiritual need at the same time.[5]

---

[1] So Anderson, *Mark*, 100; Lane, *Mark*, 94; Cranfield, *Mark*, 98; Schweizer, *Mark*, 61; Schmithals, *Markus*, I, 155f, 159f; Van der Loos, *Miracles*, 444, cf. 260–3.

[2] So Taylor, *Mark*, 195; Schmid, *Markus*, 57; cf. also Kee, *Community*, 157; Caird, *Language and Imagery*, 15; Hooker, *Son of Man*, 86.

[3] The passive formulation is a circumlocution for the divine subject (BDF, S.130.1). The present ἀφίενται is to be preferred to the perfect ἀφέωνται (Metzger, *Textual Commentary*, 77). It is an aoristic present meaning, 'your sins are forgiven at this moment' (BDF, S.320); Taylor, *Mark*, 195; Cranfield, *Mark*, 97).

[4] On this, see Klauck, 'Sündenvergebung', 236f.

[5] S. H. Travis claims in Jesus' ministry, 'there is no suggestion that simply by being healed a person necessarily participates in eternal salvation from sin and death; if he is to experience that total salvation it must be by repentance and faith in Jesus', 'The Scope of Salvation' (7th Lecture to Assn of Conservative Evangelicals in Methodism: Sheffield, 25 June, 1980) 12. But from Mark's perspective, the faith that wins healing is repentant faith and the recovery it secures is more than physical.

The stated connection between healing and forgiveness thus lies in the character of the kingdom of God on the one hand, and in the inherent structure of responsive faith on the other. In Mark, the present realisation of God's reign means the exertion of divine power over forces of evil and disease, and the immediacy of God's presence to effect the resumption of fellowship with God (cf. 2:15–17). Accordingly, to place faith in this reality entails perceiving and responding to God's presence in Jesus, thereby establishing a relationship with him, and, where necessary, trusting confidently in his power for the restoration of bodily wellbeing.

(c) Summary

Whatever its compositional pre-history, the present structure of 2:1–12 serves to contrast starkly the faith of the powerless man and his friends with the contentious unbelief of the religious authorities. In Mark's interpretation, the suppliants come to Jesus because they recognise in him the authority of God to teach and to heal. Their faith is not a simple *Wunderglaube*, but a profound conviction that if they can reach the one in whom God's power is present, the lame man will be restored. Because of this faith, the once powerless man is introduced to the realm of eschatological power. Once carried on a pallet, he now carries his pallet; once prostrate and unable to walk, he now arises and walks; once dependent on others, he now returns to his own home. The anticipation of this empowering in v 9 and its almost verbatim fulfilment in v 11 enhances the impact of the transformation wrought through faith.

The scribes' silent accusation of blasphemy (v 7) means that for the first time in the story the death of Jesus comes faintly into view. The Son of Man who here confers forgiveness will be later identified as the Son of Man who must suffer, die and rise again (8:31; 9:31f; 10:33ff). The implications of this for faith are not spelt out here. But it is worth noting that it is perservering faith in the forgiving Son of Man (cf. 10:45) that leads to divine acceptance, to the remission of sins, and finally to the command 'arise'.

The faith of Jairus (5:21–4,35–43)

This episode is one of the few cases in the gospel where a person in a position of religious or political power appears in a positive light (cf. 12:28–34; 15:39,43ff), and the content of the story further illuminates the dialectical relationship the author depicts between human power or powerlessness and the power of faith. It is also a classic example of faith being exercised on behalf of a third party, as well as of a faith that is severely and repeatedly tested before winning its remarkable desire: the restoring to life of a dead child. Through the internal construction of the account and by the use of various literary devices, such as irony and intercalation, Mark succeeds in communicating to his audience, not just the rational content of faith, but also the existential 'feel' of genuine faith. Suspense mounts as the story progresses and a series of unexpected twists enthrall, surprise and ultimately instruct the reader or hearer in the nature of faith.

(a) Composition, structure and theme

The story of Jairus' daughter has a planned scenic structure.[1] It is made up of a sequence of scenes, each introduced by a verb of motion (ἔρχεσθαι, and once εἰσπορεύσθαι), set along Jesus' journey from the lakeside (vv 21ff) to the dead girl's bedroom (vv 40ff). The steady narrowing of focus from the public domain of the seaside to the privacy of the room of death corresponds to the progressive drawing of a veil of ambiguity and secrecy over the event itself. This scenic pattern has allowed the author to sandwich an entirely separate episode into the midst of the Jairus narrative (vv 25–34), where it now functions as an additional scene. It is also introduced by ἔρχεσθαι, although after a long series of dependent participles (vv 24f) and, like all but the first scene in the story, it ends with an injunction or instruction from Jesus (v 35; cf. vv 37,40b,43). Because of this literary arrangement, we must approach the story of the woman with the haemorrhage both as an independent faith story in its own right (see later), and as an integral part of the surrounding narrative.

The intercalation of one episode within another has long been recognised[2] as one of the most characteristic compositional features of Mark's gospel (see 3:20–35; 5:21–43; 6:7–32;

---

[1] See Rochais, *Récits de Résurrection*, 54f.
[2] E. von Dobschütz first drew attention to this, 'Zur Erzählerkunst der Markus', 193–8.

11:12–26; 14:1–11 and 14:10–25; 14:54–72. Intercalations are usually attributed to the evangelist,[1] although the actual technique may have been suggested to him from the tradition. In general, Mark uses the device to bring episodes into some kind of mutually interpretative relationship, or to achieve some rhetorical effect in the narrative, such as retarding the action in order to heighten dramatic tension or to indicate the passage of time, to create irony or add emphasis, and so on.[2] The task of the interpreter is to determine in each instance what literary and/or theological function the intercalation fulfils.

The present case is the only example in the gospel of two miracle stories being dovetailed together in this manner. In fact, so skilful is their interweaving that some scholars think we have here an original unitary tradition.[3] Elements essential to the central story, like the journeying of Jesus and the presence of the thronging crowd (v 27), are anticipated in the first part of the Jairus story (vv 21,24), while the disciples, who play a role in the second part of the Jairus narrative (vv 37,40), are first introduced in the episode of the haemorrhaging woman (v 31). In addition, the latter portion of the Jairus story actually commences with a deft backward link to the intervening episode (ἔτι αὐτοῦ λαλοῦντος v 35a). On the other hand, there are some significant *stylistic differences* between the two accounts. The Jairus story is written mainly in the historic present with frequent use of καί, whereas the story of the haemorrhaging woman is predominantly in the aorist and imperfect,[4] has longer sentences, and includes no fewer than fifteen participles. These dissimilarities, though not absolute (the past tense is also found in the Jairus account: vv 21,24,

---

[1] E.g. Schenke, *Wundererzählungen*, 198; Koch, *Wundererzählungen*, 139; Hooker, *Message*, 23; Achtemeier, 'Toward the Isolation', 278.

[2] On the function of Markan sandwiches, see esp.: Burkill, *Mysterious Revelation*, 121 n.10; Dewey, *Public Debate*, 22; Donahue, *Are You the Christ?*, 60, cf. 42.

[3] E.g. Taylor, *Mark*, 289; Cranfield, *Mark*, 182; Schmidt, *Rahmen*, 148; Rengstorf, *TDNT*, II, 322. Schmithals, *Markus*, I, writes: 'Die Verbindung beider Erzählungen ist vielmehr ursprunglich und unlösbar', 284.

[4] The use of the past tense may be a stylistic device to show that this scene is subordinate to the main episode. See Osburn, 'Historical Present in Mark', esp. 498.

37,42f), convince most exegetes that two originally separate traditions have been intertwined, either by Mark,[1] or sometime in the pre-Markan phase.[2]

For our purposes, it does not really matter whether the present format of 5:21–43 is original, pre-Markan or redactional; it remains a case of the *literary* encapsulation of one self-contained episode within another, as a result of which at a narrative level each story participates in the features of the other, and together they constitute a literary whole. The two stories have several features in common. Both concern the healing through physical contact of females who are ritually unclean, one because of a menstrual disorder, the other by death, the first for a period of twelve years (v 25), the second at the age of twelve years (v 42). These similarities may have encouraged the linking of the traditions in the first place,[3] yet many of the linguistic affinities between the accounts seem more to reflect a conscious attempt to tie the episodes together at the discourse level in a mutually interpretative manner. In both cases the petitioners desire full restoration (σώζεσθαι vv 23,28,34), and both fall down before Jesus (πίπτει v 22, προσέπεσεν v 33). Jairus seeks help for his θυγάτριον (v 23; cf. v 35) and the woman is addressed as θυγάτηρ (v 34). The woman experiences great fear (φοβεῖσθαι v 33), and Jairus is told not to fear (μὴ φοβοῦ v 36). The restored woman is commended for her faith (ἡ πίστις σου v 34), and Jairus is told to keep faith (μόνον πίστευε v 36). These verbal contacts invite a comparison between the behaviour and attitudes of the synagogue ruler and those of the woman with the haemorrhage, behaviour which in each case is measured against the, by now well established, standard of judgement restated here by Jesus – the standard of faith. The faith which Jairus displays for the 'saving' of his daughter is paralleled and related to the faith the 'daughter' with the haemorrhage exhibits in order to be

---

[1] E.g. Sundwall, *Zusammensetzung*, 35; Gnilka, *Markus*, I, 210; Koch, *Wundererzählungen*, 138f; Schenke, *Wundererzählungen*, 197–200; Rochais, *Récits de Résurrection*, 59; Kelber, *Kingdom*, 52; Theissen, *Miracle Stories*, 183f; Achtemeier, 'Origin and Function', 277f; Patten, 'Thaumaturgical Element', 242–5; Kuhn, *Ältere Sammlungen*, 200–2.

[2] Kertelge, *Wunder Jesu*, 110f; Ernst, *Markus*, 160; Roloff, *Kerygma*, 153; Baarlink, *Anfängliches Evangelium*, 121f.

[3] So Gnilka, *Markus*, I, 210; Rochais, *Récits de Résurrection*, 59.

'saved' herself.[1] Indeed, in the progression of the narrative, Jairus' faith is encouraged to rise to the new challenge posed by the intervention of death straight after he has witnessed at first hand the restorative powers of the woman's faith.

In sum, we have a story of five scenes in which the theme of faith in Jesus' saving power is steadily elaborated. There is also a counter-movement set up in which this faith is repeatedly tested and proven by a series of obstacles that must be surmounted before faith is answered by miracle. The scenic structure and theme of the Jairus narrative may be set out diagrammatically as follows:

Scene	Barrier	Role of faith
Prelude: verse 21 – location by the sea with a crowd)		
Scene One (vv 22–4a)	The crowd and Jairus' social position	Believing request for salvation and life
Scene Two (vv 24b–34)	Interruption by needy woman	Example of faith's power to save
Scene Three (vv 35–7)	News and evidence of child's death	Exhortation to continued faith
Scene Four (vv 38–40a)	Mourners' scepticism	Removal of unbelievers
Scene Five (vv 40b–3)	Miracle, amazement, and command to silence as the answer to faith.	

(b) The portrayal of faith in 5:21–4,35–43

The general context for the operation of kingdom power in Mark is the condition of human powerlessness. What is distinctive about this episode, however, is that the one who experiences such power is explicitly identified as a possessor of social and religious power. He is a ruler of the synagogue (vv 22,38) – that is, one of the most influential and respected members of the community with special responsibility for the

[1] The importance of the faith theme to the interweaving of the two accounts is recognised by many scholars, e.g. Schniewind, *Markus*, 55; Koch, *Wundererzählungen*, 139; Ernst, *Markus*, 160; Lohse, 'Glauben', 99; Hurtado, *Mark*, 73; Baarlink, *Anfängliches Evangelium*, 122.

conduct of religious services and the practical observance of ceremonial law in the synagogue.[1] He is clearly a man of high standing, the owner of a many-roomed house (vv 38,40), with sufficient means and importance to attract a large gathering of (professional?) mourners when death touches his family (v 38). Religious dignitaries like Jairus are usually in Mark's story the implacable enemies of Jesus and synagogues are the source of hostility (3:1ff; 6:2ff). Not so with Jairus however, for a power greater than himself, the power of sickness, had reduced him also to the position of impotence. The staccato style of his threefold appeal for help, introduced by ἵνα recitative, imperatival ἵνα, and final ἵνα, 'like three brief gasps pronounced in one breath'[2] expresses the desperation he feels. His beloved θυγάτριον is at the point of death, beyond the reach of human remedy.

Even more significantly, and certainly not lost on Mark's first readers, Jairus shows a striking disregard for his own social rank. Although he is a prominent synagogue official, he does not send a servant but comes himself to Jesus and, despite the presence of a very large crowd, falls at his feet. He thereby adopts the same posture of humility before Jesus as the unclean leper (1:40), the demonised Gerasene tomb dweller (5:6), and the Gentile Syrophoenician woman (7:25). In so doing he evidences the same standard of judgement towards social rank and prestige that Jesus does in his teaching (e.g. 3:35; 9:35ff; 10:23ff; 10:42–5; 12:13–17,38,41–44.) and in his deeds (e.g. 2:15–17; 10:13–16,17–22 etc.). The very fact that Jesus later interrupts his journey to the ruler's house to seek out a 'mere', frightened woman confirms that he too shows no regard for the priority of social status; priority belongs to faith alone (cf. v 36).

The manner of the ruler's approach then demonstrates his condition and awareness of helplessness in face of the most extreme need. It also expresses his utter trust in Jesus' ability and readiness to save his daughter from death. Although faith is first mentioned explicitly in connection with Jairus in v 36, the synagogue ruler clearly exercises faith in coming to Jesus at the beginning. In v 36, as Rochais notes, 'the present πίστευε indicates that Jesus asks Jairus to maintain the same faith

---

[1] See Schrage, *TDNT*, VII, 844–7; *Bill.*, IV, 115–52; cf. Lk 8:49; 13:14; Acts 13:15; 18:8,17.

[2] Rochais, *Récits de Résurrection*, 57.

which he had already manifested when he first sought the healing of his daughter'.[1] Mark indicates the character and content of this initial venture of faith through the language he uses to phrase Jairus' petition. The man does not ask Jesus for special prayer or magical manipulations, as he might a miracle-working rabbi, but for the direct impartation of 'saving' and 'life giving' power through the laying on of hands.[2]

Mark employs σώζειν in healing contexts (3:4; 5:23,28,34; 6: 56; 10:52) to make two points about Jesus' ministry. First, by using the term usually associated in the Old Testament with God's deliverance of his people, he indicates that in Jesus' healing work we are to see the saving activity of God himself. And secondly, in view of the eschatological and soteriological import of σώζειν elsewhere in the gospel (8:35; 10:26; 13:13,20; cf. 15:30,31) and in wider Christian usage, his use of it in the healing narratives implies that the restoration granted to faith goes beyond bodily recovery to effect a more comprehensive salvation, entailing both physical and spiritual wholeness.[3] By placing this term on Jairus' lips in our story therefore, Mark indicates that the ruler recognised the divine origin and capacity of Jesus' power to secure full restoration (cf. 5:23). The request that his daughter might live (καὶ ζήσῃ) echoes this conviction. Elsewhere in Mark, life is associated with the nature of God (12:27) and with the future kingdom (9:43,45; 10:17,30), and Jairus here confesses the power of Jesus, like that of God, to give life to the dying by holding death at bay. Through his choice of words, then, the narrator highlights the spiritual perception underlying the man's faith. Jairus 'sees' Jesus as he really is (καὶ ἰδὼν αὐτόν), not as an ordinary wonder worker but as bearer of the saving and life-giving power of God himself. He is therefore confident that if Jesus will but intervene in his situation, his daughter will be fully restored.

---

[1] Rochais, *Récits de Résurrection*, 62, cf. 60. So also Lane, *Mark*, 75; Ernst, *Markus*, 161; O'Connor, *Faith*, 49; Derrett, 'Mark's Technique', 490.

[2] See Schmithals, *Wunder und Glaube*, 69f; idem, *Markus*, I, 285; Gnilka, *Markus*, I, 214.

[3] Cf. Foerster, *TDNT*, VII, 990; Hahn, 'Glaubens', 56; Findlay, *Jesus*, 105f. Otherwise: Turner, *Grammatical Insights*, 33; also Lemcio, 'Intention of Mark', 191.

The testing of faith

Having overcome the obstacle of social prestige to express his trust in Jesus, Jairus is now confronted by a series of circumstances that subject his faith to severe and repeated testing, and which arouse tension in Mark's audience. In the coming scenes, three grim assaults are mounted on his faith. The first is the tormenting delay created by Jesus' determination to seek out the woman who surreptitiously draws upon his power while he journeys with Jairus. This interruption threatens disaster for the sick child, whose life is ebbing away. Yet what transpires in the hold-up also gives Jairus grounds for hope, because Jesus takes pains to expose publicly the all-important place of the woman's faith in winning the kind of restoration Jairus seeks for his daughter (Θυγάτηρ, ἡ πίστις σου σέσωκέν σε). That Jesus' words are partly for the benefit of the synagogue ruler is suggested by the repetition of key words from Jairus' request (θυγάτρ[ιόν], σώζειν), and by the interlocking way in which the narrator resumes the Jairus account (ἔτι αὐτοῦ λαλοῦντος).

At this point, the narrator introduces another more extreme test. Members of the ruler's household arrive with news of his daughter's death and remonstrate with him not to bother the teacher any more (v 35). Jairus' faith is assailed on two levels. His original hope that his daughter would be spared death is shattered; the girl is now dead, the aorist ἀπέθανεν underlining the fact of her demise. What is more, the messengers implicitly call into question Jesus' ability to help: 'Why trouble the teacher any further?' There is marvellous irony in their reference to Jesus as 'the teacher'. For them Jesus is but a διδάσκαλος, not someone empowered to outreach death. But from Mark's point of view, it is virtually *because* Jesus is a teacher that he can help, for his didactic words carry the power of action, while his actions are integral expressions of his message of the presence of God's kingly might.

Jesus himself disregards the message of despair and appeals directly to Jairus' faith. The present imperative μόνον πίστευε is primarily a call for continuing trust in Jesus more than for a particular belief in his capacity to raise the dead. Resurrection is never expressly promised (if anything it is deliberately obscured, v 39), and the first part of the twofold exhortation (μὴ φοβοῦ), which functions both as a word of consolation and a summons to courage, leads us to expect the second part also to describe an existential condition, one of fearless trust before an apparently hopeless situation. Such trust does have a firm cognitive content however. Jairus resided confidence in Jesus in the first place because he believed that he embodied the saving and life-giving power of God, and it is in light of this true insight that he is now enjoined to retain his confidence in Jesus despite the spectre of death. Belief and trust are inseparable.

Jairus' retention of faith is implied in what follows in the story since, 'the little drama at vv 35–36 was written to emphasise that the Girl's rising depended on faith'.[1] Jesus now prepares for the miracle by sending away all but his three closest disciples (v 37). The reason for this dismissal is not to remove a superfluous element (the crowd) carried over from the intercalated story,[2] nor is it simply meant to enhance the secrecy theme.[3] It also secures the exclusion of sceptical unbelief (the messengers) from participation in and under-standing of the δυνάμεις (cf. 6:5f) and highlights the fact that faith is an individual reality and responsibility.

The third test of faith also involves a choice between the judgement of Jesus and the judgement afforded by human experience. The presence of mourners in Jairus' house (v 39) constitutes firm evidence that the girl is indeed dead. Jesus, however, questions the reason for their weeping and wailing, and declares, mysteriously, that the child is not dead but (ἀλλά) sleeping. The reference to sleeping is intentionally ambiguous. The mourners (and some commentators!)[4] take it literally and, knowing for certain that the child is dead, laugh Jesus to scorn.[5] Their derisive laughter manifests their un-belief (cf. 15:29–32), since they fail to discern in Jesus' words God's perspective on the situation. According to this perspec-

---

[1] Derrett, 'Mark's Technique', 490.

[2] Rochais, *Récits de Résurrection*, 63. Many exegetes claim that the crowd has no role in the Jairus story and is introduced in v 24 solely to prepare for the story of the sick woman (e.g. Kertelge, *Wunder Jesu*, 111; Theissen, *Miracle Stories*, 184; Schenke, *Wundererzählungen*, 199; Gnilka, *Markus*, I, 209). But if so, it is surprising it should be mentioned twice early in the Jairus account (vv 21,24). Also, the story of the sick woman contains its own reference to the crowd (v 31) and does not really require v 24 at all.

[3] Schenke, *Wundererzählungen*, 205.

[4] E.g. Van der Loos believes that 'Jesus aroused an apparently dead girl from a state of unconsciousness, suspended animation, or whatever else it may be called', *Miracles*, 569; cf. also Taylor, *Mark*, 285f, 295.

[5] καταγελάω is found only here and at Matt 9:24; Lk 8:53 in the New Testament; see Rengstorf, *TDNT*, I, 660.

tive, the girl is only sleeping because her death, though real, is transitory, because the eschatological life-giver is present and faith is operative.

The answer to faith

Jairus' faith in the life-giver is finally vindicated by the raising of his deceased daughter (ἀναστῆναι cf. 8:31; 9:9f,31; 10:34).[1] The puzzling reference to the girl's age encourages a flashback to the healing (v 34) of the twelve-year-long affliction of the woman with the haemorrhage as a way of completing the comparison between the accounts and once again confirming the saving power of faith.[2]

The story ends with the event being subjected to a command to secrecy (v 43). This serves a double function with respect to the faith element in the story. In view of the sceptical unbelief of the mourners, it represents an attempt by Jesus to discourage a popular following based on external wonders and divorced from genuine repentance and faith. Secondly, it subjects the event to a temporary embargo until those who have witnessed it have enough understanding of Jesus' mission for its full significance to become apparent. The selection of Peter, James and John to witness the miracle foreshadows their involvement in the Transfiguration scene (9:2–8), and there is a close verbal affinity between the commands to secrecy in 5:43 (and 7:36) and 9:9. The same three disciples reappear in the Gethsemane scene where the necessity of Jesus' passion is spelled out (14:32–42). This signals to the reader that the raising of the dead girl acquires its fullest meaning when viewed in relation to the cross and resurrection of Jesus. Although the disciples are not yet in a position to understand it, the miracle is intended as a symbolic anticipation of the impending fate of Jesus himself. It suggests, furthermore, that the faith placed in the earthly Jesus secures proleptically what is to be accomplished through the work of the cross at the end of the narrative. By faith, the synagogue ruler receives in advance the saving benefits secured when, ironically, the unbelieving (15:32) religious establishment puts the divine life-giver to death; for through his dying, death is finally defeated.

---

[1] The Aramaic may be retained here to engender a sense of the mysteriousness of Jesus' power – so Schmithals, *Wunder und Glaube*, 73.

[2] For other views, see Moiser, "'She was Twelve Years Old'", 179–86; Schmithals, *Wunder*, 73; idem, *Markus*, I, 288; Schüssler Fiorenza, *Memory*, 124; Via, *Ethics*, 110f.

Commentators frequently speak of the artificiality of the secrecy command in this episode since to maintain the secrecy of the girl's resurrection plainly would be impossible.[1] But this is to miss the subtlety of Mark's narration. The aim of the command is not to keep the girl's recovery hidden, but only the fact that she has been raised from death; the final remark about giving her a meal is to signal her return to normal human society. Even before the performance of the miracle, Jesus deliberately shrouds the impending cure in ambiguity by describing the girl's state as one of sleep (v 39). Taken at face value this provokes faithless mirth from the mourners, yet at the same time it provides these unbelievers with a 'natural' explanation for her subsequent reappearance in the community. She had, after all, been asleep! The reference to sleep does, of course, have a deeper meaning too, as we have seen, but one which only faith can penetrate.

(c) Summary

The events of the Jairus story are an illustration of the power of Jesus over the combined forces of death and unbelief, just as they are also a demonstration of the necessity of faith for the appropriation of the saving power of the kingdom's presence. Jairus' faith consisted in the cognitive perception that the saving and life-giving power of God was resident in Jesus, and a corresponding entrusting of his daughter's extreme need to this power. This entailed a concurrent recognition of his own powerlessness to help, and of the irrelevance of his social rank to winning divine aid. Such was the strength of his faith that in spite of tormenting delay, faithless scepticism and even death itself, he held firmly to the word of Jesus that faith alone was sufficient to secure the saving of his child.

By placing the miracle under a command to secrecy, and forging interpretative forward linkages to later stages in the narrative, the author shows that faith stands in an implicit relationship to the death and resurrection of Jesus.[2] Faith placed in the earthly Jesus is structurally or experientially the same as faith placed in the crucified and risen Lord, and receives in an anticipatory way the saving benefits of his passion, death and resurrection.

---

[1] Burkill, *Mysterious Revelation*, 82; Kertelge, *Wunder Jesu*, 119.
[2] Cf. Schreiber, *Theologie des Vertrauens*, 240.

The faith of the haemorrhaging woman (5:24–34)

We have seen how in its present context the story of the woman with the haemorrhage functions as an integral part of the surrounding Jairus narrative. As a self-contained episode however, the story also has its own distinctive contribution to make to Mark's broader conception and presentation of faith and deserves to be treated separately. Of all Mark's faith stories, this one places most stress on the individuation of the petitioner from the general crowd pressing around Jesus. Furthermore, the form of her petition is not only unspoken, as in 2:5, it is completely covert, intentionally hidden even from Jesus himself. The request is actually granted before Jesus is consciously aware of the presence of petitionary faith. This unusual mode of request, and the equally unusual way in which Jesus' power operates, gives the faith motif in the story an additional role in countering any possible misinterpretation of the event in an impersonal or mechanistic direction. Finally, as in the previous two accounts, this narrative emphasises the comprehensiveness of the healing granted to faith, but it does so by temporally separating the suppliant's experience of bodily recovery (v 29) and the fuller gift of wholeness (v 34).

Yet in spite of these distinctive features Mark does not present the experience of the sick woman as a unique occurrence. Elements of the story are repeated in two of his *Sammelberichte*. In 3:7–12, many people, having heard of Jesus' deeds (cf. 5:27) fall upon him to touch him for healing from their 'scourges' (cf. 5:29,34); and in 6:56 as many as touch even the fringe of his garment are healed (cf. 5:28f). In view of this, the account of the haemorrhaging woman constitutes a kind of case study of what this manner of approaching Jesus involves, and especially of the crucial place faith occupies in such encounters with his power.

(a) Composition, structure and theme

Commentators are virtually unanimous that faith is the governing theme of this miracle story. This is largely because it is not the healing itself, which is recorded half-way through the story (v 29), that forms the climax of the narrative, but rather Jesus' final saying on the saving power of faith (v 34). It is also because Mark is commonly seen as giving prominence to the concept of faith to correct, reinterpret or augment two features in the account deriving from or open to a thaumaturgical-magical understanding:[1] the conviction that healing power is concentrated like an invisible substance in Jesus' cloak (v 28), and the apparently automatic emanation of mana-like δύναμις from Jesus at the touch of the hand (v 30).

The existing narrative divides readily into two parts: the healing event itself (vv 25–29), and the account of Jesus' response and interaction with the woman (vv 30–4). The first part ends with the woman 'knowing in her body' that she is healed, and the second part begins with Jesus 'knowing in himself' that power has gone forth. The second half of the story in particular serves to bring the contact healing expressly under the control of faith, and takes the place usually occupied in miracle stories by the public demonstration of the cure and a choral ending.[2] Yet these verses cannot be regarded simply as a secondary corrective expansion of a traditional healing story which is permeated with magical motifs.[3] For the account as a whole has a unifying double narrative structure, in which the outer actions of the characters are paired with an evaluative commentary or record of their inner thoughts and intentions, as a result of which the woman's actions are interpreted as an expression of faith from the outset.

The narration consists of an external sequence of events plus an inner drama in which the essence of the event is repeated in some form of interpretative comment, thought or saying.[4] The pattern can be set out diagramatically as on the page opposite.

The comments, thoughts and sayings that make up the 'repetitive-commentary' level of the narrative climax in the identification of the woman's actions as a manifestation of saving faith (v 34), and, as we will see, it is this perspective which governs the inner drama as a whole. The commentary highlights the woman's faith in two ways. It underlines the strength of her confidence in the fact that Jesus will heal her (v

---

[1] Opinions differ on whether Mark is criticising these magical elements (Lohmeyer, Fuller, Schenke, Verweyen), or ratifying them, in the sense of accommodating his picture of Jesus to current Hellenistic models (Schmithals, Pesch, Kertelge, Roloff). On this, see Verweyen, 'Einheit und Vielhaft', 15–19.

[2] For listing of the typical miracle story elements in this narrative, see Schenke, *Wundererzählungen*, 207; cf. Bultmann, *History*, 221–6.

[3] Contra Koch, *Wundererzählungen*, 136f. See Verweyen's discussion, 'Einheit und Vielhaft', 16–18.

[4] On this see, Theissen, *Miracle Stories*, 133; Gnilka, *Markus*, I, 212f.

Event	Repetition and comment
Woman's distress and failure of doctors (vv 25–26a)	Human healers have aggravated her condition (v 26b)
Woman touches Jesus' cloak (v 27)	Inner confidence in being cured (v 28)
The healing (v 29a)	Woman's awareness of healing (v 29b) Jesus' awareness of the impartation of power (v 30a)
Jesus' question (v 30b)	Disciples' answer (v 31)
Jesus searches for suppliant (v 32)	Woman afraid and aware of what has happened (v 33)
Woman comes forward and confesses truth (v 33)	Evaluation ('your faith has saved you'), dismissal and assurance of healing (v 34)

28), despite her previous frustration at the hands of other doctors (v 26b); and it establishes an affinity in characterisation between the woman and Jesus, as well as a corresponding contrast with the disciples and the crowd. Both the sick woman and Jesus share inner perception of the operation of divine power (vv 29b,30a,33b), and whereas the disciples do not understand Jesus' apparently senseless quest for the particular person who, in the crush of the crowd, touched his garments (v 31), the woman knows that it is she whom Jesus seeks (v 33). The narrative style of the composition means therefore that in spite of formal similarities with contemporary magical conceptions and practices,[1] the actions and attitudes of the needy woman are understood and portrayed from the beginning as a demonstration of genuine faith.

(b) The portrayal of faith in 5:24–34
The suppliant in this story and Jairus in the surrounding narrative have one thing in common: their utter helplessness in face of the overwhelming power of sickness. Jairus'

[1] See the discussion in Van der Loos, *Miracles*, 313–17.

daughter is terminally ill, and the woman's complaint –
continuous or recurrent uterine bleeding[1] – has proved in-
curable. However in social, economic, and religious terms, the
woman is portrayed at the opposite end of the spectrum to
Jairus. He is a male leader, while she is a nameless woman.
He is a synagogue official, whereas her complaint renders her
ceremonially unclean and excludes her from the religious
community (ῥύσει αἵματος v 25; cf. Lev 15:25–27,33; and πηγὴ . . .
αἵματος v 29; cf. Lev 12:7; 20:18). Jairus has a family and a
large household (vv 35,40f), whereas the woman's problem
would tend to preclude or terminate marriage and child-
bearing,[2] and lead to social isolation, since ritual impurity was
communicable by mere touch (Lev 15:7; Num 5:2). Jairus is a
man of means and influence, whilst the woman is impov-
erished, having exhausted all her resources on doctors who
have only caused her pain and aggravated her condition (v 26).
It is little wonder then that the narrator twice terms her
wretched condition a μάστιξ or scourge (vv 29,34), for it entails
not only physical suffering but also isolation from social
intercourse and exclusion from the worship of God.[3]

The striking proliferation of participles in the opening
sentence (vv 25–7), unmatched elsewhere in Mark's composition,[4] conveys to the audience the relentless compounding of
the woman's need over a twelve-year span (five of the seven
participles are attributive and relate to the woman's state) as
the necessary background for perceiving the motivation of faith
behind her secret approach to Jesus.

Faith Concealed

The manner of the woman's approach from behind is often
taken as an expression of superstitious or magical belief in the
healing virtue of physical contact with the clothing of a miracle doctor or θεῖος ἀνήρ. According to J. M. Hull, the woman

---

[1] For a diagnostic analysis, see Derrett, 'Mark's Technique', 475–9.

[2] On this, see Derrett, 'Mark's Technique', 476.

[3] The suggestion being made here is that the term μάστιξ depicts the
experiential dimension of the problem more than its origin. Hooker
believes that Mark probably 'thinks of the scourge as being in the hands of
Satan', *Message*, 42; and Derrett thinks it may imply, as in the LXX and
Judaism, that the affliction is a divine punishment, 'Mark's Technique',
476 n.11.

[4] The style no doubt originates from Mark's Semitic source, see Pryke,
Redactional Style, 123.

shows no interest in the person of Jesus at all; she only seeks his impersonal magical δυνάμις. 'The faith is in the power. What the woman wants is the power, not the Christ; the water not the fireman.'[1] Many others would agree, although the faith element is more often understood not as part of the magical conception but as the author's correction or reinterpretation of the magical ideas represented by the woman. However, if such a magical conviction exists at all and needs correction or modification, it is in Mark's potential audience, not in the woman in the story. Although her act of touching Jesus' clothing is capable of evoking magical and even sexual connotations,[2] the narrator makes it quite clear from the outset that in this case it expresses not superstition, nor even a mixture of incipient faith and quasi-magical beliefs,[3] but a genuine perceptive faith.

When the narrator recounts the woman's inner thoughts in v 28, he is anticipating the concluding hermeneutical judgement on her behaviour as an expression of faith in v 34.[4] The stress on the woman's utter confidence in Jesus,[5] despite previous frustration at the hands of other human healers, and the use of σώζειν to describe her inner reflection, signify that her trust resides not in some magical source of power, but specifically in the presence of God's saving power in Jesus. Similarly her act of touching Jesus' garments does not imply magical manipulation.[6] Within Mark's broader framework (cf. 6:56), and indeed in wider Christian circles (cf. Lk 6:19; Acts 5:15; 19:12), the belief that God's healing power could be disseminated through a healer's possessions or clothing is not

---

[1] The quote is from Hull's comments on the Lukan version of the story, but he would apply it equally to Mark, *Hellenistic Magic*, 109. See also, Bultmann, *History*, 219.

[2] See Derrett, 'Mark's Technique', 495f; also Theissen, *Miracle Stories*, 134.

[3] As is, for example, claimed by Cranfield, *Mark*, 185; Lane, *Mark*, 192.

[4] Schenke rightly observes that v 28 has the same purpose as v 34a, *Wundererzählungen*, 202. Therefore, v 34 cannot be regarded as something of an afterthought, as Kertelge claims, *Wunder Jesu*, 115. Nor can the woman's act of faith be tied to her approach in v 33 alone, as Roloff implies, *Kerygma*, 154.

[5] On how the syntax of v 28 conveys this, see Turner, *Grammatical Insights*, 33.

[6] See rather the interpretations set against an Old Testament-Jewish backdrop: Derrett, 'Mark's Technique', 494f; Jeremias, *Theology*, I, 163, cf. 65f. See Kee's assessment of the presence of magic in the synoptic tradition, *Medicine, Miracle and Magic*, 112–16.

in itself regarded as suspicious. Jesus' clothing here is understood as a vital extension of his person, as is apparent from the way the disciples paraphrase Jesus' question, 'who touched my garments?', as 'who touched me?' (v 31, cf. also 9:2f; 15:24). The woman's confidence centres on the person of Jesus (cf. v 27), and the expression 'even his garments' marks the intensity of her conviction. Finally, her furtive approach from behind is best understood as expressing, not an indifference to his person, but fear and embarrassment at public exposure of her unclean condition and her act of apparently contaminating the Jewish male healer. The narrator implies this interpretation by making the verbal contacts with the relevant Levitical passages noted earlier, and by describing the woman's fear and trembling at the prospect of discovery by Jesus (v 33).

The genuineness of the woman's faith is ratified by her immediate experience of healing power (v 29). Her faith completes the circuit, as it were, and allows the power of God (δύναμις), which is constantly going forth from Jesus (τὴν ἐξ αὐτοῦ δύναμιν ἐξελθοῦσαν),[1] to leap the gap from God to the powerless human suppliant. Read in isolation, v 29f could imply an autonomous transference of healing mana, since power is appropriated by the woman without Jesus consciously imparting it. But when viewed in the wider Markan context, the description in v 29f serves to confirm both that Jesus' power is ultimately under the governance of God, and that it carries an inherent disposition towards receptive faith. Wherever faith is present, power is released – not 'automatically', but because, as Jesus declares at the beginning, God has determined to limit the present manifestation of his kingly power to the arena of repentant faith (1:15).

Despite the effectual operation of faith however, there remains at this point of the story a sense of incompleteness about the event. The woman seeks 'salvation' (v 28), but in v 29 the stress is placed upon the healing (ἴαται) of her bodily needs only (τῷ σώματι). There are social and religious dimensions to her need yet to be addressed. Also her fear at Jesus' reaction to her deed represents a defect in her understanding of his character which must yet be remedied. This explains Jesus' subsequent action, for although he perceives the transition of healing power, rather than continuing on his urgent journey he halts to seek out the beneficiary. In Markan perspective,

[1] On the syntax of this verse, see Taylor, *Mark*, 291; Cranfield, *Mark*, 185; *BDF*, S.416 (2).

while faith remains secretive and the woman afraid of discovery, the work of faith is not yet complete.

Faith Revealed

The woman's state of fear and trembling in v 33 is regarded by some exegetes as a positive expression of Mark's 'admiration motif'.[1] Her realisation that divine power has flowed into her triggers the inevitable human reaction of holy dread and awe. But if this were Mark's thought here, one would expect him to mention it along with his commentary on the woman's inner awareness of healing in v 29. Furthermore, the incompatibility of her fear (φοβηθεῖσα) with faith is confirmed by Jesus' subsequent injunction to Jairus not to fear (μὴ φοβοῦ) but only to believe (v 36). In the immediate context, it is not the miracle that occasions her fear but the feeling of imminent discovery by Jesus.[2] Her consciousness of healing (εἰδυῖα ὃ γέγονεν αὐτῇ cf. ἔγνω ... ὅτι ἴαται [v 29]), far from causing her fear, is the reason for her courageous transcending of the final obstacle of fear to reveal her presence to Jesus.

In vv 32–4, the narrator adopts an alternating narrative style, switching from Jesus to the woman and back to Jesus. By connecting the sentences, for the first time in the account, with δέ rather than καί,[3] he implies a sequence in which the action of one actor is quickly superseded by the counter-action of the other. Before Jesus has time to discover the woman, she voluntarily makes herself known to him, falls at his feet and confesses 'the whole truth' (v 33). To counter her fear and in view of her now complete turning to him, Jesus assures the woman of her full restoration in a declaration so pregnant with significance for Mark's entire understanding of the subject that we must examine it closely.

> Daughter, your faith has saved you. Go in peace and be
> healed from your scourge. (v 34)

The use once again (cf. 2:5; 5:39,41) of a familial term of affection (θυγατήρ) signals the establishment of a personal bond between Jesus and the woman. It also emphasises, along with the differentiation of the woman's touch from the physical jostling of the crowd in v 32, the *individualism* of faith. Saving

---

[1] E.g. Schmithals, *Wunder*, 88, 91; idem, *Markus*, I, 295; Pesch, *Markus*, I, 304; cf. Gnilka, *Markus*, I, 215 ('Offenbarungsformel').

[2] Luke interprets Mark in this way, Lk 8:47.

[3] Cf. Zerwick, *Markus-Stil*, 17.

faith is no communal system of belief or practice, but an immediate personal involvement: *your* (σου) faith. The woman's illness had been an individual experience, isolating her from the healthy community. Now an individual investment of faith restores her to health and well-being.

The formula is striking not just for its individual focus but, secondly, for the *apparently causative power* it ascribes to faith in winning salvation. Jesus does not say, 'God has saved you', or 'I have saved you', but 'your faith' has done it. Divorced from its narrative context, it is possible to interpret this logion to mean that faith itself, as a human disposition, is the power that has healed the petitioner; and indeed some commentators feel there is a contradiction between v 34, which mentions faith, and v 29, which mentions δύναμις, as the source of this healing.[1] However, although the object of faith is not explicitly mentioned, this is not because Mark regards the subjective experience of faith as more important than its content.[2] It is because, given the unusual manner in which God's kingdom manifests itself in Mark's story, there is an inherent ambiguity surrounding the real object of faith which the absolute formula neatly preserves. The fact that the woman seeks and finds salvation (vv 28,34), and salvation for Mark is an activity of God (10:26f; 13:13,20), means that her faith is ultimately placed in God's saving action. But the woman's entire orientation is toward Jesus as the one through whom such salvation is available. Therefore neither God nor Jesus can be removed from the object of saving faith; both are implied by the context. The absolute formula allows for this, and also has the virtue of shifting the spotlight onto the crucial importance of the human response to God's self-revelation in Jesus. There is also no discrepancy between v 29 and v 34; they are two sides of the same coin. The woman's faith has saved her because it has permitted the 'going forth power' of Jesus to do its intended work in her life. As Schmithals appositely comments,[3] to ask whether it is faith or δύναμις that heals the woman is the same as asking whether it is water or the act of drinking that quenches thirst, or whether it is our legs or the power of motion that carries us forward. Each needs the other to

---

[1] E.g. Schenke, *Wundererzählungen*, 200f; Koch, *Wundererzählungen*, 137; cf. Kertelge, *Wunder Jesu*, 115. Haenchen notes the tension but says Mark did not feel it, *Weg Jesu*, 208.

[2] Cf. Goppelt's criticism of Ebeling on this point, *Theology*, I, 152ff.

[3] Schmithals, *Wunder und Glaube*, 90; idem, *Markus*, I, 297.

achieve the desired end. Faith saves because it allows God's saving power in Jesus to save. Both πίστις and δύναμις are active agents, and it is therefore quite fitting to identify faith itself as the saving power.

As well as conveying the individualism and power of faith, the closing words underscore, thirdly, the *comprehensiveness* of the restoration granted to faith. Mark conveys the sense of the wholeness secured by the woman not only by the use of σώ-ζειν in the formula, but also by his narrative arrangement and by Jesus' words of dismissal. In v 29 the narrator stresses the bodily dimension of the woman's healing (ἔγνω τῷ σώματι ὅτι ἴαται); but simply remedying the cause of the bleeding is not enough to restore her full well-being. Her complaint had religious and social implications as well, but until she had established full relationship with Jesus these remained unresolved. Once she has directly encountered Jesus and told him 'the whole truth', the way is cleared for the work of wholeness to be completed.[1] Her sense of alienation from God is removed by the address 'daughter' and especially by the blessing, 'depart in peace'. Against its Old Testament-Jewish background, this valediction wishes God's peace or shalom on the recipient, that sense of wholeness and completeness of life which comes from standing in right relationship with God.[2] Finally, the deliberate exposure of the woman's need, and Jesus' public and authoritative assurance of the permanence of her cure (καὶ ἴσθι ὑγιής), paves the way for the reception of the outcast back into normal human society.

(c) Summary

By the time the character in this episode finally casts her lot in with Jesus she has lost her health, her wealth and her place in the religious community. She is the quintessence of powerlessness. But through profound trust in Jesus' capacity to save her

---

[1] A comparable use of ἰάσθαι and σώζειν in Lk 17:11–19 provides an interesting parallel. All ten lepers are cleansed; but only one, seeing that he was healed (ἰάθη, v15), returns to encounter Jesus again and only then is the term salvation used (ἡ πίστις σου σέσωκέν σε, v 19).

[2] Cf. Judg 18:6; 1 Sam 1:17; 2 Sam 15:9; 1 Kg 22:17; Luke 7:50; Acts 16:36; Jas 2:16. Best comments of Mk 5:34, 'peace is not merely health but peace with God, through the reconciliation that has taken place with him in healing and therefore in the restoration to the congregation of Israel', *Temptation and Passion*, 107. For similar views, see Taylor, *Mark*, 293; Cranfield, *Mark*, 186; Schweizer, *Mark*, 118; Lane, *Mark*, 194; Schmithals, *Wunder und Glaube*, 91.

and a courageous entrusting of her full need to him despite her fear and trembling, she experiences an in-flowing of eschatological power that heals her body, brings her into God's blessing (εἰς εἰρήνην), and makes possible her restoration to regular human society. By delaying any mention of faith until the end of the story, Mark effectively broadens the reference of the term from the woman's initial approach for healing to include as well her subsequent act of courage, her obeisance before Jesus, and her total honesty regarding her situation.

Because of the depiction of saving faith in this episode, some exegetes think that 'the fully Christian idea of saving-faith is meant which includes the death and resurrection of Jesus'.[1] Schreiber suggests that the woman's faith is related to the cross and resurrection both by the description of the woman 'following' Jesus (5:24,27), and by her act of touching the same garments which are divided at his death (15:24) and glisten at his exaltation (9:2f). He therefore proposes that 'the woman sees in the lowly state of the exalted one (*im Erniedrigten den Erhöhten*), the Son of God, and trusts him and is therefore saved (5:28,24)'.[2] But this somewhat outruns the evidence. To Mark, the link between the woman's faith and the cross and resurrection of Jesus lies not in her conscious awareness of Jesus' divine sonship, but in the *structure* of faith itself. Her confident reliance upon Jesus as bearer of God's saving power for release from her 'scourge' is structurally the same as the attitude required of those who encounter the crucified and risen Jesus.

The faith of the father of the epileptic boy (9:14–29)

In his article, 'The Portrayal of the Life of Faith in the Gospel of Mark', Eduard Schweizer nominates 9:14–29 as the most explicit treatment of the subject in the gospel; it is 'much more a treatise about unbelief and belief than a miracle story . . .'.[3] The story contains an explicit denunciation by Jesus of faithlessness (v 19), an affirmation of the omnipotence available to those who believe (v 23), a paradoxical confession by the petitioner of unbelieving belief (v 24), and a saying that implicitly links faith and prayer (v 29).

---

[1] Schenke, *Wundererzählungen*, 214, cf. 202. Otherwise: Haenchen, *Weg Jesu*, 207; Ernst, *Markus*, 163.

[2] Schreiber, *Theologie des Vertrauens*, 239.

[3] Schweizer, 'Portrayal of Faith', 389, 396.

In narrative terms, the faith content in the story has at least a triple focus: (i) the faith (or coming to faith) of the helpless suppliant, (ii) the failure and unbelief of the disciples, and (iii) the faith of Jesus himself. At this juncture we are concerned only with the faith of the petitioner; we shall return to the other two areas in subsequent chapters. Of course, the separation of these three facets in this way is somewhat artificial for they are complexly intertwined in the narrative itself. The location of the story in the discipleship-instruction section of the gospel (8:27–10:52), plus its opening and concluding focus on the disciples, indicates that in this episode Mark deals primarily with the question of failing faith amongst the disciples. But since one of Mark's favourite strategies for highlighting the failure of the disciples is the use of minor figures as a foil for them, it is legitimate and helpful for us to concentrate initially on the faith posture of the helpless suppliant.

(a) Composition, structure and theme

The story of the epileptic boy contains a wealth of vivid detail that makes it distinctive even in Mark's miracle collection. It exhibits many of the typical features of exorcism stories; and yet the sheer weight of the dialogue included, the extent of repetition present, the inclusion of motifs more often associated with healing accounts or discipleship narratives, and the complex interweaving of themes and sub-themes, set this account apart from other examples of the genre.

Particularly striking is the amount of duplication in the narrative. There are two descriptions of the boy's symptoms (vv 17f,22a), and he is twice brought forward for healing (vv 17,20). There are two identifications of the demon (vv 17,25), and the demon reacts twice to Jesus' presence (vv 20,26). The crowd is present and active from vv 14ff, but the assembling of a crowd is again described in v 25. There is also extensive verbal duplication throughout the narrative.[1] Commentators usually point to a number of obscurities and logical tensions in the text as well. In v 24 the motive for healing is the presence of faith, while in v 25 it seems to be the onrush of a crowd. In v 19 the

---

[1] Verbal repetition includes: μαθηταί (vv 14,18,28), ἐπερωτᾶν (vv 16,21,28), δύνασθαι (vv 22,23,28,29), ἰδεῖν (vv 14,15,20,25), εὐθύς (vv 15,20,24), ὄχλος (vv 14,15,17,25), ἄλαλον (vv 17,25), πνεῦμα (vv 17,20,25), ἄπιστος, ἀπιστία (vv 19,24; cf. 23), φέρειν (vv 17,19,20), ἀφρίζειν (vv 18,20), ἔρχεσθαι (vv 14,25,28), συζητεῖν (vv 14,16), λέγειν (vv 19,21,23,24,25,26), ἀποκρίνεσθαι (vv 17,19).

failure of the disciples is attributed to faithlessness, whereas in
v 28f it is linked with the need of prayer.

The standard critical explanations[1] for these features are
essentially variants on two basic hypotheses. The first maintains that the present format of the story is the product of the
amalgamation of two separate traditions, one centring on the
inability of the disciples to perform a miracle, the other on the
father and the paradox of unbelieving belief. Some think they
were originally independent miracle stories;[2] others that they
were two versions of the same episode.[3] Some ascribe the
combination to the pre-Markan phase,[4] others to Mark himself,[5] and opinions on how the narrative should be distributed
between each source and what is attributable to Markan
redaction, differ considerably. The second hypothesis, more
favoured in recent research, conjectures one basic story that
has been considerably expanded in the process of oral transmission and/or Markan redaction. Whether the traditional
kernel focused on the inability of the disciples to heal (vv 14–
19),[6] the discussion with the father (vv 20–7),[7] or was a basic
exorcism story elaborated to highlight discipleship failure and
the importance of faith[8] (e.g. vv 16–18,20–2,25b–27), is a matter
of dispute.

Clearly then the text of 9:14–29 presents a considerable
challenge to traditio-historical and redaction-critical analysis.
The often arbitrary and mutually exclusive ways of breaking
up the text would even suggest that the compositional prehistory of the narrative is ultimately irrecoverable and that a
greater attempt should be made to appreciate the literary and

[1] For a brief summary of the literature, see Schenke, *Wundererzählungen*,
314–20.

[2] Bultmann, *History*, 211; Fuller, *Miracles*, 34, 61; Achtemeier, 'Miracles
and Historical Jesus', 476–82.

[3] Taylor, *Mark*, 396; Schweizer, *Mark*, 187; Anderson, *Mark*, 229; Held,
'Matthew as Interpreter', 187. See also Bornkamm, 'Πνεῦμα ἄλαλον', 21–6.

[4] Bultmann, *History*, 211; Achtemeier, 'Miracles and Historical Jesus', 477;
Bornkamm, 'Πνεῦμα ἄλαλον', 24; Haenchen, *Weg Jesu*, 318 n.1; cf. Best,
Discipleship, 185.

[5] Schweizer, *Mark*, 187; Koch, *Wundererzählungen*, 119.

[6] Roloff, *Kerygma*, 145–52 (following Fridrichsen, *Problem of Miracle*, 81).

[7] Sundwall, *Zusammensetzung*, 58ff; Kertelge, *Wunder Jesu*, 174–9.

[8] Schenk, 'Epileptiker-Perikope',76–94. See also, with variations between
them, Schenke, *Wundererzählungen*, 314–49, especially 320, 332–4; Telford, *Barren Temple*, 104–9; Patten, 'Thaumaturgical Element', 254–7; cf.
Koch, *Wundererzählungen*, 125ff.

theological unity of the story as it stands.[1] For whatever its traditional make-up, within the final narrative we undoubtedly hear the voice of a single narrator whose consistent theological point of view and extensive verbal repetition give unity to the account.

The considerable duplication in the account is never strictly a matter of redundancy; it is nearly always incremental, progressively enriching the picture of the boy's need and the characterisation of those involved. L. Schenke[2] evaluates the alleged tensions and doublets listed above and concludes that there is really only one genuine contradiction in the story – the discrepancy between the crowd assembling in v 25, and yet already being present in v 14. Even here, however, the reference to it as 'a crowd', not 'the' crowd already present, allows for the possibility of a second gathering of onlookers which, as we shall see, fulfils a similar function to the second group of outsiders (the mourners) in the Jairus episode.

The complexity of the existing narrative lies partly in the number of actors involved in the drama. This is the only story in which all of the seven characters who comprise the potential *dramatis personae* of a gospel miracle story (Jesus, vicarious petitioner, sick person, demon, crowd, opponents, and the disciples) are involved. Each of the characters, apart from the scribes (v 14), has its own 'history' in the story, moving from the fringe to the centre, then back to the fringe again. The disciples, for example, figure in vv 14–19, are ignored in vv 20–7, then reappear in vv 28f. The father has a secondary role in vv 14–19, a central place in vv 20–4, and then is not mentioned again. The crowd is prominent in the first part of the story, but fades into the background in the second part. The narrative itself is crafted to bring out contrasts between the different characters. The success of Jesus in healing the boy contrasts with the failure of the disciples, while the faithless impotence of Jesus' followers is set off by the effectual faith of the father, and perhaps of Jesus too.

[1] Among those who work with the narrative as a unity are: Schniewind, *Markus*, 91; Lohmeyer, *Markus*, 184–91; Schmidt, *Rahmen*, 227; Van der Loos, *Miracles*, 397–405; Cranfield, *Mark*, 299; Dibelius, *Tradition to Gospel*, 66ff; Schmithals, *Markus*, II, 406–24, especially 408f; Pesch, *Markus*, II, 86f.

[2] Schenke, *Wundererzählungen*, 317–20. He concludes, 'Wir sehen also: die "Spannungen" und Doppelungen geben keinen Anlass, in 9:14–29 zwischen verschiedenen Traditionsschichten zu unterscheiden.'

As it stands, the narrative of the epileptic boy has a recognisable four-fold scenic structure. The scenes are distinguishable according to the different persons or groups Jesus addresses or is in conversation with. Each scene contains an authoritative declaration by Jesus and, apart from the exorcism scene, each is elaborated around a question put to or by Jesus. The arrangement is as follows.

Scene	Question	Declaration by Jesus
Scene 1: Jesus and the Crowd (vv 14–20)	'What are you discussing with them?' (v 16)	'O faithless generation! How long am I to be with you? How long am I to bear with you?' (v 19)
Scene 2: Jesus and the Father (vv 21–4)	'How long has he had this?' (v 21)	'All things are possible to the one who believes.' (v 23)
Scene 3: Jesus and the Demon (vv 25–7)	--------------------	'You deaf and dumb spirit. I command you, come out of him and never enter him again.' (v 25)
Scene 4: Jesus and the Disciples (vv 28–9)	'Why could we not cast it out?' (v 28)	'This kind cannot be driven out by anything but prayer.' (v 29)

In the first scene, Jesus is in conversation with the crowd. The disciples are present (v 14) and referred to (v 18), but it is the ὄχλος which runs up to greet him (v 15) which Jesus addresses; thereafter the impersonal plurals are most naturally read as references to this group. Also, although it is the father who answers Jesus' question, he is identified as a spokesman for the group (εἷς ἐκ τοῦ ὄχλου). Jesus does not therefore reply to the man personally at this point, but 'answers them' (v 19a). The opening scene is the most detailed and introduces all the actors who will subsequently figure in the drama. It also serves to link the episode to the preceding Transfiguration story and the passion instruction given during the descent from the mountain (9:2–13).[1]

[1] There are some verbal ties (συζητεῖν, γραμματεῖς, ἔρχεσθαι) and the plural reading ἐλθόντες . . . εἶδον implies the return of the four from the Mount

The scene closes with a dramatic demonic manifestation. The next scene is not an exorcism however, but a tension-heightening conversation between Jesus and the father that underlines the centrality of faith to the cure. H. D. Betz suggests that at this point the miracle story 'flips over' to a conversion story depicting the father's coming to faith.[1] The petitioner's faith is immediately contrasted with the spectacle-seeking crowd that converges on the boy at the opening of the third scene (v 25). Seeing the situation, Jesus orders the un-clean spirit to depart and never return again; the cure is to be total. The closing scene comprises a private discussion between Jesus and the disciples on the sole efficacy of prayer for dealing with this kind of need. Since elsewhere Mark closely links prayer and faith (11:24f), this diagnosis may be seen as an identification of what constituted the faithlessness of the disciples lamented by Jesus in v 19.

If the component scenes are differentiated by Jesus' varying conversation partners, then they are unified by the presence of Jesus in each and by the reiteration of the particular need in question — severe demonic possession (vv 17f,20,22,25f,28f). Above all, 'the unity of the entire narrative is found in the theme of faith'.[2] The first scene climaxes in a lament over unbelief; the second climaxes in a confession of unbelieving belief; the third concretely demonstrates faith at work; whilst the fourth scene relates faith to the practice of prayer.

(b) The portrayal of faith in 9:14–29

A situation of total human impotence again provides the appropriate context for the operation of faith. The sufferer is a victim of demonic possession of quite startling severity. Most of the repetition in the narrative actually concerns the boy's condition, and as a result the shifts in the main plot line all take place against a backdrop which consistently portrays the extremity of the need. The inability of the disciples to help the boy (v 18), the long duration of his affliction (v 22), the extent of demonic resistance to Jesus (vv 20,26), the vivid catalogue

---

of Transfiguration. More significantly, the opening scene picks up the themes of discipleship incomprehension, scribal opposition and 'epiphanic' appearance, present in 9:2–13.

[1] Betz, 'Early Christian Miracle Story', 79.

[2] Kertelge, *Wunder Jesu*, 177. Similarly, Lührmann, *Glaube*, 23; Loh-meyer, *Markus*, 191; Bornkamm, 'Πνεῦμα ἄλαλον', 22; Schmithals, *Mar-kus*, II, 420, amongst others.

of the boy's symptoms, usually understood as epileptic in character[1], and the closing remarks about driving out 'this kind' (of demon?), together convey the seriousness of the condition. The attributes of the demon symbolise the human and spiritual dimensions of the condition. Deafness and dumbness (vv 17,25) mean isolation from human communication; uncleanness (v 25) implies separation from God;[2] and the attempts by the demon to destroy the youth by throwing him into fire and water (v 21) evidences Satanic enmity.

In this hopeless situation the boy's father seeks help from Jesus. But since Jesus is absent, he asks the disciples instead to cast out the demon (v 18). They try and fail, and a general dispute breaks out. Jesus returns, intervenes in the situation and learns from the father the cause of the commotion and the nature of the boy's need. After reviewing the full reality of his son's case history, and whilst an attack of convulsive fits is actually in progress (v 20), the father places his halting request to Jesus: 'if you can do anything, have pity on us and help us' (v 22).

A deficient faith

Clearly at this point the man's faith is deficient. He does not query Jesus' compassion, and therefore his readiness to help, but he has a deep-seated doubt (εἰ) about his ability to cope with so great a need (contrast 1:40). The narrator underlines this sceptical note by having Jesus pick out the offending words and throw them back at the father. The construction τὸ εἰ δύνῃ (v 23a) is somewhat obscure and has occasioned some significant textual variants.[3] The most plausible explanation is that the word τό is a marker to signal that a quotation is being introduced.[4] Jesus is repeating the doubt expressed by his interlocutor in order to challenge it: 'so far as your "if you can" is

---

[1] See, e.g., Van der Loos, *Miracles*, 402–5.

[2] Cf. Taylor, *Mark*, 173f; Foerster, *TDNT*, II, 12–16.

[3] The textual variants seem to stem from a failure of copyists to understand the function of τό in the compressed sentence τὸ εἰ δύνῃ. Numerous witnesses add πιστεῦσαι after δύνῃ (or δύνασαι) which has the effect of changing the subject of δύνῃ from Jesus to the father, 'if you can believe, then . . .' (A, D, Θ, fam13, pm, lat, syp,h,). But one would expect the personal pronoun σύ if Jesus was referring to the father. Moreover, this makes the presence of τό very awkward, so that many authorities omit it altogether (P45, D, Θ, fam13 et al.). Τό should be read however since scribes are more likely to omit than include awkward constructions.

[4] See *BDF*, S.267(1), 140.

concerned, I tell you that all things are possible to the one who believes.'

Here then is a case of a request for healing being temporarily postponed on the grounds of inadequate faith so that a stronger faith may be evinced before Jesus acts (cf. 7:26ff). Whether Mark is suggesting that the man's faith had been at fault since the beginning of the story, or that it only became defective after his initial confidence had been shattered by the fiasco with the disciples, is difficult to determine. Three observations however would suggest that the former is the case.

(i) It is widely accepted that the impassioned outburst of Jesus about the 'unbelieving generation' (v 19) is aimed at the disciples, since it is news of their failure that occasions the cry, and Jesus is recorded as addressing αὐτοῖς, not αὐτῷ (= the father). But whilst the disciples are undoubtedly the principal target (cf. 4:40; 6:52; 8:17), the saying cannot be confined exclusively to them, for a number of reasons. To begin with, Jesus is in conversation with the whole crowd (v 16f), not just the disciples, and his words are described as an 'answer'. Although ἀποκριθεὶς ... λέγει is idiomatic and does not necessarily presuppose a specific question (e.g. 9:5f; 10:24; 11:14; 14:40,48; 15:12), αὐτοῖς here is still most naturally taken as referring to Jesus' existing conversation partners. As 'one of the crowd' (v 17a), this includes the father. Furthermore, as applied to the nine impotent disciples, the pejorative γενεά is not intended to distinguish them from everyone present, but to indicate that in their faithlessness they are lamentably *indistinguishable* from their unbelieving compatriots, represented by the scribes (cf. 2:6ff; 8:12), and by the people assembled (cf. 6:6), of which the father is a spokesman. Again, the two rhetorical 'how long' questions, which echo Old Testament laments over the faithlessness of Israel,[1] bring Jesus' impending passion, and thus the entire purpose of his mission, into view. This purpose is to bring the whole people to faith (cf. 1:15), not just sustain the faith of a few chosen followers. And finally, within the story the disciples do not seem to apply Jesus' outburst principally to themselves, for later they must ask about the reasons for their own particular failure to drive out the demon (vv 28f). The ἡμεῖς in v.28 is emphatic; having heard Jesus' condemnation of the faithlessness of the age, they still ask 'why could not we, for our part, cast it out?' Mark is suggesting, then, that the failure of Jesus' own followers

[1] E.g. Num 14:27; Isa 6:11; cf. Deut 32:5,20; Isa 65:2; Jer 5:21f; Ezek 12:2.

provokes in him a sense of near despair at the obduracy of unbelief in the entire contemporary generation that expresses itself in all who are present,[1] *including the father.*

(ii) Although approaching Jesus through the agency of the disciples does not represent any fundamental misunderstanding on the father's part,[2] since the disciples are authorised extensions of Jesus' ministry (3:15; 6:7,13f, 37), the fact that he ascribes their failure to their lack of 'strength' (οὐκ ἴσχυσαν v 18; cf. 5:4) may imply a misapprehension about the basis of their miraculous power, and by implication Jesus' power too. He saw it as a special technique rather than the eschatological power of God. Jesus must therefore direct his attention to the omnipotence of God (v 23; cf. 10:27; 14:36). Mark also seems to imply that the disciples in the story equated their authority with mere technique, since, as Koch notes,[3] the closing discourse presents prayer as an alternative to exorcistic praxis (οὐδενὶ δύναται . . . εἰ μὴ ἐν προσευχῇ).

(iii) Finally, the wording of the father's appeal, βοήθει μου τῇ ἀπιστίᾳ (v 24), suggests a self-identification with the γενεὰ ἄπιστος. His confession of faith (πιστεύω) entails a corresponding plea for deliverance from the entrenched unbelief of the age to which he belongs.

All this means then that the scene between Jesus and the father in vv 21–4 can be legitimately seen as an initial coming to faith by the suppliant. Before this he had recognised in the 'teacher' both compassion and a degree of power, but he had not yet identified it as the unlimited power of God to whom all things are possible. It is to this power that he is now called to direct his trust.

The call to faith

The call to faith takes the form of an ambiguous affirmation by Jesus that 'all things are possible to the one who believes' (v 23). Depending on whether our interpretation of v 23 is governed by what precedes it or by what follows, τῷ πιστεύοντι could be applied either to the petitioner, from whom faith is demanded, or else to Jesus, who declares his own possession of faith. The logic of the preceding context makes Jesus the natu-

---

[1] So O'Connor, *Faith*, 48; Focant, 'L'Incompréhension', 174f; Johnson, *Mark*, 161; Rawlinson, *Mark*, 124; Taylor, *Mark*, 398; Blackman, *IDB*, II, 229; cf. Bertram, *TDNT*, VII, 718.

[2] As Schmithals implies, *Markus*, II, 416ff.

[3] Koch, *Wundererzählungen*, 122f.

ral subject of the phrase and this best suits Greek sensibility.[1] In this case, Jesus is repudiating the father's doubt about his ability by laying claim to unlimited power on the grounds of possessing effectual faith.[2] And the implication is that the disciples failed because, unlike Jesus, they lacked such faith. Alternatively the saying could be intended to shift the focus away from the question of Jesus' ability and onto the petitioner's own need of faith.[3] The father clearly understands Jesus' words in this way and replies with a confession of faith. It is further argued by some commentators that the father is more likely to be the subject of faith since nowhere else does Mark speak of Jesus' own faith.

Now the ambiguity of v 23 has been variously ascribed to 'Mark's habitual carelessness in arranging his accounts',[4] to his misunderstanding his tradition,[5] and to his attempt to correct a defective christology by applying a statement on Jesus' faith to the father.[6] Another possibility, however, is that the ambiguity is intentional.[7] This would be to evade the issue were it not for the fact that the particular form of the statement encourages such a conclusion. The scope of the saying clearly exceeds its immediate context. The father is being pointed to a general maxim or statement of principle that limitless divine power is released through human faith. Whether it is the faith of those who seek miracles (here the father), or of those who work miracles (the disciples and Jesus), is not specified, for the principle logically embraces both. Mark would accept the view that, 'The miracles presuppose the faith of the One who performs them and also the one on whom they are performed.

---

[1] Most exegetes accept this, e.g. Nineham, *Mark*, 247n; Schweizer, *Mark*, 188; Klostermann, *Markus*, 91; Jeremias, *Theology*, I, 166.

[2] So Lohmeyer, *Markus*, 189; Grundmann, *Markus*, 190f; Martin, *Evangelist and Theologian*, 109; Van der Loos, *Miracles*, 400; Ebeling, 'Jesus and Faith', 234; Schreiber, *Theologie des Vertrauens*, 240f; Schniewind, *Markus*, 91f; Powell, *Concept of Power*, 182, 183 n.15; cf. Lührmann, *Glaube*, 24.

[3] So Theissen, *Miracle Stories*, 137; Koch, *Wundererzählungen*, 121f; Schmithals, *Markus*, II, 418; Roloff, *Kerygma*, 150f, 205; Hahn, 'Verständnis des Glaubens', 58; Bornkamm, *Jesus*, 209 n.41; Nineham, *Mark*, 247n; Anderson, *Mark*, 230; Schlatter, *Glaube*, 129; Zeller, 'Jesus als Mittler', 285.

[4] O'Connor, *Faith*, 45.

[5] E.g. Haenchen, *Weg Jesu*, 320; Held, 'Matthew as Interpreter', 190n.

[6] Achtemeier, 'Miracles and Historical Jesus', 480f.

[7] Cf. Jeremias, *Theology*, I, 166.

They are thus accomplished in a wholly personal relationship.'[1] In this instance it was the lack of effective faith of both
the father and the disciples that frustrated the first attempt at
exorcism. Aware of the disciple's failure (v 18) and now of his
own unbelief (v 24), the man correctly hears the words as
primarily a summons to full faith. At the same time however
the maxim discloses by implication the secret of Jesus' great
power, his complete confidence in God. The father is being
implicitly called to emulate the faith of Jesus, and it is the faith
of both parties that permits of success (vv 25ff).

A second area of ambiguity is more easily resolved, especially in light of our earlier discussion on the saying, 'your
faith has saved you'. The present saying could also be taken to
mean that faith itself is an autonomous source of omnipotent
power, regardless of its content or object. But this is certainly
not Mark's understanding. In the two other places he speaks
of 'all things being possible' (10:27; 14:36), he ascribes such all-
mightiness to God alone, and it is to such a recognition that the
father is here directed. Omnipotence ($\pi\acute{\alpha}\nu\tau\alpha$ $\delta\upsilon\nu\alpha\tau\acute{\alpha}$) is strictly
a divine attribute and faith is simply the means by which the
believer gains a share in the impinging rule of God. Moreover,
in all three texts the operation of such power is conditioned by a
redemptive intent – healing, discipleship and the passion.
Omnipotent power is available to faith only within an ethical-
soteriological framework, and this in turn is the only appropriate context for faith to lay claim to such resource. For Mark,
all things are possible to the believer because, actively or
passively, the believer sets no limits on God's power to break
into his or her concrete situation, for the very existence of faith
within the believer is the ground which allows God to act in his
or her context. Since faith is letting God go into action, it is
legitimate to ascribe to faith what is in fact a matter for God.

Paradoxical belief

Sudden recognition ($\epsilon\grave{\upsilon}\theta\acute{\upsilon}\varsigma$) that God's unlimited power is
available in Jesus provokes the haunting cry from the father,
'I believe, help my unbelief' (v 24). The belief he confesses is an
unreserved trust in that power, and the exorcism follows. But
the dramatic impact of the faith-confession and its theological
depth lies in the fact that it is paired with a simultaneous
acknowledgement of unbelief. Elsewhere faith and unbelief

---

[1] Grundmann, *TDNT*, II, 302f. So too Rhoads and Michie, *Mark as Story*,
108.

appear as mutually exclusive categories (e.g. 4:40; 6:6; 15:32), whereas here they seem to be contemporaneous experiences. How is this to be understood?

The paradoxical formulation of believing unbelief is certainly *not* meant to portray the man as double-minded, ambivalent, or still held fast in unbelief.[1] Nor is the second clause to be taken as a correction or a revocation of an over-hasty claim to a faith greater that he in reality possesses.[2] Nor again is the formula particularly meant to typify an emergent, weak or immature faith,[3] or a faith about to collapse into unbelief.[4] This is the only occasion where one of Mark's characters speaks of his own faith in the first person singular, and his words are intended to capture what the human experience of faith is invariably like; they express a sort of typical 'psychology of belief' that may be assumed also in other characters who are commended for their persevering faith. They show that in Mark's outlook there is within each believer a tension between faith and unfaith, and that faith can only continue to exist by dint of divine aid.

This does not mean that the presence of unbelief should be accepted with an air of resignation. The father pleads for deliverance from his ἀπιστία, and it is this that proves and constitutes his faith. At the same time he acknowledges that such deliverance is never definitive but is continually needed. The present (durative) imperative βοήθει in v 24 contrasts with the aorist imperative βοήθησον in his plea for decisive help for his son (v 22). Faith is not a secure possession attained once for all, but is ever threatened by the reassertion of unbelief from which the believer needs rescue. 'I believe, help my unbelief' is the classic expression of one of Mark's leading convictions about faith – it proves its reality by perseverance under testing.

The formula also reveals that while Mark considers faith to be a free volitional decision (πιστεύω), it is not simply a human aptitude or achievement. It is finally a gift, not only because it emerges from encounter with Jesus, but also because it remains forever contingent upon the sustaining power of the one in whom it is placed (βοήθει μου τῇ ἀπιστίᾳ). Perceiving

---

[1] So Büschel, *TDNT*, III, 947; Achtemeier, 'Miracles and Historical Jesus', 480; cf. Gould, *Mark*, 169f.

[2] So Bornkamm, *Jesus*, 131; Fuller, *Miracles*, 62; Hahn, 'Verständnis des Glaubens', 59 n.67. Cf. also Nineham, *Mark*, 244.

[3] So Swete, *Mark*, 200; Lane, *Mark*, 334.

[4] So Rawlinson, *Mark*, 124; Taylor, *Mark*, 161; Johnson, *Mark*, 400.

that he is not capable of enduring faith, the father does not place his trust in his own capacity to go on trusting and believing, but looks beyond himself to the object of his faith, the power resident in Jesus, for the necessary strength to maintain faith. It is this clear perception of unbelief as a problem, and his prayer for on-going deliverance from it, that distinguishes the father's ἀπιστία from the ἀπιστία of Nazareth (6:6) or of the unbelieving generation (9:19). There, unbelief is concealed and recalcitrant; here it is repentant.

(c) Summary

The overpowering of Satan (cf. 3:23–7) and the healing of deafness and dumbness (cf. Isa 35:5f) are evidence in Mark's story of the in-breaking kingdom of God. The present episode shows that the omnipotent, kingly power of God is manifested not only to bring release to the helpless in response to petitionary faith, but also to sustain the on-going faith of those who seek deliverance from the unbelieving age against which the kingdom stands.

The story of the epileptic boy shares a number of features in common with the Jairus story. They both have a scenic structure in which unexpected developments in the plot lead to the temporary postponement of the cure in order to bring to the surface the fundamental importance and essential character of faith. This device arouses tension in the audience and thereby heightens the didactic power of the particular motifs developed at this point. Secondly, both accounts treat vicarious or intercessory faith. In 9:14–29, the extent of the father's solidarity with the distress of his son is apparent in the petition, 'have mercy on *us* . . . help *us*' (v 22). Similarly, in each of his conversations with Jesus the man goes beyond giving the bare information sought by Jesus to speak in moving detail of his boy's need. It is *the father's* faith which is the key to the boy's cure. This is indicated by the juxtaposition of the exorcism in vv 25ff with the confession of faith in v 24, and also by the identification of the one expressing faith not simply as 'the father' but 'the father of the child', an otherwise superfluous detail.

Finally, the exorcism scene in our story (vv 25–7) is strongly reminiscent of the fourth scene of the Jairus story (5:38–40a). Here too outsiders pronounce the youth dead (v 26) until Jesus takes him by the hand and raises him up. The imagery of dying and rising has a double symbolic significance. It serves, for the disciples, as a symbolic prefiguration of the impending (v 19) fate of Jesus. The same terms are used to describe the boy's 'death' (νεκρός v 26) and rising (ἤγειρεν αὐτόν, καὶ ἀνέστη v 27) as are used in the two discussions with the disciples on the death and resurrection of the Son of Man which immediately precede (ἐκ νεκρῶν ἀναστῇ 9:9) and immediately follow (καὶ ἀποκτανθεὶς . . . ἀναστήσεται 9:31) the episode. The literary context in which Mark places 9:14–29 (i.e. after the Transfiguration scene [cf. 9:7 and 15:39] and flanked by references to the passion) indicates that the power Jesus exercises here over Satan is exercised in anticipation of his definitive victory over him through his cross and resurrection. The exorcism points beyond itself to this event. At the same time, the events of the story reveal faith as the one condition necessary for others to participate in the saving benefits of this event. Through faith in Jesus' power the father is enabled to appropriate the benefits of this triumph ahead of its narrated occurrence. The image of Jesus raising the apparently dead youth in answer to faith is an indication that faith placed in the earthly Jesus of the story is structurally the same as faith placed in the risen Lord, a faith which ultimately leads to being raised from death to be with God.

The faith of Bartimaeus (10:46–52)

The story of Bartimaeus is the last healing narrative in the gospel and marks the conclusion of Jesus' entire ministry outside Jerusalem. As such, it fulfils a three-fold structural function within Mark's overall composition. First, as we shall see further in the next chapter, it forms an *inclusio* with the opening pericopae of the Galilean narrative (1:14–20) and recapitulates the main ideas introduced there – messianic fulfilment, conversion and faith, and following Jesus. Through this framing device, the author confirms that the faith theme and its associated motifs are fundamental to the interpretation of the intervening material. The story also functions as a transitional unit, linking the themes of the preceding context to the passion material that follows. The story closes with the man Jesus heals 'following him on the way' to Jerusalem. This means that Jesus arrives in the city to a jubilant welcome accompanied by evidence of his eschatological work (cf. Isa 29:18f; 35:5; 42:16ff; 61:1ff). Thirdly, Mark uses the Bartimaeus story, together with an earlier episode in which a blind man is healed (8:22–26), to frame the discipleship-instruction section of his narrative (8:27–10:45). In so doing, he presses both accounts into service of his discipleship theme, and invests their content with a metaphorical or figurative significance[1] which we shall explore later.

Thus, 10:46–52, like 9:14–29, carries a strong discipleship orientation. But here too Mark's strategy is to use the attitudes and actions of a minor character as a foil for those of the disciples. The reader/hearer is invited to compare the two responses to Jesus and to see in the behaviour and experience of the blind beggar the answer to the spiritual myopia that afflicts the Twelve. So before drawing out the discipleship implications of the story in the next chapter, we shall look first at the positive depiction of Bartimaeus' own faith.

(a) Composition, structure and theme

The main stages in the compositional prehistory of this narrative are somewhat easier to detect than they are in the previous story we have examined. The translation of the beggar's name into Greek (v 46) reveals at least three stages of development: an early Palestinian stage (cf. *bar, rabbuni*), a phase when the story was taken over by the Greek speaking community, and the stage of integration into Mark's composition. A more precise reconstruction of the tradition-history, however, is complicated by the fact that the existing story fails to conform to the classical form critical miracle story *Gattung* in various ways. For example, there is a conspicuous lack of emphasis on the course of the miracle itself. There is no healing word or gesture, no demonstration of the cure, and no choral acclamation. The localisation of the event near Jericho, the naming of the petitioner, and the allusion to his subsequent fate, are all details not usually found in miracle stories.

This lack of a conventional structure has been construed variously as evidence for the story's great antiquity,[2] for its secondary legendary development,[3] for its original organic connection to the larger passion narrative complex,[4] and for its

---

[1] Many commentators concede a symbolic dimension to the Bartimaeus story. Some caution is needed however; Robbins observes a tendency toward 'an almost totally allegorical interpretation of the Bartimaeus story in modern criticism', 'Healing of Bartimaeus', 226 n. 15; cf. also Pesch, *Markus*, II, 175.

[2] E.g. Taylor, *Mark*, 441; Jeremias, *Theology*, I, 90.

[3] Dibelius, *Tradition to Gospel*, 51–3; Fuller, *Miracles*, 62f; cf. Bultmann, *History*, 213.

[4] Pesch, *Markus*, II, 169, 174.

extensive redactional reworking.[1] Recently it has been proposed that behind the narrative lies not a simple miracle account but the call story of a disciple.[2] But here too its conformity to other examples of the genre is far from complete.[3] That 10:46–52 does not fit neatly into either form critical category is, in fact, an important key to appreciating the literary functioning of the narrative as it stands.

The main emphasis of the story is the great faith of the blind beggar. This is clear from the climactic saying, 'your faith has saved you' (v 52), and from the almost exclusive concentration on the behaviour of Bartimaeus throughout most of the account. The content and format of the story show that this faith is given a double application. In v 49, the blind man receives a call from Jesus. Considerable stress is placed on this call (note the threefold use of φωνεῖν in v 49), for it carries two levels of meaning. On the one hand, it is a call to receive healing from Jesus, and the miracle follows. On the other, it functions as an implicit summons to discipleship, which the narrator clarifies with the closing remarks, 'and he followed him on the way' (v 52). Furthermore, as we shall see in chapter five, the manner in which Bartimaeus responds to this call seems intended to evoke earlier discipleship call accounts (1:16–20; 2:13f; 10:17–22). From this point on faith stands in a dual relationship to miracle and to discipleship. It is the internal construction of the account then, not just its broader narrative context (8:27–10:45), that gives it a discipleship atmosphere. This connection does not supplant the relationship between faith and miracle however, but stands side by side with it. This is of some significance for the question of the relationship between 'miracle faith' and 'discipleship faith'.

---

[1] Most critics think that Markan redaction is confined to the seams of this pericope. Some, such as Robbins, see much more extensive redactional interference. For a recent redactional analysis that cites most relevant literature, see Steinhauser, 'Bartimaeus Narrative', 588–92.

[2] E.g. Steinhauser, 'Call Story', 204–6; idem, 'Bartimaeus Narrative', 583–88; Achtemeier, '"And He Followed Him"', 133f; Culpepper, 'Why Mention the Garment?', 131f.

[3] See Kingsbury, *Christology*, 104f n.159. Achtemeier uses Lk 5:1ff as an example of the genre, but is forced to argue that Mark has substantially reordered the component elements in the Bartimaeus tradition, '"And He Followed Him"', 133f. Steinhauser proposes that the Bartimaeus narrative is modelled on the formal structure of the Old Testament call accounts of Gideon (Judg 6:11b-17) and Moses (Ex 3:1-12), 'Bartimaeus Narrative', 584–8.

The main structuring factor in the final narrative is the process whereby personal contact is established between Bartimaeus and Jesus. The first half of the story (vv 46–9) depicts Bartimaeus seeking this contact, and the second half (vv 50–2) narrates the making of contact and its implications. The beginning, middle and end points of the narrative are marked by three descriptions of Bartimaeus' physical posture which symbolise the different stages of his relationship to Jesus. The format of the story may be set out as follows:

(I)	Bartimaeus 'sitting by the way' (v 46)
	Part One: Seeking Personal Contact with Jesus
(II)	Bartimaeus 'springs up and comes to Jesus' (v 50)
	Part Two: Making Personal Contact with Jesus
(III)	Bartimaeus 'follows him on the way' (v 52)

The story opens with a twin focus: Jesus and his entourage journeying through Jericho, and the blind beggar sitting by the roadside on the outskirts of the city. At the end of the first half, the two foci merge, as Jesus halts his journey and sends for the beggar who in the interim has been desperately trying to catch his attention. The second half commences with the beggar physically approaching Jesus, and closes with him being dismissed by Jesus yet choosing to follow him on the way to Jerusalem. Between these two points is a conversation between the two characters, an affirmation of the beggar's faith, and the curing of his blindness.

(b) The portrayal of faith in 10:46–52
The depiction of faith in the Bartimaeus story is distinctive for the emphasis it places on two aspects in particular – the cognitive or 'christological' perception underlying the response of faith, and the volitional character of such a response. Both these elements have featured in all the stories we have examined so far, but they are brought into particularly sharp focus in this episode. We shall consider each separately.

Faith and perception
The attitude which Mark deems πίστις is founded upon a direct apprehension by the beggar of the eschatological uniqueness of

Jesus' person and mission. The content of this perception is conveyed by the four-fold identification of Jesus in the story.

(i) The beggar's crying out is precipitated by news (ἀκούσας) that 'Jesus of Nazareth' is passing by. This specific identification of Jesus, more than half-way through the gospel, indicates that the man's hope and trust had become fixed on this one particular individual. As elsewhere (cf. 1:24; 14:67, cf. 61f; 16:6), the Nazareth designation signals that something special about Jesus has been perceived, something which ironically the people of Nazareth themselves refuse to accept (6:1–6).[1] Wherein this lies is expressed in the address 'Son of David' and in the plea 'have mercy on me' (vv 47f).

(ii) This is the only occasion in Mark where Jesus is addressed as Son of David and opinions differ on the meaning of the expression and its place in Markan christology. A number of scholars have argued that because the confession comes from the man while he is still blind, together with the fact that later he changes his address to *rabbuni*, the designation 'Son of David' constitutes a misinterpretation of Jesus' true identity. By not having Jesus expressly accept the title, Mark implicitly repudiates it.[2] But this is extremely improbable. The narrator places considerable stress on the 'Son of David' confession, both by citing the expression twice and by describing the beggar's persistence in crying out the name (v 48). Hence when Jesus responds by summoning the man, commending his faith and healing him, the obvious inference is that he accepts the validity of the description. Recent studies of Markan christology have convincingly argued, furthermore, that Mark's dominant characterisation of Jesus is as the Davidic Messiah-King, the Son of God.[3] The *ben-David* address is consistent with and integral to this positive royal christology.

Bartimaeus' address expresses his conviction that Jesus is not simply of Davidic lineage but is the one who fulfils the eschatological or messianic expectations associated with

---

[1] On the 'Nazareth theme' in Mark, see Dewey, 'Peter's Curse', 99f; Kelber, *Kingdom*, 95 n.23; Kilpatrick, 'Jesus, Family and Disciples', 4–11.

[2] E.g. Johnson, *Mark*, 181f; Pesch, *Markus*, II, 98; Achtemeier, '"And He Followed Him"', 131; Kelber, *Kingdom*, 95. Via, *Ethics*, 162.

[3] E.g. Kingsbury, *Christology*, esp. 47–155; Donahue, 'Royal Christology', 72–8. See also the studies of Juel, *Messiah and Temple*, and Matera, *The Kingship of Jesus* (cf. the comments by Chronis, 'Torn Veil', 101–6). This repudiates the claim by others that the Davidic element is unimportant in Mark's christology; e.g. Achtemeier, '"And He Followed Him"', 115, 130f; Johnson, 'Davidic-Royal Motif', 136, 139.

David. More significantly, the circumstances in which the confession is made reveal that the beggar perceives the particular
kind of Davidic figure Jesus truly is. He is not the nationalistic-
militaristic warrior king as pictured in the Psalms of Solomon
17, but one whose royal authority is expressed in therapeutic
works of mercy and deliverance. Such an understanding is in
keeping with certain strands of Old Testament-Jewish Davidic
expectation,[1] and found a form of expression in healing and
magical folk-traditions associated with Solomon, the prototype
ben-David, probably current in Mark's day.[2] Bartimaeus' faith-
borne insight into Jesus' messianic status and mission
corresponds with the standard of judgement towards rule
and authority expressed by Jesus throughout the story (e.g.
9:35f; 10:21ff; 10:42–5; 12:13–17), and also with the ethical-
soteriological conditioning of Jesus' power discussed in
chapter 3.

(iii) The plea 'have mercy on me' coheres with this therapeutic evaluation of Jesus' Davidic sonship. But the narrator
probably intends a deeper significance still. In the Old Testament, this cry is directed towards God,[3] and in later Judaism
ἔλεος acquired an increasingly eschatological orientation (e.g.
2 Macc 2:7; 7:9). 'The age of salvation is the age of ἔλεος.'[4] As a
blind beggar, Bartimaeus would have been acutely aware of
his need for divine mercy. In popular thought of the period,
blindness could be interpreted as a punishment for sin (cf. Jn
9:2) and the status of being a beggar as evidence of a curse.[5]
Conscious of his need of salvation, the beggar recognises in the
man Jesus the in-breaking of God's eschatological mercy (cf.
5:19) which brings with it the possibility of the restoration of
sight to the blind.

(iv) Finally, when called by Jesus Bartimaeus uses the first
person address ῥαββουνί, 'my master'. Mark may have retained this Aramaic term because he felt it conveyed a deeper
sense of the man's recognition of Jesus' true identity (cf. Jn
20:16, the only other use in the New Testament) than the term

---

[1] E.g. Isa 29:18; 32:1ff; 35:4f; 61:1ff; 4QFlor; 4 Q Pat.Blessings; Isaiah
Commentary. See further in Kee, *Community*, 124–7, also 116f, 128.

[2] On this see especially Chilton, 'Jesus *ben David*', 88–112 and the extensive citation of literature there. Also Smith, *Magician*, 79f.

[3] E.g. Pss 4:1; 6:2; 9:13; 40:11; 41:4,10; Isa 33:2 *vl*.

[4] Bultmann, *TDNT*, II, 481.

[5] Cf. Ps 109:10; Sir 40:28–30. See Steinhauser, 'Bartimaeus Narrative', 585f,
593 n.28.

ῥαββί (9:5; 11:21; 14:45). At very least, it signals Bartimaeus'
acceptance of and submission to Jesus' authority, perhaps
especially as teacher.[1]

In these ways Mark portrays Bartimaeus' faith as grounded
upon a true, intuitive apprehension of Jesus' person and
mission. Though blind, he has concluded on the basis of
reports about Jesus' deeds ('Son of David') and words ('rabbuni') that he bears God's eschatological mercy. Consequently
all his hope had become centred on a personal meeting with
him. It is this 'christological' component that sets faith apart
from simple trust in the power of a wonder worker. The
strength of Bartimaeus' confidence in Jesus is apparent from
the persistence of his crying out for mercy. His incessant
pleading aggravates the crowd and many try to silence him,
but to no avail. Their attempt serves to confirm the beggar's
faith.[2] In this case, it is not only his perseverance in crying out
that proves his faith; it is also the way he, so to speak, goes on
the offensive against all discouragement by 'crying out all the
more'.

Faith and volition

The effort to silence Bartimaeus ultimately fails because of the
intervention of Jesus. With Jesus seizing the initiative, the
emphasis shifts, somewhat paradoxically, to the volitional
character of faith. This has two components: that of *decision*
and that of *motivation*.

Jesus stops and the beggar is called (v 49). Bartimaeus
springs to his feet, throws aside his garment, representing for
a beggar all his worldly goods and his whole way of life, and
makes his way to Jesus (v 50). This action has discipleship
overtones, but here we should note that the alacrity of his
response attests a ready volitional commitment. It is not that
Jesus' call somehow creates faith in the man; rather it creates

[1] The term is used in later Jewish writings for God, as well as for human
lords (Palestinian Targums) – see Black, *Aramaic Approach*, 24, 44, 46. In
Mark's day, it was used for 'eschatological charismatics' like Jesus who
taught informally, see Hengel, *Charismatic Leader*, 43–4. The address
does not detract from 'Son of David' (contra Achtemeier, '"And He Followed
Him"', 131; Trocmé, *Formation*, 143 n.1). On this see Kingsbury, *Christology*, 106.

[2] It has nothing to do with the Messianic Secret theme (contra Burkill,
Mysterious Revelation, 186, 190–2), for it is not Jesus who rebukes the
confession, but the crowd, and in Mark the secret relates to Jesus' divine
sonship, not his Davidic status.

the situation in which an existing inner confidence could realise itself in a decisive response of obedience, and so become capable of winning its desire. Faith and obedience are, for Mark, inseparable (1:15).

The second volitional component is uncovered in the question Jesus puts to the beggar: Τί σοι θέλεις ποιήσω; (v 51). This question is not intended to elicit information about the nature of the man's condition, since his need to be free of blindness would have been obvious to anybody! It acts rather as a narrative device to enrich the portrayal of Bartimaeus' faith. Some form of the question, 'what do you want me to do for you?', occurs no fewer than four times in Mark's story. It is a 'loaded question' intended to bring to the surface people's true motives and values. It is the question asked of Herodias (6:22f), and the result is the execution of John the Baptist. It is the question Pilate asks the crowd (15:7ff), and the outcome is the crucifixion of Jesus. It is the question Jesus puts to the sons of Zebedee (10:35f), and their disappointing request is for prestige, privilege and power. And it is the question put to Bartimaeus. But here the result is different. The man is healed and his reply embraced as a manifestation of saving faith.

The implication is that Bartimaeus' inward motivations and commitment conform to the volitional standard required by Jesus, a desire to do the will of God (3:35; 14:36). While it is not surprising that a blind man should want to see again, the real point is that by making this request of Jesus, Bartimaeus implicitly acknowledges both his power to grant it and the redemptive intent of his mission (contrast 10:35ff). Moreover, the use of ἀναβλέπειν in his petition is probably a deliberate allusion to Isaianic prophecy (61:1ff; cf. 29:18f; 35:5f; 42:16ff), and is meant to confirm that the beggar saw Jesus as the dispenser of the blessings of the eschatological age upon which he had set his heart.

The narrator closes by confirming the quality and correctness of Bartimaeus' insight and volitional commitment in three ways. First, there is an exact correspondence between his request and the answer given (ἵνα ἀναβλέψω . . . καὶ εὐθὺς ἀνέβλεψεν). Second, Jesus dismisses the man with an affirmation that his faith has secured the benefits of ultimate salvation he desired: 'depart, your faith has saved you'. Salvation means wholeness in both its physical and spiritual dimensions. The saying recalls the story of the woman with the haemorrhage (5:34) and carries the same weight of meaning here as discussed earlier. It is worth observing, however, that here the formula does not simply accompany a healing word but actually replaces it. It thus represents the climax of the whole sub-theme in the miracle narratives of the relationship between faith and human powerlessness (2:5; 5:34,36; 9: 23f; cf. 6:5f). Thirdly, the healed man is depicted as making a voluntary commitment to 'follow Jesus on the way'. By this stage of Mark's narrative, 'the way' has become a metaphor for the path of obedient suffering (8:27; 9:33; 10:32; cf. 10:17). We shall return to this later, but here we should note that by making Bartimaeus' act of following an immediate outcome of regaining his sight, Mark implies that a preparedness to tread the path of suffering in on-going commitment to Jesus is to be understood as inherent in his desire to see again.

(c) Summary

The Bartimaeus episode is a story about how a potential or inward condition of faith, founded upon a true 'christological' perception, comes to experience the operation of divine power through a decisive commitment of the will. The man's regaining of physical sight is a verification of the intuitive insight he possessed into the true character of Jesus' person and mission. Mark often uses 'seeing' and 'hearing' as metaphors for spiritual perception and understanding,[1] and here we have the paradox of a blind man who, having heard about Jesus, really 'sees' his significance, in contrast to the disciples who 'have eyes but do not see, and ears but do not hear' (8:18; cf. 4:12). Kee points to the implicit epistemology in the story: 'for Mark, understanding of reality is not achieved by availability of evidence but by revelatory insight'.[2]

But revelatory insight is not the sum total of faith. Although faith is an inner attitude, it must become visible in action in order to achieve its goal. This in turn expresses a volitional commitment which proves itself in his persistence, his obedience to Jesus' call, the nature of his request, and his willingness to follow on the way. In 1:15, Jesus requires a two-fold volitional response to the dawning kingdom – repentance and faith. Bartimaeus displays both. When confronted with Jesus, he abandons his past way of life and his possessions (his

---

[1] E.g. 4:3,9,12,15ff,23f,33; 6:11; 7:14; 8:18; 9:7; 12:29,37; 14:40; 15:39. On this see especially Donahue, 'Neglected Factor', 593 n.107.

[2] Kee, *Community*, 58.

garment), he addresses him as master, and he takes the path of suffering discipleship. In one sense, the radically powerless beggar becomes even more powerless, bereft of his only source of human security and vulnerable to suffering and death. But in another sense, he becomes the recipient of eschatological power, the power of the impinging rule of God which brings wholeness in answer to faith.

3. Conclusion: faith and the powerless

In chapter 7 we shall draw together the main conceptual threads of Mark's faith theme as uncovered in this and other chapters. Here we shall confine ourselves to some concluding observations about the literary character of the five episodes in which faith stands in positive relationship to human power-lessness.

Each of the narratives we have examined departs in some significant way from the usual compositional pattern associated with the classical form critical miracle genre. In 2:1–12 it is because of the central interchange between Jesus and the hostile scribes; in 5:21–43 it is the combination of two distinct miracle stories into a new literary unity; in the intercalated episode itself, 5:24–34, it is the internal double-narrative structure that sets it apart; in 9:14–29 it is the extensive duplication and the proportion of the text devoted to dialogue; and in 10:46–52 it is due to the coalescence of miracle and call story elements. In every instance there is a diversity of traditio-historical and redaction-critical explanations for the emergence of the final account. Yet also in every case, the existing narrative can be shown to exhibit its own coherent literary structure which not only facilitates the dramatic delivery of the story, but allows us to appreciate the way in which the explicit faith reference in the text functions as the governing theme of the whole unit. This justifies taking each account as it stands as the best way of determining what Mark means by πίστις, πιστεύειν and how he conveys this to his audience.

These faith stories are among the most detailed of Mark's miracle accounts, and it is through this detail that the final author is able to vivify and illustrate different facets of his theme and to develop characterisation. In each narrative he deploys an array of rhetorical devices and literary techniques. By use of irony and paradox, chiasmus and intercalation, framing verses and duplication, suspense, shock and surprise, riddles and rhetorical questions, ambiguity and double-meaning, foreshadowing and allusion, the narrator is able to tell his stories in a way that communicates both the rational content of faith and the experiential feel of such a disposition.

In terms of their basic message the five accounts are alike. Each portrays a petitioner, locked into a situation of radical powerlessness, who exhibits a stubborn faith in the presence of Jesus that leads to the operation of divine power on his or her behalf. The same basic ingredients of faith are present in each episode (e.g. perception, perseverance, courage), and acquire their importance partly through their reiteration. Yet each story is also quite distinctive in its treatment of these elements. The first emphasises in particular the physical and spiritual dimensions of the healing granted to faith. The second depicts a faith that is severely tested by tormenting delay, deepening need, and sceptical unbelief before it experiences the deliverance it seeks. The next account lays stress on the need for the suppliant to forge a personal bond with Jesus before faith can complete its work of adding to bodily healing the full restoration of relationships indicative of 'salvation'. The fourth story contains the most extensive 'theoretical' reflection on the subject of faith and power, and, unlike previous stories, narrates the petitioner coming to faith, or at least having his defective faith rectified. The last episode is distinctive for the explicit treatment of the christological perception undergirding faith and the volitional commitment intrinsic to the fullness of this disposition. This combination of the reiteration of basic motifs, and a distinctiveness in the treatment of these motifs, is confirmation of the value of our method of treating each story in its existing integrity rather than simply trying to distil the elements common to the depiction of faith in all five narratives.

5 FAITH AND DISCIPLESHIP

We have seen how the initial call to repentance and faith (1:14f), which reverberates throughout the narrative, finds concrete fulfilment in the response of minor characters in situations of dire need. We have also observed how at points Mark implicitly contrasts the childlike trust and spiritual insight of these figures with the want of such qualities in Jesus' closest followers. This in itself suggests that faith is a disposition which Mark thinks should typify the disciples as well. Given that Mark's Christian readers would naturally identify themselves with the disciples in the drama,[1] this may seem self-evident, though it also makes it somewhat surprising that there are so few explicit references to their faith. F. Hahn takes this to mean that Mark does not consider faith to be the leading characteristic of discipleship, but as only one feature of it, which he orients and subordinates to the theme of following.[2] From the perspective of narrative criticism however, it is not only a matter of *how much* the author says on the subject that counts, but also *of how and where* he says it. Alertness to the use of framing devices and to the strategic juxtaposition of episodes and elements within episodes to create comparisons and contrasts, and attention to the way key words or concepts brought into association with faith in certain pericopae subsequently 'fan out' in the rest of the narrative, adds much to our appreciation of Mark's views on the place of faith in discipleship.

Within the πίστις, πιστεύειν material itself, faith is related to discipleship in three main connections – to the act of becoming a disciple, to the nature of the new community which the disciples constitute, and to the functioning of the disciples in the service of Jesus. This last area is largely developed by a *via*

---

[1] See Tannehill, 'Disciples in Mark', 392f; Best, *Discipleship*, 128f. See further below, pp. 210–11.

[2] Hahn, 'Verständnis des Glaubens', 67; cf. 63.

negativa; that is, by depicting their experience of failing faith. We will therefore consider this dimension in the next chapter on unbelief; here we shall examine the first two areas and also look at the relationship in Mark's story between the call to repentance and faith and the call to discipleship.

1. Faith and becoming a disciple

One significant indication that Mark represents faith as lying at the heart of discipleship is the way he uses two units which link faith and a commitment to follow Jesus as an *inclusio* around the Galilee-oriented portion of his narrative (1:14–20; 10:46–52). Framing devices such as this serve two main literary functions: they are an internal indication of structure, marking the limits of structural units of various sizes in a narrative, and they provide a commentary on the material framed. In opening and closing his account of Jesus' ministry outside Jerusalem by relating faith to following, Mark underlines the centrality of these concerns in the intervening material. In addition to these two framing pericopae, we should also take into account 13:5f,21–3 (also framing units) which relate faith to discipleship by way of reverse application.

The faith of the fishermen (1:14–20)

In chapter 2, we isolated the major ways in which 1:14f functions as the hermeneutical key to Mark's entire narrative programme. Now we must consider the role this unit plays in its own immediate context, specifically in relation to the story of the calling of the four fishermen which follows it (1:16–20).

Mark does not simply juxtapose vv 14–15 and vv 16–20 but joins them in such a way that they form a small literary unity that is set off from the surrounding context. They are tied together by the spatial designation 'Galilee' (vv 14,16; cf. 'the wilderness' in vv 12f, and 'Capernaum' in v 21) and by the absence of any mention of temporal duration, in contrast to the 'forty days' of the preceding episode and the 'Sabbath day' of the following one. Furthermore the addition of the imperative 'come after me' (v 16) to the twin imperatives of the kingdom announcement creates a three-step progressive sequence,[1] a

---

[1] Cf. Robbins' somewhat similar proposal, 'Mark 1:14–20', 220ff; idem, *Jesus the Teacher*, 27–31.

form of arrangement for which Mark is well known. Triadic
patterns of various kinds are pervasive in his gospel.[1]

By forging such a connection between vv 14f and vv 16–20, the
author indicates that the fishermen's response of leaving and
following Jesus presupposes and expresses the conversion and
faith demanded in v 15. The relationship can be conceived
diagramatically as follows:

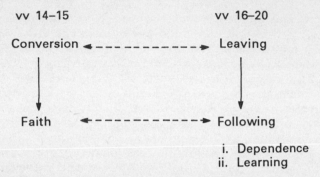

vv 14–15   vv 16–20

Conversion ◄ ─ ─ ─ ─ ─ ─ ─ ─ ─ ► Leaving

Faith ◄ ─ ─ ─ ─ ─ ─ ─ ─ ─ ► Following

                                    i. Dependence
                                   ii. Learning

The alignment of the two accounts therefore attests the centrality of repentant faith to the initiation of discipleship, and
also illustrates the concrete character and implications of such
faith for those individuals summoned to join Jesus on his
mission.

In the call account, the initiative rests entirely with Jesus.
The fishermen do not ask to become Jesus' disciples but are
approached unexpectedly by him, in the midst of their everyday
work, and issued with a summons to follow. In this sense their
discipleship is a gift more than an achievement, and in this
lies the key to future success. But it is a gift which must be
positively accepted. Jesus does not dragoon them into the
cause of the kingdom; his word, though powerful, is not on the
human plane irresistible, nor does his call 'create their obedience',[2] for the call to follow can be refused (10:21f). Instead the
call creates a situation where obedience, and thus faith,
becomes a possibility; where divine initiative and human response may meet and faith come to birth. For the disciples,

[1] See, e.g., Neirynck, *Duality*, 110–12; Burkill, *Mysterious Revelation*, 232
n.24; 243f; Robbins, *Jesus the Teacher*, 25–48; and on the rhetorical
significance of three-fold patterns, see Tannehill, *Sword of His Mouth*, 43–
5.
[2] As Schweizer says, 'Portrayal of Faith', 392ff. Similarly, Mangatt,
'Aspects of Discipleship', 239; Schürmann, 'Jungerkreis Jesu', 28.

obedience to Jesus' call is the condition of faith, and faith is the expression of their obedience.

The immediacy (καὶ εὐθύς v 18) of the fishermen's obedience evidences the intuitive nature of their apprehension of Jesus' eschatological significance. In the call accounts Jesus occupies a role analogous only to that of Yahweh in the Old Testament prophetic call stories,[1] and the immediate reaction of the fishermen is only comprehensible on the assumption of a sudden, revelatory insight into the divine authority with which Jesus addresses them and a preparedness on their part to do the will of God[2] (cf. 3:35). Mark is not implying that they instantly confess Jesus to be the Messiah (this is slow in coming, cf. 8:27ff), but that they sense his divine authorisation to proclaim and effect the dawning rule of God, which relativises all other values and evinces a commitment to him of conversion and faith.

Mark conceives discipleship faith as a condition pregnant with practical consequences. It entails a radical conversion, a decisive break with the existing order. The fishermen abandon their possessions and means of livelihood: their nets and boats (vv 18,20); they relinquish their positions of human authority over hired servants (v 20); and, most demanding of all, they detach themselves from family ties and traditions, the main source of identity for first century Palestinians.[3] This ethical rigour is not only, at least for Mark, a symptom of eschatological urgency.[4] It serves two more immediate ends.

On one side, it is a symbolic demonstration within the story world that God's kingdom lays claim to the whole of existence (cf. 12:28–34,41–4) and effects a transformation of social and economic relations, even in advance of its eschatological consummation, for those who accept it in faith. It brings a new understanding and experience of family (3:31–5; 10:29f; cf. 6:4; 13:12), a new concept of authority and servanthood (9:35; 10:31,

[1] See Hengel, *Charismatic Leader*, especially 67–71, 84–8. Cf. Robbins, who suggests that in 1:14–20, Jesus' role 'merges the authority of Yahweh and the prophets with the authority of ethical teachers who embody the system of thought and action they teach to others', 'Mark 1:14–20', 98; see also 226.

[2] On the theistic grounding of discipleship in Mark, see Donahue, 'Neglected Factor', 585.

[3] See Kee, *Community*, 153f. Lohfink, *Jesus and Community*, 39, 44.

[4] It is unlikely that Mark exhibits a markedly imminent eschatology; on this see Schweizer, 'Eschatology in Mark' 114–18; Best, *Temptation and Passion*, 176; idem, *Following Jesus*, 9f, 152–4, 249; idem, *Gospel as Story*, 42f. Otherwise: Perrin, *Introduction*, 149.

42–5), and a new attitude to wealth and possessions (10:21–7; 12:41–4). On the other side, the almost suicidal renunciation of all means of human security places the disciples in a situation of radical dependency, even of human powerlessness, for they dispossess themselves of all that gives them control or power over their own lives and over the lives of others. The realities of the old order as such are not repudiated. Simon and Andrew still exhibit familial concern (1:30; cf. 7:10–13; 10:2–12) and evidently retain their house (1:29; cf. 2:1; 3:20; 9:33) and maybe their boat (e.g. 3:9; 4:1,35). But these are put at the disposal of the kingdom and are no longer their means of support and identity. They are to be replaced by a new sense of dependency on divine provision (2:23; 6:8f,37–44; 8:1–10; 9:41; 11:24; cf. 8: 14–21) and protection (4:35–41; 6:48–52). It is an unwillingness to live at such risk that disqualifies the rich man, despite his perceptiveness and piety, from following after Jesus (10:17–22).

Because the commitment to follow Jesus plunges the fishermen into a total lack of material and personal security, the essence of their following is unconditional faith – an on-going relationship of total dependence on Jesus for all that is needed. The measure of this faith is their preparedness to entrust their destiny into Jesus' hands, both in this life, where it will bring suffering and deprivation (8:34f; 10:29; 13:9–13; 14:27; cf. 10: 32), and in relation to the future kingdom, for which they look to Jesus for participation in its consummation (cf. 8:36ff; 10:30,37; 13:26f; cf. 10:17). 'In Mark it is dangerous to follow Jesus, because it is a matter of responding totally to the kingdom of God in a time and a place in which the kingdom of God is not totally present.'[1] As well as material dependence and confidence in Jesus for eschatological salvation, the faith of the fishermen expresses itself in submission to his formative power over their lives. The goal of their following is to become 'fishers of men' (v 17). This is not simply a prophecy of their future task (cf. 13:10) but the commencement of a continual process of personal transformation (καὶ ποιήσω ὑμᾶς γενέσθαι) that runs throughout the gospel. Their ubiquitous presence as witnesses of Jesus' ministry (e.g. 5:40; 8:19f; 9:2), their private instruction (4:10ff,14–20,34; 8:27–10:45), their authorisation to preach, heal and exorcise (3:14f; 6:7,13), and the repeated appeal for them to hear and understand (e.g. 4:13,40f; 6:52; 8: 14–21,31ff; 9:5), are all part of this process of being made into something they were not before. And fundamental to this pro-

[1] Via, *Ethics*, 146.

cess is the initial commitment and on-going maintenance of (cf. 4:40; 9:19) faith in Jesus.

To recapitulate: in 1:14–20, the author establishes the norm by which the reader may judge the subsequent behaviour of the disciples, for discipleship should continue as it begins. The beginning of discipleship is depicted as an act of conversion and faith in obedience to an unsolicited call from Jesus. Conversion is marked by the spontaneous forsaking of all existing forms of security, and faith consists in embarking on a lifelong relationship of believing trust in Jesus involving material dependence, reliance on him for eschatological salvation, and a submission to a process of learning and personal transformation. In Mark's story, the attachment of disciple to master is therefore more than commitment to his teaching, and more even than fierce loyalty to his person (cf. 6:29); the bond is one of religious faith. For Mark, this does not conflict with the disciples' faith in God (cf. 11:22), for even in contemporary Jewish tradition, following after and placing faith in God's messianic envoy was considered the same as placing faith in God himself.[1]

Following on the Way (10:46–52)

Mark reiterates the connection between faith and following in the Bartimaeus episode, which forms the other part of the *inclusio*. In the interim narrative the disciples have time and again failed to match up to what the reader would expect from their initial commitment, and the author uses the case of Bartimaeus to underscore their shortcomings by way of contrast, and also to indicate the remedy for them. The strategic placement of the story and its thematic connection with the preceding context enable it to function in this way. As noted earlier, Mark uses the two accounts of the healing of blind men to frame the portion of his narrative in which Jesus relentlessly seeks to rid the disciples of their spiritual blindness (8:27–10:45). What Jesus does at the beginning and end of the section he is in effect trying to do throughout – open the eyes of the uncomprehending disciples (cf. 8:18).

The healing of the blind man at Bethsaida (8:22–6), which flanks the beginning of the section, is unique for depicting a progressive healing. In Mark's treatment, the two stages symbolise the need for the disciples to link their apprehension

---

[1] See Hengel, *Charismatic Leader*, 21–2 for references and discussion.

of Jesus' *messianic identity*, the first stage of understanding finally achieved at Caesarea Philippi (8:27–33), with an appreciation of his *messianic mission* of suffering and death and an acceptance of the corresponding demands of discipleship, the second stage of insight.[1] When this happens, their eyes will be fully opened and their understanding complete. Bartimaeus, whose healing closes the section, exemplifies such an understanding, and the disciples are implicitly beckoned to emulate his faith and insight. Only a combination of their faith and Jesus' restorative power will grant them true understanding and sustain their commitment to follow Jesus.

In the framed section itself, widely recognised to be one of the most carefully structured portions of the gospel,[2] the disciples' failings are exposed both by corrective teaching from Jesus and by the actions of minor characters who appear in this part of the story. A marked contrast is drawn between Bartimaeus, for example, and the sons of Zebedee who figure in the immediately preceding episode. In both accounts Jesus asks the same question: Τί σοι θέλεις ποιήσω; (vv 36,51). The disciples reveal their blindness by seeking places of prestige and power in the coming age (v 37; cf. 15:27!), which Jesus cannot grant, while Bartimaeus seeks eschatological healing, which Jesus can give (v 51f). While the disciples' minds are filled with sitting in glory (καθίσωμεν ἐν τῇ δόξῃ σου v 37), the blind beggar is sitting on the way (ἐκάθητο παρὰ τὴν ὁδόν v 46) which leads to the city of rejection. Whereas the disciples understand the messianic kingdom in terms of worldly hierarchies of power and crass nepotism (v 37), Bartimaeus intuitively perceives the Son of David to be a merciful healer (vv 48f). The faithless self-confidence of James and John concerning their ability to share in Jesus' redemptive passion (δυνάμεθα v 39) contrasts with the helpless beggar's pleading faith (ἐλέησόν με vv 47f) which leads him to follow Jesus on the way of suffering (v 52).

As well as highlighting the inadequacies of the disciples, the Bartimaeus story reaffirms the norm of discipleship established at the beginning as the remedy for them. The existing narrative represents a coalescence of miracle story and call-

---

[1] For various interpretations of the two-stage symbolism, see E. Johnson, 'Blind Man from Bethsaida', 379–83.

[2] See, e.g., Perrin, *Redaction Criticism*, 40–63; idem, 'Towards an Interpretation', 6–21; Swartley '"Way" in Mark', 74–7; Koch, 'Inhaltliche Gliederung', 147–9; Best, *Discipleship*, 1–16; Senior, *Passion*, 28–36.

story elements,[1] with the faith of the suppliant standing in a twofold relationship to healing and discipleship. The discipleship elements pick up the main motifs of 1:14–20, but with some significant differences that reflect developments in the intervening plot.

The discipleship orientation first becomes apparent in v 49, where the blind man receives a call from Jesus, the significance of which is enhanced by the threefold use of φωνεῖν. The man is not simply being called forward for healing; he is being implicitly summoned to a discipleship commitment.[2] The naming of Bartimaeus adds to the call story atmosphere. This is the only miracle story where the sick person is named (cf. 5:22), whereas in discipleship call accounts the characters are regularly named (1:16,19; 2:14; 3:13–19; but cf. 10:17–22).

The manner of Bartimaeus' response to Jesus' call is also suggestive of a discipleship commitment. The depiction of him casting off (ἀποβαλών) his cloak has occasioned much discussion. A weakly attested variant has him putting on (ἐπιβαλών) his garment, and some exegetes favour this reading since it corresponds better to the usual Oriental custom of a man being properly attired when called before a superior.[3] But this is to miss the real significance of ἀποβαλών. Common to Mark's call stories is the way the person summoned leaves his occupation and possessions behind in order to go after Jesus (1:18,20; 2:14; 10:21,28ff). According to the Old Testament, a person's cloak was one of his most valued possessions, so indispensable that even a debtor could not be deprived of it (Ex 22:26f; Deut 24:12f). A beggar's mantle would represent all his worldly goods, as well as his only means of livelihood, since Oriental beggars commonly spread their cloaks before them to collect alms.[4] Bartimaeus' instinctive discarding of his cloak is, therefore, tantamount to the fishermen leaving their nets, Levi his occupation and the rich man being called to surrender

---

[1] For our purposes, it matters not whether the story is a miracle story elaborated into a discipleship story (e.g. Gnilka, *Markus*, II, 111f; and most exegetes), or if a genuine call story underlies the narrative (e.g. Steinhauser, 'Call Story'; idem, 'Bartimaeus Narrative'; Achtemeier, '"And He Followed Him"'). Either way, the final narrative has a call story character (contra, Kingsbury, *Christology*, 104f n.159).

[2] Mark uses καλεῖν (1:18; 2:17), προσκαλεῖσθαι (3:13; 6:7; 7:14; 8:1,34; 10:42; 12:43) and φωνεῖν (9:35; 3:31 TR) for Jesus' summoning of disciples.

[3] E.g. Lohmeyer, *Markus*, 226 n.2; Grundmann, *Markus*, 221; Johnson, *Mark*, 182; Findlay, *Jesus*, 27.

[4] See Steinhauser, 'Call Story', 205.

his wealth. Like the fishermen in 1:16–20, the beggar's faith is shown in his willingness to allow the call of Jesus to dispel all concern for his own security and material well-being. Having known the powerlessness of destitution, in an act of radical conversion he leaves behind his one source of support and identity to follow Jesus.

This act of following (v 52) is the third discipleship element in the narrative. The Bartimaeus story is unique for depicting the healed man following Jesus (cf. 5:18f), and some interpreters think it simply demonstrates the reality of the miracle.[1] However such a demonstration would be more appropriate for the healing of lameness than blindness and, more importantly, ἀκολουθεῖν and ἐν τῇ ὁδῷ belong to Mark's repertoire of discipleship terms. Although ἀκολουθεῖν does not invariably imply committed discipleship (e.g. 3:7; 5:24; 11:9; cf. 14:13), when the narrator uses it of individuals and of those designated μαθηταί, it does carry the sense of personal allegiance to Jesus (1:18; 2:14f; 10:21,28,32; 15:41; cf. 9:38). In this case, he may have chosen the durative imperfect tense to draw attention to the significance of the act[2] and to connote an enduring way of life rather than a single journey to Jerusalem (cf. 2:15; 9:38; 15:41). The phrase 'on the way' gives a specific content to his lifestyle. In Mark, ὁδός mainly denotes a literal road or journey.[3] Jesus' wanderings, however, are invested with a special eschatological purposiveness in light of the injunction at the beginning of the story to 'prepare the ὁδός of the Lord' (1:2). This purpose becomes more focused after 8:27 where ἐν τῇ ὁδῷ specifically denotes Jesus' journey from Caesarea Philippi to Jerusalem (8:27; 9:33; 10:32,52; cf. 10:17). Because Jesus uses this journey to speak of the fate that awaits him in Jerusalem, 'the way' becomes a symbol for the path of suffering and rejection that the Messiah must tread. And because in Mark messiahship and discipleship are cut from the same cloth, it also becomes a metaphor for the suffering nature of discipleship (cf. 8:34ff; 10:32). Bartimaeus is thus

---

[1] E.g. Pesch, *Markus*, II, 174; Meye, *Twelve*, 79, 164f; Lane, *Mark*, 389.

[2] The choice of tense may carry no special significance; the aorist is used in 1:18 and 2:14. Burkill, however, has suggested that Mark 'feels that the imperfect tense is more appropriate than the aorist in a statement whose general import he wishes to emphasise', *Mysterious Revelation*, 65f.

[3] For a review of scholarly opinion on Mark's 'way' motif, see Swartley, '"Way" in Mark', 77–9. See also Kelber, *Kingdom*, 67–85; Best, *Following Jesus*, 15–18.

depicted as embarking in faith on the path of obedient suffering as a disciple of Jesus.

Now it might be objected that Bartimaeus' action cannot be an act of discipleship since, unlike earlier call episodes, he is not explicitly enjoined by Jesus to follow but does so on his own initiative, in contravention of Jesus' command to go away (ὕπαγε).[1] But this overlooks a crucial development in the discipleship theme earlier in the gospel. In the first half of the story, the explicit call to follow is directed to specific individuals only. Straight after the first major passion announcement however, Jesus calls together the crowd with the disciples and issues a new general call: 'If anyone wishes to come after me, let him deny himself and take up his cross and follow me' (8:34). Within the plotted narrative, this manoeuvre represents an attempt by Jesus, as he approaches Jerusalem, to restrict his physical accompaniment to those willing to tread the path of suffering. But at the same time, it effects a universalising of the call to follow to 'anyone who wishes to. . .' This opens up a new pattern of discipleship, based not on personal selection by Jesus, but on the voluntary acceptance of certain demands by those who entrust their salvation to the gospel of Jesus (v 35).

Bartimaeus exemplifies this new pattern. By making his act of 'following on the way' a direct consequence of his healing, the narrator implies that a preparedness to identify himself fully with the destiny of Jesus was inherent in the faith he placed in Jesus for healing. The voluntary and whole-hearted character of his commitment is enhanced by the way the beggar chooses to follow despite being permitted to depart (ὕπαγε). This does not amount to disobedience, since ὕπαγε is not so much an instruction ('go away') as a farewell dismissal ('you may go').[2] As Jesus reaches the city of his death, Bartimaeus demonstrates that faith in Jesus has consequences beyond the experience of miracle; it requires following Jesus on the way of his passion.

To summarise: the Galilee-oriented section of the narrative closes on a similar note to which it opened with an account of a named character making a commitment to discipleship as an expression of a radical conversion and an on-going, dependent faith. These elements however are modified in two important ways.

[1] So Roloff, *Kerygma*, 126 n.67; Meye, *Twelve*, 165; Lane, *Mark*, 389.
[2] See R. G. Bratcher and E. Nida, *A Translator's Handbook on the Gospel of Mark*, (Leiden: E. J. Brill, 1961), 340.

(i) No longer is discipleship confined to a specific injunction by Jesus to follow him but is now a path open to all who identify with Jesus in faith. For Bartimaeus, the call to follow is implicit in the call forward for healing (v 49) and his response is paradigmatic of the convergence of the call to faith and the call to discipleship consequent upon the death and resurrection of Jesus (cf. 13:10; 14:9).

(ii) The path Bartimaeus takes in following Jesus is specified as the way of the cross. The disciples have been introduced to this dimension in 8:27–10:45 but they have been slow to grasp it. They have insight into Jesus' messianic identity (8:29), but this is only partial sight for they cannot comprehend his messianic destiny of death and resurrection (8:31–3; 9:9f,32). By 10:32 their fear and amazement perhaps suggest that they have begun to accept what will happen to Jesus, but 10:35–45 shows that they still do not understand what this means for themselves. Bartimaeus, however, exemplifies what is required of them. In response to his persevering faith he is assured of salvation, given new sight, and follows on the way of the cross (10:52). This ordering of elements at the end of the account is significant. Salvation is given to faith, not earned through discipleship, yet salvation only becomes visible and is finally only assured through a preparedness to follow Jesus on the *via crucis* (8:34–8).

Future fidelity (13:5f,20–3)

The warning found in the Olivet Discourse against believing false prophets and messiahs is relevant to Mark's portrayal of discipleship faith by way of reverse application. That is to say, inasmuch as the discourse is addressed to four disciples (v 3), and in it they are forbidden to believe (μὴ πιστεύετε) other claimants to messiahship, the implication is that their belief or faith should be steadfastly directed to the true Messiah alone. Moreover such an attitude is transposed, by its literary setting, to the time beyond the end of Jesus' earthly ministry, to the post-Easter period.

In the main storyline, Mark 13 constitutes Jesus' farewell discourse to his followers in which, after the model of Deut 32, he prepares them for what will happen after his departure. Through the vehicle of prophecy he transports the disciples, and the reader/hearer, to the time between the resurrection and the parousia (cf. 14:28; 16:7). It is common opinion, even among literary critics,[1] that in opening up this future world Mark wishes to touch directly upon the real-life situation – whether current, impending, or just past – of his readers (note especially vv 14,23,37). This situation is usually identified as the turbulent period of the Jewish War of AD 66–70, which is known to have sparked a general upsurge in eschatological expectancy.[2] Mark's intention is not to inflame apocalyptic speculation in his audience but rather to warn them against being misled into thinking that their present distress signals the arrival of the τέλος and to encourage steadfastness in face of the inevitable woes which must precede the End. Presumably then the false prophets and messiahs, who with the 'elect' are new to Mark's cast of characters, correspond with people known by the author to be active among his first readers/ hearers. His aim is to encourage an identification and an evaluation of such people in accordance with the standard of judgement adopted towards them by Jesus in advance of their emergence. By this predictive device, he thus incorporates the real world of his audience into the past world of his plotted narrative.[3]

Much scholarly debate has centred on the authenticity and original form of the traditions contained in chapter 13 and on the extent of their redactional reworking by Mark. Whatever the answer to these questions, and some experts have changed their positions from one publication to another,[4] Mark himself is ultimately responsible for the shape and message of the final narrative. One feature of this is the way he integrates chapter 13 into the wider gospel programme. Its focus on the destruction of the temple (vv 1ff) caps the preceding section dealing with Jesus' conflict with the temple authorities (11:11–12:44), whilst forward linkages in the discourse to the following passion narrative[5] imply a connection between the demise of the temple and the death and resurrection of Jesus. Hence, chapter 13 should not be viewed in isolation but as an integral part of Mark's whole composition.

[1] E.g. Petersen, *Literary Criticism*, 78–80; Stock, *Discipleship*, 174.

[2] As a recent example, see Hengel, *Studies*, 14–28.

[3] Cf. Petersen, 'When is the End not the End', 157f.

[4] See the discussion by Beasley-Murray, 'Eschatology in Mark', 37ff. Also see idem, 'Second Thoughts on Mark 13', 414–20.

[5] On these linkages, see Lightfoot, *Gospel Message*, 51f; Stock, *Discipleship*, 175–80; Gaston, *No Stone*, 478f; and Cousar, 'Eschatology and Mark's "Theologia Crucis"', 321–35.

In terms of literary structure, the discourse falls into three parts[1] (vv 5–23,24–7,28–37), and is unified by a string of parenetic injunctions such as βλέπετε (vv 5,9,23,33), μὴ θροεῖσθε (v 7), μὴ προμεριμνᾶτε (v 11), ὁ ὑπομείνας (v 13), μὴ πιστεύετε (v 21), μάθετε (v 28) γινώσκετε (v 29) ἀγρυπνεῖτε (v 33) and γρηγορεῖτε (vv 35–7). The injuction 'believe not' occurs in the first part of the discourse, which has its own symmetrical structure.

			Signs of the End	
v 5	βλέπετε	(A)	Deceivers (vv 5b–6)	
		(B)	War (vv 7–8)	– 'when you hear ... (v 7)
v 9	βλέπετε	(C)	Persecution (vv 9–13)	– 'when you are delivered up' (v 11)
		(Bi)	War (vv 14–20)	– 'when you see ...' (v 14)
v 23	βλέπετε	(Ai)	Deceivers (vv 21–3)	

The significant thing for us about this structure is the way Mark encloses the whole section with a double warning about false prophets and messiahs (vv 6,21f), each of which is associated with the imperative βλέπετε, used by Mark throughout the chapter to draw the reader's attention to the issue under discussion (vv 5,9,23,33). The repetition of the warning indicates that the danger of being led astray from the truth poses an even greater threat to the community than persecution and physical distress. Moreover, as an instance of Mark's familiar framing device,[2] some relationship is implied between the historical events taking place in vv 7–20 and the activity of the messianic impostors; presumably their false claims will be fuelled by the political turmoil, natural disasters and intense persecution depicted here.

Now while both framing units describe the same phenomenon, there is an internal development in the intervening verses which gives each warning a different temporal reference. The framed section contains three temporal signposts (vv

[1] See Lambrecht, *Markus-Apocalypse*, 263–97; Standaert, *Marc*, 231–59; Kelber, *Oral and Written Gospel*, 100.

[2] So Lambrecht, *Markus-Apocalypse*, 173, 273f; Standaert, *Marc*, 232; Weeden, *Traditions in Conflict*, 88; Achtemeier, *Mark*, 106f; Kelber, *Kingdom*, 114; idem, *Mark's Story*, 69.

7,11,14). The first two, 'when you hear of wars and rumours of wars', and 'when you are delivered up', are joined with injunctions not to be alarmed and not to be anxious. The third case, 'when you see the desolating sacrilege' is, however, linked with a call to immediate action – flee to the mountains! This one historical event is singled out as the decisive sign to look out for; the earlier occurrences are only preliminary signs and should not be seen as proof that the parousia is imminent (ἀλλ' οὔπω τὸ τέλος, v 7).

Accordingly, the first warning against deceivers relates to the period before the decisive event in vv 14ff, and their claims are countered by a denial that the signs they appeal to are anything more than what is to be expected in post-Easter history. The second warning however refers to the later period of flight (καὶ τότε v 21) when further ψευδόχριστοι καὶ ψευδο-προφῆται will claim that the parousia has already occurred covertly and will justify their claims with signs and wonders. They are not to be believed, for when the Son of Man does come – 'after that tribulation' (v 24) – it will be with attendant signs that none shall miss seeing (vv 24–7). By placing warnings against messianic imposters at the beginning and end of a period of historical development, the author suggests that this threat spans the entire period before the return of the Son of Man. The injunction μὴ πιστεύετε is not then to be limited to the final wave of pretenders alone, but applies throughout the post-resurrection period when Jesus is physically absent from the community (cf. vv 34–7).

The historical spread and numerical diversity (πολλοὶ ἐλεύ-σονται, v 6) envisaged for these false claimants warns against an overly-specific identification of them;[1] in the New Testament, 'false prophet/messiah' is a catchall term embracing a variety of aberrations.[2] One thing seems plain however. They are portrayed as members of the Christian community rather than as Jewish messianic figures. They invoke the authority of Jesus (ἐπὶ τῷ ὀνόματί μου, v 6; cf. 9:37–41; 13:13),[3] and use the

[1] Weeden, for example, identifies them as *theios aner* Christians (*Traditions in Conflict*, 74–6, 95); Kelber as 'politically committed Jewish-Christian prophets', (*Oral and Written Gospel*, 99); and many commentators identify them as the Jewish messianic personalities spoken of by Josephus during the siege of Jerusalem (*Jos. Ant.* XX v.1; viii.5–6,10; *War*, II, xiii.3, xvii.8–9; VI v.2, viii.1; xi.1).

[2] See Weeden, *Traditions in Conflict*, 74; Friedrich, *TDNT*, VI, 855f.

[3] On the meaning of this phrase, see n. 3, p. 157 below.

epithet ἐγώ εἰμι, which occurs elsewhere in Mark as a self-designation of Jesus with overtones of divine dignity (6:50; 14:62). This suggests that they either claim literally to be Jesus himself, or else arrogate to themselves his messianic title and divine authority. (Ironically, when at his trial the true Messiah declares ἐγώ εἰμι, he is rejected as a false prophet! 14:62ff). In the second warning the deceivers claim to be (v 22), and are hailed by others as (v 21), ὁ Χριστός. 'The title "Messiah" in 13:21, construed as a reference to Jesus and not some other figure quite simply connotes the "Jesus of Mark's story". . . whom his followers, in the time before the Parousia, await with eager anticipation.'[1] The impostors then are 'parousia pretenders'[2] who justify their claim to be Christ returned with signs and wonders.

Now the sole response which Jesus requires of the disciples to such imposters is: μὴ πιστεύετε (v 21). The dividing line between the disciples and the elect on one side, and the deceivers and those led astray on the other, is the matter of belief or disbelief in their messianic claims. As we have found in other πίστις, πιστεύειν references in Mark, the construction μὴ πιστεύετε is unqualified; its object is to be derived from the context. In this case, the phrase 'do not believe' could be completed either by 'it' (i.e. the news of Messiah's presence), or by 'him' (i.e. the pseudo-messiah himself, or the one proclaiming him). Either way, the primary meaning of μὴ πιστεύετε is to refuse to believe the truthfulness of the claims of Jesus' reappearance. However, more is at stake than a 'non-religious act of crediting';[3] it implies at the same time that the disciples should in no sense trust the pseudo-messiahs or bind themselves to them in faith. This can be confirmed from a number of directions.

(i) Mark 13:21 is the negative counterpart of 1:15, and recalls the understanding of faith conveyed there. The two texts have several features in common: they both use the present imperative πιστεύετε (cf. 5:36); both demands are spoken by Jesus; and both are eschatologically qualified. In 1:15, Jesus summons faith in the hidden, proleptic manifestation of God's kingdom; in 13:21, he summons disbelief in a hidden consummation of the same. In the first demand, cognitive perception of God's kingly presence should lead to trustful reliance on Jesus as kingdom-bearer. In the second cognitive disbelief in false

---

[1] Kingsbury, *Christology*, 138.

[2] This is Kelber's phrase, *Kingdom*, 114–16; cf. Perrin, *Introduction*, 149.

[3] As Warfield judges it, *Biblical Doctrines*, 478; also Shearer, 'Faith', 4.

eschatological claims is to forestall being led astray into mis-placed reliance on false messiahs.

(ii) As Mark presents it, the danger posed by messianic impostors lies in their mimicry of the person and activity of Jesus. They claim the name, messianic status and divine authority of Jesus; they impersonate his parousia; they work miraculous signs and wonders; and they create a following of people whom they lead astray. The injunction μὴ πιστεύετε is best seen, then, as an attempt to deny these characters the full faith response they seek, but which must be reserved for the genuine Messiah alone, Jesus. It is significant that their σημεῖα καὶ τέρατα, unlike Jesus' redemptive δυνάμεις, are not given in response to an existing faith but are intended (πρὸς τό) to compel belief, even , if possible, among the elect (v 22). They are spectacular 'signs' that pander to unbelief (8:11–13; 15:29–32) and relieve the recipient of the need for genuine repentant faith.[1]

(iii) An essential component of genuine faith, in Markan perspective, is dogged perseverance in face of all difficulties. As we have seen, it is such persevering faith that 'saves' those in need in the miracle stories (5:34, cf.23; 10:52). In the farewell discourse, the exhortation μὴ πιστεύετε belongs to the broader parenetic framework through which Mark seeks to foster perseverance in his audience until the End. 'For the one who endures to the end will be saved' (σωθήσεται v 13). For Mark 'the faith that survives is authentic faith',[2] and his fear is that his readers will reject the authentic faith of Jesus for the escapism proffered by the deceivers. The demand 'do not be-lieve them' is more than an intellectual rejection of christo-logical error; it is, in effect, a summons to preserve a genuine, persevering faith in Jesus.

(iv) The farewell address as a whole quotes and alludes to many Old Testament texts.[3] The warning in vv 21f has clear verbal and thematic links with the admonition against false prophecy in Deut 13:1–5. Mark's μὴ πιστεύετε corresponds to Deuteronomy's οὐκ ἀκούσεσθε, the practical meaning of which is given as maintaining a whole-hearted love for God, follow-ing him (!), fearing him and obeying his voice (vv 3f). It is such

---

[1] See above, pp. 66–70.

[2] Weeden, *Traditions in Conflict*, 82.

[3] See Hartmann, *Prophecy Interpreted*, 145–59; Kee, 'Scriptural Quo-tations', 169.

undivided allegiance to Jesus that Mark implies in the command μὴ πιστεύετε.

To conclude, we may note that Mark 13:21 is the only case in the gospel where unbelief on the part of the disciples is actually sanctioned by Jesus, and the clear implication of such a denial of believing trust to others is that an exclusive faith commitment to himself forms the heart of their discipleship. A demand is made of them, and through them of Mark's audience (cf. v 37), that tests be applied and discernment exercised. The reality of their faith will then manifest itself in the deliberate rejection (disbelief) of whatever does not bear the hallmark of truth. Behind this demand lies a concern that false christological perception will make shipwreck of their faith and, by undermining their commitment to Jesus, threaten their salvation (cf. v 13b).

In 1:14–20 and 10:46–52, the initiation of discipleship comprises an act of conversion and faith which leads to an ongoing relationship of trustful dependence on Jesus. As it turns out this relationship does not survive the traumas of the passion and the disciples all desert Jesus. But, contrary to what some interpreters claim[1], the last state envisaged for the disciples is not one of failure but one of faith. The plot may not narrate the restoration of the failed disciples but Mark's narrative world assumes it. In 14:28 and 16:7, Jesus predicts a reconstitution of the community in Galilee (i.e. after the model of 1:14–20),[2] and in 13:5f,21–3 the scenario is one of Jesus' followers being exhorted to maintain their faith in Messiah-Jesus up until the parousia. The faith depicted here has the character of fidelity or exclusive allegiance to Jesus. But this faithfulness is not simply a matter of personal loyalty to his teaching or to his person; it is the continuation of the relationship of dependent trust on Jesus for provision, protection and ultimate salvation

---

[1] E.g. Weeden, *Traditions in Conflict*, 45–51; Crossan, 'Empty Tomb', 149; Kelber, *Oral and Written Gospel*, 127–9. For a refutation, see especially Petersen, 'When is the End not the End', 151–66. Also see Best, *Gospel as Story*, 47f, 72f; Rhoads and Michie, *Mark as Story*, 96–100; Tannehill, 'Narrative Christology', 83f; Catchpole, 'Fearful Silence', 3–10. On 16:8 as the intentional end of the gospel, see, e.g., Boomershine/Bartholomew, 'Narrative Technique', 213–23; Boomershine, 'Apostolic Commission', 225–39; Meye, 'Ending of Mark's Gospel', 33–43; Via, *Ethics*, 50–7, and especially the full-scale study of Magness, *Sense and Absence*, passim.

[2] See above, pp. 41–2.

embarked upon at the beginning. Faithfulness is, for Mark, where faith has become a habitual way of life.

2. The call to faith and the call to discipleship

The relationship between the demand for repentance and faith on the one hand, and the call to discipleship on the other, is one of the more difficult issues in Markan interpretation. Does Mark envisage all who repent and believe becoming disciples,[1] or does he view faith and discipleship as two separate paths to the kingdom?[2] A related question is whether the term 'disciple' designates only the Twelve,[3] or a wider body of adherents inclusive or exclusive of the Twelve.[4] The spread of exegetical opinion on these questions shows that the evidence is ambiguous enough to be construed in several different ways. To my mind however, it seems clear that Mark portrays various forms of positive response to Jesus, all of which presuppose repentance and faith but not all of which constitute full discipleship or 'followingship'.

(i) First of all, there are the twelve specially appointed disciples, or 'apostles', who form the inner circle of adherents (3: 13–19; 4:10; 6:7,30; 9:35; 10:32; 11:11; 14:10,17,20,43). Of these, three and sometimes four appear as Jesus' most intimate friends (e.g. 1:29–31; 5:37; 9:2ff; 13:3; 14:33ff).

(ii) Then there is a wider circle of adherents who physically follow Jesus around as an expression of personal attachment to him and acceptance of the demands of such following as laid down in 1:16–20 (cf. 10:21,28). Levi belongs to this group (2: 13; cf. 10:21f), along with the many other tax-gatherers and sinners who follow Jesus in response to his call (2:15–17).[5] It includes those περὶ αὐτόν whom Jesus deems his true family

---

[1] 'It is Mark who depicts clearer than anyone else in the New Testament that faith always means discipleship, following Jesus', Schweizer, 'Mark's Contribution', 432; idem, 'Portrayal of Faith', 396. Cf. Goetzmann, *NIDNTT*, 358.

[2] Cf. Goppelt, *Theology*, I, 207–13; Hengel, *Charismatic Leader*, 62–73; Cook, 'Faith', 693–700; Hahn, 'Verständnis des Glaubens', 63, 66f.

[3] So Meye, *Twelve*, especially chapters 4, 5, 9; Freyne, *Twelve*, 109–14; Turner, 'Marcan Usage', *JTS* 28, 22–30.

[4] E.g. Best, *Discipleship*, 103f, 127, 157f; idem, *Following Jesus*, 180–9; Peacock, 'Discipleship', 555f; Schweizer, 'Portrayal of Faith', 391; Munro, 'Women Disciples', 231ff; Trocmé, *Formation*, 182f n.2; Kelber, *Mark's Story*, 45.

[5] On this passage, see Dewey, *Public Debate*, 81; Best, *Following Jesus*, 176f.

(3:34) and to whom, with the Twelve, has been given the mystery of the kingdom (4:10). Presumably it is these who occupy the 'other boats' on Lake Galilee in 4:36. The mutual sharing and fellowship of this group of men, women and children is meant to compensate for the loss suffered by its members who have left all to follow Jesus (10:28; cf. 3:34). These supporters follow Jesus up to Jerusalem (10:32), and Bartimaeus joins their ranks (10:52). From their number are drawn the women present during the passion (15:40; 16:1ff) who followed Jesus in Galilee.[1]

Mark implies that the Twelve are selected from this larger circle (3:13), and are distinguished from them by a combination of greater personal intimacy (ὦσιν μετ' αὐτοῦ), which includes companionship and a sharing of Jesus' fate (cf. 5:40; 6:50; 14:14,18,27), and a special commissioning to preach, exorcise and heal; in other words, to extend Jesus' ministry as his authorised representatives (3:14f; 6:7f,30). They also have a symbolic role, constituting a backward reference to Old Testament Israel and a forward reference to the new messianic community.[2] It is the *combination* of factors that is distinctive. The Gerasene demoniac is refused permission to join this inner group (ἵνα μετ' αὐτοῦ ᾖ, 5:18), but is sent away to preach (5:19; cf. 3:14). Others similarly preach and exorcise on Jesus' behalf (1:45; 9:38–41), but do not share the personal proximity to Jesus of the Twelve. Despite their special role however, the Twelve possess no special dignity or authority within the larger body of followers. When they try to arrogate such to themselves, conflict develops and corrective teaching is given (e.g. 9:33ff; 10:35ff). It is noteworthy that the incomprehension of the disciples, which is writ large in Mark's narrative, includes a misunderstanding or abuse of the role of power and authority in the new community (e.g. 9:38–41; 10:13–15).

It is difficult to decide whether Mark uses μαθηταί to refer to the Twelve only or to the wider circle of committed followers. Virtually all of the forty-or-so uses of the term could denote either or both groups. However since Mark nowhere uses the phrase 'twelve disciples' (though cf. 14:14,17), nor on the other

---

[1] See Munro, 'Women Disciples', 230–6; also Malbon, 'Fallible Followers', 29–48; Selvidge, "'And Those who Followed Feared'", 396–400; Schmitt, 'Women in Mark', 228–33; Schüssler Fiorenza, *Memory*, 320–3; Gill, 'Women Ministers', 14–21.

[2] Cf. Schürmann, 'Jüngerkreis Jesu', 21–35; Lohfink, *Community*, 9–12, 33–5, 75–8. See also Sanders, *Jesus*, 95–106, cf. 222–8.

hand does he use the term 'disciple' to differentiate other followers from the Twelve when he mentions both groups together (4:10; 9:35; 10:32), it seems best to take μαθητής as a generic term for all those who take on the full demands of physically following Jesus.[1] After all, the four fishermen (and others?) are described as μαθηταί (2:15) before their special commissioning in 3:13–19.

(iii) Another form of allegiance, also grounded in conversion and faith, is represented by those who do not physically accompany Jesus on his wanderings, but who are adherents to his message and may even minister on his behalf.[2] Jesus refers to this group in 3:35 when he extends the definition of his family[3] from those sitting around him to 'whoever does the will of God', presumably as expressed in 1:15. It includes those who are healed and depart 'preaching the word' (1:45; 5:20; cf. 7:36); those who bring children to Jesus for his blessing (10:13); the 'strange exorcist' who does not follow but ministers in Jesus' name and exemplifies those who are 'for us' (9:38–41); Simon the leper in Bethany and the woman who anoints Jesus (14:3ff); and the local sympathisers who provide the donkey for Jesus' entry to Jerusalem (11:1–6), the room for his last supper (14:13ff) and the tomb for his burial (15:43ff). The characters in the miracle stories who are commended for their faith presumably represent this group as well.

(iv) Finally, there are the crowds which follow Jesus about or flock to him in local areas (e.g. 1:45; 3:7,20; 5:21,24; 6:33,53–6). Mark's portrayal of the ὄχλος is neither wholly positive,[4] nor wholly negative.[5] For whilst the multitude plays its own distinctive role in the drama, constituting the background scenery for much of Jesus' activity and representing the audience to whom Jesus addresses the message and demands of the kingdom (e.g. 2:2,13; 4:1ff; 7:14; 8:34; 10:1), nonetheless Mark does

---

[1] In 4:34, Mark speaks of τοῖς ἰδίοις μαθηταῖς. This may denote just the Twelve, but the phrase implies there are others who are disciples as well.

[2] Cf. Theissen's sociological study of the Jesus movement in which he distinguishes 'local sympathisers' and 'wandering charismatics', *First Followers*, 1–30.

[3] For a discussion of natural family and eschatological family in Mark, see Via, *Ethics*, 139–55.

[4] As Weeden claims, *Traditions in Conflict*, 22f; Achtemeier, *Mark*, 94.

[5] As Robinson claims, *Problem of History*, 71ff; cf. Burkill, *Mysterious Revelation*, 62ff. For literature on the 'crowd' in Mark, see Best, *Following Jesus*, 46 n.6.

not present them as a single, monolithic character group. We would propose that the perspective which governs Mark's depiction of the crowd is expressed in the parable of the sower (4:3–20), according to which the word of the kingdom suffers different fates among its recipients. Basically three kinds of response are envisaged: outright rejection (v 15), genuine acceptance (v 20), and a contingent reception of the word that, for various reasons, proves non-durable (vv 16–19), despite in some cases an initial enthusiasm (v 16). This alone would suggest that Mark considers Jesus' broad following to be something of a mixed bag. Accordingly, although for the most part the crowd responds favourably to Jesus, listening to his teaching (e.g. 2:13; 3:32; 4:1ff; 6:34; 7:14) and bringing their sick to him for healing (1:32ff; 3:9f; 6:53–6), and are considered by the ruling authorities to be supporters of Jesus (11:18; 14:2; cf. 11:32; 12:37–40), nevertheless not all who respond so enthusiastically possess true understanding (6:14; 8:27f) or durable faith. Eventually in Jerusalem the crowd or a faction of it turns against Jesus and is implicated in his arrest (14:43) and execution (15:6–15; cf. 15:29,35f).

In Mark's presentation, then, discipleship, 'twelveship' and localised allegiance are all derivative expressions of the universal demand for repentance and faith (1:15). He does not depict discipleship and faith as two different expressions of repentance,[1] nor does he consider repentance and discipleship as two distinct responses sought by Jesus.[2] Rather repentance and faith find different forms of concrete expression and are fundamental to each form. With this background in mind, we are better able to understand an otherwise obscure reference to believers in 9:42.

Believing little ones (9:42)

Included in the teaching that forms the sequel to the second passion prediction (9:33–50) is a threat of severe punishment for offences against 'believing little ones':

> For whoever causes one of these little ones who believe [in me] to stumble, it would be better for him if a great millstone were hung around his neck and he were thrown into the sea.   (v 42)

---

[1] As Goppelt suggests of the synoptic tradition generally, *Theology*, I, 208.
[2] As Hengel suggests of the historical Jesus, *Charismatic Leader*, 62.

The recipients of this ominous warning are the Twelve (cf. v 5). But who are 'these little ones possessing faith' (ἕνα τῶν μικρῶν τούτων τῶν πιστευόντων)? And how are the Twelve at risk of scandalising them?

In identifying the μικροί, our concern is with the internal narrative reference of the term, not its 'original' or traditional meaning. It is generally accepted that in composing 9:33–50, Mark has utilised a collection of sayings already joined together by the catchword principle and by poetic parallelism, rather than by strict logical association.[1] How far Mark has extended this catchword composition, and the extent to which he has reworked the sayings themselves, is virtually impossible to say.[2] However the fact that he presents the material in the form of an extended discourse (cf. 9:33 and 10:1) suggests that he intends some logical progression in the sequence of elements, while his use of two references to discord among the disciples as an *inclusio* around the discourse (9:34,50) gives it a certain unity of thought.

Verse 42 itself has two main clues as to the identity of the μικροί – the use of the articular participle of πιστεύειν, which recalls the only other occasion in Mark where this construction occurs, in the dialogue with the father of the epileptic boy (9:32); and the demonstrative adjective τούτων, which implies that the μικροί have been referred to earlier in the text. This is because in its present setting, the expression 'these believing little ones' acts as a summary designation for all the characters depicted in the preceding interchange between Jesus and the Twelve. This is apparent from the logical progression of the discourse up until this point and by the parallelism between the three 'whoever' sayings in vv 37,41,42 (ὅς ἂν + subj.). The story of the strange exorcist (vv 38–40) intervenes between the first and second of these sayings, which may have once stood adjacent,[3] and is linked to them by the key word ὄνομα. In its

---

[1] The catchwords include: ὄνομα (vv 37,38,39,41); παιδία, μικροί (vv 36,37,42); (ἐκ)βάλλειν (vv 38,42,45,47); σκανδαλίζειν (vv 42,43,45,47); καλόν ἐστιν (vv 42,43,45,47); πῦρ (vv 43,48,49), ἅλας (ἁλισθήσεται) (vv 49,50). Note also the extensive use of γάρ (vv 34,39,40,41,49). On Aramaic alliterations in the passage, see Black, *Aramaic Approach*, 169–71, 218–22.

[2] So Kee, *Community*, 42. Recent studies on the composition of the discourse include Catchpole, 'Poor on Earth', 361–73; Wenham, 'A Note on Mk 9:33–42', 113–18; Fleddermann, 'Discipleship Discourse', 57–75; Best, *Following Jesus*, 73–98.

[3] Some ascribe the insertion to Mark (e.g. Kuhn, *Ältere Sammlungen*, 186; Catchpole, 'Poor on Earth', 361; cf. Schmithals, *Markus*, II, 430f); others to a

present position, it serves to illustrate and widen the scope of the παιδία and μικροί sayings that flank it. Verse 41 functions in a similar way.

The first group of characters included in the μικροί designation are the 'children' Jesus speaks of in vv 36ff. A dispute has developed among Jesus' followers over who is the greatest (v 34). The fact that Jesus reacts by summoning the Twelve (v 35) and reproving them as a group about their attitude to people outside their circle, could suggest that the argument was the result of the Twelve asserting their priority over other followers whom they regarded in a lesser light to themselves. After ruling that those who would be first must be last of all and servant of all (v 35), Jesus sets a child in their midst and declares that to receive 'one such child' in his name is the same as receiving Jesus himself and even the One who sent Jesus (vv 36f).

There is some debate as to whom the phrase ἕν τῶν τοιούτων παιδίων refers.[1] The action with the child in v 36 suggests ordinary children; yet the use of a *shaliach*-based principle in v 37 and mission-type terminology like δέχεσθαι (cf. 6:11; 10:14) and 'in my name' (cf. vv 38f), is more indicative of disciples or missionaries. This merging of features, often ascribed to a traditio-historical or redactional change of reference in the saying from disciples to children, or vice versa,[2] makes some sense within the horizons of the immediate story world. For here Jesus' wider body of adherents and sympathisers evidently includes children[3] as well as men and women (10:29f – νῦν ἐν τῷ καιρῷ τούτῳ . . . τέκνα; cf. 3:34f; 10:13–16; 14:51f [?]). The παιδίον Jesus uses to illustrate his teaching presumably belongs to the company of adherents since he is present with the Twelve in the house at Capernaum, the setting in Mark usually associates with the private instruction of the disciples (e.g. 1:29ff; 2:15; 3:19,31ff; 7:17; 9:28f; 10:10). Since in the ancient world children were regarded as the least significant

---

pre-Markan editor (e.g. Best, *Following Jesus*, 80–2; Nineham, *Mark*, 253; Anderson, *Mark*, 235f).

[1] For the various options, see Légasse, *Jésus et L'Enfant*, 101–4.

[2] For various versions of this, see T. W. Manson, *The Sayings of Jesus* (Norwich: Jarrold & Sons, 1949) 78, 138ff; Taylor, *Mark*, 411, cf. 405; Bultmann, *History*, 142, 144; Catchpole, 'Poor on Earth', 372f.

[3] On the synoptic evidence generally, see Agourides, '"Little Ones"', 329–34.

members of society,[1] the young ones attached to Jesus' company would naturally be considered, in terms of existing
values, the very least of his adherents (cf. ἔσχατος v 35) and
would thus serve as a ready symbol (τοιοῦτος)[2] for all those in
Jesus' circle considered 'least great' in the eyes of the Twelve.
In a radical reversal of this evaluation, Mark deems service
and reception of the smallest members of Jesus' society –
children and those most like children in terms of status and
influence – to be the mark of true greatness. That these figures
belong to the community of faith is indicated by Jesus' (and
God's) complete self-identification with them, which according
to Mark's prevailing point of view demands the presence of
active faith (cf. 2:5; 5:34; 10:24). Further, if the phrase 'in my
name' qualifies 'one such child' rather than the act of receiving, which is possible,[3] it marks them out as those who confess
or appeal to the name of Jesus.

At this point Mark has one of the Twelve recount an episode
with an unknown exorcist who was appealing to the name of
Jesus and whose actions the disciples forbade (vv 38–40). Their
opposition to him was not only out of concern for Jesus' honour
but principally because 'he was not following us' – that is, he
did not belong to the circle of disciples specially commissioned
to cast out demons (3:15; 6:7,13). In their opinion, he was arrogating to himself what did not belong to him. Once more the
Twelve evidence a mistaken sense of their own importance or
greatness. Jesus resists such exclusivism. Access to kingdom
power (ποιήσει δύναμιν v 39) is not the sole prerogative of the
Twelve but open to all who adhere to Jesus' name. Such people
work not against the mission of Jesus and the Twelve (καθ'
ἡμῶν), but on behalf of it (ὑπὲρ ἡμῶν).

The strange exorcist is one who acts in genuine faith outside
the immediate following of Jesus (he is not a magician or a

---

[1] See Oepke, *TDNT*, v, 639–48; *Bill.* I, 569f, 607, 780ff; II, 373; Légasse, *Jésus
et L'Enfant*, 276ff, cf. 168ff.

[2] This correlative adjective should probably be given more of a comparative than a demonstrative force, as in 10:14f, where 'such' means 'these and
others who though not literal children, share the characteristics of children', (C. Brown, *NIDNTT*, I, 284).

[3] See the discussion in Via, *Ethics*, 83, 87f. The phrase, 'in my name' carries
the general sense of acting on behalf or in the authority of the one named;
the more specific nuances vary according to the context (such as, 'invoking
or calling upon', 'being commissioned by', 'fulfilling the will of', 'in
obedience to', 'in the sphere of the power of' etc). See Bietenhard, *TDNT*, v,
271; also Kelber, *Kingdom*, 114.

pagan).[1] His possession of faith is indicated by his appeal to
Jesus' name and by his success in exorcism. This success
shows how misplaced the disciples' claim to superiority is, for
their failure to deliver the epileptic boy (9:14–29) has already
demonstrated that special commissioning alone does not
guarantee power over demons. Faith, expressed as prayerful
dependence (9:28f), is the only key, and it is these elements that
account for the effectiveness of the unknown exorcist. He too is
'one such child' whom the Twelve must receive and one of the
'believing little ones' they are in danger of causing to stumble
by their elitist attitudes. Finally, in v 41 the group of 'believing
little ones' is expanded to include those who offer simple kindness to the disciples. That such action is cited as an example
(γάρ) of those who are 'for us', is motivated by the messianic
allegiance of the disciples (ἐν ὀνόματι ὅτι Χριστοῦ ἐστε),[2] and is
guaranteed an eschatological reward, all suggests that these
sympathisers belong to the circle of faith.

In sum, the μικροί are those characters who have responded
in faith to Jesus' message, some of whom may have joined
Jesus' broader following, but who, according to the human
standards of judgement used by the Twelve (cf. 8:33), and by
Mark's audience, rank of least account. They include believing
children and the humblest people who share their lack of
influence and power, those exercising kingdom power outside
the immediate following of Jesus, and all those who offer the
lowliest service to the itinerant disciples (cf. 6:7–10). In Mark's
total cast of characters, the μικροί stand in absolute contrast to
the μεγάλοι (10:42) who abuse the social and political power
they possess and refuse to reside faith in Jesus.

The description of these figures as 'believers' makes explicit
what is implied in the characterisation of them in the preceding verses, especially by their relation to the name of Jesus.
The constant reiteration of the phrase 'in my/your name' (vv
37,38,39,41) is echoed in the addition of the words εἰς ἐμέ after τῷ
πιστεύοντι in some weighty MSS of v 42.[3] Mark's preference for
unqualified faith language argues against the originality of

---

[1] As claim Hull, *Hellenistic Magic*, 72 n.101; Smith, *Magician*, 35; Rawlinson, *Mark*, 128f.

[2] The precise wording of v 41 is textually uncertain. ℵ* has ἐμοῦ instead of
Χριστοῦ. Many MSS also insert μοῦ after ἐν ὀνόματι (ℵ* C³ D W Δ Θ Φ fam[1,13],
28 565. *pc*).

[3] Included by A B C² L W Θ fam[1,13]. Metzger brackets the words, *Textual
Commentary*, 101f; cf. Lührmann, *Glaube*, 17.

these words and they probably reflect the influence of Matt 18:6. Nevertheless the addition accurately captures the emphasis of the preceding verses – the faith of the little ones places them in unique relation to the name or person of Jesus. Their faith is also apparent from their actions. In vv 38–41, the narrator firmly stresses the decisive importance of action inspired by faith, whether it be a successful work of power or a simple deed of kindness. Mark has already made clear that 'all things are possible τῷ πιστεύοντι' (9:23), and the little ones are termed οἱ πιστεύοντες because their faith manifests itself in manifold action.

With respect to these people, the Twelve are solemnly warned against 'scandalising' them. This means more than causing them to sin; it means causing them to abandon their faith, and thus their adherence to Jesus, and so lose their salvation.[1] To deprive another of his or her salvation carries the corresponding penalty, for 'the only thing more terrible than being drowned with a millstone about one's neck is damnation at the Last Judgement'.[2] So in the following sayings (vv 43–50) the Twelve are advised to subject all actions and behaviour that threaten the faith of the 'believing little ones', and hence their own salvation, to radical surgery. We now go on to examine the main passage in which Mark characterises the new society of Jesus as a community of faith.

3. The new community of faith

The first call story, which establishes the norm for discipleship, narrates the summoning of several disciples at the same time and in the same place, indicating that discipleship involves, besides personal conversion and faith, integration into a new discipleship community. Indeed the convening of a new community, in which the rule of God may be concretely and visibly realised, is the first thing Jesus does in Mark's story after the initial kingdom announcement.

Within the story world, this discipleship community is paradigmatic of the wider gospel movement which comprises all who adhere to Jesus' message in faith (cf. 13:37). At the same time it points beyond itself to the post-Easter community (cf. 1:17; 13:10), of which it forms the foundation and nucleus

[1] So Rawlinson, *Mark*, 130; Cranfield, *Mark*, 365; Nineham, *Mark*, 255; Ernst, *Markus*, 281; O'Connor, *Faith*, 33, 141 n.10.
[2] Stählin, *TDNT*, VII, 351.

(14:28; 16:7). Mark uses a variety of images or metaphors for this new community – house (e.g. 7:17; 9:28,33; 10:10), family (10:28–30; cf. 3:31–5), ship (4:35–41; 6:45–52; 8:14–21), flock (14: 27; cf. 6:34), and a temple not made with hands (14:58; 15:29). In addition to these, he depicts it as a community of miracle-working faith, prayer and forgiveness, which is destined to supplant the existing religious establishment centred on the temple cultus (11:20–5). This passage represents Mark's most extensive reflection on faith outside the miracle collection. Before examining this passage we shall consider its narrative setting, since an appreciation of this is crucial to its interpretation.

The narrative setting

The sayings on faith, prayer and forgiveness constitute a small discourse attached to the second half of the story of the cursing of the fig tree (11:12–14,20ff), which is the only miracle Jesus performs in the Jerusalem phase of his ministry. In a classic example of his intercalation technique,[1] Mark sandwiches the story of the 'cleansing' of the temple between the two parts of the fig tree episode, thereby establishing a mutually interpretative relationship between the dovetailed episodes and bringing the discussion on faith into connection with the whole complex.

The fig-tree episode has long troubled and perplexed commentators. Yet the symbolism and dramatic impact of the story would certainly not have escaped Mark's original audience, as the exhaustive study of W. R. Telford[2] makes clear. For them, the blasting of the fig tree could only be a token of eschatological judgement against the nation,[3] directed in this case, by means of the intercalated story, specifically against the corrupt temple cultus. Mark intends the elements of the story to have both a literal and a symbolic significance.[4] Only Jesus is said to be hungry because 'Jesus alone can demand faith'.[5] The absence of fruit on the tree, despite external appearances, typifies the spiritual barrenness at the religious

---

[1] On this technique, see above, pp. 91–2.

[2] Telford, *The Barren Temple and the Withered Tree* (1980). On the history of interpretation, see 1–38.

[3] Cf. Jer 8:12; Isa 28:3f; Mic 7:1; Joel 1:7,12; Hos 9:15f.

[4] Telford, *Barren Temple*, 205.

[5] Giesen, 'Feigenbaum', 104.

heart of the nation; 'fruitfulness' is Mark's metaphor for a believing response to Jesus' message (4:1–20; 12:1–12).[1] The incongruity of Jesus seeking figs, though 'it was not the season (καιρός) for figs', underlines the tragic paradox of Israel's plight in the story. Her καιρός of eschatological fulfilment (1: 15; 12:2) has not become the καιρός of her fruitfulness because her religious leaders have spurned the demand for repentance and faith.[2] Judgement now looms.

In cursing the fig tree, Jesus enacts parabolically for the benefit of the disciples the terminal condition of the Jerusalem cultus: 'henceforth no one will ever eat fruit from you again'. In the temple-cleansing scene, he enacts the same message publicly before the religious authorities. In Mark's presentation, Jesus' action in the temple is not merely a cleansing preparatory to its restoration, as anticipated in Old Testament-Jewish tradition,[3] but a definitive disqualification of its legitimacy.[4] In a prophetic-symbolic gesture prefiguring the ultimate cessation of the temple's normal functioning, Jesus closes down, at least momentarily and in one location, both the commercial and cultic sides of temple worship. He drives out the buyers, sellers and money-changers who provide the animals for sacrifice and money for offerings (v 15), and he prevents the carrying of vessels, probably sacred cult vessels bearing gifts and offerings,[5] through the temple (v 16).

---

[1] Telford, *Barren Temple*, 211f; Giesen, 'Feigenbaum', 106f.

[2] On the *Entscheidungscharakter* of καιρός in Mark, see Giesen, 'Feigenbaum', 105. Mark's comment is certainly not an indication that he 'has made a hash of the overall tale', as Meagher claims, *Clumsy Construction*, 67. Cotter, to the contrary, claims that by 11:13d, 'Mark has exerted a great deal of care to present Jesus' approach to the tree as a reasonable act', '"Season for Figs"', 65.

[3] Temple purification was associated with the restoration of the Israelite kingdom (2 Kg 18:4ff; 22:3–23:5; 2 Chron 29:12ff; 34:3ff; Neh 13:4–9), and the coming of the messianic kingdom (Ezek 22:8,26; 23:37–9; 37:6–8,40–8; Tb 14:5f; Jub 1:28f; En 90:28f; Sib Or 5:414–33; Pss Sol 17:33). See Telford, *Barren Temple*, 260f; Juel, *Messiah and Temple*, 169–209. Sanders argues that an expectation for the destruction and rebuilding of the Temple was also part of contemporary Jewish expectation, *Jesus*, 77–90.

[4] So Achtemeier, *Mark*, 24; Fleddermann, 'Warning About the Scribes', 63–6; Watty, 'Jesus and the Temple', 235–9; Kelber, *Mark as Story*, 60f; Gaston, *No Stone*, 82, 85f, 88; Schweizer, *Mark*, 233; Telford, *Barren Temple*, 93, 103, 261; Stock, *Discipleship*, 163–70.

[5] See Kelber, *Kingdom*, 100f; Achtemeier, *Mark*, 24; Telford, *Barren Temple*, 92f n.102. For the more traditional interpretation, see Taylor, *Mark*, 463.

The Jerusalem establishment stands condemned both for what the temple has become, 'a den of robbers', and for what it has not become, 'a house of prayer for all nations'. The 'den of robbers' charge is drawn from Jeremiah 7:11 and is intended to evoke the whole situation of moral degeneracy and religious hypocrisy which Jeremiah denounces and which leads to the destruction of the first temple, as a valid parallel for the corruption of the religious establishment of Jesus' day, which apparently includes the sanctioning of exploitative practices in the temple precincts by the merchants Jesus expels.[1] Jeremiah denounces those who 'trust in the temple of the Lord' (7:4,14), relying vainly on the maintenance of cultic practice as a way of evading Yahweh's displeasure at their lying, stealing, violence, adultery, and the like. Mark depicts Jesus condemning a similar false faith in cultic performance, for God's rule demands a repentant or ethically qualified faith (cf. 7:1–23) expressed in love of God and neighbour, which is more than all burnt offerings and sacrifice (12:28–34).

Such abuse of the temple has effectively abrogated its destined role as 'a house of prayer for all nations'. In applying this quotation from Isaiah 56:7 to Jesus' situation, the author plays upon both the imprecatory and predictive features of prophetic speech. On the one hand, the existing temple set-up is condemned. This is not just because the rights of Gentiles to use the outer court have been nullified by the location of commercial practices there.[2] And it is not because the temple has failed to have yet realised its eschatological destiny as a centre of universal worship.[3] Rather it is because its rulers have comprehensively failed to make it a genuine house of *prayer*, worthy of God's eschatological designs for the nations. In the Old Testament and post-exilic Judaism, the temple was regarded as a place where prayer was particularly efficacious.[4] But Mark insists that such efficaciousness is not

[1] The term ληστής means bandit, robber, insurrectionist (see *BAG*, 473; cf. Mk 14:48; 15:27). It seems inappropriate for sharp business practices, although it may imply here the use of official structures of violence to support extortion. Mark applies it principally to the temple authorities, not the merchants, though they may be implicated too. Some feel the term reflects the use of the temple as a Zealot stronghold during the siege of Jerusalem – Gaston, *No Stone*, 474; Barrett, 'House of Prayer', 13–20.

[2] So Giesen, 'Feigenbaum', 107; Lane, *Mark*, 403–5; Anderson, *Mark*, 266.

[3] See Achtemeier, *Mark*, 24f; Stock, *Discipleship*, 165ff.

[4] Cf. 1 Sam 1:1–28; 1 Kings 8:30–51; 2 Kings 19:14–33; Jon 2:7; Jud 4:9–15; 3 Macc 1:20–4. See Hre Krio, 'Prayer Framework', 326f.

simply dependent on the maintenance of cultic worship. By becoming a den of thieves and practising an exploitative and hypocritical piety, the Jerusalem temple has disqualified itself as the place where Isaiah's prophecy shall be fulfilled.

On the other hand, the prophetic prediction is reaffirmed. There shall indeed be a house of prayer open to all nations, not the temple house of Jerusalem, but the 'house' of Jesus ('my house'), the community of his disciples. Prayer is an activity in Mark almost exclusively associated with Jesus and the disciples (1:35; 6:46; 9:29; 11:24f; 13:33; 14:38; cf. 12:40), and the house is a regular setting for the instruction of the disciples (7:17; 9:28,33; 10:10) and the operation of kingdom power (1:29–31; 2:1–12). A replacement motif (cf. 12:9) is thus introduced to balance the rejection motif, and it is this that explains the ensuing discourse. In this double rejection-replacement motif, Mark draws a significant parallel between the fate of the temple and the fate of Jesus. It is Jesus' condemnation of the temple that unites priests and scribes to plot his condemnation and death (v 18); yet ironically it is this death that finally seals the condemnation of the temple (cf. 15:38) and the substitution of the new temple 'not made with hands' (14:58; 15:29).[1] (We will examine official reaction to Jesus' actions in the temple more closely in the next chapter).

Faith, prayer and forgiveness (11:20–5)

The intended connection of the sayings of faith, prayer and forgiveness with the fig-tree episode has often eluded Markan interpreters. Some think it is a matter of simple catchword linkage, with no real conceptual connection at all.[2] Others ascribe the sayings to a pre-Markan[3] or post-Markan[4] interpretation of the fig-tree miracle as an object lesson in the wonder-working power of faith and prayer, which is fundamentally at variance with Mark's own symbolic use of the story as a commentary on the temple incident. But the present placement of the sayings is more than an accident of tradition. Mark employs the material positively to give content to the new 'house of prayer' destined to supplant the old 'den of robbers'.

---

[1] On this expression, see Juel, *Messiah and Temple*, 143–57.

[2] E.g. Taylor, *Mark*, 24f; Nineham, *Mark*, 300; Roloff, *Kerygma*, 167f.

[3] Best, *Discipleship*; 42f; Anderson, *Mark*, 267f.

[4] Telford, *Barren Temple*, 40, 49ff, 59.

The passage begins with Peter's exclamation over the state of the cursed tree (vv 20f). The narrator goes to some lengths to indicate that Peter's outburst reflects on this occasion, not incomprehension,[1] but a profound sense of the portentousness of what he sees. Whereas in 8:18 the incomprehension of the disciples is typified as an inability to see, hear or remember the import of Jesus' deeds, here their positive 'hearing-seeing-remembering'[2] ties both halves of the fig-tree narrative together:

> (v 14) And his disciples heard . . . (v 20) And . . . they saw the fig-tree withered . . . (v 21) And Peter remembering said . . .

Peter's words are occasioned by the fact that the symbolic fig tree, which had only been consigned to fruitlessness by Jesus, has now completely withered from the roots up, and he wonders how such total destruction on the old order could be possible (cf. 13:1f).

Centrality of Faith

Jesus does not respond with an explanation of the miracle, but with a summons to participate in the activity of God: ἔχετε πίστιν θεοῦ (v 22). This verse is best taken as an independent imperative summoning faith in God. Although several important textual witnesses[3] place εἰ before ἔχετε, most scholars regard this as an assimilation to Lk 17:6 (cf. Matt 21:21). Even if it is accepted, εἰ is probably not an ordinary conditional particle since nowhere else is an ἀμήν-saying preceded by a protasis.[4] A few MSS also omit θεοῦ, and some exegetes consider this word to be a later scribal gloss.[5] This is the only

---

[1] As claim Ernst, *Markus*, 325f, 332; Giesen, 'Feigenbaum', 109, 111; Malbon sees it as 'lack of faith', 'Characters and Readers', 119.

[2] This is not mitigated by the fact that Mark uses different verbs for 'seeing' in 8:18 and 11:22; both verbs can carry a literal and a figurative sense in Mark (cf. 4:12).

[3] ℵ D Θ fam[13] 28. 33[c]. 565. 700 *pc* it sy[s].

[4] The particle could be interrogative ('Do you have faith in God?'), see Metzger, *Textual Commentary*, 109 n.1; or an aposiopesis, expressing a strong wish, ('if only you had faith in God') or an emphatic denial ('you have no faith at all'), see Telford, *Barren Temple* 120 n.4; or the imperative may be taken concessively ('Granted you possess faith in God, truly . . .'), see Black, *Aramaic Approach*, 90f.

[5] Lohmeyer, *Markus*, 239; Nineham, *Mark*, 305; Telford, *Barren Temple*, 57. The word is omitted in 28 a c k r[1] r[2] bo[ms].

place in the New Testament where θεοῦ occurs as an objective genitive after πίστις, and Mark himself usually prefers unqualified faith language. However the construction could have a Semitic *Vorlage*,[1] and Mark includes similar expressions of confidence in God's omnipotence elsewhere (10:27; 14:36). Here he presents God expressly as the object of a call to faith, although some thought of him as the source of faith may also be implied.[2]

This call to faith is, at the discourse level, conditioned by the preceding judgement-replacement theme. The disciples are beckoned to trust actively in God, for although the existing temple has been disqualified, *they* are the beginning of God's new 'house of prayer for all nations'. It is through their faith that God's eschatological work shall be brought to pass. Mark conceives of faith then not simply as the basis for entry to the new community, but as its continuing *modus operandi*.

This is dramatically illustrated in the subsequent adage about mountains being moved into the sea (v 23). This comment on faith, more than any other in the gospel tradition, has fascinated scholars, both for its elemental force and for its particularly strong claim to dominical origin.[3] Usually it is analysed from a traditio-historical perspective as an isolated logion, but our concern is with the meaning it carries as a result of its integration into Mark's narrative programme. It is important to recognise, however, that even within its Markan setting the saying stands apart as a kind of proverbial expression or metaphor placed on the lips of Jesus. Its proverbial ring derives from its solemn introductory formula (ἀμὴν λέγω ὑμῖν), its indeterminate reference ('whoever says . . .'), its vivid imagery, also used in contemporary Jewish proverbs, and the way in which the following verse derives a more generalised lesson from it. It is a characteristic of proverbial sayings to have their own encapsulated meanings independent of their

---

[1] See Jeremias, *Theology*, I, 161; Schlatter, *Glaube*, 586f.

[2] Cf. Powell, *Concept of Power*, 182f; Schlatter, *Glaube*, 587; Carrington, *Mark*, 244; O'Connor, *Faith*, 136. Derrett seems to take the expression to mean holding onto God with the faithfulness God displays towards humankind, *Making of Mark*, II, 193. Silva insists that an exegetical choice must be made between objective and subjective senses, *Biblical Words*, 150.

[3] E.g. Ebeling, 'Jesus and Faith', 229f; Perrin, *Rediscovering*, 137ff; Lohse, 'Glauben', 95; Lührmann, *Glaube*, 18f; Telford, *Barren Temple*, 118; Jeremias, *Theology*, I, 161. On the tradition-history of the logion, see Telford, *Barren Temple*, 95–109; Barth, 'Glaube und Zweifel', 271–6.

use in any given circumstance, yet to acquire added poignancy or significance when employed in a particular situation. Accordingly, Mark's mountain-moving saying achieves its narrative significance partly from the range of associations and comparisons the imagery and language themselves evoke, and partly from the ironical aptness of these associations to the point under discussion, namely the replacement of the old temple mount with a new eschatological community.

The imagery of the saying could have evoked various associations for Mark's audience. In Jewish circles the picture of moving mountains was used, both figuratively and literally, for feats of an exceptional, extraordinary or impossible nature.[1] Even more decisive for the Markan saying, with its flanking references to faith in God and to believing prayer, is the fact that in the Old Testament the establishing and moving of mountains is the work of God alone,[2] and the levelling of mountains is one of the characteristics of the eschatological age.[3] The mountain-moving saying applies this traditional imagery associated with the sovereign power and eschatological activity of God to 'whoever' speaks in faith. In the miracle stories, faith permits the reception of divine power; here faith enables the believer to dispose of that power, to exercise with respect to the mountain not just a prayer of petition but an authoritative word of power.

Some interpreters insist that Mark intends the idea of moving mountains to be taken literally; he is thinking of the disciples' power to perform major nature miracles.[4] But while real miraculous works are undoubtedly in view,[5] the saying's figurative language should not be 'flattened out' in this one-dimensional way. Powerful imaginative language is used elsewhere in the gospel (e.g. 7:27f; 9:42–8; 13:24–7), and as Tannehill explains, there is a whole strategy of communication involved with such language. Whereas 'plain speech' by-

---

[1] Telford documents examples in legal, legendary, thaumaturgical and eschatological contexts, *Barren Temple*, 109–19.

[2] E.g. Ex 19:18; Job 9:5; Pss 68:8; 90:2; 97:5; 114:4–7; 144:5; Jer 4:24; Nah 1:5.

[3] E.g. Ps 6:2,6; Isa 40:4; 49:11; 54:10; 64:1–3; Ez 38:20; Mic 1:4; Hab 3:6; Zech 14:1–4; cf. Jud 16:15 [LXX]; Sir 16:19; Bar 5:7.

[4] Coutts, 'Authority of Jesus and Disciples', 115–16; Beavis, 'Mark's Teaching', 140 ; cf. Dunn, *Jesus and the Spirit*, 72.

[5] Contra Derrett, who claims Mark uses the image metaphorically to denote the internalising of the desire to achieve messianic prosperity, *Making of Mark*, II, 192.

passes the imagination and works within established interpretations of the world, forceful and expressive language
administers an 'imaginative shock' which challenges old per-
ceptions and suggests new visions of reality. Imaginative
language seeks to

> touch those fundamental images, those prerational
> visions of self and the world, which determine how we
> think and what we are. Such force, in spite of some clear
> tendencies towards hyperbole in the Gospels, is not just
> a matter of shouting loudly and going to extremes. By a
> variety of means the Gospels speak with strong personal
> impact, challenging fundamental assumptions, thereby
> acquiring the imagination to awake from its slumbers
> and interpret the world anew.[1]

This is precisely the impact of the mountain-moving saying. By
ascribing to faith what is a prerogative of Yahweh alone, it
opens up the awe-inspiring proportions of the injunction to
have faith in God (v 22). It is not an invitation to a state of
placid reliance on God but to active participation in his kingly
dominion. For whoever moves mountains is, *ipso facto*, wield-
ing the creative and judging word of God himself.

Mark stresses that this cannot be done apathetically.
Between the conditional form, 'whoever says to this mountain',
and its consequence, 'it will be to him', is the lengthy and
unwieldy qualification: 'and does not doubt in his heart but
believes what he says will happen'. This condition has a very
precise focus. It does not relate to the believer's general state of
being but only to the situation in which he seeks to exercise
divine power. Undoubting belief is required specifically with
respect to the authoritative word (πιστεύῃ ὅτι ὃ λαλεῖ) addressed
to this mountain. When one seeks to activate God's omnipotence in a definite situation, there must be an enduring
conviction that the seemingly impossible will certainly happen.
This means the exclusion of any 'doubt in the heart', any
hesitancy, wavering, or ambivalence toward the efficacy or
authority of one's word to the mountain. To attempt a work of
power without being fully assured of its outcome brings no
guarantee of success.

Some exegetes feel that this emphasis on complete subjective
certainty runs the risk of transposing faith, and indeed mountain moving, into an outstanding human achievement, and for

[1] Tannehill, *Sword of His Mouth*, 1–58 (quote from p. 27).

this reason consider the mustard seed analogy of Matt 17:19f and Lk 17:5f more fitting.[1] Others consider the saying grossly unrealistic and destined to cruelly disappoint those who accept it. Mark himself, however, would probably understand faith's certainty as stemming from two things: a clear awareness of having been commissioned to exercise delegated authority (cf. 3:14f; 6:7,12f), and an implicit perception of God's will in a specific situation (cf. 1:38f,40f; 3:4; 14:36). The exertion of God's transcendent power, which faith seeks, is always subject to the constraint of God's will. The certainty of faith, in other words, presupposes revelatory insight into the divine intention, though this must be actualised by the believer's volitional commitment to refuse doubt and seek undivided faith (cf. 5:36; 9:22–4).

Now the placement and wording of the saying brings these background associations to bear specifically on the temple-replacement theme. The demonstrative 'this mountain' seems to imply that Jesus is to be thought of as pointing illustratively to a particular mountain. If so, and this need not be the case,[2] it is usually identified either as the Mount of Olives,[3] in accordance with Zech 14:4; cf. 4:7, or as the temple mount, Mount Zion.[4] It is unlikely to be an allusion to the Mount of Olives. Mark usually identifies this mountain by name, and in this part of his story it serves positively as the base from which he challenges the temple establishment (11:1,11f; 13:1–3; cf. 14:3ff). Also the fate of the mountain in 11:23 does not accord with that of the Mount of Olives in Zech 14:4, which moves north and south but not into the sea. A reference to the temple mount, on the other hand, is consistent with the preceding emphasis on the condemnation and supplanting of the existing temple cultus. In this connection, 11:23 exerts an 'imaginative shock' comparable to the withering of the fig tree. Faith in God is not directed towards the exaltation of the 'mountain of the

[1] E.g. Barth, 'Glaube und Zweifel', 274, 290f; Schweizer, *Mark*, 235; Anderson, *Mark*, 268.

[2] 'Das Sprichtwörtliche verbietet es zu fragen welcher Berge gemeint ist', Schmithals, *Markus*, II, 501. Cf. Schmid, *Markus*, 214; see also Matt 17:19f.

[3] E.g. Smith, 'No Time for Figs', 322; Lane, *Mark*, 410; Taylor, *Mark*, 466; Cranfield, *Mark*, 361; Ernst, *Markus*, 333; Beavis, 'Mark's Teaching', 139f.

[4] Carrington, *Mark*, 242f; Trocmé, *Formation*, 106; Kelber, *Kingdom*, 103–6; Telford, *Barren Temple*, 59; Gaston, *No Stone*, 475f; Lightfoot, *Gospel Message*, 78; Lohmeyer, *Lord of the Temple*, 101f.

Lord's house' above all other hills (Mic 4:1; Isa 2:2) but towards its casting down into the sea.

This shock is intensified by the significance of the sea in Mark's symbolic universe, where it represents forces hostile to faith and therefore the fitting place of judgement. It is upon the sea that the faith of the disciples is assaulted and tested (4:35–41; cf. 6:37–52; 8:14–21), with Jesus' authority being attested in his dominance over the elements (4:39; 6:49). The sea is where the demonised pigs rush to their deaths (5:13), and it is the preferred destiny for those who cause believing little ones to lose their faith (9:42). The verbal contacts between 9:42 (καὶ βέβληται εἰς τὴν θάλασσαν) and 11:23 (καὶ βλήθητι εἰς τὴν θάλασσαν) in particular corroborates the suggestion that the mountain going into the sea is a picture of judgement, and further implies that the cause of this judgement is its intransigent opposition to the faith of the kingdom community.[1]

For all this, 11:23 should not be equated with other references to the physical destruction of the literal temple (13:1ff; 14:58; 15:29).[2] If it is, it follows that the task of razing the temple to the ground rests with the disciples who are to seek its destruction through miracle-working faith. But Mark regards the ultimate demise of the temple as an act of God; Jesus foretells and enacts its downfall, but the suggestion that he will be instrumental in its commission is deemed by the narrator as false (14:57–9; 15:29). And the falsity is hardly because the responsibility really lies with his followers! Besides, the temple can be destroyed literally only once, whereas 11:23 promises mountain-moving power to anyone who believes, and the abiding validity of the promise is vouchsafed by the introductory ἀμήν-formula. Instead, Mark uses 'this mountain' as a figure for the unbelieving temple system as such, with its hostile ruling authorities and entrenched resistance to the message and demands of Jesus. One word of undoubting faith is sufficient to overcome the massive weight of such institutionalised opposition. For the strength of faith springs not from 'whoever' possesses it but from the God in whom it is placed and with whose work it joins. The 'war of faith' waged against the 'mountain of unbelief' anticipates and parallels God's final judgement on the literal temple, but it is not equivalent with it.

---

[1] It is not, as Gaston proposes, a symbol of the place of God's presence going out to the Gentiles, *No Stone*, 83f, 475f.

[2] Contra Kelber, *Kingdom*, 104; Telford, *Barren Temple*, 59; Trocmé, *Formation*, 59.

The praying community

If faith is the *modus operandi* of the eschatological community, prayer is the vehicle and expression of this faith; the community of faith is therefore a 'house of prayer'. Significantly, vv 24f do not enjoin prayer but presuppose it as the prevailing life-condition of the community (καὶ ὅταν στήκετε προσευχόμενοι). The present imperatives in vv 24f specify two conditions for answered prayer: faith and forgiveness.

(i) Verse 24 is not a simple restatement of v 23. Rather it extends the principle underlying the fiat of faith to the sphere of petitionary prayer. Just as the command of faith moves mountains, so the prayer of faith receives answers. The two sayings have a similar format:

v 23		*v 24*
ἀμὴν λέγω ὑμῖν	----	διὰ τοῦτο λέγω ὑμῖν
πιστεύῃ ὅτι	----	πιστεύετε ὅτι
ἔσται αὐτῷ	----	ἔσται ὑμῖν

A close relationship between faith and prayer is implicit in Mark's[1] alignment of the two sayings. Although the word of faith to the mountain is not itself couched as a petition, the faith and authority which give it its power derive ultimately from prayer (cf. 1:35 and 39; 6:41 and 43; 6:46 and 48; 14:32 and 36). What is exercised in faith before the mountainous obstacle must first be requested in prayer; otherwise it is no act of faith (cf. 9:18f,28f).

But v 24 is not only concerned with prayers to exercise or receive miraculous powers; it concerns the whole range of petitionary prayer (πάντα ὅσα προσεύχεσθε καὶ αἰτεῖσθε). A direct correlation is made between the certainty of the request (πιστεύετε ὅτι ἐλάβετε), and the certainty of the fulfilment (καὶ ἔσται ὑμῖν). The degree of certainty envisaged for the petition is conveyed grammatically by the proleptic use of the aorist

---

[1] Telford argues that v 24 could well be a later gloss, echoing Matt 7:7f or 18:19; 21:22 etc., *Barren Temple*, 54–6. However, (i) the textual evidence for its inclusion is overwhelming; (ii) awkward syntax and grammar in Mark are hardly evidence of a glossator's activity; the tendency in the textual tradition is towards smoothing out the syntax, e.g. ἐλάβετε to λαμβάνετε or λήμψεσθε; (iii) 'Diese Verbindung von Glaube und Gebet ist typisch für das Markusevangelium, wie sich in dem anderen Komplex der Wundergeschichten noch zeigen wird', observes Lührmann, *Glaube*, 19. The author's thought in 9:14–29 only makes any sense in light of 11:24 (although Telford suspects 9:29 as a scribal gloss too, 106f, 109).

ἐλάβετε in the ὅτι clause, indicating that the outcome is regarded with such certitude that it is assumed to have been realised even before the request is made.[1] Mark does not say that an absolute assurance that the request has already been granted is the unvarying prerequisite for all answered prayer. Rather he affirms that *when* prayer is made with such certitude, it is *always* answered, not by a cause-and-effect mechanism but because the believer's certainty, which is more than hopeful optimism, is firm evidence that the petition is in accord with God's will. 'Prayer is therefore for Mark the final and ultimate expression of faith because as dialogue with God it implies an unconditional commitment to the divine will.'[2] It is praying faith, rather than ceremonial prayer (12:40), that is to be typical of the new community.

The πιστεύειν ὅτι clauses in vv 23–4 underscore the concrete character of wonder-working and petitionary faith in Mark's conception. Essentially expressions of active trust in God (πίστις θεοῦ), such faith nevertheless demands rational assent, not to general theological propositions but to specific convictions concerning the concrete situation in which faith is exercised – that God wills *this* mountain moved, *this* specific prayer (e.g. 13: 18; 14:38) fulfilled. Inasmuch as Mark sees prayer as faith-verbalised, like faith it is not acquiescent acceptance of situations as given by God but urgent, confident request that divine power be set in motion. Mark envisages praying faith as the active redefining of what is possible, the transcendence of actual limitations.

(ii) When such prayer is offered, a second factor besides faith conditions its efficacy – forgiveness (v 25). If a person prays while failing to forgive others, that prayer will not be heard, for the person himself or herself remains unforgiven and therefore severed from God. The forgiveness of God is consequent upon the petitioner's forgivingness, for, as Schmithals notes, Mark holds the belief, attested also in Judaism, that divine and human forgiveness form a unity.[3] One must live out the forgiveness of God in human relationships, or else the pardon one has received is denied and nullified. This ethical orientation of faith-inspired prayer is consistent with Mark's broader treatment of these themes. True faith is repentant faith, entailing

---

[1] See M. Zerwick, *Biblical Greek* (Rome: Pontificio Institutio Biblico, 1979), s.257; cf. Gnilka, *Markus*, II, 125.

[2] Schreiber, *Theologie des Vertrauens*, 241.

[3] Schmithals, *Markus*, II, 501.

the redirection of one's life in both its ethical and religious dimensions (1:15). When such faith is exhibited, divine forgiveness is secured (2:5,11f); when it is refused, divine pardon is withheld (3:28f; 4:11f; cf. 2:5–10). The existing religious establishment, centred on a failed house of prayer (11:17), has leaders who honour God with their lips (7:6) and say long prayers for pretence (12:40), yet pervert the law (7:9–13) and devour widows' houses (12:38–40; cf. 41–4). Incumbent therefore on the new house of prayer for all nations is the practice of forgiveness, not only toward fellow members but toward anyone against whom aught is held.

Summary

In the sequel to the cursing-cleansing complex, the focus shifts from the corrupt temple community to the new eschatological community of Jesus, which has become the locus of salvation. In this community faith is not only the sole criterion for entrance, enabling it genuinely to be 'for all nations'; it is also the concrete means by which the community itself functions. Through miracle-working faith, the community gains a share in the cosmic dominion of God himself and is empowered to overcome the mountain of unbelief represented by the institutional cultus. The vehicle of faith is prayer. Prayer is the source of its power, the sovereignty of God its only limitation. Therefore to pray in the certainty of faith is to be assured of being heard. The power of praying faith, however, is not for thaumaturgical display but, as always in Mark, is ethically conditioned. Only those who pray in a forgiving spirit are heard; only to them is divine power released.

Excursus: the status of verse 25

The contribution of the saying on prayer and forgiveness to Mark's faith theme would, of course, be vitiated if v 25 was not part of the text he produced. Its sequel, v 26, is almost universally regarded as a post-Markan scribal gloss based on Matt 6:15 and occasioned by the similarity of v 25 with Matt 6:14, and a number of scholars have proposed that v 25 is also a later scribal addition, though by a different scribe.[1] There are three

---

[1] See Telford, *Barren Temple*, 51–3, 58; Sparks, 'Divine Fatherhood', 244f; Klostermann, *Markus*, 119; cf. Bultmann, *History*, 25, 61; Nineham, *Mark*, 305.

main supports for this suggestion. (i) The vocabulary and phraseology of v 25 are distinctly 'Matthean' and unparalleled elsewhere in Mark. The phrase ὁ πατὴρ ὑμῶν ὁ ἐν τοῖς οὐρανοῖς occurs some twenty times in Matthew but only here in Mark, and παράπωμα is a *hapax legomenon* in Mark, yet found in Matt 6:14f. Other expressions in v 25 are also reminiscent of various passages in Matt 5-6. (ii) Matthew follows Mark in this pericope only as far as v 24, which would suggest that his copy of Mark did not include vv 25f. (iii) The subject matter of v 25 seems unrelated to that of the fig-tree episode and its sequel.

Although these observations place a question mark beside the originality of the verse, there is sufficient reason to give v 25 the benefit of the doubt.

(i) The external evidence for its genuineness is unassailable. No textual authorities omit it, in contrast to v 26.

(ii) Unlike v 26, which is an almost exact parallel to Matt 6:15, v 25 differs from Matt 6:14 a good deal more than is usually the case in scribal harmonisations or interpolations.[1] This may be due to the scribe working from memory, but it is difficult to see what would have called Matt 6:14 to mind in the first place. Neither προσεύχεσθαι nor αἰτεῖσθαι are found there, and the immediate Matthean setting, the Lord's Prayer, is not about praying in faith or the power of prayer. Conversely there is no mention of forgiveness in Mark 11:24. Even if v 25 is not based solely on Matt 6:14 but is a pastiche of elements drawn from Matthean logia on prayer and forgiveness (Telford), the difficulty of accounting for its interpolation remains.

(iii) Matthew does not follow Mark so slavishly in his parallel to this pericope that the omission of v 25 necessarily indicates its absence in his *Vorlage*. Matthew deviates from Mark considerably already in v 24 (Matt 21:22), and the omission of v 25 may be because this teaching on prayer is covered in Matt 6:14f.

(iv) Some exegetes feel that the similarity of v 25 with Matt 6:14 reflects Mark's knowledge of the Lord's Prayer,[2] although this would require an acquaintance with the Matthean version (cf. Lk 11:2) and it is hard to conceive of Mark omitting the Prayer from his gospel if he knew of it. It is possible, however, that v 25 was available to him as an independent logion whose formulation had been shaped by liturgical language also used

---

[1] Stendahl, 'Prayer and Forgiveness', 76f.

[2] E.g. Taylor, *Mark*, 467; Rawlinson, *Mark*, 159; cf. Schmithals, *Markus*, II, 503.

in the Lord's Prayer (παράπτωμα is a *hapax legomenon* in Matthew too [cf. 18:35 *v.l.*], and the phrase 'your father in heaven', though a Matthean favourite, was not invented by him; it was common Jewish-Aramaic).[1]

(v) The language of v 25 is not totally un-Markan. Jeremias[2] ascribes καὶ ὅταν στήκετε προσευχόμενοι to Mark since he is the only synoptist to use στήκω (3:31; 11:25), and ὅταν with the indicative (3:11; 11:19,25). Telford[3] still asserts that ὅταν στήκετε is 'distinctly non-Markan', citing rather fine syntactical distinctions between v 25 and the comparable constructions in 3:11 and 11:19. But since this syntax and verb are extremely rare elsewhere in the New Testament, yet attested on more than one occasion in Mark, it seems natural to accept the Markan provenance of the construction in v 25.

(vi) We have outlined the thematic coherence of v 25 with its broader Markan context. One further observation may be added here. The notion in v 25 that divine forgiveness is conditioned by fraternal behaviour serves to anticipate the following pericope in which Jesus asks the religious authorities whether John's baptism, which was for the forgiveness of sins (1:4), was from heaven or from a human source. The linguistic parallel between v 25 and vv 30f (ἐν τοῖς οὐρανοῖς v 25, cf. ἐξ οὐρανοῦ vv 30f) and the the thematic association of divine forgiveness facilitates the transition from one pericope to the other.

Taken together, these points add internal probability to the overwhelming weight of external evidence to support the presence of v 25 in the original text of Mark. It may therefore be justifiably included in our description of the faith theme in Mark's narrative.

4. Conclusion: faith and discipleship

In Mark's story faith and discipleship are distinguishable but inseparable realities. Not all who display faith become disciples, but all who become disciples require faith. Following Jesus entails both an initial act of conversion and faith, and the on-going maintenance of the same attitude, by which the

[1] On Matthew's formula, see Traub, *TDNT*, V, 538. For the notion of a liturgically shaped logion, see Stendahl, 'Prayer and Forgiveness', 77 n.8; Lane, *Mark*, 410f.

[2] Jeremias, *The Prayers of Jesus* (London: SCM, 1967) 39 n.53.

[3] Telford, *Barren Temple*, 51f.

disciples may carry out the tasks laid upon them. Despite the limited number of explicit references to the subject, Mark clearly regards faith as the controlling and integrating factor in discipleship existence.

One gauge of the importance of faith in Mark's conception of discipleship is the way he mentions it in connection with each of the major temporal phases his narrative envisages. By bracketing the Galilean narrative with two units relating faith to following (1:14–20; 10:46–52), he underscores its importance for their participation in Jesus' earthly ministry. In the Jerusalem section, where the locus of salvation is shifted from the existing religious establishment to the circle of Jesus' adherents, faith, prayer and forgiveness are given as the distinguishing characteristics of the new community (11:12–25). In the eschatological discourse, which telescopes the post-Easter period right up until the parousia, the elect are those who maintain faith in Messiah Jesus and deny it to all others (13:5–23). Those who endure to the end will be saved (13:13), though the disciples have earlier been warned of eternal judgement should they, through their arrogance and exclusivism, cause one of the 'little believers' in Jesus' company to lose their faith (9:33–42).

In this discipleship material, faith has the character of a relationship of trustful dependence on Jesus for provision, protection, instruction and ultimate salvation. At heart it involves the voluntary assumption of social powerlessness, comparable to the powerlessness of those in the miracle narratives. For in Mark, faith is the power of those without power, and it is experienced as power only in relation to human powerlessness. This power is expressed not only in miraculous mountain moving and omnipotent prayer (11:23f), but also in following Jesus on the way of the cross (10:52). In both these respects – miracles and suffering – the example of Jesus is the pattern for the disciple.

Another leading feature of discipleship faith is complete fidelity to Jesus. The personal bond between disciple and master is one of faith, entailing an exclusive allegiance to Jesus, a sharing in his destiny, and a continuing reliance upon him for material needs and for participation in the consummated kingdom. Discipleship faith is ultimately faith in God (11:22) and participation in his eschatological activity, both as the companions of Jesus during his ministry, and as the community of Jesus, the 'temple not made with hands', after his resurrection. Faith is fundamental to this new community, not just as the basis of entry but as the very means by which the community operates. The massive, institutionalised power of the existing religious establishment must give way to the kingdom community whose power lies solely in faith-borne prayer.

6 THE NATURE OF UNBELIEF

The call to conversion and faith, which commences Mark's story of Jesus, is comprehensive in its intent. All who appear in the drama are subject to the demand and all, except perhaps demons,[1] have the opportunity to respond. Up until this point we have been principally concerned with examining the positive response to the call by minor characters in situations of extreme need and by the disciples. But at the very outset of the story an ominous note is also sounded. By launching the kingdom programme against the backdrop of the 'handing over' of John the Baptist (1:14), who also demanded repentance (1:4), the narrator warns us that the eschatological initiative of God has already encountered opposition. Similar opposition to Jesus soon begins to emerge (2:6ff) and in 9:19 the entire generation which Jesus addresses is evaluated as chronically 'faithless' (γενεὰ ἄπιστος), locked fast in unbelieving resistance to the reality and demands of the dawning kingdom (cf. 8: 12,38). In this chapter we will examine six passages which deal with the issue of unbelief. But first by way of introduction something may be said about the larger pattern which the motif of unbelief creates in the narrative.

The intersection of the universal demand for faith and the entrenched unbelief of the contemporary age has two main effects in Mark's story. First it creates a distinction between 'insiders' and 'outsiders' (3:31–5; 4:10–12), between those who perceive the mystery of God's kingly presence in Jesus and respond in repentant faith, and those who do not. The dividing line falls unexpectedly. Those physically closest to Jesus, his kith and kin, and those supposedly closest to God, the religious leaders, are consigned to the outside, while publicans, sinners and fishermen are found on the inside. It is important to note,

---

[1] 'The demons, although grasping the truth, are . . . volitionally so corrupt that they cannot bring themselves to repentance and faith', Burkill, *New Light*, 162.

however, that Mark does not simply divide his cast of characters into two fixed, mutually exclusive groups. The inside/outside categories denote rather two ideological or existential positions which actors may adopt (cf. ἔξω στήκοντες 3:31) with respect to the message and demands of Jesus. Even the disciples, who have been given the mystery of the kingdom, frequently relapse into the faithlessness (4:40; 9:18) and incomprehension of outsiders (cf. 8:17–21 and 4:11f). Conversely some religious dignitaries exhibit the understanding (12:28–34), faith (5:36), and actions (15:43–6) appropriate to those inside the kingdom community, and a member of Jesus' family is present at the crucifixion[1] (cf. 15:40 and 6:3).

Secondly the collision between the call to faith and the resistance of the unbelieving age generates tremendous conflict between Jesus and those who represent the interests and standards of judgement of the γενεὰ ἄπιστος. This conflict takes different forms depending on whether Jesus is in dialogue with the demons, whom he dominates, the disciples, whom he instructs, or the religious authorities, with whom he debates. But behind these conflicts lies a fundamental contest between the power of the kingdom and the only power able to withstand it: the power of unbelief (cf. 6:5f). Mark's depiction of unbelief is best viewed in such dynamic, combative terms. For he seems to conceive of unbelief not so much as a fixed state of existence but as an active power, which some characters are held fast by, and which others, in spite of their initial faith commitment, remain ever vulnerable to. Hence at different points in the story Mark predicates unbelief of the crowds, the opponents of Jesus, and even the disciples. Before examining the material relating to opponents and disciples in some detail, we should recall the element of unbelief among the crowd evident in some of the miracle stories we have already looked at.

The motif of unbelief among spectators or members of the crowd is particularly pronounced in the Jairus story (5:21–43).[2] In proportion as this story moves forward, Jesus eliminates the unbelieving world from witnessing his work of power. First he excludes the messengers who bring news of the girl's death and who implicitly call into question the capacity of the 'teacher' to help (vv 35–7). Then at Jairus' house, he reacts forcefully to a second expression of unbelief from the mourners

---

[1] On this identification, see Fenton, 'Mother of Jesus', 434f. Her presence is meant to be evaluated positively, however. See p. 207 below.

[2] See above, pp. 97–9.

who laugh scornfully at his perspective on the girl's plight: he
expels them from the house (v 40). The emphatic position of
αὐτὸς δέ at the head of the sentence and the choice of the strong
verb ἐκβάλλειν – used some eleven times in Mark for driving
out demons (cf. also 1:12,43; 11:15; 12:8) – underlines the
strength of Jesus' oppposition to unbelief, and implies that the
banishment of unbelief is an important part of his assault on
Satan's kingdom.

The role of the unbelieving mourners in the Jairus narrative
is paralleled in the story of the epileptic boy (9:14–28) by the
members of the crowd who declare that the youth Jesus has
just exorcised is dead (v 26). It is the convergence of this crowd
that hastened Jesus into action in the first place (v 25), and
their judgement on the situation expresses the perspective of
the 'faithless generation' which they represent (v 19). Inasmuch as the 'raising' of the dead youth and raising of Jairus'
daughter are used by Mark to prefigure the raising of Jesus,[1]
the reaction of the outsiders in both stories foreshadows the
scepticism which the author anticipates will greet news of
Jesus' resurrection, beyond the end of the story.

In the other miracle narratives we have examined, the faith
of the petitioner is often set off in contrast to the attitude of
other participants in the episode. But this is more of a dramatic device to enhance the response of the petitioner and tells
us little about what Mark conceives unbelief to be. In a number
of pericopae relating to Jesus' opponents and to the disciples
however, the notion of unbelief is in the foreground, and to
these episodes we now turn.

1. The unbelief of Jesus' adversaries

Before examining the four passages in which the attitude of
Jesus' opponents is expressly diagnosed as unbelief, we should
consider the broader thematic context of which they are a part.

Narrative role and characterisation of Jesus' opponents

The major antagonists of Jesus in Mark's story are the ruling authorities: scribes, Pharisees, Herodians, chief priests,
elders, Sadducees, the High Priest and the Sanhedrin, as well
as Herod, Pilate and the Roman soldiers. Each of these groups
could be characterised individually, but they fulfil the same

---

[1] See above, pp. 99–100; 122–3.

overall function in the plot and, with a few notable exceptions, are evaluated by the narrator in the same negative terms.[1]

Collectively, these characters work against the establishment of God's new order. They refuse to acknowledge the authority of Jesus (1:22; 2:10; 11:28ff) and accuse him of blasphemy (2:7; 14:64), unlawful conduct (2:24; 3:1–5), disregard for tradition (2:16,18; 7:5), and demonic possession (3:22). Because of their hardness of heart (3:5; cf. 8:15 and 17f; 10:5) and their unwillingness to repent (4:11f; 11:30ff; cf. 2:17), they cannot accept God's kingly presence in Jesus' works of restoration (2:1–12; 3:1–5; 9:14), and demand instead signs of their own design (8:11f; 15:30ff). They regard themselves as guardians of Israel's law and cult, but they are deceitful, hypocritical, and preoccupied with preserving their own power (7:1–13; 11:17f; 12:13,15,38–40). They are ruthless in their prosecution of their enemies (6:14–28; 12:1–12; 13:9–11; 15:10ff). They not only seek the life of Jesus without just cause (3:6; 8:31; 10:32; 11:18; 12: 12), but are prepared to use trickery (12:13; 14:1f), treachery (14:10f,44f), perjury (14:55f), mob rule (14:43–50; 15:11–15), and the machinery of the heathen state (15:1–15) to secure it. They then mock and deride the victim in his agony (15:27–36; cf. vv 16–20).

This starkly negative portrayal of the Jewish leadership groups is frequently seen as part of a polemic by Mark against Judaism or Jewish-Christianity,[2] or even as outright anti-Semitism.[3] But this is an inadequate explanation of Mark's narrative strategy. The great majority of Mark's characters are Jewish by race and religion, and the fact that Jesus sanctions priestly practice (1:44), occasionally advocates Mosaic teaching (7:10–13; 10:17–19; 12:28–34), ministers in synagogues (1:21,39; 3:1; 6:2; cf. 13:9), and enjoys popularity with the Jewish crowds (e.g. 1:45; 3:7; 6:31; 11:18), argues against a thoroughgoing anti-Jewish polemic[4] (even if the

---

[1] See Rhoads and Michie, *Mark as Story*, 117–22; Senior, '"Swords and Clubs"', 14–17; cf. Cook, *Jewish Leaders*, 16, 21, 79.

[2] E.g. Trocmé, *Formation*, 87–119; Fenton, 'Paul and Mark', 98f, 102; Burkill, *Mysterious Revelation*, 118f, 123, 224f, 227, 323; idem, *New Light*, 126, 129, 146f, 164f; cf. Hultgren, *Adversaries*, 180–4.

[3] See, e.g., Burkill, *New Light*, 78 n.11; S. G. F Brandon, *Jesus and the Zealots. A Study in the Political Factor in Primitive Christianity* (Manchester University Press, 1967), 279f. S. Sandmel, *Anti-Semitism in the New Testament*, (Philadelphia: Fortress Press, 1978), 25–48.

[4] See esp. Baarlink, 'Antijudaismus im Markusevangelium', 166–93.

content of Jesus' debates with his adversaries would have been useful for Mark's audience in its Christian self-definition *vis-à-vis* Judaism).[1] This does not mean that the theme of Jewish rejection of Jesus is absent from Mark's story. As we shall see, the episodes with Jesus' family (3:21,31ff) and *patris* (6:1–6), together with some other references and allusions (e.g. 7:3,6; 14:43; 15:11ff), are probably intended to prefigure the repudiation of the Messiah by the whole nation. But Mark points the accusing finger for this not at the Jewish people as such, but specifically at her religious leaders; it is the abuse of power by those in positions of authority that he is most concerned to highlight. Nor is his reproach confined to the *Jewish* religious groups alone. Three types of civil authorities appear in Mark's story – Herod Antipas, the Herodians and the Romans – and each of these is also depicted in a critical light (3:6; 6:14–29; 10:42; 12:16; 13:9; 15:1–20; cf. 5:9; 12:17). Pilate may be more reluctant to see Jesus crucified than the Jewish authorities are, but Mark's intention is hardly to exonerate Roman involvement in the crime, for he narrates at length how Jesus is condemned to death by the Roman governor, mocked and tortured by Roman soldiers and put to death by a Roman execution squad.[2]

Within the story world, what is most characteristic of Jesus' opponents is not race or religion, but the fact that they occupy positions of religious, political and military power within the ruling establishment of Palestine, both Jewish and Gentile.[3] The basis of their conflict with Jesus is not purely theological in nature, for it must be remembered that the religious leaders of the day also exercised social and political power. The law of

---

[1] See, e.g., Dunn, 'Jesus and Paul', 400–3.

[2] So also Senior, '"Swords and Clubs"', 15–17; Myers, 'Obedience and Upheaval', VI, 34–6.

[3] See further Rhoads and Michie, *Mark as Story*, 79–89, 117–22; Kee, *Community*, 113, 146–51; Weeden, *Traditions in Conflict*, 20; Juel, *Messiah and Temple*, 212f. Even Burkill concedes that Mark's 'anti-Semitic feeling is tempered through the influence of an implicit distinction between government and people', *New Light*, 100f, 174. Similarly Hare writes that 'it is the religious leaders whom Mark castigates, not Israel as a whole', and concludes that 'Mark contains only the barest traces of prophetic and Jewish-Christian anti-Judaism, and not the slightest evidence of that gentilizing anti-Judaism that was later to dominate Christian theology' [p.33, 35], 'The Rejection of the Jews in the Synoptic Gospels and Acts', in A. T. Davies, *Anti-Semitism and the Foundations of New Testament Christianity* (New York/Toronto: Paulist Press, 1979), pp.27–47.

Moses was the law of the land; the temple was the centre of spiritual and civil authority for the nation and the power-house of the Jerusalem economy; the Sanhedrin was the major arm of local government; and the Jerusalem authorities were responsible finally to the Roman procurator. Within this setting, Jesus' message and lifestyle, his disregard for certain traditions and customs, his reinterpretation of the law, his claim to messianic authority, and his high-handed action in the temple would be perceived not simply as an offence to religious sensibilities, but as a challenge to the very corner-stones of Jewish society and ultimately to Roman provincial peace.

In the narrator's evaluation, it is those with vested interests in the existing order who are most antagonistic to Jesus' proclamation of the rule of God. They have most to lose from his claim to embody and represent that rule (12:1–12), and from his call for submission to it (faith) and for the reordering of existing social and personal relationships consequent upon it (repentance). The way God expresses his rule in Jesus collides head-on with the way the civil and religious rulers exercise theirs (cf. 9:35f; 10:15,31 and 10:42; 13:9), and it is this that generates conflict in the story. Jesus provokes political opposition because his message challenges the legitimacy of the way in which the existing religio-political establishment exercises its ruling power.

In Mark's account the scribes are the main or typical opponents of Jesus. They are mentioned more frequently than any other group;[1] they alone are active throughout the entire plot (1:22; 15:31) and provide the unifying link between the opponents in the first and second parts of the gospel (8:31; 10:33); only they are denounced as a group (12:38–40; cf. 7:6ff) and negatively contrasted by the people with Jesus (1:22); and it is against them that the charge of the eternal sin is laid (3:28–30). They appear to be legal experts (2:7,16; 7:1ff; 9:11; 12:28ff,35ff), and the extent of their hatred for Jesus is underscored by their seemingly improbable alliance with the priestly aristocracy (8:31; 10:33; 11:18,27; 14:1,43,53; 15:1,31; cf. 14:10; 15:3,11) as well as with the Pharisees (2:16; 7:1). The scribes are the first to appear in conflict with Jesus, and it is in connection with them that the narrator first evaluates such opposition in terms of unbelief.

[1] For the comparative statistics, see Cook, *Jewish Leaders*, 66.

Unbelief in Capernaum (2:1–12)

In our previous discussion of 2:1–12, we examined the literary structure of the pericope as a whole and noted how the duplicate framing verses around the central controversy section serve to establish a contrast between the faith of the paralytic and the unbelief of the questioning scribes.[1] We shall now look more closely at the unbelieving response of the scribes.

The central controversy section also exhibits a balanced literary structure. The scribes debate in their hearts two unspoken questions, beginning with τί and τίς respectively (vv 6–7), and Jesus responds with two counter-questions beginning with τί (vv 8–9). Furthermore, as Maisch observes,[2] the section has two high-points which are related as question and answer. The scribal ruminations climax in the question 'who but God can forgive sins?' (v 7), which is meant rhetorically, implying the negative reply 'no one', while the response of Jesus climaxes in the Son of Man saying (v 10), which answers the scribal question in positive terms: 'not only God but also the Son of Man'. The pattern then is as follows:

Who but God? The Son of Man!

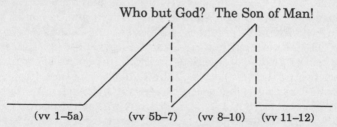

(vv 1–5a)   (vv 5b–7)   (vv 8–10)   (vv 11–12)

The Son of Man saying is therefore part of the rhetorical structure of the debate with the scribes and is addressed directly to them. It is not a parenthetical aside to Mark's readers or a later interpolation.[3] Mark intends the response of the scribes to Jesus' declaration of forgiveness to be seen as a fundamental expression of unbelief, in contrast to the πίστις of the paralytic and his party (v 5). Wherein then lies this unbelief?

---

[1] See above, pp. 83–6.

[2] Maisch, *Heilung des Gelähmten*, 80f, 101f. See also Dewey, *Public Debate*, 70.

[3] As advocated by: Perrin, 'High Priest's Question', 92; idem, 'Christology of Mark', 477, 481 n.24; Lane, *Mark*, 96ff; Cranfield, *Mark*, 96, 100; Trocmé, *Formation*, 173; Hay, 'Son of Man', 71f; cf. Anderson, *Mark*, 101; Theissen, *Miracle Stories*, 164, 192; Schmithals, *Markus*, I, 151ff.

(a) The portrayal of unbelief

The passive formulation of the pronouncement of forgiveness is ambiguous and thus invites interpretative involvement from its hearers. Jesus could be making a declarative judgement about an act of God, or else exercising the divine prerogative himself.

If the former is the case, Jesus would in effect be arrogating to himself the task of the High Priest, who had power to proclaim God's forgiveness on the basis of repentance and sacrifice (Lev chs. 4, 5, 16, 17:11). In this connection, some exegetes interpret the scribes' response as an objection to Jesus' encroachment on the cultic domain[1] or to his granting of forgiveness without demanding restitution and expiation[2] (cf. 2 Sam 12:12–23). But even if Jesus' action was an infringement of cultic jurisdiction, Mark makes it clear by the wording of the scribes' question, 'who is *able* (δύναται) to forgive sins but God alone?' (v 7), that what they are reacting to is Jesus' implicit claim to possess the ability to remit sins, which of right belongs to God alone. In this deduction they were quite correct. Since Jesus was obviously not a priest and did not require the man to offer sacrifice at the temple, he could not be declaring divine forgiveness within the provisions of the law; since he did not promise the man forgiveness at the end of time on the grounds of penitent action, but spoke of forgiveness as an event already accomplished in the present (ἀφίενταί)[3] without ceremony, he was plainly not acting in a prophetic-symbolic capacity (cf. 1:4); and since it was not anticipated that the Messiah or any other eschatological figure would possess authority to pardon sins,[4] the only conclusion left was that Jesus was venturing to exercise the divine privilege himself (cf. Ex 34:6f; Isa 43:25f; 44:22).

This is important. For where the scribes' unbelief becomes apparent is in their *evaluation* of Jesus' implied claim to act in God's stead. Given their own theological presuppositions, only two responses were open to them. They could either conclude

---

[1] So Lohmeyer, *Lord of the Temple*, 26; Gaston, *No Stone*, 77.

[2] Branscomb, 'Thy Sins are Forgiven', 59; idem, *Mark*, 46ff; Johnson, *Mark*, 56f; cf. Rawlinson, *Mark*, 93. See also Sander's recent discussion, *Jesus*, 200–8, 273f. On the significance of 2 Sam 12:12–23, see Klauck, 'Sündenvergebung', 236f.

[3] See above, pp. 89 n.3.

[4] On this, see Klauck, 'Sündenvergebung', 238f.

that Jesus' actualisation of divine forgiveness was consistent with, and evidence of, his message (ὁ λόγος, v 2) of the present assertion of eschatological salvation, which was expected to bring in its train forgiveness of sins (Isa 33:24; Jer 31:34; Mic 7:18). Or else they could construe his words as a conceited act of blasphemy[1] and thereby worthy of death (Lev 24:11ff; Num 15:30f; cf. Mk 3:6; 14:64). In opting for this latter interpretation instead of the former, or like the scribe in 12:38–40 seeking further illumination, they manifest entrenched unbelief.

Now the narrator indicates in various ways that this reaction to Jesus is not motivated purely by a justifiable concern for the honour of God. The use of the term οὗτος (v 7) is probably meant to signal a deep-seated contempt for Jesus.[2] Similarly the description of them 'reasoning in their hearts' denotes not a spirit of genuine inquiry but a volitional resistance to the truth, a hardening of heart (3:5). Διαλογίζεσθαι 'is a bad word in Mark; it suggests doubt, lack of faith, even hostility'[3] (cf. 8:16f; 9:33; 11:31). Again, the whole matter turns on the issue of the ἐξουσία of Jesus, with which the Capernaum crowds have already begun to contrast scribal authority unfavourably (1:22). By encouraging this retrospection to 1:22, 27, the narrator invites us to see the scribal reaction to Jesus in 2:6–10 as fuelled by rivalry and jealousy.

It is striking that Jesus takes the initiative against such unbelieving hostility. The scribes never verbalise their thoughts, but Jesus rounds on them nonetheless and, ironically by taking over another privilege of Yahweh,[4] the capacity to read thoughts and intentions, he provokes the first direct confrontation with the religious establishment in Mark's story. In v 9, Jesus poses a riddle: 'which is easier to say to the paralytic, "your sins are forgiven", or to say, "arise, take up your bed, and walk"?'. By means of this riddle and its sequel, the narrator enables Jesus both to confirm his fundamental claim to divine

---

[1] For the purposes of the story, it does not matter whether or not Jesus' words are technically blasphemy under Jewish law; it is the attitude of the scribes that is pivotal to Mark's message.

[2] See Black, *Aramaic Approach*, 121f; Maisch, *Heilung des Gelähmten*, 80; *BAG*, 596; Taylor, *Mark*, 195f; Nineham, *Mark*, 90; Cranfield, *Mark*, 98.

[3] Carrington, *Mark*, 167.

[4] Cf. 1 Sam 16:7; 1 Kg 8:39; 1 Chron 28:9; Ps 7:9; Jer 11:20; 17:10; Sir 42:18; Pss Sol 14:6. There is no need to attribute this to *theios aner* elements in the tradition, as do Maisch, *Heilung des Gelähmten*, 79, 123; and Schenke, *Wundererzählungen*, 159.

authority and yet, by doing so indirectly, to avoid immediate indictment for blasphemy.

The riddle is a snare for the scribes[1], for however they answer it they must end up conceding Jesus' unique authority. If they say forgiveness is easier, then Jesus' performance of the more difficult healing would automatically prove his capacity to do the lesser deed too (*ad majus a minori*). If alternatively they say healing is easier, then they must concede that Jesus has already done the more difficult thing, which the man's physical recovery would ratify. And if, in an attempt to avoid such a conclusion, they should say both works are of equal difficulty, they would then be unwittingly concurring with the fundamental truth Jesus is seeking to convey. For the question cannot be answered in the either/or terms in which it is framed. Since both the healing of lameness and the forgiveness of sins are eschatological works of God[2], they are both as equally easy to God as they are equally impossible for humans (cf. 10:26f, note εὐκοπώτερον in v 25). In view of this, the fact that Jesus speaks a word of forgiveness (v 5) and a word of healing (v 10) with equal ease, and the authenticity of both is confirmed by the cure of the paralytic, demonstrates that he has power to do what only God can do.

It is in this sense that the healing is offered as proof of Jesus' authority to pardon sins. Mark's logic seems to be that if Jesus' word of forgiveness was blasphemous, then the word of healing would be ineffectual, since God would not honour the word of a blasphemer, and in any case the root of the man's condition, his sins, would remain unremedied. Consequently, the effectiveness of the healing word may be used to authenti-

---

[1] Cf. Hooker, *Son of Man*, 87f. It has also been a snare for commentators who divide over whether Mark considers forgiveness as 'easier', because it is unverifiable (e.g. Best, *Temptation and Passion*, 35f; Hultgren, *Adversaries*, 108; Klostermann, *Markus*, 23; Gnilka, *Markus*, I, 100; Ernst, *Markus*, 88; Anderson, *Mark*, 101), or healing as 'easier', because humans may heal, but only God can forgive (e.g., Lane, *Mark*, 96). Those who see the point of the riddle as equating the two works include Budesheim, 'Jesus and the Disciples', 192; Dewey, *Public Debate*, 70; Schmithals, *Markus*, I, 152, 161f. In a recent formal analysis of the logical principles in the eleven confrontation narratives in Mark, Keller comments with respect to 2:6–12: 'Jesus by demonstration has negated the alternatives he had proposed by combining physical healing with spiritual. The resulting conjunction (because negated disjunctions convert to conjunctions) thus strongly implies the reality: that Jesus can both forgive sins and heal the body', 'Jesus and his Critics', 31.

[2] Cf. Isa 35:6; Jer 31:8 and 34; Zech 13:1; Ezek 36:25–7.

cate the authority of the pronouncement of forgiveness. In this way the miracle serves as a refutation of unbelief and as a renewed summons to repentance and faith. For if the charge of blasphemy is proved groundless, then according to the scribes' own theology God himself must be exercising his prerogative in this Son of Man.

The 'Son of Man' designation raises a plethora of critical problems which cannot detain us here.[1] Suffice it to note that the title does not serve here or elsewhere in Mark's story as an overt claim to a messianic or divine status, and there is no hint of Jesus' enemies taking exception to it. It contains an oblique reference to the figure in Daniel 7, but at the same time may be heard by characters in the story as a self-designation by Jesus as 'the man' or 'the human being'. The healing miracle is not intended therefore to legitimate Jesus' status as Son of Man but rather to establish that the one who calls himself 'Son of Man' has authority to forgive.

(b) Summary

By his stylistic arrangement of 2:1–12 Mark draws a contrast between the faith of the paralytic and his friends, and the faithlessness of the contentious scribes. Faith receives pardon and healing, while unbelief leads to an overt clash with Jesus. The unbelief of the scribes lies not in a failure to perceive the import of Jesus' word of forgiveness; it lies rather in their attempt to evade the full implications of Jesus' possession of divine authority by charging him with blasphemy.

Although he is able to refute their accusation in both word (v 9) and deed (v 10), official hostility does not abate but intensifies. In fact Mark uses 2:1–12 to introduce a series of *Streitgespräche* (2:1–3:6) in which the reader/hearer is made aware of the depth and seriousness of official opposition to Jesus, despite his overwhelming popularity with the people in the flanking material (1:45; 3:7). In this controversy collection, there is both a concentric arrangement of the five accounts, with the opening and closing episodes reflecting each other in

---

[1] The origin and meaning of the phrase, e.g., remains one of the most controverted issues in gospel research, and there are numerous recent monographs devoted to it. On the special issues associated with Mk 2:10,28, see Tuckett, 'Son of Man', 58–81; Doughty, 'Son of Man', 161–81. On the phrase, 'upon the earth', see Hooker, *Son of Man*, 90–3. And for a recent, fresh treatment of the title in Markan christology, see Kingsbury, *Christology*, 157–79.

structure, content and theme, and an internal linear progression, in which there is a steady accumulation of forces
opposing Jesus and an intensifiction of opposition from silent
resistance (2:6ff) through to plotting his death (3:6).[1] The
pairing of 2:1–12 and 3:1–6 implies a direct connection between
the religious leaders' refusal of faith in face of Jesus' evident
authority and the plot to kill him. Their unbelief is more than
doubt or an absence of faith; it is an active, even murderous,
opposition to the bearer of the kingdom (cf. 12:7f).

It is noteworthy too that in the linear progression we find not
so much a steadily deepening hostility towards Jesus, as an
increasingly overt expression of a hostility that appears at its
most profound from the very beginning; for it is the charge of
blasphemy that finally seals the condemnation of Jesus (2:7;
14:64). From their first appearance in the story, the unbelieving scribes nurse 'in their hearts' the convictions that lead to
Jesus' death (why this is so will become apparent in the third
episode we look at below). That this attitude will eventually
infect the whole nation is implied in the scene we now turn to.

Unbelief at Nazareth (6:1–6)

In 6:1–6, Jesus encounters unbelief in his own *patris*. In this
story the narrator does not expressly single out the religious
leaders for blame but speaks more generally of the response of
the πολλοί (v 2). It should be noted, however, that the action
takes place in the synagogue, a setting which Mark regularly
associates with the religious authorities (1:21f; 3:1f; 12:38; cf.
13:9), and their presence in the Nazareth synagogue is no
doubt to be presumed. Even so, in this particular episode Mark
is probably wanting to portray a more thorough-going repudiation of Jesus than solely by the scribes and Pharisees. There
are various indications that he felt that the response of Jesus'
home town as a whole would serve as a suitable metaphor for,
or foreshadowing of, the final rejection of Jesus in Jerusalem
by the entire nation.[2]

---

[1] On the literary unit, 2:1–3:6, see: Dewey, 'Controversy Stories', 394–401;
eadem, *Public Debate*, 16–52, 105f, 111, 118, 124; Stock, 'Chiastic Awareness',
23–7; Maisch, *Heilung des Gelähmten*, 107–120; Rhoads and Michie, *Mark
as Story*, 51–4; Cook, *Jewish Leaders*, 43–8; Kuhn, *Ältere Sammlungen*, 53–
95; Schenke, *Wundererzählungen*, 149–52; Dunn, 'Jesus and Paul', 397–
409; Pesch, *Markus*, I, 149–51.

[2] Similarly, Lightfoot, *History and Interpretation*, 188, 191; Burkill,

(i) The movement within the story from amazement (v 2) to hostility (v 3) expresses *in nuce* the overall direction of Mark's plotted narrative. Mention of amazement (ἐξεπλήσσοντο) recalls Jesus' first public appearance (1:22), while mention of stumbling points forward to the comprehensive spurning of Jesus at the end of the story (cf. 14:27).

(ii) Mark establishes a tight connection between the Nazareth episode and the preceding narrative (καὶ ἐξῆλθεν ἐκεῖθεν καὶ . . . v 1). In the Jairus story, the raising of the dead girl serves as a symbolic anticipation of the death and resurrection of Jesus. Immediately after, the process by which this comes about is acted out symbolically in Jesus' home town.

(iii) It is not coincidental that the following pericope deals with the mission of the Twelve (6:7–13), in which the disciples rehearse their post-Easter task (13:10). This mission, anticipated in 3:14, thus emerges as a *result* of the rejection of Jesus by his own people, and also follows an analogous path, combining rejection (vv 3,11) and success (vv 5b,13). It is also significant that Mark sandwiches the story of the passion of the Baptist between the sending out and return of the apostles (6:14–29). In light of Mark's comment in 1:14, the reader can easily catch the menacing parallel between John's fate and the fate awaiting Jesus as opposition intensifies, as just witnessed in Nazareth.

(iv) Finally, Mark stresses the comprehensiveness of Jesus' rejection by mentioning three circles that 'dishonour' the prophet in v 4 (compared to Matthew's two and Luke's one). It is generally accepted that οἰκίᾳ and συγγενεῦσιν are intended to include Jesus' family and relatives mentioned in v 3 among those who refuse him faith,[1] although συγγενής, a *hapax legomenon* in Mark, is a flexible term and could even denote fellow

---

Mysterious Revelation, 138f; idem, *New Light*, 62f, 103, 236 n.79; Martin, *Evangelist and Theologian*, 117; Davies, *Gospel and Land*, 239; Nineham, *Mark*, 123, 125; Best, *Temptation and Passion*, 119 (but cf. idem, *Gospel as Story*, 60); Gnilka, *Markus*, I, 28, 233; Buby, 'Christology of Relationship', 153.

[1] E.g. Grässer, 'Jesus in Nazareth', 16; Nineham, *Mark*, 165. Many scholars see here a deliberate polemic against Jesus' family (e.g. Trocmé, *Formation*, 130–7; Crossan, 'Relatives of Jesus', 105; Kelber, *Kingdom*, 54f; idem, *Oral and Written Gospel*, 103; Schreiber, 'Christologie des Markusevangeliums', 175–83). It is improbable that this is because they espouse a Jerusalem theology which Mark rejects; for a critique, see Lambrecht, 'Relatives of Jesus', 241–58; Gnilka, *Markus*, I, 232f.

members of the same nation.[1] In any event, the thought is that
Jesus' compatriots in general oppose him. The reference to
Jesus' relatives recalls 3:20f,31–5, where their attitude to him
is paralleled with that of the Jerusalem scribes who ultimately
conspire in his death.

The episode at Nazareth thus represents on a small scale
what will happen to Jesus at the end of the story, and presents
its cause as ἀπιστία. For a man to be rejected by his *patris* and
family was, after all, no small matter in the ancient world and
it serves appropriately in Mark's narrative as a foreboding of
things to come.

(a) Composition, structure, and theme

Scholarly judgements on the origin, development and redactional handling of 6:1–6 differ considerably. Some[2] speak of an
'ideal scene' built up around the proverbial saying in v 4, while
others[3] concede an underlying historical tradition, and the
extent to which the literary complexities[4] in the final text, such
as the tension between v 5a and v 5b, or between the positive
response in v 2 and the negative response in v 3d, are the
product of Markan redaction is a matter of dispute.[5] At any
rate, in whatever way it is explained, the present shape of the
narrative is, as Gnilka points out, *sui generis*; it is not comparable to any known form.[6] And it is the final format that
conveys Mark's message to the reader/hearer.

As it stands, the narrative comprises third-person narration
in the opening and closing sections, and direct speech in the
middle section (vv 2b–4). The direct speech consists of two sets

---

[1] Cf. Rom 9:3; 11:11,21. See *BAG* , 772.

[2] E.g. Bultmann, *History*, 31, 60, 102, 386; Burkill, *New Light*, 235 n. 79;
Koch,*Wundererzählungen*, 150; Kee, *Community*, 51.

[3] E.g. Smith, *Jesus the Magician*, 15f; Taylor, *Mark*, 298; Cranfield, *Mark*,
192; Gnilka, *Markus*, I, 229; Pesch, *Markus*, I, 322.

[4] For a fuller listing of such complexities, see Grässer, 'Jesus in Nazareth',
4–6; Lightfoot, *History and Interpretation*, 188 n.2; Schmithals, *Markus*, I,
299.

[5] Extensive redaction is detected by Grässer, 'Jesus in Nazareth', 10–18;
Crossan, 'Relatives of Jesus', 105 (for summary). A more moderate reworking is advocated by Mayer, 'Überlegungen zu Mk 6,1-6a', 198 (summary);
Patten, 'Thaumaturgical Element', 88f. Limited redactional interference
is found by Pesch, *Markus*, I, 315, 324f. Another view postulates a conflation
of traditions, Schmidt, *Rahmen*, 152ff; Best, *Temptation and Passion*, 75
n.1.

[6] Gnilka, *Markus*, I, 229.

of rhetorical questions posed by the synagogue congregation and a proverbial saying quoted by Jesus. The rhetorical question is a dramatic device much used in Mark to heighten the drama and involve the audience by putting responsibility on them to find the answer,[1] while proverbs contain encapsulated knowledge with a provocative aptness to the situation in view. The central dialogue section is flanked by narrative descriptions of Jesus' teaching (v 2a) and therapeutic (v 5) activity. Both these aspects are also picked up in the dialogue itself, and the literary arrangement of the narrative brings out the two-way relationship that exists between the activity of Jesus and the sort of response it evinces.

After the introductory verse, the account falls into two parts. The first part (vv 2b–3) depicts the negative impact of Jesus' activity on 'many' in the synagogue and ends with an evaluative commentary by the narrator: 'and they took offence at him'. The second part (vv 4–6) deals conversely with the negative effect this reaction has on the activity of Jesus, in that only a 'few' are healed, and it also closes with an evaluative commentary: 'and he marvelled at their unbelief'. We thus have the following arrangement:

(I)	*Activity*:	Teaching in the Synagogue (v 2a)
	Dialogue:	Questions of Source and Identity (v 2b–3)
	[Evaluation:	'and they took offence at him' v 3d]
(II)	*Dialogue*:	Proverb of Rejected Prophet (v 4)
	Activity:	Strictly Limited Healings (v 5)
	[Evaluation:	'and he marvelled at their unbelief' v 6a]

The central theme of the story is that when Jesus' attempt to win faith founders on unbelief there is a consequent impeding of kingdom δύναμις, and it is this message[2] that governs the literary arrangement of the pericope.

(b) The portrayal of unbelief
The Nazareth story contains a clear exposition of the intrinsic character of unbelief and its consequences. The renunciation

---

[1] Rhoads and Michie, *Mark as Story*, 49–51; Kee, *Community*, 117.

[2] Grässer describes the story as a 'paradigm for the structure of faith', and maintains that 'the problem of "belief" or "unbelief" [is] the essential point of the whole story', 'Jesus in Nazareth', 21f. So also Pesch, *Markus*, I, 316; Schweizer, *Mark*, 124.

of Jesus by the synagogue congregation is depicted as a conscious and deliberative and therefore culpable response to Jesus' teaching and healing activity. The verb διδάσκειν in v 2 is probably meant to embrace both the σοφία and the δυνάμεις in v 3. The narrator makes it clear that there is no real doubt among the people as to the objective virtue of Jesus' activity – it astonishes them. Their unbelief lies not in a failure to perceive the quality of Jesus' words or the reality of his miracles; it lies rather in a refusal to admit the true *source* of this wisdom and power (v 2) and to accept the unique *identity* of the one who manifests them (v 3).

The three interrogatory clauses in v 2 all concern the origin of Jesus' words and deeds. Πόθεν τούτῳ ταῦτα states the general question, while the next two clauses define ταῦτα as his wisdom (parables?) and miracles.[1] The issue of source or origin emerges at a number of points in Mark's story, and it is evident that there are only three possible answers for the question in 6:2: a human source (11:30b), a divine source (11:30a), or a demonic source (3:22). The wording of the 'whence' questions indicates that a human origin has been ruled out. The LXX background of πόθεν[2], the passive form δοθεῖσα, and the instrumental διὰ τῶν χειρῶν αὐτοῦ γινόμεναι, all presuppose a superhuman origin for Jesus' activity. In fact, by having the speakers characterise his work as 'Wisdom and Power', epithets used of God in Job 12:13 (cf. 28:12,28) and Messiah in Isa 11:2; Pss Sol 17:24f (cf. 1 Cor 1:24), Mark even implies that they recognise a correspondence between the words and deeds of Jesus and those of God.

Yet despite the evidence they refuse to draw the natural corollary and admit God's agency (which leaves, by elimination, only one option: a diabolical source). What prevents them from accepting the conclusion suggested by the 'astonishing' evidence emerges in v 3: they are offended by the *person* of Jesus himself. They cannot reconcile the extraordinariness of his wisdom and power with the excessive ordinariness of his vocational training (ὁ τέκτων) and his local family origins (ὁ υἱὸς τῆς Μαρίας κτλ.). Given the Palestinian setting of the episode, nothing derisory is probably intended in their descrip-

---

[1] The τίς before σοφία also means 'where does it come from', rather than being a query about content (as Taylor, *Mark*, 299, maintains). So *BDF*, S.298[2]; Grässer, 'Jesus in Nazareth', 14; Pesch, *Markus*, 318.

[2] On this, see Quesnell, *Mind of St Mark*, 164–8.

tion of Jesus as a manual worker,[1] nor in their identification of him by reference to his mother rather than his father,[2] although Gentiles in Mark's audience might understand their words this way. Both comments are simply meant to draw attention to his humble background circumstances which, according to established standards of judgement, forbid the possibility that God is active in his ministry. They are 'offended *at him*' (v 3). The use of σκανδαλίζεσθαι here signifies 'a denial of faith which has eschatological importance'.[3] It does not necessarily imply an eternal loss of salvation[4], since elsewhere Mark allows for the restoration of other characters who are scandalised (cf. 14:27 and 14:28,72b; 16:7).[5] It does mean, however, that they cannot share in the immediate benefits afforded by the availability of eschatological power in Jesus.

The presence of pervasive unbelief therefore has a direct impact on Jesus' synagogue activity: 'and he could do no mighty work there except he laid his hands on a few sick people and healed them' (v 5). The presence of the exceptive clause in v 5b is usually explained[6] as a redactional attempt to mitigate the implication of v 5a in Mark's tradition that Jesus was rendered totally impotent by the Nazarenes' unbelief. The weakness of this suggestion is that it does not explain why Mark retained οὐκ ἐδύνατο in the first place (cf. Matt 13:53), nor does it give adequate enough account of the narrative significance of the extant form of v 5, which Mark obviously felt as a whole suited his purposes. The logical tension between v 5a and v 5b should

---

[1] A number of textual witnesses (P45vid, fam13 565 pc it bomss) describe Jesus as 'son of a carpenter' (cf. Matt 13:55), and some explain this as reflecting embarrassment over the inference that Jesus himself was a tradesman. The point to note is that the Jews, unlike Greeks and Romans, did not despise manual labour (*Bill.*, II, 101f), and to Semitic ears both designations would have been more or less equivalent.

[2] As claim Stauffer, 'Jeschu ben Mirjam', 119–28; Nineham, *Mark*, 166; Cranfield, *Mark*, 195; Smith, *Magician*, 26f; Lightfoot, *History and Interpretation*, 187; Martin, *Evangelist and Theologian*, 123. But see McArthur, 'Son of Mary', 38, 58.

[3] Davies, *Gospel and Land*, 239. Also Stählin, *TDNT*, 7, 350.

[4] Contra Grässer, 'Jesus in Nazareth', 21; Lightfoot, *History and Interpretation*,189 n.2; Burkill, *Mysterious Revelation*, 137–40.

[5] Best sees 14:72 as indicating Peter's repentance and restoration, *Discipleship*, 554.

[6] E.g. Grässer, 'Jesus in Nazareth', 17; Crossan, 'Relatives of Jesus', 104; Smith, *Magician*, 16; Koch, *Wundererzählungen*, 152; Mayer, 'Uberlegungen zu Mk 6,1–6a', 196; Gnilka, *Markus*, I, 233.

not be overrated. The construction οὐδείς . . . εἰ μή is found
frequently in New Testament Greek, including again in Mk
10:18, as a way of stating a limited exception to a general rule
which thereby adds emphasis to the rule.[1] On such a comparison, Mk 6:5 constitutes a very strong, though qualified,
assertion. The reason for the qualification is not to mitigate the
force of v 5a but to make room for the miracles referred to
previously in the story. The phrase αἱ δυνάμεις τοιαῦται in v 2 is
commonly related back to the miracles in the previous chapter,[2] but equally it could anticipate v 5b. Indeed the three-fold
use of demonstrative pronouns in v 2 strongly suggests matters
witnessed in the immediate setting, and the phrase διὰ τῶν
χειρῶν αὐτοῦ (v 2a) anticipates ἐπιθεὶς τὰς χεῖρας in v 5b. The
accomplishment of these healings in the synagogue indicates
that at the outset a few people possessed real faith. But when
the πολλοί who witnessed these miracles did not accept their
significance and the atmosphere of wonder turned to hostility,
the unbelief was such that no further miracles were possible.
By οὐκ ἐδύνατο Mark obviously does not mean an involuntary,
physical powerlessness (cf. 3:1–6; 4:35–41), but a moral or
volitional limitation. As Glöckner explains,

> Unbelief makes a miracle not so much impossible as
> meaningless, and therefore in most cases unaccom-
> plishable (cf. otherwise 3:1–6). A miracle leads nowhere
> if the externally astonishing event is not received and
> experienced in faith as a sign of salvation.[3]

The function of v 5 then is to underscore forcefully the ham-
pering effect of unbelief on Jesus' mission, yet at the same time
to record the significant fact that even in the midst of such
resistance those few individuals who exhibited true faith
towards Jesus experienced healing.

(c) Summary

The people of Nazareth in this episode are faced with an identification crisis. Jesus' words and deeds astound them and point

---

[1] E.g. Matt 17:8; Matt 11:27 = Lk 10:22; Jn 14:6; 1 Cor 1:14; 8:4b; Rev 2:17;
14:3; 19:12; see especially Phil 4:15.

[2] E.g. Grässer, 'Jesus in Nazareth', 13; Pesch, *Markus*, I, 318; Lane, *Mark*,
201 n.4.

[3] Glöckner, *Biblischer Glaube*, 81. Similarly Richardson, *Miracle-Stories*,
43f; Van der Loos, *Miracles*, 192 nn.2,3; 118; Roloff, *Kerygma*, 159; Lane,
Mark, 204.

towards a mandate from God, but his local origins, humble family circumstances and occupational background depart radically from conventional expectations of what a divine emissary should be like. Hence they refuse to respond in believing trust. Their unbelief consists not in a failure to perceive the potential implications of Jesus' ministry; it is not some kind of preordained blindness. It consists rather in a conscious refusal to surrender established standards of judgement in view of clear evidence that God's ruling power is present in Jesus.

The narrator underlines the seriousness and culpability of ἀπιστία in various ways. While not expecting ready acceptance in his *patris* (v 4), Jesus also does not expect such firm resistance and he marvels at their unbelief (v 6a). So powerful is this unbelief that it succeeds in frustrating Jesus' best intentions and he is 'unable' to extend kingdom power to the degree he wishes. 'According to the self-same rule by which Jesus granted everything to faith, he also denied everything to unbelief.'[1] By placing this episode after a series of dramatic miracles (4:35–5:43), Mark shows how the powerful Son of God who calms storms, expels demons, banishes diseases and raises the dead, is finally checkmated by entrenched unbelief in his hometown. Such unbelief will ultimately lead to his death in Jerusalem. In the next scene we consider, the Jerusalem authorities will set in train their attempt to incriminate him.

Unbelief in Jerusalem (11:27–33)

In chapter 5 we discussed the temple-cleansing incident and the discourse on the new community of faith destined to replace the existing cultic centre (11:12–25). We now turn to the immediate sequel, the so-called *Vollmachtsfrage*, in which Mark picks up and develops the reference he makes in the cleansing scene to the determination of the Jerusalem authorities to destroy Jesus because his popularity with the people had made him a direct threat to their position (11:18).

In 11:27 Jesus returns to the temple and as he walks sovereignly around its precincts, a delegation of Sanhedrin members (cf. v 27 and 14:43,53; 15:1) challenges him to declare the nature and source of the authority which gave him the right to do 'these things' (i.e. in the temple).[2] In the ensuing

---

[1] Schlatter, *Glaube*, 51.

[2] Most relate ταῦτα to the cleansing incident, though some apply it more

dialogue, the Jewish leaders' rejection of Jesus' authority is brought into connection with their failure to have believed John the Baptist (οὐκ ἐπιστεύσατε αὐτῷ). This is the only case in Mark where πιστεύειν is referred to a personal object other than Jesus or God. It could be that the verb does not signal the same faith-conception here as it does in other Markan passages. Yet even if it simply denotes intellectual assent, the choice of πιστεύειν may well be a conscious strategy by the narrator to indicate an important relationship between the religious leaders' attitude to the Baptist and their denial of faith to Jesus. We should therefore consider 11:27–33 as part of Mark's faith theme.

(a) Composition, structure and theme

This pericope has a number of features in common with 2:1–12. In both accounts Jesus responds to official criticism with a counter-question or riddle; both have the opponents 'reasoning' (διαλογίζεσθαι) within or among themselves; in both cases the ἐξουσία of Jesus is at issue; and each pericope introduces a larger cycle of conflict stories[1] which further illustrate the unbelief specially highlighted in the initial story. There is also an affinity in literary style and structure. Both narratives have features that particularly suit them to dramatic oral delivery. As in 2:1–12, there is considerable repetition in 11:27–33 which gives emphasis to the central issues at stake. Some variation of the phrase ἐν ποίᾳ ἐξουσίᾳ ταῦτα ποιεῖς occurs four times in the account and the alternatives ἐξ οὐρανοῦ/ἐξ ἀνθρώπων are repeated twice each. The preponderance of direct speech (λέγειν is used nine times; ἀποκρίνεσθαι three times; and λόγος and ἐπερωτᾶν once each) is also suggestive of oral communication, where it heightens the immediacy and impact of the story.[2]

There is a striking anacolouthon in 11:32 (similarly in 2:10) which is perhaps also explicable in terms of oral dynamics. The second conditional sentence suddenly breaks off after ἐξ ἀνθρώπων, and instead of an apodosis there is a change to third-person narration (cf. Matt 21:26; Lk 20:6). According to Shae, 'literary rupture of this nature often points to a change of hand in the developmental history of the tradition', and he

generally to Jesus' ministry. For literature and discussion see Hultgren, *Adversaries*, 70–2.

[1] On the Jerusalem controversies, see Dewey, *Public Debate*, 55f, 63ff, 152–67; Cook, *Jewish Leaders*, 34, 48ff; Rhoads and Michie, *Mark as Story*, 53f.

[2] See above, pp. 18–19.

ascribes the break to Markan redaction.[1] In oral performance, however, leaving the conditional sentence incomplete could, with the appropriate inflection of the voice, convey with dramatic effect the hierarchs' sudden realisation that Jesus' trick question has set them on the horns of a dilemma. The narrator then explains in an aside to the audience the cause of the dilemma – they feared the people.

The literary arrangement of 11:27–33 is also not unlike that of 2:1–12. There the debate with the scribes is sandwiched between two halves of a healing account. Here the interchange between Jesus and the hierarchs loosely frames a central section (vv 31,32) in which the opponents deliberate among themselves over how to answer Jesus' counter-question. The counter-question material is bracketed by nearly identical phrases at the beginning and end.

v 29c ἐρῶ ὑμῖν ἐν ποίᾳ ἐξουσίᾳ ταῦτα ποιῶ

v 33b οὐδὲ ἐγὼ λέγω ὑμῖν ἐν ποίᾳ ἐξουσίᾳ ταῦτα ποιῶ.

The second phrase returns the reader/hearer to the question posed by the religious leaders at the beginning of the conflict (v 28); the authority they query has now been further demonstrated by Jesus' refusal to give account of his actions.

(b) The portrayal of unbelief

The interrogation of Jesus in this episode is probably meant to be understood, in view of 11:18, as an attempt by the Jerusalem leaders to secure grounds for moving against Jesus. They implicitly recognise that he has acted with authority in the temple, but their intention is to use this as a means of incriminating him (cf. 12:13). The two questions they pose have a slightly different focus: the 'what' question inquires as to the *nature* of Jesus' authority (prophetic, messianic, etc.), and the 'who' question as to its ultimate *source* (human, divine, Satanic). The conjunction 'or' indicates however that they are alternative ways of eliciting the same confession from Jesus.[2] Has he interfered with temple worship on his own human

---

[1] Shae, 'Question on Authority', 8. Also, Stein, 'Proper Methodology', 189. Shae attempts a thorough redaction-critical and traditio-historical analysis. For a different estimate, see Schmithals, *Markus*, II, 504–6.

[2] The ascription of the two questions to different layers of tradition by Hultgren (*Adversaries*, 68–70) and Shae ('Question on Authority', 11) over-rates the difference between them. This is rather a case of duality or two-step progression in which the second member adds clarity to the first. See above pp. 12, 19.

authority (!), or does he dare to claim divine authorisation for his cynical disrespect for the place of the divine presence (cf. 14:58–62)?

Jesus agrees to answer this question if the leaders are prepared to declare whether John's baptism was of divine or human origin. He thereby turns the tables on his opponents. If they admit John's divine commission, they must then acknowledge their own disregard for his message. If they deny John's prophetic authority, they will discredit themselves in the eyes of the people, whose animosity they plainly fear (11: 18,32). They are therefore forced to declare themselves agnostic on the issue, which Jesus then uses to deny them the explicit declaration they seek concerning his own authority.

Jesus' counter-question functions rhetorically to direct attention back to John's baptising ministry at the beginning of the story. There, dressed as Elijah (1:6; cf. 2 Kg 1:8), the Baptist fulfilled even scribal expectations (9:11f), and proclaimed a baptism of repentance in anticipation of the Coming One who would baptise in the Holy Spirit (1:7f). By evoking John's baptism in connection with Jesus' authority, the narrator is able simultaneously to expose, diagnose, and answer the unbelief of the Jerusalem authorities.

(i) Their unbelief is *exposed* in their private deliberations over how to reply to Jesus' question. They obviously perceive in his allusion to John's baptism an implicit application of John's witness to himself, otherwise they could freely concede John's divine mandate. The reason they cannot do so is in case Jesus asks them: διὰ τί οὖν οὐκ ἐπιστεύσατε αὐτῷ; (i.e. accept his message of the coming Mightier One). This would have posed no threat to them had they not recognised Jesus' implied claim to be that One. Once again Mark indicates that the unbelief of Jesus' adversaries consists not in a failure to apprehend his possible significance, but in a stubborn refusal to accept it.

Now πιστεύειν with the dative is the normal construction in secular Greek for accepting the truth of what someone says.[1] This is the only time Mark employs this locution and the primary meaning is clearly to give credence to John's message, though 'in a somewhat pregnant sense'.[2] For belief in John's message involved more than detached mental assent; it required submission to a baptism of repentance, entailing trust in God for remission of sins. Moreover, inasmuch as Mark

---

[1] Harris, 'Prepositions and Theology', 1213.

[2] See Warfield, *Biblical Doctrines*, 475.

portrays John as a prophet (v 32), the belief directed towards him was, in accordance with Old Testament-Jewish thought[1], ultimately placed in God. To have believed John then means to have received his eschatologically motivated call for conversion as a demand of God and to have responded in obedience and expectancy. To have disbelieved him means to have rejected the divine imperative and the prediction of the Coming One as groundless.

Mark both parallels and differentiates the belief rendered to John and the belief rendered to Jesus. They are distinguished by their content. In the case of John, belief is the inner dynamic of repentance in view of a future act of God. With Jesus, it is a trustful reliance on the present action of God's kingly power. Faith is not expressly demanded by John but is implicit in the act of repentant baptism. With Jesus, however, faith emerges as a distinct demand, and is the on-going condition-of-being appropriate to the new reality he brings.[2]

(ii) At the same time, 11:30–2 implies a close connection between belief in John and faith in Jesus. In fact Mark *diagnoses* the leaders' rejection of John's baptism of repentance as the cause of their denial of faith in Jesus. The unbelief displayed towards Jesus had already formed with respect to John (cf. 12:1–5), which is why the religious leaders are depicted as hostile to Jesus from their very first appearance in Mark's story (2:6f, cf. 1:22). This correlation at the level of faith is part of a larger motif in the gospel in which Mark parallels the careers of John and Jesus.[3] Suffice it to note here that both God's end-time messengers produce fear in the ruling authorities (6:20; 11:18,32; 12:12), both are denied belief, and both suffer violent fates. Disbelief in John leads ultimately to the passion of Jesus.

(iii) Finally the retrospection in 11:30f to John's baptism provides a veiled *answer* to the question about Jesus' authority. Mark's audience would see in the reference to John's baptism, especially in connection with the phrase ἐξ οὐρανοῦ, an allusion to Jesus' own baptism, where he receives the Spirit and a

---

[1] Cf. Ex 4:1–9; 14:30f; 19:9; 2 Chron 20:20; Jn 5:46; Acts 8:12.

[2] See above, pp. 51–2. On the role of faith in the Baptist's ministry, see Schlatter, *Glaube*, 80–94, 143f, 150, 155.

[3] On this see: Kelber, *Mark's Story*, 17, 34; Matera, *Kingship of Jesus*, 98–100; Wolff, 'Johannes des Täufers', 858–65; Marxsen, *Mark the Evangelist*, 42f; Patten, 'Thaumaturgical Element', 193–201; Senior, *Passion of Jesus*, 16–20. See also Theissen, *First Followers*, 104f.

voice ἐκ τῶν οὐρανῶν declares: 'this is my beloved son' (1:9–11). This is the real source of Jesus' ἐξουσία. The one who walks imperiously around the temple, who claims authority to 'cleanse' it, who announces the foundation of a new community of faith, and whom the ruling establishment seeks to destroy, is none other than the Son of God.

(c) Summary

In 2:1–12 and 11:27–33, Mark locates the religious leaders' unbelief in their reaction to Jesus' ἐξουσία. In 2:1–12, his authority is demonstrated in his forgiveness of sins; in 11:27–33, in his sovereignty over the temple. In both cases Mark shows that their unbelief lies in their rejection of the clear implications of what they witness rather than in an inability to perceive the truth. In 11:27–33, the reason why official opposition to Jesus appears full-blown right at the beginning of his ministry (2:6–10) becomes evident: unbelief with respect to God's eschatological initiative had already taken root before Jesus' work began. A refusal by the nation's rulers to believe John and repent was the first step on the road to the passion of Jesus. And it is at the last moments of his passion that we find the crudest display of unbelief in Mark's entire story.

Unbelief before the cross (15:27–32)

Jesus begins his ministry in Mark by calling people to repentant faith in view of the dawning βασιλεία. He ends his ministry however with his enemies assembled before the cross deridingly offering faith to the βασιλεύς in return for a distorted display of divine power. The scene at the cross represents for Mark both the ultimate repudiation of the gospel as he understands it and the clearest demonstration of the paradoxical relationship that exists between faith, power and powerlessness.

(a) Composition, structure and theme

There has been a notable shift of emphasis in treatments of the Markan passion narrative over recent years. The 'decompositional' approach of the 1970s, in which attempts were made to break the passion account down into its various traditional and redactional components, with widely divergent results, has increasingly given way to a concern to treat the story in its full narrative integrity.[1] The current tendency is to ascribe this

---

[1] For reviews of recent scholarly trends, see: Kelber, *Oral and Written*

integrity to Mark's own compositional activity, although the form-critical hypothesis of a sequential pre-Markan passion narrative enjoying an independent existence prior to the writing of the gospel has also been reasserted by Rudolf Pesch.[1] For our purposes, the important point to note is that whether Mark received an extended passion narrative from tradition and then 'composed backwards' (Marxsen), or whether he put the story of chapters 14–16 together himself from a diversity of sources, the fact remains that Markan style, purposes and themes are as much in evidence in the last two chapters of the gospel as in the previous thirteen. They cannot be divided into separate theological units.

The passion narrative has two thematically-connected high-points: the trial scene in 14:53–65 and the crucifixion account in 15:20b–41, in which the faith reference we are interested in occurs. The crucifixion account is part of the larger rhetorical unit of chapter 15,[2] which is arranged into the format of a single crucifixion day divided into three-hour periods (vv 1,25, 33,34,42). The governing theme of the chapter – the kingship of Jesus (vv 2,9,12,18,26,32,39) – is carried forward in an alternating pattern. Each of the narrated events leading up to the death of Jesus is followed by a mockery scene, representing a sort of 'anti-confession' of Jesus' true messianic identity.

Event	Mockery
(1) Trial (vv 1–15)	Soldiers mock (vv 16–20a)
(2) Crucifixion (vv 20b–7)	Passers-by and Religious Leaders Mock (vv 29–32)
(3) Darkness and Cry of Dereliction (vv 33–4)	Bystanders Mock (vv 35–6)

Gospel, 185–99; Matera, *Kingship of Jesus*, 1–5, 35–44; and the essays in Kelber, *Passion in Mark*, esp. 153–9. See also Donahue, *Are You the Christ?* 191–6; Kee, *Community*, 30–2; Achtemeier, *Mark*, 82ff; Cook, *Jewish Leaders*, 52–8; Güttgemanns, *Candid Questions*, 337–40.

[1] Pesch, *Markus*, II, 1–27. Cf. Nickelsburg, 'Genre and Function', esp. 182ff. A convenient review of the case for a pre-Markan passion narrative is found in J. A. Fitzmyer, *The Gospel According to Luke* (AB. Garden City, New York: Doubleday, 1985), II, 1359–62.

[2] See especially Matera, *Kingship of Jesus*, 21–34 and passim.

Our principal concern is with the second mockery scene, which Mark locates between the third and sixth hours (vv 25,33). Senior regards this as 'one of Mark's most skillful narratives, catching up the major motifs of christology and discipleship that have run throughout the gospel and bringing them to their final expression'.[1] The scene is bracketed by two references to those crucified with Jesus (καὶ σὺν αὐτῷ σταυροῦσιν, v 27; καὶ οἱ συνεσταυρωμένοι σὺν αὐτῷ, v 32) and, like the rest of the crucifixion narrative, is highly stylised to bring out the basic 'agreement with scripture' in what befalls Jesus. Allusions to Psalm 22 in particular contribute to Mark's characterisation of Jesus here as the Suffering Righteous One.[2]

The action involves three groups of characters whose taunts rehearse for the reader/hearer the major issues of the trial scene and indeed the outstanding features of Jesus' ministry as a whole. The first group are simply described as passersby (v 29, cf. v 21). However, although no direct connection is indicated, their derision of Jesus as temple-destroyer and their appearance in the same scene as chief priests and scribes is strongly evocative of the false witnesses at Jesus' trial (14:56–9), and their function here may be similar (cf. Pss 27:12; 35:11). Their derisory words and gestures conclude with a challenge to Jesus to save himself and descend from the cross. Both these taunts are taken up by the second group, though in a different configuration.[3] The chief priests and scribes deny that the crucified one is able to save himself, in contrast to his saving others, and they make witnessing his descent from the cross a condition for their belief in him as messianic king. The third group have no part in the dialogue. But the fact that Jesus' two fellow victims renounce their solidarity with him in pain also to revile him conveys the extent of his aloneness. It now remains only for God to forsake him (v 34) and his abandonment will be total.

Crucial to understanding this scene, and indeed the whole passion narrative, is the narrator's conscious use of ironic

---

[1] Senior, *Passion of Jesus*, 117.

[2] See Reumann, 'Psalm 22 at the Cross', 39–58; Matera, *Kingship of Jesus*, 129; and for a thorough analysis of Old Testament citations in Mark 11–16, Kee, 'Scriptural Quotations', 164–88.

[3] We have here a case of Markan duality (see above, n.1, p. 197). The verses are not 'doublets' (Bultmann, *History*, 273; Schweizer, *Mark*, 348f).

speech and imagery.[1] Irony is where a character speaks from one point of view but makes an evaluation from another. Here what the scoffers declare about Jesus is in fact true, although they mean the very opposite of what they say. He *is* the one whose death signals the end of the temple and who in three days (cf. 8:31; 9:31; 10:34) will establish a new temple 'not made with hands' (14:58). He *is* the 'saviour' who, by refusing to save his own life, saves others (8:35; 10:45). He *is* the Christ, the King of Israel, enthroned between two criminals who occupy the places of royal honour sought by James and John (10:37f). His cross itself *is* the sign of faith his tormentors demand in order to believe, though they cannot 'see' it. For Mark's audience, then, the words of mockery point to the hidden truth about Jesus.

Now the derisory offer of faith in the dying messiah (κατα-βάτω . . . καὶ πιστεύσωμεν) is placed only on the lips of the chief priests and scribes, and thus represents the climax of the sub-theme of the unbelief of the religious authorities. But since the narrator expressly likens (ὁμοίως καί, v 31) the ridicule of the first and second groups of mockers, and they both demand the same self-serving miracle, we may safely consider the dialogue as a whole as constitutive of Mark's representation of unbelief in this scene. Furthermore although we must confine ourselves mainly to this scene, linguistic contacts and the-matic comparisons and contrasts will inevitably carry us into the wider crucifixion narrative to round out Mark's presen-tation of the subject.

(b) The portrayal of unbelief

Mark employs faith terminology ironically in this scene in order to represent the converse state in the spectators at the crucifixion. This means that by πιστεύειν more is implied than giving intellectual credence to Jesus' messianic identity. It denotes the withholding of that full commitment of believing trust in the person of Jesus demanded throughout the gospel in response to his proclamation of the kingdom. The absolute usage of the verb is in keeping with Mark's preferred way of signalling such a response, and the association of πιστεύειν with βασιλεύς (v 32) is deliberately reminiscent of the linking of the same verb with ἡ βασιλεία in 1:14f. Faith in the presence of

[1] On Markan irony, see esp. Fowler, *Loaves and Fishes* 182–219; Rhoads and Michie, *Mark as Story*, 59–62; Tannehill, 'Narrative Christology', 79f; Juel, *Messiah and Temple*, 47ff.

God's kingdom is here paralleled with faith in the crucified king.

The unbelief of Jesus' detractors in 15:27-32 has two aspects: their implied disavowal of the eschatological significance which they know Jesus lays claim to, and their demand for compelling proof as a ground for accepting his claim. Let us consider each in turn.

(i) The words which the narrator places on the lips of the scoffers serve to confirm, albeit with ironical intent, that they clearly apprehend the eschatological status which Jesus has claimed for himself during the course of his ministry. They ridicule him as a messianic pretender (v 32) because they know from his trial that he considers himself to be the royal Messiah (cf.14:61f – even at the trial Jesus does not need to volunteer this information but only to confirm what the authorities already suspect). Their denunciation of him as one who would destroy and rebuild the temple (v 29) also derives from his trial (14:58). In itself the charge is false,[1] a parody of Jesus' attitude towards the temple (11:17; 12:1–12,32–4; 13:2), though in light of his execution their charge is not without some ironic truth. (Indeed, it is doubly ironic because it is in the act of destroying Jesus that the temple establishment seals its own demise.) The point to note however is that behind the accusation lies an implicit recognition of Jesus' scandalous claim to sovereignty over the temple (11:28) and to the right to establish a new temple order (11:17,20–5). The scornful reference to Jesus' 'saving others' (v 29) discloses an apprehension of his therapeutic powers (3:4; 5:23,28,34; 6:56; 10:52) and of their intended role in attesting his message of the presence of ultimate salvation. And finally even their insincere offer of faith in return for miracle reveals an understanding of the kind of response sought by Jesus to his mission.

Their unbelief then lies not in a failure or inability to discern Jesus' potential significance, but in a conscious repudiation of him and of his works. For this reason the narrator describes

---

[1] Scholars are divided on whether the falsity lies in the intent of the witnesses or in the charge itself, or both. On the temple word and Mark's whole anti-temple posture, see: Juel, *Messiah and Temple*, 117–26, 143–57, 169–209; Donahue, *Are You the Christ?*, 71–7; idem, 'Royal Christology', 66–71; Kelber, *Mark's Story*, 57–70; idem, 'Passion Narrative', 170–2; Weeden, 'Power in Weakness', 121–9; Matera, *Kingship of Jesus*, 67–91; Best, *Following Jesus*, 213–25; Lührmann, 'Zerstörung des Tempel', 457–74; Vögtle, 'Tempelworte', 362–83; Chronis, 'Torn Veil', 109–14. See also Gaston, *No Stone*, 65–243; Lohmeyer, *Lord of the Temple*, 24–52.

their invective as 'blasphemy' (v 29), a culpable violation of
God's honour. Ironically they are thus doing the very thing for
which they condemned Jesus (2:7; 14:64), and so bring condemnation on themselves (3:28f).

(ii) The other aspect of the depiction of unbelief before the
cross is the demand for immediate (νῦν), visible (ἵνα ἴδωμεν),
incontrovertible proof as the condition of faith. The phrase 'see
and believe', which incidentally is unique to Mark's version
of the crucifixion narrative, reverses the pattern established
throughout his entire story where faith is the presupposition of
miracle, not its inevitable consequence. The demand does violence to the volitional character of true faith, whilst evading the
concomitant demand for ethical repentance.[1] But even more
significant is *what* is demanded: namely, the repudiation by
Jesus of the prevailing pattern of his entire ministry. His
enemies concede that he has 'saved others' but they refuse to
'see' such activity as the work of God. Instead they demand of
him what they think is physically — but in fact is morally —
impossible: that he contradict his own teaching (8:34f), abandon the purpose of his mission (10:45), reject the witness of
scripture (9:12; 14:21,49), and deny the divine δεῖ (8:31; cf. 9:11)
by descending from the cross. In requiring this kind of
'seeing', they reveal their failure to truly 'see' the action of God
(cf. 4:11f).

Their unbelief, therefore, is a combination of correctly seeing
Jesus' implied claims to messianic dignity and yet failing to
see God's own validation of them. The cross itself is not the
primary stumbling block, since it is their unbelief that has put
Jesus there in the first place. The cross is however a dramatic
symbol of the mainspring of their repudiation of him as
Messiah.

(c) Summary

The whole scene beneath the cross turns on the issue of *power*
— Jesus' power to destroy the temple, and his power to save
others yet not to save himself. At the heart of official unbelief,
as Mark treats it here, is a disdain for the ethically and
soteriologically qualified use of power by Jesus. His adversaries can neither accept that God's rule is evidenced in Jesus'
works of restoration, his 'saving others' (cf. 2:1–12; 3:1–6), nor
in his inability to 'save himself'. They consider his voluntary
self-giving (10:45; 15:4f), his powerless dependence on God

---

[1] See above, pp. 66–70.

(14:36), as a fatal weakness (ἑαυτὸν οὐ δύναται σῶσαι) and they appeal to his apparent impotence to discredit his claims. They thus evaluate divine power purely in human, self-serving terms, according to their own standards of practice (e.g. 11:18; 12:1–9; 14:43,48f; cf. 14:65 and 15:19).[1] They are therefore closed to faith, since Mark portrays faith as the sole possession of those who recognise their own powerlessness and who accept the demand it brings to relinquish conventional notions of rule and power (e.g. 10:42–5).

To complete the scene, we may note that the sequel to the second mockery scene confirms this correlation between unbelief and the scandal of powerlessness. In the third mockery scene,[2] the bystanders witness the darkness of judgement[3] and the cry of dereliction.[4] But unable to comprehend the meaning of these happenings, they mockingly twist Jesus' words into a last desperate cry for Elijah's aid and cruelly seek to prolong his life to 'see' if Elijah will save the Messiah who cannot save himself. In reality they expect Elijah's appearance as much as the priests expect Jesus to descend from the cross.

Then, upon Jesus' death, the narrator describes two striking events. The first is the splitting of the temple veil (v 38). Commentators divide over whether the inner or outer veil is meant and whether its tearing symbolises judgement on the temple or the unveiling of God's majesty.[5] In fact it is 'a rich image with both positive and negative poles'.[6] Whilst in the context of Mark's wider anti-temple motif (11:17; 12:1–12; 13:1f; 14:58; 15:29) it is a portent of the destruction of the temple, its immediate narrative function is to symbolise that here, at the

---

[1] Mark parallels the actions of the priests and soldiers; 'nearly everything the soldiers do the priests do', Matera, *Kingship of Jesus*, 96, cf. 24.

[2] This scene is not always seen as a case of mockery, but see Best, *Temptation and Passion*, 101f; Matera, *Kingship of Jesus*, 29–32, 122–5.

[3] See Best, *Temptation and Passion*, 97f; Culpepper, 'Passion and Resurrection', 585f.

[4] Some see this as a shout of eschatological victory (e.g. Matera, *Kingship of Jesus*, 127–35; cf. Burchard, 'Markus 15,34', 8f), but see Best, *Temptation and Passion*, 100f; Culpepper, 'Passion and Resurrection', 587.

[5] On this see the commentaries, and also: Best, *Temptation and Passion*, 98f; Juel, *Messiah and Temple*, 127f, 140–2; Matera, *Kingship of Jesus*, 137–40; Culpepper, 'Passion and Resurrection', 589–91; Donahue, *Are You the Christ?*, 201–3; Linnemann, *Passionsgeschichte*, 158–63; Vögtle, 'Tempelworte', 368–78; Senior, *Passion of Jesus*, 126–8; Chronis, 'Torn Veil', 97–114; Motyer, 'Rending of the Veil', 155–7; Jackson, 'Death of Jesus', 22–7.

[6] Matera, *Kingship of Jesus*, 139.

point of his final and supreme powerlessness, the divine sonship of Jesus is manifest. The use of σχίζεσθαι recalls the only other time Mark employs the verb: at Jesus' baptism,[1] where the heavens are split and a voice declares 'this is my beloved son' (1:10f).

The second event is the acknowledgement of this sonship by the Roman centurion (v 39).[2] In Mark's ideological framework, the intended significance of this is not only that the first person to make the climactic confession of the gospel is a Gentile, but that he is also a *centurion*, the commander of the execution squad (v 44), a symbol of military might and imperial power. Whereas the mockers demand to 'see' the supernatural deliverance of Jesus from death in order to believe, the soldier, who also 'stands opposite' (or opposed) to Jesus (vv 35,39) 'sees' (ἰδών) in his manner of dying an expression of his real dignity.[3] He thus displays the perception of faith, a perception predicated on his surrendering of preconceived notions of coercive power in order to perceive in the contradictions of the cross, in the very antithesis of worldly standards of divinity or royalty, the redemptive power of God revealed in the death of his son.[4] Perhaps the same sort of insight is also implied for the women at the cross and Joseph of Arimathea.

Thus as Jesus' earthly life ends Mark contrasts two types of seeing: the seeing of unbelief, which remains wedded to human notions of rule and power, and the seeing of faith, which perceives in apparent powerlessness the hidden, saving power of God. Faith alone can penetrate the ultimate paradox of the gospel: that the kingly power of God is manifest in the suffering and death of Jesus on the pagan cross, transforming

---

[1] On other linkages between these two passages, see Motyer, 'Rending of the Veil', 155.

[2] There are many exegetical issues associated with v 39 which cannot be discussed here, such as the significance of the anarthrous construction, the implications of the past tense of the verb, whether the confession should be understood in Hellenistic or Palestinian categories, and how it relates to Markan christology.

[3] Precisely what it is about Jesus' death that stimulates the centurion's confession is perplexing. See the thorough discussion of options by Jackson, 'Death of Jesus', 16–37.

[4] This interpretation should not be confused with the 'divine man' approach which contrasts the power of the cross with the power of miracles (e.g. Weeden, *Traditions in Conflict*, 53f, 67; idem, 'Power in Weakness', 120ff). We wish to contrast soteriological power, also evidenced in miracles, with 'worldly' or coercive power, displayed by the adversaries.

the cross into a power that is infinitely greater than any human power.

Before turning to the passages dealing with failing faith among the disciples, we should summarise what we have learned so far. A remarkably consistent picture of unbelief has emerged from these four pericopae dealing with the unbelief of Jesus' opponents. Mark portrays their unbelief as a mixture of seeing and not seeing, of correctly perceiving Jesus' implied claim to a unique status, yet refusing to accept it. They recognise Jesus as one who dares to act in God's stead (2:7), who (like God) possesses wisdom and remarkable therapeutic powers (6:2; 15:31), who claims authority over the temple (11:28), and who considers himself to be messianic king (15:32). They clearly understand his demand for repentant faith; indeed, the only characters in Mark's story to use faith terminology apart from Jesus are his enemies (11:31; 15:32). Where their unbelief becomes apparent is in their refusal to concede a divine source for what seem to be divine works, preferring instead to charge Jesus with blasphemy (2:7) and demonic allegiance (implied in 6:3; cf. 3:22,28ff). The root of this unbelief lies in the refusal of the religious authorities to have accepted John the Baptist's demand for conversion and his message of the coming Mightier One (11:30f), with the result that they display hostility towards Jesus from the very beginning of his ministry (2:6–10).

Their unrepentance expresses itself, we have proposed, especially in their refusal to do what the centurion does: to surrender their established notions of rule, power and prestige. It is Jesus' ordinariness (6:1–6) and his apparent powerlessness (15:29–32) that cry out against his claims to be God's emissary, despite his evident authority over sin (2:5,10f), sickness (2:11f; 6:2; 15:31), and even the temple system (11:28). A messianic king who merely saves or heals others and will not save himself is not worthy of faith. They are antagonistic to his concept of God's rule, for to accept it would mean an ending of the kind of rule which they exercise and from which they benefit.

2. Unbelief among the disciples

There are two pericopae in which Mark deals explicitly with faithlessness among the disciples. But again, before examining these passages we should briefly consider the thematic context to which they belong.

The theme of discipleship failure

Whereas Mark portrays the ruling authorities in an almost uniformly bad light, his characterisation of the disciples is more intricately developed, and hence more difficult to interpret. They are more 'rounded' characters who exhibit conflicting character traits. They appear as Jesus' companions, confidants, and co-workers, and yet the longer they are with Jesus, the more pronounced becomes their failure in each of these areas.

As the story unfolds, the author spares nothing in emphasising their shortcomings. The motif of failure begins in 4:13,[1] and is initially associated with their imperviousness to the meaning of Jesus' words (4:13; 5:31; 6:37; 7:18; 8:4,15f) and miracles (4:38ff; 6:52; 8:19–21), both of which betoken a failure to perceive his unique identity (4:41; 6:51). In the journey to Jerusalem, they fail to understand Jesus' passion teaching (8:32f; 9:10f,32; 10:32) and the true nature of their own discipleship (9:18f,28f,33f; 10:13–16,24,26,35ff). And once in Jerusalem, the Twelve not only fail to offer the support Jesus seeks (14:32–42), but one of their number betrays him (14:10f, 17–21), another disowns him (14:26–32,66–72), and they all forsake him (14:50, cf. v 27).

Now Mark's relentless exposure of the disciples' failings has been interpreted in various ways. Earlier generations appealed to Peter's historical reminiscences or to the constraints of Mark's tradition. However, most scholars now agree that, 'In comparison to his *Vorlage* and to his successors Matthew and Luke, Mark has clearly heightened the misunderstanding, rebuke and failure of the disciples.'[2] A second view understands the failure motif as a christological device intended to show that a true understanding of Jesus was not possible

---

[1] Some scholars locate the beginning as early as 1:35f; e.g. Kuby, 'Konzeption des Markus-Evangeliums', 55; Kelber, *Kingdom*, 45f; idem, *Mark's Story*, 22; Schenke, *Wundererzählungen*, 403; Weeden, *Traditions in Conflict*, 27ff, 149 n.17. But Mark's strategy seems to be first to paint the disciples in positive terms, then plot their failings. See our own explanation below.

[2] Klauck, 'Erzählerische Rolle', 26.

before his death and resurrection. The disciples do not understand because they *cannot* understand, nor are they meant to.[1] But even our own investigations of Mark's faith concept thus far would call this interpretation into question. For Mark portrays faith as founded upon an indispensable, even if incomplete, intuitive insight into Jesus' person, and he depicts unbelief as a culpable rejection of the truth. Easter is not the only effective revelatory event in Mark's story.[2] A third approach has Mark actively polemicising against the disciples, with whom he identifies theological opponents of his own day.[3] But this view fails to do justice to the positive elements of Mark's discipleship theme and leaves the readers or hearers bereft of any 'good' characters, apart from Jesus, with whom they may identify.[4]

The most helpful explanation, in our view, is one that relates the failure motif to Mark's pastoral or parenetic concern on the one hand, and to his narrative technique on the other.[5]

---

[1] See, e.g., Achtemeier, 'Mark as Interpreter', 123–7; idem, *Mark*, 100; Burkill, *Mysterious Revelation*, 168–87; idem, *New Light*, 239–41; Schenke, *Wundererzählungen*, 87f, 403f. This view owes much to the influence of Wrede, *Messianic Secret*, 101ff, although most scholars now accept that discipleship failure cannot be subsumed under the general rubric of the Messianic Secret. On this generally see Kingsbury, *Christology*, 1–23; Tuckett, *Messianic Secret*, 1–34.

[2] For a critique, see Tannehill, 'Disciples in Mark', 393. See also Lemcio, 'External Evidence', 333–6. At one point, even Burkill concedes that Mark 'is liable to forget they are historically located in a period of obscurity. . . .', *New Light*, 125.

[3] Some see Mark's opponents as advocates of a divine man christology (Weeden, 'Heresy', 245–58; idem, *Traditions in Conflict*, 159–68 and passim); others as representatives of the Jerusalem church or its royal theology (e.g. Tyson, 'Blindness of the Disciples', 261–8; Kelber, *Kingdom*, e.g. 83f, 144–7; idem, *Mark's Story*, 88–95; Crossan, 'Form for Absence', 49f).

[4] For more thorough critiques, see: Tannehill, 'Disciples in Mark', 393f; Best, *Discipleship*, 101–16; idem, *Gospel as Story*, 45–8; *Following Jesus*, 244f; 'Purpose of Mark', 24–6; Focant, 'L'Incompréhension des Disciples', 182–4; Martin, *Evangelist and Theologian*, 152f. See also Kingsbury's helpful critique of such 'corrective' approaches to Mark's christology, *Christology*, 25–45.

[5] Variations on this approach are advocated by, e.g., Tannehill, 'Disciples in Mark', 386–405; Best, *Discipleship*, 98–130; Rhoads and Michie, *Mark as Story*, 89–100, 122–9; Peacock, 'Discipleship in Mark', 555–64; Moloney, 'Vocation of the Disciples', 487–516; Mangatt, 'Aspects of Discipleship', 239–53; Malbon, 'Markan Characters and Readers', 104–30. See also, Reploh, *Lehrer*, 75–86; Kee, *Community*, 87–100; Hooker, *Message*, 105–21;

Knowing that his audience would naturally identify with the disciples, and wishing to challenge them with the full demands and reality of Christian discipleship, Mark depicts following Jesus as a constant dialectic between success and failure. He begins by reinforcing the tendency of his audience to identify with the disciples by presenting them in a positive light. They respond to Jesus' call (1:14–20; 2:13–15) and are allied with him against his foes (2:18–28). They participate in the new kingdom order (2:15,19–22,23), possess its mystery (4:10f), and are authorised to extend its powers (3:13–19). Then, having enouraged solidarity with and high expectations of the disciples, Mark introduces the element of growing conflict with Jesus. Yet he also continues to foster the readers' identification with them in two ways: by still portraying positive features in their behaviour – such as loyalty and courage (10:32; 14:29), obedience and assistance to Jesus (6:41; 8:6; 11:2–7; 14:13–16), self-sacrifice (10:28), success in ministry (6:7,12f,30), occasional insight (8:29), intimacy with Jesus (e.g. 6:31; 14:17ff), and intimations of a future role (9:9; 13:10,34; 14:28) – and by attributing to them the kinds of failings and weaknesses his audience could identify with. The narrator's evaluative point of view on the disciples is admirably expressed in 14:38: 'the spirit is indeed willing, but the flesh is weak'.

Given this alignment with the disciples, the failure motif can be understood as an effective and 'economical' literary device that enables the author to accomplish his parenetic and narrative goals. A single episode of discipleship failure, at one and the same time, (i) allows the true ideal of discipleship to stand out more clearly by its non-attainment; (ii) provides an opportunity for corrective teaching from Jesus and often for a demonstration of the power available to remedy the failing (5:31ff; 6:37ff,48ff; 8:4; 8:4ff; 9:18ff); (iii) enhances, by way of contrast, the characterisation of Jesus, who himself embodies the ideal the disciples fall short of; and (iv) encourages self-criticism in the reader or hearer, who perceives in himself or herself the same kind of failing.

One further point should be made before moving on to examine the specific area of faithlessness in this failure theme. In 8:14–21, the whole catalogue of vices associated with outsiders and opponents (2:7; 3:6; 4:11f) are attributed to the disciples: incomprehension, blindness, deafness, 'reasoning',

Hawkin, 'Incomprehension of the Disciples', 491–500; Freyne, 'At Cross Purposes', 331–9.

forgetfulness and hardness of heart. The use of this terminology is not meant to imply that the disciples are now the enemies of Jesus. Rather, it is indicative of an attempt by Jesus, by bombarding them with a series of rhetorical questions, to shock his disciples (and Mark's audience) into appreciating the existential seriousness of their condition. They are in mortal danger of succumbing to the same resistance to the truth that afflicts the religious leaders and against which he has just warned them (v 15).

The linguistic contacts do imply, however, that Mark perceives an essential kinship between the failure of the disciples and the mentality of Jesus' opponents. They are both exemplary of the γενέα ἄπιστος which stands opposed to the kingdom, and both come into conflict with Jesus. Yet, significantly, Mark largely isolates the two arenas of conflict and distinguishes between the nature of each. The conflict with the disciples usually takes place in private, as part of their ongoing community with Jesus, whereas the conflict with the opponents takes place in public, often in synagogues and the temple, where they oppose Jesus on their own ground.[1] Tension arises with the authorities because they are actively hostile to Jesus' words and deeds; it develops with the disciples because they passively fail to understand the significance of what he says and does. For all their failings, the disciples are never rejected by Jesus and are even promised a restored relationship after their climactic desertion of him (14:27; 16:7f).[2] By contrast, the ruling authorities are ultimately repudiated (cf. 15:29 and 3:28), for their failure is not one of cognition or courage, but of deliberate suppression of the truth.

In short, Jesus and the ruling authorities are at opposite poles in Mark's story and conflict between them is perpetual. The disciples however vacillate between both poles and are rebuked by Jesus only insofar as they revert to the values and attitudes of the γενέα ἄπιστος. We now turn to the two episodes in which the disciples manifest unbelief to see how this compares to the portrayal of unbelief in the above pericopae.

---

[1] Cf. Rhoads and Michie, *Mark as Story*, 100, 119, 123f.

[2] The polemical school argues that 16:8 condemns the disciples to ultimate failure. This is most improbable. See above n.1, p. 150. Also see pp. 41–2.

Unbelief in the storm at sea (4:35–41)

The first clear indication the narrator gives of a defect in the disciples' understanding comes in 4:13. Despite possessing the mystery of the kingdom, in distinction to outsiders who see and hear but do not understand (4:10–12), the disciples have failed to understand the parable of the sower. Jesus' ensuing explanation appears at first to have remedied the problem but, at the end of the day, the depth and disastrous consequences of their cognitive impairment are evidenced during a stormy crossing of the sea of Galilee.

The storm-stilling episode and the other sea story in 6:45–52 are the only two miracles performed in Mark directly on behalf of the disciples. More strikingly, they are worked in the absence of petitionary faith. Indeed, far from presupposing the faith of those involved, the miracle in 4:35–41 is followed by a denunciation of the faithlessness of those present. This in itself may suggest that Mark is dealing here with a different kind of unbelief than we have encountered thus far.

(a) Composition, structure, and theme
It is widely recognised that, as it stands, 4:35–41 contains two prominent themes: a christological theme which, drawing on various Old Testament motifs,[1] sets forth Jesus as one greater than Jonah, as one who himself exercises Yahweh's cosmic dominion over the natural elements; and a discipleship-failure theme, which describes the disciples' loss of courage and faith before the threatening storm. The first theme climaxes in the wondering question: 'who is this that even wind and sea obey him?' (v 41), and the second in the rebuke: 'why are you afraid? Do you still have no faith?' (v 40).

It is often felt that a certain tension exists between these two motifs. Verse 40 disrupts the narrative flow between the miracle (v 39) and the choral response (v 41), and seems ill-placed after the accomplishment of the miraculous deed. Many scholars therefore propose that v 40, and probably v 38c as well, have been secondarily interpolated in order to transpose a nature miracle or epiphany story into a new discipleship key.

---

[1] For a discussion of Old Testament motifs, as well as *religionsgeschicht-liche* parallels, see Schenke, *Wundererzählungen*, 59–69; Kertelge, *Wunder Jesu*, 95f; Theissen, *Miracle Stories*, 99–103; Smith, *Magician*, 119; Van der Loos, *Miracles*, 641–4; cf. Derrett, *Making of Mark*, 96–8. The influence of the Jonah story is disputed; see Pesch, *Markus*, I, 271ff.

Mark himself is usually credited with this revision.[1] Another possibility however is that the narrator has simply moved v 40 forward from its earlier location before v 39 to its present conspicuous position in order to give prominence to the charge of unbelief[2] (cf. Matt 8:26). Furthermore even if the christological and discipleship emphases do represent different layers of tradition, in the final narrative both themes are equally pronounced and thoroughly interrelated. The failure of the disciples is directly related to their unawareness of the true identity of their passenger, whilst Jesus' unique power stands out even more boldly by way of contrast to their cowardly fear.

Now Mark draws attention to the didactic significance of 4:35–41 for his discipleship theme in a number of ways. He takes some pains,[3] for example, to create a connection between this episode and the preceding parable material. The doubled time reference in v 35 locates it at the end of the same day that has been filled with the teaching of vv 1–34; it commences with the same formula used to introduce each earlier piece of parabolic instruction (καὶ λέγει αὐτοῖς, v 35, cf. vv 2,11,13,21, 24,26,30); and it takes place in the same boat that has served all day as Jesus' pulpit (ὡς ἦν ἐν τῷ πλοίῳ, v 36, cf. 4:1). Mark stresses the seclusion of Jesus with his disciples in the boat by commenting on the departure of the crowd and by noting the presence of other boats, which, by implication, Jesus is *not* in. The address διδάσκαλε (v 38) in the centre of the narrative also alludes to the instructional significance of this episode for Mark's discipleship concerns.

The narrative style of 4:35–41 is vivid and colourful. With the exception of v 37c, the whole account is built up on the basis of καί-parataxis, with a notable mixing of present, imperfect and aorist tenses. Although differing somewhat in their colometric reckoning, a number of scholars have detected rhythmic strophic patterns in the narrative,[4] suggestive perhaps of an

---

[1] So, e.g., Koch, *Wundererzählungen*, 97; Kelber, *Kingdom*, 49; Schenke, *Wundererzählungen*, 33–44, 82; Pesch, *Markus*, I, 268, 276; Gnilka, *Markus*, I, 193. Schmithals is virtually alone in claiming that v 41 is a Markan addition, *Wunder*, 57f.

[2] Schenke's arguments against this possibility are not compelling, *Wundererzählungen*, 38, 41, 44.

[3] Schenke argues that Mark is responsible for this linkage, *Wundererzählungen*, 1–17. Kertelge considers it pre-Markan, *Wunder Jesu*, 91.

[4] E.g. Lohmeyer, *Markus*, 89; Grundmann, *Markus*, 102f; cf. Pesch, *Markus*, I, 269 n.3; Kertelge, *Wunder Jesu*, 93f. Schille uses metric structure as a way of eliminating secondary elements, 'Seesturmerzählungen', 34f.

oral ballad. The narrative advances through three stages. The introduction (vv 35–6) sets the scene and includes two important elements for understanding the charge of unbelief: the initiative of Jesus in undertaking the journey and announcing its goal, and the comment on his presence with the disciples in the boat. The latter element is emphasised by the clumsy construction παραλαμβάνουσιν αὐτὸν ὡς ἦν ἐν τῷ πλοίῳ, as well as by the reference to 'other boats'.[1] In the plotted context, these boats are presumably for the wider circle of followers mentioned in 4:10, but the effect of their mention in v 36 is to underline the fact that the disciples whose faith fails are the very ones with whom Jesus is quartered.

The second section, which narrates the storm itself, opens and closes on contrasting notes.

v 37 καὶ γίνεται λαῖλαψ μεγάλη ἀνέμου
v 39 καὶ ἐγένετο γαλήνη μεγάλη

In between these verses, a contrast is drawn between the faithless anxiety of the disciples and the trustful repose of Jesus. The use of the technical term ἐπιτιμᾶν for Jesus' action suggests that the storm is conceived of as a violent demonic onslaught aimed at destroying the kingdom community in the ship (cf. 4:39 and 1:25).[2]

The third section (v 40–1) begins, like the first, with Jesus addressing the disciples (καὶ εἶπεν αὐτοῖς) and comprises the didactic commentary on what has just transpired. The behaviour of the disciples is diagnosed as a case of cowardice (δειλός) and faithlessness, and the reason for this state is intimated in their fearful reaction to Jesus' awesome demonstration of power: they have not yet plumbed the full identity and capacities of this man whom even wind and sea obey.

(b) The portrayal of unbelief

Mark employs two of his favourite dramatic devices in framing Jesus' denunciation of the disciples' unbelief: the rhetorical question, which heightens the drama and encourages self-questioning in the audience, and two-step progression or

---

[1] This reference is usually seen, however, as a vestige of an earlier form of the tradition. For various opinions on the role of these boats, see Pesch, *Markus*, I, 270 n.7; Schmithals, *Wunder und Glaube*, 59f; Schenke, *Wundererzählungen*, 8, 32.

[2] See Kee, 'Terminology of Exorcism', 243f; idem, *Community*, 121; Kertelge, *Wunder Jesu*, 92. Otherwise, Cranfield, *Mark*, 174; Lenski, *Mark*, 199.

duality, by which the second rhetorical question clarifies and interprets the first.[1] The disciples' state of fear is thus explained as a manifestation that they 'still' (οὔπω) have no faith. A well-attested variant has πῶς οὐκ instead of οὔπω and this reading is favoured by the RSV and a number of commentators.[2] The inclusion of οὔπω, however, 'has by far the best external support'[3] and derives some internal probability from a likely thematic linkage with the twofold use of οὔπω in Mark's third and climactic boat scene (8:17,21).

Wherein does the faithlessness of the disciples lie in this episode? Schenke[4] argues that it lies in their unwillingness to die with Jesus. Instead of trusting him to lead them through death to eternal life (cf. 8:34ff), they plead for miraculous intervention, for a 'sign' of divine power (cf. 8:11f; 15:29ff). This interpretation is hard to sustain however. Elsewhere in Mark's story, pleading for miraculous intervention in situations of genuine need is positively evaluated: 'sign seeking' is something quite different to what transpires here.[5] Also, the corollary of Schenke's interpretation is that the disciples should have read in Jesus' composure an acceptance of his own impending death. But this is hardly in Mark's mind. The storm is demonically inspired and there would be nothing 'redemptive' in the death of Jesus or of his disciples in this context. The image of Jesus going quietly to his death sleeping peacefully in the stern contrasts markedly with the fear and anguish he experiences in Gethsemane, where it is the disciples who sleep! (14:32–42).

The faithlessness of the disciples consists not in their unwillingness to die with Jesus, but rather in their mistaken conviction that they are surely about to die with him (ἀπολλύμεθα) and that he appears not to care (οὐ μέλει σοι). Within the story, the ambiguity of Jesus' state of sleep symbolises the challenge posed to their faith. They could either interpret his slumber as an expression of confidence in God's care (Pss 3:5; 4:8; Prov 3:23f; Job 11:18f; cf. Ps 121:3f) and, since they are called 'to be with him' (3:14), be reassured of their

---

[1] On rhetorical questions, see above p. 191.

[2] πῶς οὐκ (A C K Π 33 al.) οὔπω (ℵ B D L Δ Θ 565 700 892*)

[3] Metzger, Textual Commentary, 84. Schenke evaluates the external evidence more evenly, but favours this reading on internal grounds, Wundererzählungen, 35–7. See also Koch,Wundererzählungen, 97 n.29.

[4] Schenke, Wundererzählungen, 83–93.

[5] See above, pp. 66–70.

ultimate safety. Or they could construe it as a sign of his indifference to their plight (cf. Pss 44:23; also 35:23; 59:5; 78:65), and give way to fear. And this is precisely what they do.

The evaluation of their response as 'cowardice' and the use of the word 'still' imply that, given the circumstances, better could have been expected of the disciples. They had witnessed Jesus' power on many previous occasions; he was present with them in the boat facing the same danger; he had initiated the journey and declared its goal; in his parabolic teaching that day, after exhorting them to understand his words (4:13), he had warned of the danger of succumbing during times of trial (4:16–19), and had given reassurance that even when the sower sleeps they may be confident of God's continuing activity (4:26–9) – and yet they 'still' had no faith in his power and readiness to rescue them. For they had still not yet grasped his full identity (v 41).

Some interpreters suggest that the charge of faithlessness is levelled against the disciples here not so much because they failed to trust in Jesus' miraculous intervention, but because they did not exercise miracle-working power themselves against the elements.[1] This view has much to commend it. The storm scene is depicted as an exorcism, and in 3:15 the Twelve had been specially authorised to cast out demons. It is this kind of failure they experience again in 9:14–29, where they are also accused of unbelief. Furthermore, there is a network of passages in which the narrator seems to imply that Jesus expected the disciples to effect miracles. In 6:37 he instructs the empty-handed disciples to feed the multitude in the desert (cf. 8:4f); in the second storm episode (6:45–52) Jesus comes to the toiling disciples walking on water, but his intention is to by-pass the boat (v 48), as if his aim was simply to put them in mind of their delegated powers; in 8:14–21 he expresses exasperation at their concern over having only one loaf of bread with them so soon after witnessing the feeding miracles;[2] and,

---

[1] E.g. Rhoads and Michie, *Mark as Story*, 47, 90f, 93, 124f, 129; Coutts, 'Authority of Jesus', 112f.

[2] 8:14–21 is traditionally understood as depicting a failure by the disciples to trust in Jesus for material provision. Gibson has recently argued strongly against this view, proposing instead that the disciples failed to bring extra bread on the boat in order to discourage Jesus from a further display of divine favour to those outside Israel, such as he had shown in 8:1–10, 'Rebuke of the Disciples', 31–47. But why would choosing not to bring bread prevent this; after all in the feeding miracles Jesus *multiplied* limited resources? Perhaps a better way to interpret this difficult passage is

as we have seen, in 11:22–5, he depicts miracle-working faith as characteristic of the new discipleship community.

The main difficulty with such a reading of 4:35–41, however, lies in reconciling the christological import of v 41 – that Jesus' unique identity is evidenced in his sovereignty over the elements – with the fact that in v 40 the disciples are reproved for not having first exercised such dominion themselves! On the other hand, Mark consistently ascribes to faith the capacity to do what God alone can do, and his thought in v 41 may be that the disciples failed to exercise miraculous power because they failed to perceive that Jesus had such cosmic authority to delegate to them in the first place.

Whether this is the case, or whether, as on balance seems more likely, their faithlessness lay in a lack of confidence in Jesus' power to deliver them, the result is the same: a belief that the situation is hopeless and that Jesus does not care. The disciples thus display the reverse attitude to what Jairus is encouraged to show. He is exhorted not to fear but only to have faith (5:36); they are reproached for not having faith but being overcome with fear (4:40). It would be out of keeping with the dramatic style of the narrative to take οὔπω ἔχετε πίστιν; to imply an absolute absence of faith on the part of the disciples.[1] It is better to see the narrator as employing 'shock tactics', as in 8:14–21, to drive home the seriousness of their plight. The intended tone of the two rhetorical questions in v 41 is one of horrified indignation that those cloistered with Jesus in the boat, 'insiders' who have received so much, are still unable to manifest faith in times of crisis.

Clearly then Mark does not conceive faith as the automatic or continuous possession of those who follow Jesus. The foundation of their discipleship is total reliance on Jesus for provision, protection and ultimate salvation,[2] and insofar as they continue to follow him, this remains their basic posture. But in specific situations of need, their general reliance upon him must manifest itself in an immediate, concrete expression of trust that will overcome fear and release power. A failure in

---

to understand Jesus rebuking the disciples for failing to grasp that his miraculous provision in the wilderness had implications *for them and their material needs too*. Just as *they* did not go without in the wilderness feedings, because supply greatly exceeded demand (8:19–21), so they will not lack now.

[1] As does Schille, 'Seesturmerzählungen', 38.

[2] See above, pp. 138–9.

this respect does not invalidate their commitment to Jesus, but it is a serious inconsistency. And since the essence of their commitment is faith, the corresponding failure can only be, in Mark's eyes, faith-*lessness*.

The absence of faith in 4:35–41 then is not the entrenched unbelief of Jesus' enemies (otherwise no miracle would have been possible), nor the non-faith of *vorgläubigen Menschen*, but a particular failure by those within the community of faith to manifest active reliance on Jesus' power in a crisis. Matthew has his own technical term for such faltering faith on the part of believers: ὀλιγοπιστία/ὀλιγόπιστος.[1] But for Mark the line between faith and unfaith is more sharply drawn. When believers fail to act in faith, they are not simply 'small in faith'; they are actually succumbing to the power of the γενεά ἄπιστος that stands opposed to God's rule.

(c) Summary

The disciples are depicted in 4:35–41 as 'unbelieving believers'. They have faith enough to follow Jesus – to be with him in the boat in the first place – but cowed by the storm they lose all confidence in his power to help, whether directly through personal intervention, or indirectly through their own use of his delegated authority. And the reason for their failure of faith is that they still have not grasped the unique identity of Jesus.

The fact that Jesus' power is not hampered by the disciples' unbelief (contrast 6:5f) is perhaps explicable in two ways. First, the deed is performed within the community of those committed to Jesus, secluded from outsiders and hostile sign-seekers. However faltering their faith, the disciples are at least aware of God's presence with Jesus and open to his demands. The story is really about an existing faith that fails in time of testing, and the miracle is as much about Jesus' rescue of fragile faith as about a display of supernatural power to meet physical need. Secondly, the storm is depicted as a demonic assault presumably aimed at destroying Jesus. The attack provides an occasion for the testing of the disciples' faith, but ultimately it comes down to a contest between Jesus and the demonic. In such circumstances, the power of Jesus is not dependent on the faith of others, but on his own identity as the

---

[1] On this term, see Barth, 'Glaube und Zweifel', 283–9; Held, 'Matthew as Interpreter', 294ff; Bornkamm, 'Stilling of the Storm', 56.

Mightier One (1:7) who has already bound the strong man (3: 27; cf. 1:12f).

The power of Jesus prevails. The 'great fear' the disciples experience at his conquest of the elements (v 41) bespeaks an awareness of having witnessed divine revelation and activity, and is at the same time a gauge of how inadequate their understanding of Jesus' person has been to date. But the interrogatory format of their response leaves Mark's audience unsure as to whether the disciples yet have sufficient insight to answer their own question and avoid similar failure in the future. It soon becomes apparent that they do not. The episode in 4:35–41 is the first in a cycle of three related boat scenes[1] in which the basic cause of the disciples' failure of faith reveals itself as a continuing, even deepening malaise (6:45–52; 8:14–21). In the third and climactic scene, the disciples who 'still' had no faith in 4:40, 'still' do not understand (8:17,21). So long as they lack an adequate understanding of who Jesus is they remain vulnerable to failing faith, and in 9:14–29 we again encounter a display of unbelief.

Unbelief and exorcism (9:14–29)

Whereas the failure of faith in 4:35–41 takes place in the presence of Jesus, in 9:14–29 a similar failure occurs during his absence on the Mount of Transfiguration. This lack of success is made all the more serious by the two flanking references to Jesus' passion (9:9–13,30–2) and by the 'how long' questions within the story (v 19), which indicate that the time of Jesus' final separation from his followers is fast approaching. Despite the urgency of the time, the disciples' grasp of faith remains equivocal.

In our earlier treatment of this pericope[2] we discussed its literary construction and its portrayal of the petitioner's faith. We also noted that the location of the story in the discipleship instruction section (8:27–10:52), plus its opening and closing focus on the disciples, indicates that Mark's principal concern in this episode is the condition of the disciples as ἄπιστοι, and it is this aspect we shall now examine. This depiction of the

---

[1] See especially Meye, *Twelve*, 63–72. Mk 4:35–41 is also tightly connected to the miracle narratives that follow it. On the question of Markan or pre-Markan 'miracle collections' in Mark chs. 4–8, see Fowler, *Loaves and Fishes*, 5–37, who cites most other relevant literature.

[2] See above, pp. 110–23.

disciples centres on their failure, despite special authorisation (3:15; 6:7) and past success (6:12f), to cope with a particularly severe case of demonic possession (9:18). Within the logic of the narrative, this failure is characterised in two related ways: as an absence of faith (v 19), and as a lack of prayer (v 28f).

(a) The portrayal of unbelief

We have already argued that the lament over the faithless generation in v 19 is not addressed solely to the disciples, but embraces everyone present. Nevertheless it is news of the disciples' failure that occasions the outburst, and they are certainly included in the designation. As applied to the disciples, the term γενεὰ ἄπιστος carries a particular sting. It indicates that in their failure they are discreditably indistinguishable from the 'adulterous and sinful generation' that opposes the kingdom (8:38) and, more pointedly, from 'this generation' that seeks miraculous displays outside a genuine faith relationship to Jesus (8:12). Schenke[1] thinks that the ἕως πότε formulation may be intended, by allusion to the same phrase in Isa 6:11, to recall the description of 'outsiders' in Mark 4:11 (which draws on Isa 6:10). Indeed the language of v 19 as a whole evokes a complex of negative associations from the Old Testament which are here attributed, by implication, to the shamed disciples.[2]

Mark thus implies that in their abortive attempt to exorcise the boy, the disciples were acting no differently than those who stand outside and opposed to the kingdom. They not only failed to recognise the inadequate faith of the petitioner – which Jesus addresses before delivering the boy – but they also failed to grasp the indispensable place of faith in their own use of delegated authority. This constitutes a culpable negation of their task as disciples, and time is running out to remedy the situation (ἕως πότε πρὸς ὑμᾶς ἔσομαι;).

In the closing scene of the story (v 28f), which is conventionally held to be a redactional addition,[3] the disciples ask Jesus about the reasons for their earlier lack of success. Evidently they have either not applied Jesus' reproachful outburst in v 19 to themselves at all, or else they remain

---

[1] Schenke, *Wundererzählungen*, 322–5.

[2] E.g. Deut 32:5,20; Jer 5:21f; Ezek 12:2; Isa 65:2.

[3] For the main evidence cited in support of this view, see Reploh, *Lehrer*, 211–16; Koch, *Wundererzählungen*, 120f; Schenk, 'Epileptiker-Perikope', 77–9; Schenke, *Wundererzählungen*, 330–2.

unclear on precisely what their faithlessness entailed, since they had clearly expected success. In reply Jesus explains that 'this kind' (of demon? of miracle?) can only be driven out by prayer (and fasting?).[1]

Now some interpreters insist that there is a stark contradiction between this explanation, which suggests a failure of technique, and the explanantion in v 19, which cites a lack of faith. And if it is true that 'this kind' only goes out by prayer, why is it Jesus is not represented as having prayed? Schmithals claims that the redactor has done violence to the intention of the earlier narrative by now requiring a special praxis for particularly severe cases of possession,[2] and Telford suspects post-Markan scribal activity aimed at ameliorating the ignomy of the disciples.[3] Others propose that Mark is addressing needs in his own community more than commenting directly on the preceding episode.[4]

Two observations would suggest, however, that Mark intends the reference to prayer to serve as an interpretative commentary on the charge of faithlessness in v 19. First, we have already found in our discussion of 11:23f that for Mark faith and prayer form a tight unity.[5] He conceives of prayer as the source of faith's power and the expression of its presence. It is not a special technique but the end of all technique (cf. 12:40), for prayer is simply the verbal expression of faith which looks wholly to God for the release of his power. In the exorcism scene, therefore, it is not simply a matter of whether Jesus' words are framed as a petition, but whether Mark conceives of his authority to act as being received and exercised in prayerful dependence on God (cf. 1:35; 6:41,46; 14:32ff).[6] In keeping with this, v 29 specifies that the faithlessness of the disciples lay in their self-confident reliance upon their own strength (cf. οὐκ ἴσχυσαν, v 18) and not upon God. Presumably they had come to regard their power to heal and exorcise as

---

[1] The words have wide textual support (P^{45vid} ℵ^2 A C D L W Θ Ψ fam$^{1\ 13}$, Byz. texts generally) but the internal arguments against their originality are strong – see Cranfield, 'St Mark 9:14–29', 62 n.1.

[2] Schmithals, *Markus*, II, 423f.

[3] Telford, *Barren Temple*, 106f, 109.

[4] E.g. Reploh, *Lehrer*, 217, cf. 50; Roloff, *Kerygma*, 141; Best, *Following Jesus*, 69.

[5] See above, pp. 170–2.

[6] Cf. Oepke, *TDNT*, III, 210. Also Findlay, *Jesus,* 104; Van der Loos, *Miracles*, 271–3.

their own autonomous possession rather than being a commission from Jesus to realise his delegated authority afresh each time through dependent prayer. Mark is suggesting then that self-confident optimism may 'feel' like faith, but it is in fact unbelief, because it disregards the prerequisite of human powerlessness and prayerful dependence on God.

The second observation is that the reference to prayer in v 29 does not introduce an entirely new element into the narrative. On the contrary, the rhetorical function of vv 28f is to direct attention back to the example of the one whose 'prayer' in this episode did lead to the demon's expulsion, namely the father of the boy. The central part of the story is devoted to the way Jesus elicits a prayer of faith from the father (vv 21–4) because it exemplifies the attitude required of the disciples in their own exercise of healing power,[1] and also the requisite attitude they must seek in those to whom they minister (cf. 6:11). They had failed on both counts. The father moves from the defective 'if you can'-prayer to the prayer of trustful dependence: 'I believe, help my unbelief.' This prayer simultaneously confesses confidence in the omnipotence of God's power in Jesus, and a radical lack of confidence in his own subjective ability to maintain faith without external aid. To this attitude the disciples are now summoned, and at the same time reminded that 'all things are possible to one who believes' – and *only* to one who *truly* believes!

(b) Summary

The ἀπιστία in this episode is not the fearful despair of 4:35–41, but a blasé self-assurance that fails to see the centrality of dependent prayer in deploying Jesus' delegated power, treating it almost as a technique learned from him. Both kinds of unbelief – anxious self-concern and misplaced self-confidence – are inconsistent with the disciples' commitment to trust in Jesus for provision, protection and ultimate salvation.

Mark does not portray discipleship as a steady progress from unbelief, through doubt to the inviolate certainty of faith, but as

---

[1] That the father is set forth as a *Gegenbild* and/or *Vorbild* for the disciples is recognised by Kertelge, *Wunder Jesu*, 177f; Koch, *Wundererzählungen*, 121; Schenke, *Wundererzählungen*, 327, 345f; Lührmann, *Glaube*, 25. Best disagrees, partly because, 'There is a distinction between the faith which moves mountains and the faith which is the believing response to God's acts', *Following Jesus*, 72 n.35. However, whilst these are different expressions of faith, Mark regards the faith as *structurally* the same in both. See further below, pp. 229–30.

a constant to-and-froing between the values and outlook of the γενεὰ ἄπιστος and the values and perspective of God's rule. When the disciples fail to act in concrete situations in a manner consistent with their initial faith commitment, they are indistinguishable from those without faith and those hardened in unbelief. In Mark's estimate, discipleship evidently involves a continuing struggle for the victory of faith over unbelief.

3. Conclusion: The nature of unbelief

Analysis of the literary format of individual pericopae, set within the wider context of related themes in the narrative, has again proved a viable and useful method for exploring Mark's conception of unbelief. In particular, an appreciation of his use of such literary devices as irony, riddles, and rhetorical questions has been crucial for comprehending both the dramatic and conceptual aspects of his presentation of this motif.

Conflict is the central driving force of Mark's story. Jesus is found in conflict with demons, disciples, the crowds, and the ruling authorities, a conflict that leads ultimately to his comprehensive isolation and rejection. We have proposed that behind this conflict, Mark conceives a fundamental contest between the dawning rule of God and the γενεὰ ἄπιστος which resists its coming. Only Jesus stands in total contrast to the 'faithless generation' (9:19); all other characters are, to greater or lesser degrees, vulnerable or totally subject to its power. Mark therefore predicates unbelief not only of the crowds and the ruling authorities, but also of the disciples, despite the fact that they otherwise belong to the community of faith.

Although at different points of his story Mark applies the same battery of terms used to describe outsiders and opponents to the disciples, he nevertherless retains a distinction between the two groups. This applies also to his depiction of the unbelief of both groups. The unbelief of the ruling authorities is not primarily a want of insight, but a refusal to accept the claims and demands of Jesus – which they well understand – because they fear the existential consequences of doing so. It is a problem of volition more than cognition. They not only refuse to respond in repentant faith; they actively work to prevent the potential they perceive in Jesus becoming a reality. Scepticism, mockery and overt hostility are the hallmarks of their unbelief.

The disciples, on the other hand, are those who have already accepted the claims and demands of Jesus and who now struggle to follow him in faith. Their unbelief consists in periodic failures to act in a manner that is consistent with their commitment of radical dependency on the power of Jesus. This relapse into the values of the γενεὰ ἄπιστος is caused, paradoxically, by a failure of cognition, a persistent inability to understand who Jesus is and what he is about. Misunderstanding and fearful amazement are the hallmarks of their unbelief. This cognitive defect obviously has a volitional component, otherwise Jesus would not employ 'shock tactics' to jolt the disciples out of their spiritual myopia (which at times appear to work, cf. 8:17–21 and 8:27–30). But their problem is not so much a deliberate rejection of the truth as a failure to ensure that the intuitive insight into Jesus' significance upon which their faith was founded developed into a fuller understanding of his identity and mission, and of their relation to it.

7 CONCLUSIONS

We have now completed our exegetical and literary treatment of all the πίστις, πιστεύειν references in the Markan text. In this concluding chapter, we will briefly review the narrative methodology we have used, and then attempt to draw together the main conceptual threads of Mark's understanding of faith.

1. Methodological review

At the outset, we asked whether a predominantly literary or narrative approach would prove serviceable for the analysis of such a distinctly theological conception as 'faith', and for a motif which is developed in the course of the gospel not by progressive enrichment but by reiteration. We are now justified in answering the question affirmatively. The element of belief and unbelief plays an important role in shaping how Mark tells his story, and the use of narrative critical procedures and insights has allowed us to delineate this role with some precision. The method we have adopted has entailed two main strategies.

First, we have applied the categories and insights of literary criticism to individual pericopae, treating them as small narratives in their own right, comprising of plot, characterisation and a range of literary devices. The merit of doing this is that it has enabled us to appreciate how Mark communicates his notion of faith through the literary mode he has chosen: the narrative or story mode. There is limited abstract reflection or even direct teaching on faith in the gospel; Mark's theological perspective is implicit in the way he tells his story – both the single overall story about Jesus, and the component episodes or stories which make up the larger narrative. Analysis of the literary structure and dynamics of each faith story has allowed us to grasp the narrative techniques employed by Mark in order to give content, life and didactic power to his subject.

The various compositional features and rhetorical devices

226

we have identified have proved crucial for comprehending both the dramatic and conceptual aspects of Mark's faith theme. His use of such techniques as repetition and duplication to underline points of emphasis; intercalations and framing verses to suggest comparisons and contrasts; irony and paradox to point to deeper levels of meaning; riddles, proverbs and rhetorical questions to intensify the drama and involve the audience, all combine to give a richness to his faith motif that would have eluded us had we simply examined a set of isolated logia. It has also allowed us to see distinctive emphases in each of the individual pericopae which treat the subject.

But Mark's gospel is more than a string of isolated units; it is one unified narrative in which the individual pericopae are no longer experienced by the reader or hearer as separate tales but as cumulative scenes in a single coherent story. For this reason, in addition to treating individual passages, we have employed a second methodological strategy of seeking to relate Mark's faith emphasis to some of the broader thematic concerns of the narrative, such as the kingdom of God, discipleship and discipleship failure, official opposition and the anti-temple motif, eschatology, and so on.

This partly explains our method of organisation. We have not simply retold Mark's entire story or dealt with the faith references in the same order in which he presents them, for there is no internal development in the faith-theme itself. There is no indication of a steady movement over time of any individual or group from a condition of unbelief, through doubt to full faith. The faith of Bartimaeus in Mark 10 does not represent, in its inner structure, a progression on that of the paralytic in Mark 2. Nor is the unbelief of the priests and scribes at the foot of the cross an intensification of that of the scribes in Capernaum at the beginning of the story. Instead, the faith motif is interwoven with the major progressive themes in the narrative and contributes to the plot largely by supplying an interpretative commentary on developments in the story. The initial call to repentance and faith provides the main standard of judgement by which the reader is to assess the various reactions to Jesus he or she will encounter, and later references to faith reinforce this evaluative viewpoint with respect to events transpiring in the immediate context or within the broader thematic setting.

Mark uses various devices to integrate the faith-pericopae into the larger narrative: the reiteration of key words or concepts; prospective and retrospective references; the use of phrases, verses or whole pericopae to frame longer sections of narrative; and of course the consistent presence of Jesus and the disciples in each scene. One of Mark's important techniques is to use the faith-response of minor characters as a foil for the behaviour of the disciples and religious authorities, either within the same scene (e.g. 2:1–12) or in the wider context (e.g. 10:46–52).

In sum, our method has allowed us to combine an exegetical treatment of each of Mark's πίστις, πιστεύειν references within the integrity of the episodes in which they occur, with an appreciation of the wider significance of these references for Mark's unfolding drama. While traditio-historical and source-critical analyses have an important role in the investigation of Markan themes, it is literary or narrative critical procedures that are best suited to elucidating the intended message of the final text.

2. The Markan conception of faith

1. The expressions of faith

In Mark's story, it is possible to distinguish two main expressions or applications of faith, which we may call 'kerygmatic faith' and 'petitionary faith'.

(a) Kerygmatic faith denotes the believing acceptance of Jesus' proclamation of the dawning kingdom, a response entailing ethical conversion and a commitment of reliant trust upon Jesus as bearer of the kingdom (1:15). The main form this takes in Mark is the commitment of discipleship. Although Jesus has adherents in Mark who are not full disciples, it is the response of the disciples, and especially the Twelve, that the author focuses on as paradigmatic of the repentant faith demanded in view of the impinging kingdom.

(b) Petitionary faith denotes the concrete act of believing trust required of those who seek the operation of kingdom power. This has at least four different forms in Mark.

(i) There is the faith of needy petitioners who seek miraculous help directly for their own physical needs (2:1–12; 5:24–34; 6:5; 10:46–52).

(ii) There is the faith of vicarious petitioners who seek aid for a third party. Of the three episodes where Mark depicts Jesus interacting not with the patient but with a representative suppliant, faith is expressly mentioned in two of them (5:21–4,35–43; 9:14–29) and implied in the third (7:24–30) – both by way of

analogy and by verbal links with the Jairus narrative (cf. 5:22f and 7:25). Within these stories there are perhaps three clues as to why Mark regards intercessory faith as equivalent to the faith of the patient himself or herself. In the first place, those in need of restoration are physically unable to manifest faith themselves. Jairus' daughter is at the point of death, and the other two patients are demon-possessed (7:25; 9:18,20,22,26). Secondly, in each case the vicarious petitioner is the parent of the one in need, and thus their recognised representative in other spheres of life as well. And thirdly, the perseverance and words of the suppliants disclose complete identification with the need of the patient. Jairus lays aside his social rank and the Syrophoenician woman transcends racial and sexual barriers in order to secure Jesus' help, and both use the affectionate term θυγάτριον. The father of the epileptic boy so thoroughly identifies with his son's need that he includes himself in the petition: 'have pity on *us* and help *us*' (9:22). Evidently Mark sees a close relationship between compassion and vicarious faith.

(iii) Next there is the faith required of those who seek to effect miracles. Such 'mountain-moving' faith (11:23) may express itself as a direct word of command but Mark stresses the role of petitionary prayer as the source of faith's power (9:28f).

(iv) Finally there is the faith required for the whole range of petitionary prayer, for 'whatever' one seeks and 'whenever' one stands praying (11:25f).

Now whilst these distinctions are valid and helpful, Mark himself allows for no essential difference in the *structure or inner reality* of the faith involved in each case, in other words, in what the exercise of faith subjectively entails for the believer. Kerygmatic and petitionary faith are two expressions of the same fundamental attitude. In chapter two, we saw how 'kerygmatic faith' is not simply a matter of intellectual acceptance of Jesus' words but involves an existential entrusting of oneself to the ruling power of God as it is being established through the kerygma of Jesus. Accordingly the 'kerygmatic faith' of the disciples is portrayed as an on-going commitment of radical reliance on Jesus for miraculous provision, protection, personal transformation and ultimate salvation. In specific situations of need, this general posture of faith must realise itself in an immediate, concrete investment of trust comparable to that required of petitioners in the miracle narratives. On the other hand, within these narratives Mark depicts the 'petitionary faith' that seeks miracle as a response

to the kerygma of Jesus or as conditioned by an apprehension of the presence of God's ruling power in him. Such faith secures therefore not just bodily healing but the full experience of salvation proffered in the kerygma. The miracles themselves furthermore, in Mark's understanding, embody an implicit challenge to those who witness them to respond in 'kerygmatic faith' to the dawning kingdom. The very fact that Mark uses the response of Bartimaeus to illustrate simultaneously petitionary faith and kerygmatic faith (10:46–52) is clear evidence that he conceives of no fundamental structural difference between both expressions of πίστις.

U. Luz and G. Barth may be correct in regarding Matthew's term ὀλιγοπιστία/ὀλιγόπιστος as a 'terminological experiment' and 'conceptual balancing act' between kerygmatic faith and miracle faith.[1] But although Mark lacks the terminology, our investigations have established that he too presents both dimensions of faith as belonging together and as being mutually interpretative.

2. The object of faith

Faith of its very nature must have an object; it is always directed towards something or someone as being true or trustworthy. Mark shows a distinct preference for unqualified faith language – i.e. where the object of faith is not explicitly mentioned but must be derived from the context (2:5; 4:40; 5:34,36; 6:6; 9:19,23f,42; 10:52; cf. 1:15; 11:22,31). This results in some ambiguity concerning the intended object of faith. Is it directed towards God, towards Jesus, or towards the inherent powers of faith itself as a human disposition?

The third option[2] may be ruled out straightaway. Not only does faith have a specific 'religious' content in Mark (see below), but 9:24 shows that in the author's view true faith entails a profound distrust in one's own capacity to express and maintain faith without divine aid. The place he gives to vicarious faith also proves that it is not the psychological structure of faith itself that is the key, but the external object in which it is placed.[3]

---

[1] Luz, 'Die Jünger', 155; Barth, 'Glaube und Zweifel', 291; cf. 269f.

[2] For such a treatment of gospel faith references (though not solely in relation to Mark) see Jackson, *Role of Faith*, passim.

[3] Mark would agree with Nolan that: 'the power of faith does not come from the fact that it is a firm decision or strongly held conviction. Faith derives

We have suggested that the ambiguity surrounding the absolute linguistic construction corresponds to the unusual manner in which God's kingdom manifests itself in Mark's story – i.e. proleptically through the words and deeds of Jesus. This means that, on the one hand, Mark clearly conceives of God as the ultimate object of faith. Of the three non-absolute faith references in the story, one mentions God as the object (11:22); another cites the 'gospel', which in context is shorthand for the 'gospel of God' concerning his dawning kingdom (1:14f); and the third mentions John the Baptist, which, we have suggested, involves acceptance of his message as a word from God, and trust in God's readiness to remit sins (11:31). The ascription of omnipotence to faith (9:23; 11:23f) points in the same direction, since Mark regards omnipotence as an attribute of God alone (10:27; 14:36). Equally significant is the fact that he defines faith as an attitude that reaches out for 'salvation' (5:23,28,34; 10:52; cf. 6:56; 15:31), since salvation is the eschatological action of God (cf. 10:26; 13:13,20) which brings wholeness to minds, bodies and relationships.

Yet, on the other hand, faith for Mark is not a generalised confidence in God 'out there', but a specific commitment of trust in him insofar as he is active and present in the person and ministry of Jesus. Or, to put it the other way around, faith is believing confidence in Jesus inasmuch as he concretely embodies and manifests the saving action of God. In Mark's story, Jesus is, directly or indirectly, the sole mediator of the kind of faith in God required by the dawning kingdom.[1] From Mark's perspective, God is so uniquely present in Jesus that when people in the drama encounter him they are at the same time encountering God (cf. 5:19,20), so that either to exclude Jesus from the object of faith by defining it simply as faith in God,[2] or to exclude God by regarding it merely as trust in the miraculous power of Jesus,[3] is equally to obscure the reality. Faith in Jesus for Mark coincides with faith in God; one

---

its power from the *truth* of what is believed and hoped for. If the kingdom of God were an illusion, faith would be powerless to achieve anything . . . The power of faith is the power of truth', *Jesus*, 84.

[1] See Zeller, 'Jesus als Mittler', 280f.

[2] Along the lines of, e.g., Hatch, *Pauline Idea of Faith*, 24f, 39; Gogarten, *Christ the Crisis*, 239f, 260; Fuchs, 'Jesus and Faith', 50.

[3] See, e.g., Bultmann, *TDNT*, 6, 206 n.240; Dibelius, *Tradition to Gospel*, 75. See the critique of this so-called *Wunderglaube* in Lührmann, *Glaube*, 26–30; Maisch, *Heilung des Gelähmten*, 73ff, 127.

demands the other. J. M. Robinson[1] is therefore somewhat
misleading when he remarks that 'Mark has no single person
or act as the object of faith, and no specific credal statement as
the content of faith. Rather it is faith in the action recorded in
Marcan history . . .'. This is much too vague, for the object of
faith is, in a sense, quite specific: the presence of God's eschatological power in the person of Jesus.

With the exception of 15:32, Mark does not explicitly associate
faith with the death and resurrection of Jesus. We have found,
however, that an implicit relationship is insinuated in those
faith stories which contain forward linkages to the fate of
Jesus at the end of the story. In 2:1–12, for example, the charge
of blasphemy brings Jesus' death into view (cf. also 6:1–6),
while the paralytic's faith in the Son of Man – later identified
as a suffering, dying and rising figure – brings forgiveness of
sins and the command 'arise'. In 5:21–4,35–43 and 9:14–29,
the use of the same death and resurrection terminology used
elsewhere to depict the destiny of the Son of Man suggests that
the miracles are meant to serve as symbolic anticipations of
the impending experience of Jesus. Again, in 10:46–52, the
faith of the beggar issues in following Jesus on the way of the
cross. By such forward linkages, Mark indicates that faith
placed in the earthly Jesus is structurally the same as faith
placed in the crucified and risen Jesus, and within the story it
receives in an anticipatory way the saving benefits secured by
Jesus' passion and resurrection at the end of the story.

3. The context of faith

In chapters 2 and 3, we suggested that in Mark the phrase
'kingdom of God' signals the present manifestation of God's
eschatological power. When released through faith, this power
impinges directly on maladjustment in all areas of life: the
spiritual and the physical, the ethical and the social, the
religious and the political. Perhaps one of our most important
findings has been the consistent relationship Mark portrays
between the power available to faith and the possession or
absence of human power.

[1] Robinson, *Problem of History*, 75. So too Kelber, *Kingdom*, 13; Rigaux,
Testimony, 115; Martin, *Evangelist and Theologian*, 110. Lemcio contrasts
'faith in Jesus to perform a cure' from 'Jesus as the object of faith', and
perplexingly concludes that in the Markan narrative Jesus 'is not the
subject or object of faith or believing', 'Intention of Mark', 190.

Mark seems to regard the recognition and acceptance of one's own human impotence as the essential prerequisite for the experience of faith's power. In chapter 4, we noted that the suppliants in the miracle stories are all characterised by their utter powerlessness in the face of overwhelming need, a condition compounded (except in the case of Jairus) by a social and religious powerlessness as well. Through faith, these characters are introduced to the realm of divine power which completely transforms their situations, enabling them to transcend the limits of human possibility.

Now this positive connection between human helplessness and the power of faith is a widely recognised feature of Mark's miracle stories, and of the miracle genre in general.[1] What is not as widely recognised is that Mark extends this principle beyond the miracle accounts to his wider narrative. In chapter 5, we saw that discipleship-faith also entails the adoption of a situation of voluntary powerlessness, or radical dependency, through the renunciation of existing means of human security, identity and control (1:14–20; 10:43–52). This is the presupposition of the disciples' access to the power of praying faith, a power which both moves mountains (11:22–5) and enables one to tread the way of the cross (cf. 14:36). Whenever the disciples revert to self-reliance, as in 9:18,28f, or lose sight of the security afforded by 'being with him', as in 4:35–41, they are charged with faithlessness.

Within the discipleship community, this paradoxical understanding of power and powerlessness is meant to express itself in human relationships. Thus one of the most serious offences in Mark's eyes is to cause one of the least influential (or powerful) members of the community, 'believing little ones' (9:42), to stumble in their faith through elitism or exclusivism. Outside the kingdom community, it is the unwillingness of the ruling authorities – who possess human power – to relinquish conventional notions of rule and authority and accept the new conception of God's rule embodied and demanded by Jesus that closes them to faith. What is required of them is exemplified by the synagogue ruler (5:21–45) who lays aside his social rank and adopts a position of humility before Jesus, and by the Roman centurion who lays aside preconceived notions of royal

[1] Theissen comments: '"Faith" is therefore not just one motif among other motifs of boundary-crossing associated with human characters, but the essence of all motifs of boundary-crossing', *Miracle Stories*, 139; cf. 75–80.

or divine dignity to perceive in the humiliation of Jesus the revelation of God (15:39).

Put succinctly, faith for Mark is the power of those without power and it is experienced as power only in relation to human powerlessness. Mark thus challenges his audience to embrace the powerlessness of faith as the way of encountering God's power and of fulfilling the mandate of cross-bearing discipleship. Such sole reliance on the power of praying faith must also bring with it a concomitant reordering of social relationships based on prevailing concepts of rule and authority.

4. The necessity of faith

For Mark, repentant faith is the one condition necessary for participation in the dawning kingdom (1:14f) and for the appropriation of its unlimited powers (9:23). Mark seems to conceive of God's kingly power as carrying an inherent disposition towards receptive faith, so that saving power is never withheld from those with real faith (even if Jesus is not immediately conscious of its presence, 5:28ff), while, conversely, it is firmly denied to resistant unbelief (6:5f; 15:31).

The necessity of faith is not, as far as Mark is concerned, due to some psychological cause-and-effect mechanism that exercises external constraint over Jesus' capacities.[1] Rather, it is because the attitude of perceptive dependence – which is Markan faith – is alone capable of receiving Jesus' deeds as revelatory acts of God. Accordingly, the presence of disbelieving witnesses does not always preclude miracle (2:1–12; 3:1–5; cf. 6:5), as long as the suppliants themselves possess faith (2:5). Miracle is also possible in situations where the nature of the need would seem to make faith impossible (e.g. 5:1–20, though note v 6), or where the faith of believers is failing (4:35–41; cf. 6:45–52), or in sympathetic environments where miracles are not necessarily expected (6:34–44; 8:1–10; 11:12–14). For in these situations at least the potential for understanding is present (e.g. 5:20). It is only hardened unbelief that demands non-redemptive signs as a condition for faith that is totally excluded from kingdom power (8:11f; 15:24–31). It would follow from this that 'whether or not faith is actually named and

---

[1] Contra Hatch, *The Idea of Faith*, 6; C. G. Montefiore, *The Synoptic Gospels* (London: Macmillan, 1927[2]) 119; J. Klausner, *Jesus of Nazareth. His Life, Times and Teaching* (London: George Allen & Unwin, 1928), 272.

required in each miracle story, it is nonetheless for Mark the basic presupposition for access to the miracles of Jesus'.[1]

5. The experience of faith

Through the development of characterisation and the employment of various literary devices Mark is able to communicate something of the experiential dimension of faith. The following elements stand out in particular.

Individualism: Faith in Mark is more than a communal system of belief or practice which people subscribe to as a matter of course; it is instead the immediate, personal investment of individuals in crisis situations. In the miracle narratives this individualism is conveyed in three ways: by depicting Jesus turning aside from or even against pressing crowds to interact with individuals who possess faith (cf. 2:2 and 5; 5:21 and 24,30f; 6:5; 9:24 and 25; 10:48 and 49); by recording him using terms of affection for suppliants and patients[2] (2:5; 5: 34,39,41; cf. 9:42); and by the use of personal pronouns: 'their faith' (2:5), 'your faith' (5:34; 10:52). The corollary of this is that faith is no partial gesture by the believer but something that demands the involvement of all the faculties of the personality – thinking, feeling, willing and acting. Fundamentally, Markan faith has a knowledge aspect and an action aspect, which we will consider separately.

Knowledge or Perception: Although Mark never equates πίστις, πιστεύειν with purely intellectual belief, he nevertheless gives prominence to the cognitive element.[3] We have seen repeatedly how the response of suppliants in the miracle stories and of those called to follow is grounded upon an intuitive or revelatory insight into the identity of Jesus as bearer of God's eschatological power and mercy. Such insight is also required in order to 'see' the δυνάμεις as signs of God's dawning kingdom and to perceive his will in specific instances where miracles are to be effected or confident prayer made.

---

[1] Kertelge, *Wunder Jesu*, 198.

[2] It is therefore quite suprising that Theissen should comment of the miracle stories: '"Faith" may be central, but it does not mean a personal relationship with Jesus, but that unconditional desire which receives the promise πάντα δυνατά (Mk 9:13)', *Miracle Stories*, 285. See rather Powell, *Concept of Power*, 116.

[3] So too Robinson, *Problem of History*, 75f; Telford, *Barren Temple*, 82; Zeller, 'Jesus als Mittler', 281–3; cf. Theissen, *Miracle Stories*, 134–9.

It would be a mistake to think that Mark equates faith simply with messianic recognition. The very drama of Mark's narrative derives from the fact that Jesus' true identity as Messiah and Son of God is only gradually disclosed to the disciples. Yet they are expected to exhibit faith (4:40) long before they fully grasp Jesus' messianic status or his unique identity (cf. 4:41; 8:27ff), and even after doing so may still be chided for their lack of active faith (9:18,28f). Mark does not link faith primarily to intellectual illumination concerning Jesus' messiahship or divine sonship but to intuitive perception of God's presence and power within him. For the message of the kingdom is so permeated with irony and paradox, the identity of Jesus so clothed in ambiguity, that they defy purely rational comprehension. Unless one has revelatory insight into Jesus' significance and responds in faith, fuller understanding is impossible. Perception should lead to faith, and faith to understanding, although not all who perceive find faith (10:17–27) and not all who believe necessarily understand (e.g. 4:13; 6:52; 8:17–21). In Mark's story, the perception of faith anticipates the fuller insight available after Jesus' resurrection (16:7) and the unimpeded vision which will come with the kingdom's consummation and the parousia of the Son of Man (13:26).

Action: Although faith is an inner attitude, Mark insists that faith must become visible (2:5) in order to win its desire. The self-confession of faith in Mark is committed action, and faith can only be said to exist inasmuch as it proves itself in action. As J. A. Findlay[1] puts it:

> Faith, as illustrated in Mark's gospel, may be defined as a painstaking and concentrated effort to obtain blessing for oneself or for others, material or spiritual, inspired by a confident belief that God in Jesus can supply all human need.

More specifically, there are at least three aspects to the activity dimension of Markan faith:

(i) *Repentance*: For Mark, repentance and faith are inseparable (1:14f). The response of faith presupposes the comprehensive break with the past and that reorientation of life in both its ethical and religious dimensions connoted by μετανοεῖν. Mark's initial definition of faith as repentant faith means that

[1] Findlay, *Jesus*, 173.

in the subsequent narrative, Jesus 'interprets the desire for healing as an indication of repentance'.[1]

(ii) *Persistence*: Without doubt, the leading characteristic of Markan faith is sheer dogged perseverance. In the miracle stories, the courageous surmounting of difficulties is the overt sign of faith. The paralytic and his companions must transcend the human barrier of the crowd and the physical barrier of the roof to reach Jesus; Jairus persists in trust despite the obstacles of delay, death and prevalent scepticism; the haemorrhaging woman contravenes public strictures against women and ritual uncleanness; the father of the possessed boy overcomes the setback caused by the impotent disciples; and Bartimaeus cries out 'all the more' when people attempt to silence him. Conversely, it is the lack of courageous perseverance that the disciples are rebuked for during the storm at sea.

The corollary of persevering faith in quest of miracle is an on-going, persevering fidelity to Jesus by his adherents in face of suffering, persecution and the competing demands of other messianic claimants. Scholars often drive a wedge between the concepts of 'faith' and 'faithfulness', but for Mark they are two sides of the same coin, as the case of Bartimaeus shows. The same faith that secured his healing issues in a subsequent following of Jesus, if need be to the cross itself (10:52). For the disciples, the fidelity of faith is not a matter of simple loyalty to Jesus, but a continuation of the relationship of dependent trust on him for provision, protection and ultimate salvation.

(iii) *Obedience*: Because it is specifically demanded (1:15), the experience of faith itself is regarded by Mark as a kind of obedience, a submission of the will to the rule of God (cf. 3:35). Volitional commitment takes different forms in his story. For the disciples, it involves acceptance of the call to follow. For needy suppliants, it entails heeding their intuitions concerning Jesus, a determination to surmount all difficulties to reach him, and obedience to his specific demands (e.g. 2:11; 5:36; 10:49). The first step of faith, for Mark, is a step of obedience.

Overall then, for Mark faith demands the involvement of the volitional, cognitive, and affective dimensions of the believers' personality. It is a total commitment.

---

[1] Rhoads and Michie, *Mark as Story*, 110.

6. The origin of faith

Although the capacity to place trust in a reality beyond oneself is innately human and plays an essential part in nearly all aspects of life,[1] the actual act of trusting is not automatic or arbitrary. It is always a response to the reality towards which it is directed, and by which in a measure it is evoked. In this sense, all faith is a gift,[2] though a gift that must be actualised through a free volitional commitment.

In Mark's story, it is the person and activity of Jesus that engenders faith in others. The ground of the call to faith is the definite realisation of God's kingdom in his words and deeds, and it is therefore necessary for other characters to see and hear him (e.g. 1:17f; 2:1,5; 5:22; 6:2,5) or hear about him (e.g. 5: 27; 9:17; 10:47; cf. 6:12f) in order to believe. In addition, Jesus is typified as one who has power to sustain faith in others (9:23). Some interpreters maintain that in the gospels it is Jesus' own powerful faith in God that arouses similar faith in others.[3] But from Mark's perspective, it is not any single feature in particular that has this effect, but the sum total of what is implied by the presence of God's sovereignty within him.

But does Mark present Jesus as the exemplar of faith? This is affirmed by a number of commentators,[4] and denied by others.[5] In our view, there are a number of indications, albeit oblique ones, that Mark does indeed characterise Jesus as a man of faith.

(i) We have argued that the principle 'all things are possible to him who believes' (9:23) embraces both those who seek miracles and those who work miracles. By implication, the saying discloses the channel of Jesus' miraculous power: his faith.[6]

---

[1] This has been variously called 'innate faith', 'animal faith', 'creation faith', 'human faith', and so on.

[2] Cf. Clements, *Faith*, 23f; Richardson, *Theology*, 31.

[3] E.g. Ebeling, 'Jesus and Faith', 234; Fuchs, 'Jesus and Faith', 60ff; Nolan, *Jesus*, 32f; Gogarten, *Christ the Crisis*, 260, cf. 38–41; Cook, 'Call to Faith', 693.

[4] See n. 2, p. 119 and n. 4, p. 239, below.

[5] E.g. Best, *Following Jesus*, 72 n.32; Zeller, 'Jesus als Mittler', 285f; Schmithals, *Markus*, II, 418; cf. Barth, 'Glaube und Zweifel', 279f; O'Connor, *Faith*, 45f; Lemcio, 'Intention of Mark', 190; cf. also the comments of Dunn, *Jesus and the Spirit*, 75, 90.

[6] See pp. 118–20 above.

(ii) The formulation of 9:19 implies a distinction between Jesus and the γενεὰ ἄπιστος. He stands alone, as the authentic believer, in contrast to his faithless contemporaries.[1]

(iii) As Mark employs it, the 'mountain-moving saying' in 11:23 may carry an implicit backward reference to Jesus' action in the temple and perhaps his cursing of the fig-tree. If so, he is included in the 'whoever' empowered by faith to remove mountains.[2]

(iv) Inasmuch as Mark understands prayer as faith-verbalised (cf. 11:24f; 9:28f), the repeated portrayal of Jesus at prayer (1:35; 6:41,46; 8:6; 14:33,35,39; 15:34) reinforces the image of him as a person of faith.[3] The phrase πάντα δυνατά in the Gethsemane prayer (14:36) is, in light of 9:23, particularly evocative of petitionary faith.

(v) Finally, we should recall that Mark portrays Jesus as a figure of integrity, who lives by the values he teaches and whose lifestyle inteprets his teaching. It is therefore very likely that the author seeks to show Jesus in a practical attitude that coincides with his teaching on faith.[4] His convictions about the dawning kingdom, the certainty expressed in his *amen*-sayings, his itinerant lifestyle, his composure in the storm-tossed boat, his assurance that Jairus' daughter is only asleep, his acceptance of the cup of suffering from the Father, and so on, can all be taken as an implicit expression of his complete faith in God.

We may accept then that Mark pictures Jesus as sharing the attitude of faith he encourages others to adopt. Yet the lack of explicit comment on his personal faith suggests that this is not Mark's primary focus. Jesus functions chiefly as the concrete object of faith in Mark's gospel. It is part of the paradox of the characterisation of Jesus that he is depicted both as one who

---

[1] See Hooker, *Message*, 39; Lane, *Mark*, 332. The 'mythical' interpretation, following Dibelius, *Tradition to Gospel*, 278, sees Jesus cast here as part of the divine world.

[2] See Bird, 'γάρ-clauses', 77; Lane, *Mark*, 410 n.55. Cf. also Lührmann, *Glaube*, 23; Haenchen, *Weg Jesu*, 391; Dunn, *Jesus and the Spirit*, 75.

[3] Rhoads and Michie, *Mark as Story*, 108; Schreiber, *Theologie des Vertrauens*, 242; Powell, *Concept of Power*, 182, 183 n.15; Shaw, *Cost of Authority*, 214f; Senior, *Passion of Jesus*, 123f. Cf. also Gogarten, *Christ the Crisis*, 252f; Cairns, *Faith*, 88f; Fuchs, 'Jesus and Faith', 62f.

[4] So Rhoads and Michie, *Mark as Story*, 108ff; Martin, *Evangelist and Theologian*, 110; cf. Ebeling, 'Jesus and Faith', 234ff; Heijke, *Faith*, 43–5. Donahue suggests that Mark portrays Jesus as 'a model of trusting fidelity', 'Neglected Factor', 592.

actualises God's presence and power, and one who exemplifies the response sought from others to this reality. This somewhat ambivalent portrayal of Jesus as a man of faith provides an interesting point of comparison with wider New Testament data on this question, which is an area of current theological and exegetical interest.[1]

The aim of this book has been to elucidate another comparatively 'neglected factor in Markan theology', to reapply Donahue's phrase. We have used a method which has sought to combine an understanding of the author's theological conception with an appreciation of how this is conveyed to his readers or hearers through the medium of the gospel narrative. We have found that Mark is a writer of considerable literary and theological competence who has a definite perspective on the meaning and role of faith. This perspective invites comparison with other New Testament writers, especially Matthew and Luke (it also incidentally warrants comparison with the longer, secondary ending of Mark which contains a striking conglomeration of faith terminology).[2] A greater appreciation by scholars of Mark's perspective on faith and the central role it occupies in his narrative would, we suggest, have ramifications for the wider field of Markan interpretation. Not least of these would be its value in moderating the hermeneutical dominance still exercised by the variously understood[3] element of 'messianic secrecy' and its related motifs. There is no denying the place of secrecy and incomprehension in Mark's scheme. But the tendency to interpret the whole gospel through this grid seems at best one-sided in view of the considerable body of material we have found showing that Mark considers that an authentic understanding of the earthly Jesus is open to those with perceptive faith.

---

[1] See, e.g., the recent views of Paul's material discussed by : L. T. Johnson, 'Rom 3:21–26 and the Faith of Jesus', *CBQ* 40 (1978) 77–90; A. J. Hultgren, 'The *Pistis Christou* Formulation in Paul', *NovT* 22 (1980), 248–63 ; S. K. Williams, 'Again *Pistis Christou*', *CBQ* 49 (1987), 431–7. See also Mackey, 'Faith of the Historical Jesus', 155–74.

[2] O'Connor deals very briefly with this material, *Faith*, 28–30, 65–8. See also W. R. Farmer, *The Last Twelve Verses of Mark*, SNTSMS (CUP: 1974), 89f, 96.

[3] See initially W. Wrede, *The Messianic Secret*; J. L. Blevins, *The Messianic Secret in Markan Research 1901–1976*; C. M. Tuckett, *The Messianic Secret*; also recently Watson, 'Mark's Secrecy Theme', 49–69.

BIBLIOGRAPHY

Works appearing below are cited in the notes by short titles only. Where books (usually relevant to a single exegetical point) are cited in full in the notes, they do not reappear in the bibliography.

Commentaries on Mark

Achtemeier, P. J. *Mark*. Proclamation Commentaries (Philadelphia: Fortress Press, 1975).

Anderson, H. *The Gospel of Mark*. New Century Bible (London: Oliphants, 1976).

Carrington, P. *According to Mark, A Running Commentary on the Oldest Gospel* (London: Cambridge University Press, 1960).

Cranfield, C. E. B. *The Gospel According to Saint Mark* (London: Cambridge University Press, 1959).

Ernst, J. *Das Evangelium nach Markus*, Regensburger Neues Testament (Regensburg: Verlag Friedrich Pustet, 1981).

Branscomb, B. H. *The Gospel of Mark*. Moffatt New Testament Commentary (London: Hodder & Stoughton, 1937).

Gnilka, J. *Das Evangelium nach Markus*. Evangelisch-Katholischer Kommentar zum Neuen Testament. 2 vols. (Zürich, Einsiedeln, Köln: Benziger/Neukirchener Vluyn: Neukirchener Verlag, 1978/9).

Gould, E. P. *The Gospel According to St. Mark*. International Critical Commentary (Edinburgh: T. & T. Clark, 1896).

Grundmann, W. *Das Evangelium nach Markus*. Theologischer Handkommentar zum Neuen Testament, 2 (Berlin: Evangelische Verlagsanstalt, 1959²).

Haenchen, E. *Der Weg Jesu. Eine Erklärung des Markus-Evangeliums und der kanonischen Parallelen* (Berlin: A. Töpelmann, 1966).

Hurtado, L. W. *Mark*. Good News Bible Commentary (Basingstoke: Pickering & Inglis, 1983).

Johnson, S. E. *The Gospel According to St. Mark*. Black's New Testament Commentaries (London: Adam & Charles Black, 1972²).

Klostermann, E. *Das Markusevangelium*. Handbuch zum Neuen Testament 3 (Tübingen: Verlag J. C. B. Mohr [Paul Siebeck], 1950⁴).

Lane, W. L. *The Gospel of Mark*. The New International Commentary on the New Testament (Grand Rapids, Mich.: Eerdmans, 1974).

Lohmeyer, E. *Das Evangelium des Markus* (Göttingen: Vandenhoeck & Ruprecht, 1953).

Lenski, R. C. H. *The Interpretation of St Mark's Gospel* (Minneapolis, Minnesota: Augsburg Publishing House, 1946).

Nineham, D. E. *The Gospel of St. Mark*. Pelican New Testament Commentaries (London: Pelican, 1963).

Pesch, R. *Das Markusevangelium*, 2 vols., Herders Theologischer Kommentar zum Neuen Testament (Freiburg/Basel/Wien: Herder, 1977).

Rawlinson, A. E. J. *St. Mark*. Westminster Commentary Series (London: Methuen, 1925).

Schmid, J. *Das Evangelium nach Markus*. Regensburger Neues Testament 2 (Regensburg: Verlag Friederich Pustet, 1963).

Schmithals, W. *Das Evangelium nach Markus*. 2 vols. Ökumenischer Taschenbuchkommentar zum Neuen Testament 2/1 & 2/2 (Gütersloh: G. Mohn/Würzburg: Echter Verlag).

Schnackenburg, R. *The Gospel According to St Mark*. 2 vols. (London: Sheed & Ward, 1971).

Schniewind, J. *Das Evangelium nach Markus*. Das Neue Testament Deutsch 1 (Göttingen: Vandenhoeck & Ruprecht, 1960).

Swete, H. B. *The Gospel According to St Mark* (London: Macmillan & Co, 1898).

Taylor, V. *The Gospel According to St Mark* (London: Macmillan & Co, 1957).

Other Works

Achtemeier, P. J. 'Person and Deed. Jesus and the Storm-Tossed Sea', *Int* 16 (1962) 169–76.

'Toward the Isolation of Pre-Markan Miracle Catenae', *JBL* 89 (1970) 265–91.

'The Origin and Function of the Pre-Markan Miracle Catenae', *JBL* 91 (1972) 198–221.

'Miracles and the Historical Jesus: A Study of Mark 9:14–29', *CBQ* 37 (1975) 471–91.

'"And He Followed Him": Miracles and Discipleship in Mark 10:46–52', *Sem* 11 (1978) 115–45.

'Mark as Interpreter of the Jesus Traditions', in J. L Mays, ed., *Interpreting the Gospels* (Philadelphia: Fortress Press, 1981) pp. 115–29.

Alter, R. *The Art of Biblical Narrative* (London: George Allen & Unwin, 1981).

Agourides, S. '"Little Ones" in Matthew', *TBT* 35 (1984) 329–34.

Ambrozic, A. M. *The Hidden Kingdom. A Redaction-Critical Study of the References to the Kingdom of God in Mark's Gospel* (Washington, D.C.: Catholic Biblical Association, 1972).

Arichea, D. C. Jr. '"Faith" in the Gospels of Matthew, Mark and Luke', in *TBT* (Practical Papers) 29 (1978) 420–4.

Aune, D. E. *The New Testament in its Literary Environment* (Philadelphia: Westminster Press, 1987).

Baarlink, H. *Anfängliches Evangelium. Ein Beitrag zur näheren Bestimmung der theologischen Motive im Markusevangelium* (Kampen: J. H. Kok, 1977).

'Zur Frage nach dem Antijudaismus im Markusevangelium', *ZNW* 70 (1979) 166–93.

Barr, J. *The Semantics of Biblical Language* (London: Oxford University Press, 1961).
'Common Sense and Biblical Language', *Bib* 49 (1968) 377–87.
'Reading the Bible as Literature', *BJRL* 56 (1973/4) 10–33.
Barrett, C. K. 'The House of Prayer and the Den of Thieves', in Ellis, E. and Grässer, E., ed., *Jesus und Paulus*. Fs. W. G. Kümmel (Vandenhoeck & Ruprecht, 1975) pp. 13–20.
Barth, G. 'Glaube und Zweifel in den synoptischen Evangelien', *ZTK* 72 (1975) 269–92.
Baltensweiler, H. 'Wunder und Glaube im Neuen Testament', *TZ* 23 (1967) 241–56.
Beardslee, W. A. *Literary Criticism of the New Testament* (Philadelphia: Fortress Press, 1969).
Beasley-Murray, G. R. 'The Parousia in Mark', *Rev Exp* 75 (1977) 565–81.
'Eschatology in the Gospel of Mark', *SWJT* 21 (1978) 37–53.
'Second Thoughts on the Composition of Mark 13', *NTS* 29 (1983) 414–20.
Jesus and the Kingdom of God (Grand Rapids, Mich.: Eerdmans/Paternoster, 1986).
Beavis, M. A. 'Mark's Teaching on Faith', *BTB* 16 (1986) 139–42.
Beck, N. A. 'Reclaiming a Biblical Text: The Mark 8:14–21 Discussion About Bread in the Boat', *CBQ* 43 (1981) 49–56.
Benoit, P. 'Faith in the Synoptic Gospels', in Benoit, P., *Jesus and the Gospel*, Vol. 1 (London: Darton, Longman & Todd, 1973) pp. 71–86.
Berger, K. L. *Exegese des Neuen Testaments. Neue Wege vom Text zur Auslegung* (Heidelberg: Quelle & Meyer, 1977).
Berlin, A. 'Point of View in Biblical Narrative', in S. A. Geller (ed.), *The Sense of Text. The Art of Language in the Study of Biblical Literature*. JQR Supplement (The Dropsie College. Wiona Lake: Eisenbrauns, 1982) pp. 71–113.
Poetics and Interpretation of Biblical Narrative (Sheffield: Almond Press, 1983).
Best, E. *The Temptation and the Passion: The Markan Soteriology*. SNTSMS 2 (Cambridge University Press, 1965).
'Mark, Some Problems', *IrBibStud* 1 (1979) 77–98.
Following Jesus. Discipleship in the Gospel of Mark. JSNTSS 4 (Sheffield: JSOT, 1981).
'The Purpose of Mark', *Proceedings of the Irish Biblical Association* 6 (1982) 18–35.
Mark the Gospel as Story (Edinburgh: T. & T. Clark, 1983)
Disciples and Discipleship. Studies in the Gospel According to Mark (Edinburgh: T. & T. Clark, 1986).
Betz, H. D. [ed.] *Christology and a Modern Pilgrimage. A Discussion with Norman Perrin* (Missoula, Montana: Scholars Press, 1974).
'The Early Christian Miracle Story: Some Observations on the Form Critical Problem', *Sem* 11 (1978) 69–81.
Betz, O. 'Jesu Evangelium vom Gottesreich', in Stuhlmacher, P., ed., *Das Evangelium und die Evangelien* (Tübingen: J. C. B. Mohr [Paul Siebeck], 1983) pp. 55–77.
Bird, C. H. 'Some γάρ-clauses in St. Mark's Gospel', *JTS* n.s.4 (1953) 171–87.

Black, M. *An Aramaic Approach to the Gospels and Acts* (Oxford: Clarendon Press, 1967[3]).

Blevins, J. L. *The Messianic Secret in Markan Research 1901–1976* (Washington, University Press of America, 1981).

Blomberg, C. L. 'Synoptic Studies: Some Recent Methodological Developments and Debates', *Themelios* 12 (1987) 38–46.

Boobyer, G. H. 'Galilee and the Galileans in St. Mark's Gospel', *BJRL* 25 (1953) 334–48.

'Mark 11,10a and the Interpretation of the Healing of the Paralytic', *HTR* 47 (1954) 115–20.

'The Redaction of Mark IV,1–34', *NTS* 8 (1961/62) 59–70.

Boomershine, T. E. and Bartholomew, G. L. 'The Narrative Technique of Mark 16:8', *JBL* 100 (1981) 213–23.

Boomershine, T. E. 'Mark 16:8 and the Apostolic Commission', *JBL* 100 (1981) 225–39.

Booth, W. C. *The Rhetoric of Fiction* (Chicago: University of Chicago Press, 1961).

Boring, M. E. 'The Christology of Mark: Hermeneutical Issues for Systematic Theology', *Sem* 30 (1984) 125–53.

Bornkamm, G. *Jesus of Nazareth* (London: Hodder & Stoughton, 1960).

'"Πνεῦμα ἄλαλον". Eine Studie zum Markus-Evangelium', in Bornkamm, G., *Geschichte und Glaube*, 11 (München: Chr. Kaiser Verlag, 1971) pp. 21–36.

Branscomb, B. H. 'Mark 2,5 "Son Thy Sins are Forgiven"', *JBL* 53 (1934) 53–60.

Breck, J. 'Biblical Chiasmus: Exploring Structure for Meaning', *BTB* 17 (1987) 70–4.

Brown, R. E. and Meier, J. P. *Antioch and Rome. New Testament Cradles of Catholic Christianity* (London: Geoffrey Chapman, 1983).

Buby, B. 'A Christology of Relationship in Mark', *BTB* 10 (1980) 149–54.

Budesheim, T. L. 'Jesus and the Disciples in Conflict with Judaism', *ZNW* 62 (1971) 190–209.

Bultmann, R. *Theology of the New Testament* 2 vols. (London: SCM, 1952).

'πιστεύειν, κτλ.', *TDNT* 6:174–228 (182–96 by A. Weiser).

The History of the Synoptic Tradition (Oxford: Blackwell, 1972).

Burchard, C. 'Markus 15,34', *ZNW* 74 (1983) 1–11.

Burkill, T. A. *Mysterious Revelation. An Examination of the Philosophy of St. Mark's Gospel* (Ithaca, N.Y.: Cornell University Press, 1963).

New Light on the Earliest Gospel. Seven Markan Studies (New York & London: Cornell University Press, 1972).

Caird, G. B. *The Language and Imagery of the Bible* (London: Duckworth, 1980).

Cairns, D. S. *The Faith That Rebels. A Re-examination of the Miracles of Jesus*. Torch Library Series (London: SCM, 1933[5]).

Catchpole, D. 'The Fearful Silence of the Women at the Tomb: A Study in Marcan Theology', *JournTheolSAfr* 18 (1977) 3–10.

'The Son of Man's Search for Faith (Luke XVIII 8b)', *NovT* 19 (1977) 81–104.

'The Poor on Earth and the Son in Heaven. A Reappraisal of Matt XXV 31–46', *BJRL* 61 (1978/9) 355–97.

Chatman, S. *Story and Discourse: Narrative Structure in Fiction and Film* (Ithaca, N.Y.: Cornell University Press, 1978).

Childs, B. S. *The New Testament as Canon: An Introduction* (London: SCM, 1984).

Chilton, B. D. 'Regnum Dei Deus Est', *SJT* 31 (1978) 261–70.

God in Strength. Jesus' Announcement of the Kingdom. SUNT 1 (Linz: Plöchl Freistadt, 1979).

'Jesus *ben David*: reflections on the *Davidssohnfrage*', *JSNT* 14 (1982) 88–112.

The Kingdom of God in the Teaching of Jesus. Issues in Religion and Theology 7 (London: SPCK/Philadelphia: Fortress Press, 1985).

Chouinard, L. 'Gospel Christology: A Study in Methodology', *JSNT* 30 (1987) 21–37.

Chronis, H. L. 'The Torn Veil: Cultus and Christology in Mark 15:37–39', *JBL* 101 (1982) 97–114.

Clements, K. W. *Faith* (London: SCM, 1981).

Colpe, C. 'Traditionsüberschreitende Argumentationen zu Aussagen Jesu über sich selbst', in Jeremias, G., Kuhn, H. W., and Stegemann, H., ed., *Tradition und Glaube. Das frühe Christentum in seiner Umwelt.* Fs. H. G. Kuhn (Göttingen: Vandenhoeck & Ruprecht, 1971) pp. 230–45.

Cook, M. J. *Mark's Treatment of the Jewish Leaders.* SNovT 51 (Leiden: E. J. Brill, 1978).

Cook, M. L. 'The Call to Faith of the Historical Jesus: Questions for the Christian Understanding of Faith', *Theological Studies* 39 (1978) 679–700.

Cotter, W. J. '"For it was not the Season for Figs"', *CBQ* 48 (1986) 62–6.

Cousar, C. B. 'Eschatology and Mark's Theologia Crucis. A Critical Analysis of Mark 13', *Int* 24 (1970) 321–35.

Coutts, J. 'The Authority of Jesus and of the Twelve in St. Mark's Gospel', *JTS* n.s. 8 (1957) 111–18.

Cranfield, C. E. B. 'St. Mark 9:14–29', *SJT* 3 (1950) 57–67.

Crossan, J. D. 'Mark and the Relatives of Jesus', *NovT* 15 (1973) 81–113.

'Empty Tomb and Absent Lord (Mark 16:1–8)', in Kelber, W., ed., *The Passion in Mark. Studies on Mark 14–16* (Philadelphia: Fortress Press, 1976) pp. 135–52.

'A Form for Absence: The Markan Creation of Gospel', *Sem* 12 (1978) 41–55.

Culpepper, R. A. 'The Passion and Resurrection in Mark', *RevExp* 75 (1978) 583–600.

'Mark 10:50: Why Mention the Garment?', *JBL* 101 (1982) 131–2.

Daube, D. 'Responsibilities of Master and Disciples in the Gospels', *NTS* 19 (1972/3) 1–15.

Dautzenberg, G. 'Die Zeit des Evangeliums. Mk 1,1–15 und die Konzeption des Markusevangeliums', Part I. *BZ* 21 (1977) 219–34; Part 2. *BZ* 22 (1978) 76–91.

Davies, W. D. *The Gospel and the Land. Early Christianity and Jewish Territorial Doctrine* (Berkeley & Los Angeles: University of California Press, 1974).

Derrett, J. D. M. 'Mark's Technique: The Haemorrhaging Woman and

Jairus' Daughter', *Bib* 63 (1982) 474–505.

The Making of Mark. The Scriptural Bases of the Earliest Gospel, 2 vols. (Shipton-on-Stour, Warwickshire: P. Drinkwater, 1985).

Dertweiler, R. 'After New Criticism. Contemporary Methods of Literary Analysis', in R. A. Spencer, *Orientation by Disorientation. Studies in Literary Criticism and Biblical Literary Criticism* (Pittsburgh: Pickwick Press, 1980) 3–23.

Dewey, J. 'The Literary Structure of the Controversy Stories in Mark 2:1–3:6', *JBL* 92 (1973) 394–401.

Markan Public Debate: Literary Technique, Concentric Structure, and Theology in Mark 2:1–3:6. SBLDS 48 (Chico, Calif.: Scholars Press, 1980).

Dewey, K. E. 'Peter's Curse and Cursed Peter (Mk 14:53–54, 66–72)', in Kelber, W., ed., *The Passion in Mark. Studies on Mark 14–16* (Philadelphia: Fortress Press, 1976) pp. 96–114.

Dibelius, M. *From Tradition to Gospel* (London: Ivor Nicholson & Watson, 1934).

Donahue, J. R. *Are You the Christ? The Trial Narrative in the Gospel of Mark.* SBLDS 10 (Missoula, Montana: SBL, 1973).

'From Passion Traditions to Passion Narrative', in Kelber, W., ed., *The Passion in Mark. Studies on Mark 14–16* (Philadelphia: Fortress Press, 1976) pp. 1–20.

'Temple, Trial, and Royal Christology (Mark 14:53–65)', in Kelber, W., ed., *The Passion in Mark. Studies on Mark 14–16* (Philadelphia: Fortress Press, 1976) pp. 61–79.

'Jesus as the Parable of God in the Gospel of Mark', in Mays, J. L., ed., *Interpreting the Gospels* (Philadelphia: Fortress Press, 1981) pp. 148–67.

'A Neglected Factor in the Theology of Mark', *JBL* 101 (1982) 563–94.

Dormeyer, D. 'Die Kompositionsmetapher "Evangelium Jesu Christi, des Sohnes Gott", Mk 1.1. Ihre Theologische und Literarische Aufgabe in der Jesus-Biographie des Markus', *NTS* 33 (1987) 452–68.

Doudna, J. C. *The Greek of the Gospel of Mark.* SBL Monograph Series 12 (Ann Arbor: SBL, 1961).

Doughty, D. J. 'The Authority of the Son of Man (Mark 2:1–3:6)', *ZNW* 74 (1983) 161–81.

Dunn, J. D. G. *Jesus and the Spirit. A Study of the Religious and Charismatic Experience of Jesus and the First Christians as Reflected in the New Testament* (London: SCM, 1975).

'Mark 2:1–3:6: A Bridge Between Jesus and Paul on the Question of the Law', *NTS* 30 (1984) 395–415.

Dyson, A. O. *We Believe* (Oxford: Mowbrays, 1977).

Ebeling, G. 'Jesus and Faith', in Ebeling, G., *Word and Faith* (ET. London: SCM, 1963) 201–47.

Ellis, E. E. 'Gospels Criticism: A Perspective on the State of the Art', in Stuhlmacher, P., *Das Evangelium und die Evangelien.* WUNT 28 (Tübingen: J. C. B. Mohr [Paul Siebeck], 1983) 27–54.

Evans, C. F. 'I Will Go Before You into Galilee', *JTS* n.s.5 (1954) 3–18.

The Beginning of the Gospel. Four Lectures on St. Mark's Gospel (London: SPCK, 1968).

Evans, D. 'Faith and Belief', *RelS* 10 (1974) 1–19, 199–212.

Fenton, J. C. 'Paul and Mark', in Nineham, D. E., ed., *Studies in the Gospels. Essays in Memory of R. H. Lightfoot* (Oxford: Blackwell, 1955) pp. 89–112.

'The Mother of Jesus in Mark's Gospel and its Revisions', *Theol* 86 (1983) 433–7.

Findlay, J. A. *Jesus as They Saw Him* (London: Epworth, 1921).

Fisher, K. M. 'The Miracles of Mark 4:35–5:43. Their Meaning and Function in the Gospel Framework', *BTB* 11 (1981) 13–16.

Fleddermann, H. 'The Discipleship Discourse (Mark 9:33–50)', *CBQ* 43 (1981) 57–75.

'A Warning About the Scribes (Mark 12:37b–40)', *CBQ* 44 (1982) 52–67.

Focant, C. 'L'incompréhension des disciples dans le deuxième évangile', *Revue Biblique* 82 (1975) 161–8.

Foerster, W. 'σῴζω κτλ', *TDNT* VII, 965–1003.

Fowler, R. M. *Loaves and Fishes. The Function of the Feeding Stories in the Gospel of Mark.* SBLDS 54 (Chico, Calif.: Scholars Press, 1981).

France, R. T. 'Mark and the Teaching of Jesus', in Wenham, D. and France, R. T., ed., *Gospel Perspectives*. Vol. 1 (Sheffield: JSOT Press, 1980) pp. 101–36.

Freyne, S. *The Twelve: Disciples and Apostles. A Study in the Theology of the First Three Gospels* (London: Sheed & Ward, 1968).

'At Cross Purposes. Jesus and the Disciples in Mark', *Furrow* 33 (1982) 331–9.

'The Disciples in Mark and the *Maskilim* in Daniel. A Comparison', *JSNT* 16 (1982) 7–23.

Fridrichsen, A. *The Problem of Miracle in Primitive Christianity* (Minneapolis, Minn.: Augsburg Publishing House, 1972).

Frye, R. M. 'A Literary Perspective for the Criticism of the Gospels', in Miller, D. G. and Hadidian, D. Y., ed., *Jesus and Man's Hope* II (Pittsburgh: Pittsburgh Theological Seminary, 1971) pp. 193–221.

'Literary Criticism and Gospel Criticism', *Today* 36 (1979) 207–19.

Fuchs, E. 'Jesus and Faith', in Fuchs, E., *Studies of the Historical Jesus.* SBT 42 (London: SCM, 1964) pp. 48–64.

Fuller, R. H. *Interpreting the Miracles* (London: SCM, 1963).

Fuller, R. H. and Perkins, P. *Who is This Christ? Gospel Christology and Contemporary Faith* (Philadelphia: Fortress Press, 1983).

Funk, R. W. 'The Form of the New Testament Healing Miracle Story', *Sem* 12 (1978) 57–96.

Gaston, L. *No Stone on Another. Studies in the Significance of the Fall of Jerusalem in the Synoptic Gospels.* SNovT 23 (Leiden: E. J. Brill, 1970).

Geller, S. A. 'Through Windows and Mirrors into the Bible. History, Literature and Language in the Study of the Text', in S. A. Geller (ed.), *The Sense of Text. The Art of Language in the Study of Biblical Literature*, JQR Supplement (The Dropsie College. Wiona Lake: Eisenbrauns, 1982) pp. 3–40.

Gerhardsson, B. *The Gospel Tradition* (C. W. K. Gleerup, 1986).

Guelich, R. '"The Beginning of the Gospel" Mark 1:1–15', *BR* 27 (1982) 5–15.

'The Gospel Genre', in Stuhlmacher, P., ed., *Das Evangelium und die Evangelien.* WUNT 28 (Tübingen: J. C. B. Mohr [Paul Siebeck], 1983) pp. 183–219.

Gibson, J. B. 'The Rebuke of the Disciples in Mark 8. 14–21', *JSNT* 27 (1986) 31–47.

Giesen, H. 'Der verdorrte Feigenbaum – Eine symbolische Aussage? Mk 11,12 14–20f', *BZ* 20 (1976) 95–111.

Gill, A. 'Women Ministers in the Gospel of Mark', *Australian Biblical Review* 35 (1987) 14–21.

Gilmour, T. C. 'The Dynamic of Faith', *ExpT* 98 (1987) 365–9.

Glasswell, M. E. 'The Use of Miracles in the Markan Gospel', in C. F. D. Moule, *Miracles. Cambridge Studies in Their Philosophy and History* (London: A. R. Mowbray & Co. Ltd., 1965) 149–62.

Glöckner, R. *Biblischer Glaube ohne Wunder?* (Einsiedeln: Johannes Verlag, 1979).

Gnilka, J. 'Das Elend vor dem Menschensohn (Mk 2,1–12)', in Pesch, R. and Schnackenburg, R., ed., *Jesus und der Menschensohn*. Fs A. Vögtle (Freiburg: Herder, 1975) pp. 196–209.

Gogarten, F. *Christ the Crisis* (London: SCM, 1970).

Goppelt, L. *Theology of the New Testament*. Vol. 1: *The Ministry of Jesus in its Theological Significance* (Grand Rapids, Mich.: Eerdmans, 1981).

Grässer, E. 'Jesus in Nazareth (Mk VI 1–6a). Notes on the Redaction and Theology of St. Mark', *NTS* 16 (1969/70) 1–23.

Gros Louis, K. R. R. (ed.) *Literary Interpretations of Biblical Narratives.* Vol. 2 (Nashville: Abingdon, 1982).

Güttgemanns, E. *Candid Questions Concerning Gospel Form Criticism. A Methodological Sketch of the Fundamental Problems of Form and Redaction Criticism.* Pittsburgh Theological Monograph Series (Pittsburgh: The Pickwick Press, 1979).

Haacker, K. 'Glaube', *Theologische Realenzyklopädie* 12 (Berlin: Walter de Gruyter, 1984) 277–304.

Hahn, F. 'Das Verständnis des Glaubens im Markusevangelium', in Hahn, F., and Klein, H., ed., *Glaube im Neuen Testament*. Fs H. Binder (Neukirchen/Vluyn: Neukirchener Verlag, 1982) pp. 43–67.

Hamilton, R. 'The Gospel of Mark: Parable of God Incarnate', *Theol* 86 (1983) 438–41.

Harris, M. J. 'Prepositions and Theology in the Greek New Testament', *Appendix to NIDNTT* 3, 1171–1215.

Hartman, L. *Prophecy Interpreted. The Formation of Some Jewish Apocalyptic Texts and of the Eschatological Discourse Mark 13 Par* (Uppsala: CWK Gleerup Lund, 1966).

Hatch, W. H. P. *The Pauline Idea of Faith in its Relation to Jewish and Hellenistic Religion.* Harvard Theological Studies II 1917 (London: Cambridge Harvard University Press, 1917).

The Idea of Faith in Christian Literature from the Death of St. Paul to the Close of the Second Century (Oxford University Press, 1925).

Hawkin, D. J. 'The Incomprehension of the Disciples in the Marcan Redaction', *JBL* 91 (1972) 491–500.

Hay, L. S. 'The Son of Man in Mark 2:10 and 1:28', *JBL* 89 (1970) 69–75.

Hedrick, C. W. 'The Role of "Summary Statements" in the Composition of the Gospel of Mark: A Dialogue with Karl Schmidt and Norman Perrin', *NovT* 26 (1984) 289–311.

Heijke, J. *The Bible on Faith* (ET. De Pere, Wisc.: St. Norbert Abbey, 1966).

Held, H. J. 'Matthew as Interpreter of the Miracle Stories', in Bornkamm, G., Barth, G., and Held, H. J., *Tradition and Interpretation in Matthew* (London: SCM, 1963) pp. 165–300.

Hengel, M. *The Charismatic Leader and His Followers* (T & T Clark, 1981).

Studies in the Gospel of Mark (London: SCM, 1985).

Hickling, C. J. A. 'A Problem of Method in Gospel Criticism', *RelS* 10 (1974) 339–46.

Hooker, M. D. *The Son of Man in Mark. A Study of the Background of the Term 'Son of Man' and its Use in St. Mark's Gospel* (London: SPCK, 1967).

'In His Own Image?', in Hickling, C., and Hooker, M., ed., *What About the New Testament?* Fs. Christopher Evans (London: SCM, 1975) pp. 28–44.

The Message of Mark (London: Epworth Press, 1983).

Hre Krio, S. 'A Prayer Framework in Mark 11', *TBT* 37 (1986) 323–8.

Hull, J. M. *Hellenistic Magic and the Synoptic Tradition* (London: SCM, 1974).

Hultgren, A. J. *Jesus and His Adversaries. The Form and Function of the Conflict Stories in the Synoptic Tradition* (Minneapolis: Augsburg, 1979).

Inge, W. R. *Faith and its Psychology* (London: Duckworth, 1909).

Jackson, E. N. *The Role of Faith in the Process of Healing* (London: SCM, 1981).

Jackson, H. M. 'The Death of Jesus in Mark and the Miracle from the Cross', *NTS* 33 (1987) 16–37.

Jeremias, J. *New Testament Theology*. Vol. 1: *The Proclamation of Jesus* (London: SCM, 1971).

Johnson, E. S. Jr. 'Mark 10: 46–52: Blind Bartimaeus', *CBQ* 40 (1978) 191–204.

'Mark 8:22–26. The Blind Man From Bethsaida', *NTS* 25 (1979) 370–83.

Juel, D. *Messiah and Temple. The Trial of Jesus in the Gospel of Mark*. SBLDS (Missoula, Montana: Scholars Press, 1977).

Keck, L. E. 'The Introduction to Mark's Gospel', *NTS* 12 (1965/6) 352–70.

Kee, H. C. 'The Terminology of Mark's Exorcism Stories', *NTS* 14 (1967/8) 232–46.

'The Function of Scriptural Quotations and Allusions in Mark 11–16', in Ellis, E., and Grässer, E., ed., *Jesus und Paulus*. Fs. W. G. Kümmel (Göttingen: Vandenhoeck & Ruprecht, 1975) pp. 164–88.

The Community of the New Age. Studies in Mark's Gospel (London: SCM, 1977).

Miracle in the Ancient World. A Study in Sociological Method (New Haven/London: Yale University Press, 1983).

Medicine, Miracle and Magic in New Testament Times. SNSTSMS 55 (Cambridge University Press, 1986).

Kelber, W. H. *The Kingdom in Mark. A New Place and a New Time* (Philadelphia: Fortress Press, 1974).

[ed.] *The Passion in Mark. Studies on Mark 14–16* (Philadelphia; Fortress Press, 1976).

'The Hour of the Son of Man and the Temptation of the Disciples', in Kelber, W. H., ed., *The Passion in Mark. Studies on Mark 14–16*

(Philadelphia: Fortress Press, 1976) pp. 41–60.
'From Passion Narrative to Gospel', in Kelber, W. H., *The Passion in Mark. Studies on Mark 14–16* (Philadelphia: Fortress Press, 1976) pp. 153–80.
Mark's Story of Jesus (Philadelphia: Fortress Press, 1979).
'Mark and Oral Tradition', *Sem* 16 (1980) 7–55.
The Oral and Written Gospel. The Hermeneutics of Speaking and Writing in the Synoptic Tradition, Mark, Paul and Q (Philadelphia: Fortress Press, 1983).
'The Work of Norman Perrin: An Intellectual Pilgrimage', *JR* 64 (1984) 452–67.
Keller, J. 'Jesus and his Critics. A Logico-Critical Analysis of the Marcan Confrontation', *Int* 40 (1986) 29–38.
Kennedy, G. A. *New Testament Interpretation Through Rhetorical Criticism* (London: University of North Carolina Press, Chapel Hill 1984).
Kermode, F. *The Genesis of Secrecy. On the Interpretation of Narrative* (Cambridge, Mass./London: Harvard University Press, 1979).
Kertelge, K. *Die Wunder Jesu im Markusevangelium.* SANT (München: Kösel-Verlag, 1970).
'Die Vollmacht des Menschensohnes zur Sündenvergebung (Mk 2,10)', in Hoffmann, P., ed., *Orientierung an Jesus: zur Theologie der Synoptiker*: Fs. J. Schmid (Freiburg im Breisgau: Herder, 1973) pp. 205–13.
Kilpatrick, G. D. 'The Gentile Mission in Mark and Mark 13:9–11', in Nineham, D. E., ed., *Studies in the Gospels. Essays in Memory of R. H. Lightfoot* (Oxford: Blackwell, 1955) pp. 145–58.
Kingsbury, J. D. 'The "Divine Man" as the Key to Mark's Christology – The End of an Era?', *Int* 35 (1981) 243–57.
The Christology of Mark's Gospel (Philadelphia: Fortress Press, 1983).
Kirkland, J. R. 'The Earliest Understanding of Jesus' Use of Parables: Mark IV.10–12 in Context', *NovT* 19 (1977) 1–21.
Klauck, H.-J. 'Die Frage der Sündenvergebung in der Perikope von der Heilung des Gelähmten (Mk 2,1–12 Par)', *BZ* 25 (1981) 223–48.
'Die Erzählerische Rolle der Jünger im Markusevangelium', *NovT* 24 (1982) 1–26.
Koch, D.-A. *Die Bedeutung der Wundererzählungen für die Christologie des Markusevangeliums* (Berlin: Walter de Gruyter, 1975).
'Inhaltliche Gliederung und geographischer Aufriss im Markusevangelium', *NTS* 29 (1983) 145–66.
Kuby, A. 'Zur Konzeption des Markus-Evangeliums', *ZNW* 49 (1958) 52–64.
Kuhn, H.-W. *Ältere Sammlungen im Markusevangelium.* SUNT 8 (Göttingen: Vandenhoeck & Ruprecht, 1971).
Lake, K. *The Stewardship of Faith. Our Heritage from Early Christianity* (London: Christopher's, 1915).
Lambrecht, J. *Die Redaktion der Markus-Apokalypse. Literarische Analyse und Strukturuntersuchung.* AnBib 28 (Rome: E Pontificio Instituto Biblico, 1967).
'The Relatives of Jesus in Mark', *NovT* 16 (1974) 241–58.
Lane, W. L. '*Theois Aner* Christology and the Gospel of Mark' in R. N. Longenecker and M. C. Tenney (eds.), *New Dimensions in New*

Testament Study (Grand Rapids, Mich.: Zondervan, 1974) pp. 144–61.

Lee-Pollard, D. A. 'Powerlessness as Power: A Key Emphasis in the Gospel of Mark', *SJT* 40 (1987) 173–88.

Légasse, S. *Jésus et L'Enfant. 'Enfants', 'Petits' et 'Simples' dans la Tradition Synoptique* (Paris: J. Gabalda et Cie Editeurs, 1969).

Lemcio, E. E. 'External Evidence for the Structure and Function of Mark iv 1–20, vii 14–23 and viii 14–21', *JTS* 29 (1978) 323–38.

'The Intention of the Evangelist Mark', *NTS* 32 (1986) 187–206.

Lightfoot, R. H. *History and Interpretation in the Gospels.* The Bampton Lectures 1934 (London: Hodder & Stoughton, 1935).

Locality and Doctrine in the Gospels (New York/London: Harper & Bros., 1938).

The Gospel Message of St. Mark (London: Oxford University Press, 1950).

Linnemann, E. *Studien zur Passionsgeschichte* (Göttingen: Vandenhoeck & Ruprecht, 1970).

Lohfink, G. *Jesus and Community. The Social Dimension of Christian Faith* (Philadelphia: Fortress Press; New York/Ramsey: Paulist Press, 1984).

Lohmeyer, E. *Galiläa und Jerusalem.* FRLANT n.s.34 (Göttingen: Vandenhoeck & Ruprecht, 1936).

Lord of the Temple. A Study of the Relation Between Cult and Gospel (Edinburgh/London: Oliver & Boyd, 1961).

Lohse, E. *'Emuna* und *Pistis* – Jüdisches und urchristliches Verständnis des Glaubens', *ZNW* 68 (1977) 147–63.

'Glauben im Neuen Testament', in Hermission, H-J. und Lohse, E., *Glauben* (Stuttgart, Berlin, Köln, Mainz: Verlag W. Kohlhammer, 1978) pp. 79–132.

Louw, J. P. *Semantics of New Testament Greek* (Philadelphia: Fortress Press/Chico, Calif.: Scholars Press, 1982).

Lührmann, D. *'Pistis* im Judentum', *ZNW* 64 (1973) 19–38.

Glaube im frühen Christentum (Gütersloh: Gütersloher Verlaghaus Gerd Mohn, 1976).

'Markus 14,55–64. Christologie und Zerstörung des Tempels im Markusevangelium', *NTS* 27 (1981) 457–74.

Luz, U. 'Die Jünger im Matthausevangelium', *ZNW* 62 (1971) 141–71.

Mackey, J. P. 'The Theology of Faith: A Bibliographical Survey (And More)', *Horizons* 2 (1975) 207–37.

'Faith of the Historical Jesus', *Horizons* 3 (1976) 115–74.

Magness, J. L. *Sense and Absence. Structure and Suspension in the Ending of Mark's Gospel*, SBA Semeia Studies (Atlanta, Georgia: Scholars Press, 1986).

Maisch, I. *Die Heilung des Gelähmten. Eine exegetisch-traditionsgeschichtliche Untersuchung zu Mk 2,1–12.* Stuttgarter Bibelstudien 52 (Stuttgart: KBW Verlag, 1971).

Malbon, E. S. 'Galilee and Jerusalem: History and Literature in Marcan Interpretation', *CBQ* 44 (1982) 242–55.

'Fallible Followers: Women and Men in the Gospel of Mark', *Sem* 28 (1983) 29–49.

'Disciples/Crowds/Whoever: Markan Characters and Readers', *NovT* 28 (1986) 104–30.

'Mark: Myth and Parable', *BTB* 16 (1986) 8–17.

Mangatt, G. 'Aspects of Discipleship', *Bible Bashyam* 7 (1981) 239–53.

Martin, R. P. *Mark: Evangelist and Theologian* (Exeter: Paternoster Press, 1972).

'The Theology of Mark's Gospel', *SWJT* 21 (1978) 23–36.

Marxsen, W. *Introduction to the New Testament. An Approach to its Problems* (Oxford: Basil Blackwell, 1968).

Mark the Evangelist. Studies on the Redaction History of the Gospel (Nashville/New York: Abingdon, 1969).

The Beginnings of Christology. Together with the Lord's Supper as a Christological Problem (Philadelphia: Fortress Press, 1979).

Matera, F. J. *The Kingship of Jesus. Composition and Theology in Mark 15*. SBLDS 66 (Chico, Calif.: Scholars Press, 1982).

'The Plot of Matthew's Gospel', *CBQ* 49 (1987) 233–53.

Mayer, Bernhard. 'Überlieferungs- und redaktionsgeschichtliche Überlegungen zu Mk 6,1–6a', *BZ* 22 (1978) 187–98.

McArthur, H. A. 'Son of Mary', *NovT* 15 (1973) 38–58.

McKnight, E. V. 'The Contours and Methods of Literary Criticism', in R. A. Spencer, *Orientation by Disorientation. Studies in Literary Criticism and Biblical Literary Criticism* (Pittsburgh: Pickwick Press, 1980) pp. 53–69.

The Bible and the Reader. An Introduction to Literary Criticism (Philadelphia: Fortress Press, 1985).

Mead, R. T. 'The Healing of the Paralytic – A Unit?', *JBL* 80 (1961) 348–54.

Meagher, J. C. 'Die Form- und redaktionsgeschichtliche Methoden: The Principle of Clumsiness and the Gospel of Mark', *JAAR* 43 (1975) 459–72.

Clumsy Construction in Mark's Gospel. A Critique of Form- and Redaktionsgeschichte. Toronto Studies in Theology. Vol. 3 (New York/Toronto: The Edwin Mellen Press, 1979).

Mercer, C. R. *Norman Perrin's Interpretation of the New Testament. From 'Exegetical Method' to 'Hermeneutical Process'* (Macon, Georgia: Mercer University Press, 1986).

Metzger, B. M. *A Textual Commentary on the Greek New Testament. A Companion Volume to UBS Greek New Testament, 3rd edition* (New York/London: UBS, 1975 [corrected edition]).

Meye, R. P. *Jesus and the Twelve. Discipleship and Revelation in Mark's Gospel* (Grand Rapids, Mich.: Eerdmans, 1968).

'Mark 16:8 – The Ending of Mark's Gospel', *BR* 14 (1969) 33–43.

Moiser, J. '"She was Twelve Years Old" (Mk 5:42) A Note on Jewish-Gentile Controversy in Mark's Gospel', *IrBibStud* 3 (1981) 179–86.

Moloney, F. J. 'The Vocation of the Disciples in the Gospel of Mark', *Salesianum* 43 (1981) 487–516.

Montefiore, C. G. *The Synoptic Gospels* (London: Macmillan & Co., 1927[2]).

Moore, W. E. '"Outside" and "Inside": A Markan Motif', *ExpT* 98 (1986) 39–43.

Motyer, S. 'The Rending of the Veil: A Markan Pentecost?' *NTS* 33 (1987) 155–7.

Moule, C. F. D. *Miracles*. Cambridge Studies in Their Philosophy and History (London: A. R. Mowbray & Co., 1965).

Munro, W. 'Women Disciples in Mark?', *CBQ* 44 (1982) 225–41.

Myers, C. 'Obedience and Upheaval. Six studies in the Gospel of Mark', *Sojourners* (Vol. 16, 1987).

Neirynck, F. *Duality in Mark: Contributions to the Study of the Markan Redaction.* BETL 31 (Louvain: Leuven University, 1972).

'The Redactional Text of Mark', ETL 57 (1981) 144–62.

Nickelsburg, G. W. E. 'The Genre and Function of the Markan Passion Narrative', *HTR* 73 (1980) 153–84.

Nolan, A. *Jesus Before Christianity. The Gospel of Liberation* (London: Darton, Longman & Todd, 1976).

O'Connor, E. D. *Faith in the Synoptic Gospels. A Problem in the Correlation of Scripture and Theology* (South Bend, Ind.: University of Notre Dame Press, 1961).

Osburn, C. D. 'The Historical Present in Mark as a Text-Critical Criterion', *Bib* 64 (1983) 486–500.

Parrott, H. W. 'Blind Bartimaeus Cries Out Again', *Evangelical Quarterly* 32 (1960) 25–9.

Patten, B. R. 'The Thaumaturgical Element in the Gospel of Mark', Ph.D. Dissertation (Madison, N.J.: Drew University, 1976).

Peacock, H. L.'Discipleship in the Gospel of Mark', *RevExp* 75 (1978) 555–64.

Perrin, N. *Rediscovering the Teaching of Jesus.* SCM NT Library (London: SCM, 1967).

'The Interpretation of the Gospel of Mark', *Int* 30 (1967) 115–24.

What is Redaction Criticism? (London: SPCK, 1970).

'The Evangelist as Author: Reflections on Method in the Study and Interpretation of the Synoptic Gospels and Acts', *BR* 17 (1972) 5–18.

'Historical Criticism, Literary Criticism, and Hermeneutics: The Interpretation of the Parables of Jesus and the Gospel of Mark Today', *JR* 52 (1972) 361–75.

'Eschatology and Hermeneutics: Reflections on Method in the Interpretation of the New Testament', *JBL* 93 (1974) 3–14.

The New Testament. An Introduction. Proclamation and Parenesis. Myth and History (New York, Chicago, San Francisco, Atlanta: Harcourt Brace Jovanovich Inc., 1974).

'Towards an Interpretation of the Gospel of Mark', in Betz, H. D., ed., *Christology and a Modern Pilgrimage. A Discussion with Norman Perrin* (Missoula, Montana: Scholars Press, 1974) pp. 1–52.

'The High Priest's Question and Jesus' Answer (Mark 14:61–62)', in Kelber, W., ed., *The Passion in Mark. Studies on Mark 14–16* (Philadelphia: Fortress Press, 1976) pp. 80–95.

Jesus and the Language of the Kingdom. Symbol and Metaphor in New Testament Interpretation (London: SCM, 1976).

'Mark, Gospel of', *IDB supp* (1976) 571–3.

Pesch, R. *Naherwartungen. Tradition und Redaktion in Mk 13.* Kommentare und Beiträge zum Alten und Neuen Testament (Düsseldorf: Patmos, 1968).

'Anfang des Evangeliums Jesu Christi: Eine Studie zum Prolog des Markusevangeliums (Mk 1,1–15)', in Bornkamm, G., and Rahner, K., ed., *Die Zeit Jesu.* Fs Heinrich Schlier (Freiburg/Basel/Vienna: Herder, 1970) pp. 108–44.

Petersen, N. R. *Literary Criticism for New Testament Critics* (Philadelphia: Fortress Press, 1978).

'"Point of View" in Mark's Narrative', *Sem* 12 (1978) 97–121.
'The Composition of Mark 4:1–8:26', *HTR* 73 (1980) 185–217.
'When is the End not the End? Literary Reflections on the Ending of Mark's Narrative', *Int* 34 (1980) 151–66.
'Literary Criticism in Biblical Studies' in R. A. Spencer, *Orientation by Disorientation. Studies in Literary Criticism and Biblical Literary Criticism* (Pittsburgh: Pickwick Press, 1980) pp. 25–50.
Polhill, J. B. 'Perspectives on the Miracle Stories', *RevExp* 74 (1977) 389–99.
Powell, C. H. *The Biblical Concept of Power* (London: Epworth Press, 1963).
Pritchard, J. P. *A Literary Approach to the New Testament* (Norman, Okla.: University of Oklahoma Press, 1972).
Pryke, E. J. *Redactional Style in the Marcan Gospel.* SNTSMS 33 (Cambridge University Press, 1978).
Quesnell, Q. *The Mind of St. Mark.* AnBib 38 (Rome: Pontifical Biblical Institute, 1969).
Reicke, B. 'The Synoptic Reports of the Healing of the Paralytic', in Elliott, J. K., ed., *Studies in New Testament Language and Text.* Fs G. D. Kilpatrick (Leiden: E. J. Brill, 1976) pp. 319–29.
Remus, H. 'Does Terminology Distinguish Early Christian From Pagan Miracles?', *JBL* 101 (1982) 531–51.
Reploh, K.-G. *Markus – Lehrer der Gemeinde. Eine redaktionsgeschicht-liche Studie zu den Jüngerperikopen des Markus-Evangeliums.* Stuttgarter Biblische Monographien 9 (Stuttgart: Verlag Katholisches Bibelwerk, 1969).
'"Evangelium" bei Markus. Das Evangelium des Markus als Anruf an die Gemeinde zu Umkehr und Glaube (1,14–15)', *BK* 27 (1972) 110–14.
Reumann, J. 'Psalm 22 at the Cross. Lament and Thanksgiving for Jesus Christ', *Int* 28 (1974) 39–58.
Rhoads, D. & Michie, D. *Mark as Story. An Introduction to the Narrative of a Gospel* (Philadelphia: Fortress Press, 1982).
Rhoads, D. 'Narrative Criticism and the Gospel of Mark', *JAAR* 50 (1982) 411–34.
Richardson, A. *The Miracle-Stories of the Gospels* (London: SCM, 1941).
An Introduction to the Theology of the New Testament (London: SCM, 1958).
Rigaux, B. *The Testimony of St. Mark* (Chicago: Franciscan Herald Press, 1966).
Robbins, V. K. 'Dynameis and Semeia in Mark', *BR* 18 (1973) 5–20.
'The Healing of Bartimaeus (10:46–52) in Marcan Theology', *JBL* 92 (1973) 224–43.
'Last Meal: Preparation, Betrayal, and Absence', in Kelber, W., ed., *The Passion in Mark. Studies on Mark 14–16* (Philadelphia: Fortress Press, 1976) 21–40.
'Summons and Outline in Mark: The Three Step Progression', *NovT* 23 (1981) 97–114.
'Mark 1:14–20: An Interpretation at the Intersection of Jewish and Graeco-Roman Traditions', *NTS* 28 (1982) 220–36.
Jesus and Teacher: A Socio-Rhetorical Interpretation of Mark (Philadelphia: Fortress Press, 1984).
'The Woman who Touched Jesus' Garment: Socio-Rhetorical Analysis of the Synoptic Accounts', *NTS* 33 (1987) 502–15.

Robertson, D. 'Literature, The Bible As', *IDB Supp*, 547–51.

Robinson, J. M. *The Problem of History in Mark*. SBT 11 (London: SCM, 1957).

Rochais, G. *Les Récits de Résurrection des Morts dans le Nouveau Testament*. SNTSMS (Cambridge University Press, 1981).

Roloff, J. *Das Kerygma und der irdische Jesus. Historische Motive in den Jesus-Erzählungen der Evangelien* (Göttingen: Vandenhoeck & Ruprecht, 1970).

Sanders, E. P. *Jesus and Judaism* (London: SCM, 1985).

Schenk, W. 'Tradition und Redaktion in der Epileptiker-Perikope Mk 9,14–29', *ZNW* 63 (1972) 76–94.

Schenke, L. *Die Wundererzählungen des Markusevangeliums* (Stuttgart: Verlag Katholisches Bibelwerk, 1974).

Schille, G. 'Die Seesturmerzählung Markus 4,35–41 als Beispiel neutestamentlicher Aktualisierung', *ZNW* 56 (1965) 30–40.

Schlatter, A. D. *Der Glaube im Neuen Testament* (Stuttgart: Calwer Vereinsbuchhandlung, 1927[4]).

Schmidt, K. L. *Der Rahmen der Geschichte Jesus: literarkritische Untersuchungen zur ältesten Jesusüberlieferung* (Darmstadt: Wissenschaftliche Buchgesellschaft, 1964).

Schmithals, W. *Wunder und Glaube. Eine Auslegung von Markus 4,35–6,6a* (Neukirchen-Vluyn: Neukirchener Verlag, 1970).

Schmitt, J. J. 'Women in Mark's Gospel', *BTB* 19 (1981) 228–33.

Schnackenburg, R. '"Das Evangelium" im Verständnis des ältesten Evangelisten', in Hoffmann, P., ed., *Orientierung an Jesus zur Theologie der Synoptiker*. Fs J. Schmid (Freiburg im Breisgau: Herder, 1973) pp. 309–24.

Schreiber, J. 'Die Christologie des Markusevangeliums', *ZTK* 58 (1961) 154–83.

Theologie des Vertrauens. Eine redaktionsgeschichtliche Untersuchung des Markusevangeliums (Hamburg: Furche-Verlag, 1967).

Schürmann, H. 'Der Jüngerkreis Jesu als Zeichen für Israel (und als Urbild des kirchlichen Rätstandes)', *Geist und Leben* 26 (1963) 21–35.

Schüssler Fiorenza, E. *In Memory of Her. A Feminist Theological Reconstruction of Christian Origins* (London: SCM, 1983).

Schweizer, E. 'Anmerkungen zur Theologie des Markus', in Schweizer, E., *Neotestamentica* German and English Essays, 1951–1963 (Zürich/Stuttgart: Zwingli Verlag, 1963) 93–104.

'Mark's Contribution to the Quest for the Historical Jesus', *NTS* 10 (1963/4) 421–32.

'Eschatology in Mark's Gospel', in Ellis, E. E. and Wilcox, M. ed., *Neotestamentica et Semitica* Fs M. Black (Edinburgh: T & T Clark, 1969) pp. 114–18.

'The Portrayal of the Life of Faith in the Gospel of Mark', *Int* 32 (1978) 387–99.

Seal, W. O. 'Norman Perrin and his "School": Retracing a Pilgrimage', *JSNT* 20 (1984) 87–107.

Selvidge, M. J. '"And Those Who Followed Feared" (Mark 10:32)', *CBQ* 45 (1983) 396–400.

Senior, D. *The Passion of Jesus in the Gospel of Mark* (Wilmington, Delaware: Michael Glazier, 1984).

'"With Swords and Clubs . . ." The Setting of Mark's Community and his Critique of Abusive Power', *BTB* 17 (1987) 10–20.

Shae, G. S. 'The Question on the Authority of Jesus', *NovT* 16 (1974) 1–29.

Shaw, G. *The Cost of Authority. Manipulation and Freedom in the New Testament* (London: SCM, 1983).

Shearer, T. 'The Concept of "Faith" in the Synoptic Gospels', *ExpT* 69 (1957) 3–6.

Silva, M. *Biblical Words and Their Meanings. An Introduction to Lexical Semantics* (Grand Rapids, Mich: Zondervan, 1983).

Smith, M. *Jesus the Magician* (London: Victor Gollancz Ltd., 1978).

Snoy, T. 'Les miracles dans l'évangile de Marc. Examen de quelques études récentes', *Revue Théologique de Louvain* 3 (1972) 449–66; 4 (1973) 58–101.

Sparks, H. F. D. 'The Doctrine of the Divine Fatherhood in the Gospels', in Nineham, D. E. ed., *Studies in the Gospels. Essays in Memory of R. H. Lightfoot* (Oxford: Blackwell, 1955) pp. 241–62.

Spencer, R. A. *Orientation by Disorientation. Studies in Literary Criticism and Biblical Literary Criticism* (Pittsburgh: Pickwick Press, 1980).

Standaert, B. *L'Évangile selon Marc. Composition et genre littéraire* (Zevenkerken/Brugge: Sint-Andriesabdij, 1978).

Stanton, G. N. 'Form Criticism Revisited', in Hooker M. & Hickling, C., ed., *What About the New Testament?* Fs C. Evans (London: SCM, 1975) pp. 13–27.

Stauffer, E. 'Jeschu Ben Mirjam: Kontroversgeschichtliche Anmerkungen zu Mk 6,3', in Ellis, E. E. & Wilcox, M. ed., *Neotestamentica et Semitica* Fs M. Black (Edinburgh: T & T Clark, 1969) pp. 119–28.

Stein, R. H. 'What is Redaktionsgschichte?', *JBL* 88 (1969) 45–56.
'The "Redaktionsgeschichtliche" Investigation of a Markan Seam (Mk 1:21f)', *ZNW* 61 (1970) 70–94.
'The Proper Methodology for Ascertaining a Markan Redaction History', *NovT* 13 (1971) 181–98.
'A Short Note on Mark xiv.28 and xvi.7', *NTS* 20 (1974) 445–52.

Steinhauser, M. G. 'Part of a Call Story?', *ExpT* 94 (1983) 204–6.
'The Form of the Bartimaeus Narrative (Mark 10. 46–52)', *NTS* 32 (1986) 583–95.

Stendahl, K. 'Prayer and Forgiveness', *Svensk exegetisk årsbok* 22–23 (1957/8) 204–6.

Stock, A. *Call to Discipleship A Literary Study of Mark's Gospel* (Dublin: Veritas Publications/Wilmington, Delaware: Michael Glazier, 1982).
'Chiastic Awareness and Education in Antiquity', *BTB* 14 (1984) 23–7.

Sundwall, J. *Die Zusammensetzung des Markusevangeliums* (Abo Abo Akademi, 1934).

Swartley, W. 'The Structural Function of the Term "Way" in Mark', in Klassen, W., ed., *The New Way of Jesus* (Newton, Kansas; Faith and Life Press, 1980) pp. 73–86.

Swinburne, R. *Faith and Reason* (Oxford: Clarendon Press, 1981).

Synge, F. C. 'A Plea for Outsiders: Commentary on Mark 4:10–12', *JournTheolSAf* 30 (1980) 53–8.
'A Matter of Tenses – Fingerprints of an Annotator in Mark', *ExpT* 88 (1977) 168–71.
'Intruded Middles', *ExpT* 92 (1981) 329–33.

Taber, R. C. 'Semantics', *IDB supp*, 801–7.

Tannehill, R. C. *The Sword of His Mouth* (Missoula, Montana: Scholars Press/Philadelphia; Fortress Press, 1975).

'The Disciples in Mark: The Function of a Narrative Role', *JR* 57 (1977) 386–405.

'The Gospel of Mark as a Narrative Christology', *Sem* 16 (1980) 57–95.

Telford, W. R. *The Barren Temple and the Withered Tree. A Redaction-Critical Analysis of the Cursing of the Fig-Tree Pericope in Mark's Gospel and its Relation to the Cleansing of the Temple Tradition* JSNTSS 1 Sheffield: JSOT, 1980).

The Interpretation of Mark Issues in Religion and Theology 7 (London: SPCK/Philadelphia: Fortress Press, 1985).

Theissen, G. *The First Followers of Jesus. A Sociological Analysis of Earliest Christianity* (London: SCM, 1978).

Miracle Stories of the Early Christian Tradition (Edinburgh: T & T Clark, 1983).

Thiselton, A. C. 'Semantics and New Testament Interpretation', in Marshall, I. H. ed., *New Testament Interpretation. Essays in Principles and Methods* (Exeter: Paternoster, 1977) pp. 75–104.

Trocmé, E. *The Formation of the Gospel According to Mark* (London: SPCK, 1975).

Tuckett, C. M. 'The Present Son of Man', *JSNT* 14 (1982) 58–81.

The Messianic Secret, Issues in Religion and Theology 1 (London: SPCK/ Philadelphia: Fortress Press, 1985).

Turner, C. H. 'Marcan Usage: Notes, Critical and Exegetical, on the Second Gospel', *JTS* 25 (1924) 377–86; 26 (1925) 12–20, 145–56, 225–40; 27 (1926) 58–62; 28 (1927) 9–30, 349–62; 29 (1928) 275–89, 346–61.

Turner, N. *Grammatical Insights into the New Testament* (Edinburgh: T & T Clark, 1965).

Tyson, J. B. 'The Blindness of the Disciples in Mark', *JBL* 80 (1961) 261–8.

van der Loos, H. *The Miracles of Jesus* SNovT 9 (Leiden: E. J. Brill, 1965).

Verweyen, H. 'Einheit und Vielfalt der Evangelien am Beispiel der Redaktion von Wundergeschichten (inbesondere Mk 5, 25–44 parr)', *Didaskalia* 2 (1981) 3–24.

Via, D. O. Jr, *Kerygma and Comedy in the New Testament. A Structuralist Approach to Hermeneutic* (Philadelphia: Fortress Press, 1975).

The Ethics of Mark's Gospel. In the Middle of Time (Philadelphia: Fortress Press, 1985).

Vögtle, A. 'Das markinische Verständnis der Tempelworte' in Luz, U. and Weder, H., ed., *Die Mitte des Neuen Testaments. Einheit und Vielfalt neutestamentlicher Theologie* Fs E. Schweizer (Göttingen: Vandenhoeck & Ruprecht, 1983) pp. 362–83.

von Dobschütz, E. 'Zur Erzählerkunst der Markus', *ZNW* 27 (1928) 193–8.

Vorster, W. S. 'Mark: Collector, Redactor, Author, Narrator?', *JournTheol SAf* 31 (1980) 46–61.

'Kerygma/History and the Gospel Genre', *NTS* 29 (1983) 87–95.

Warfield, B. B. *Biblical Doctrines* (New York: OUP, 1929) pp. 467–508.

Watson, F. 'The Social Function of Mark's Secrecy Theme', *JSNT* 23 (1985) 49–69.

Watty, W. W. 'Jesus and the Temple-Cleansing or Cursing?', *ExpT* 93 (1983) 235–9.

Weder, H. '"Evangelium Jesu Christi" (Mk 1,1) and "Evangelium Gottes" (Mk 1,14)', in Luz, U. & Weder, H., ed., *Die Mitte des Neuen Testaments. Einheit und Vielfalt neutestamentlicher Theologie* Fs E. Schweizer (Göttingen: Vandenhoeck & Ruprecht, 1983) pp. 399–411.

Weeden, T. J. 'The Heresy that Necessitated Mark's Gospel', *ZNW* 59 (1968) 145–58.

Mark. Traditions in Conflict (Philadelphia: Fortress Press, 1971).

'The Cross as Power in Weakness (Mark 15:20b–41)', in Kelber, W., ed., *The Passion in Mark. Studies on Mark 14–16* (Philadelphia: Fortress Press, 1976) pp. 115–34.

Wenham, D. 'A Note on Mk 9:33–42/Mt 18:1–6/Lk 9:46–50', *JNTS* (1982) 113–18.

Werner, M. *Der Einfluss paulinischer Theologie im Markusevangelium Eine Studie zur neutestamentlichen Theologie* BZNW (Giesen: Verlag von Alfred Töpelman, 1923).

Wilder, A. N. *Early Christian Rhetoric. The Language of the Gospel* (London: SCM, 1964).

'Story and Story World', *Int* 37 (1983) 353–64.

Wire, A. C. 'The Structure of the Gospel Miracle Stories and Their Tellers' *Sem* 11 (1978) 83–113.

Wolff, C. 'Zur Bedeutung Johannes des Täufers im Markusevangelium' *Theologische Literaturzeitung* 102 (1977) 858–65.

Wrede, W. 'Zur Heilung des Gelähmten (Mc 2,1ff)', *ZNW* 5 (1904) 354–8.

The Messianic Secret (Cambridge/London: James Clarke, 1971).

Wuellner, W. 'Where is Rhetorical Criticism Taking Us?', *CBQ* 49 (1987) 448–63.

Zeller, D. 'Jesus als Mittler des Glaubens nach dem Markusevangelium', *Bible und Leben* 9 (1968) 278–86.

Zerwick, M. *Untersuchungen zum Markus-Stil. Ein Beitrag zur stilistischen Durcharbeitung des Neuen Testaments* (Rome: E Pontificio Institutio Biblico, 1937).

INDEX OF MAIN PERICOPAE DISCUSSED

INDEX OF MAJOR SUBJECTS DISCUSSED